W9-CFO-301

The Longman Handbook of
Modern American History
1763–1996

Longman Handbooks to History

The Longman Handbook of Modern British History 1714–1995, 3rd edition (*Chris Cook and John Stevenson*)

The Longman Handbook of Modern European History 1763–1997, 3rd edition (*Chris Cook and John Stevenson*)

The Longman Handbook of Modern American History 1763–1996 (*Chris Cook and David Waller*)

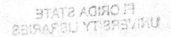

The Longman Handbook of Modern American History 1763–1996

Chris Cook
David Waller

LONGMAN
Longman and New York

Addison Wesley Longman Limited
Edinburgh Gate,
Harlow, Essex CM20 2JE, United Kingdom
and Associated Companies throughout the world.

*Published in the United States of America by Addison Wesley Longman,
New York.*

© Chris Cook and David Waller 1998

The right of Chris Cook and David Waller to be identified as authors of
this Work has been asserted by them in accordance with the Copyright,
Designs and Patents Act 1988.

First published 1998

ISBN 0–582–08489–X CSD
ISBN 0–582–08488–1 PPR

British Library Cataloguing in Publication Data

A catalogue entry for this title is available from the British Library

Library of Congress Cataloging-in-Publication Data

Cook, Chris, 1945–
    The Longman handbook of modern American history, 1763–1996 /
Chris Cook and David Waller.
        p.   cm. — (Longman handbooks to history)
    Includes bibliographical references and index.
    ISBN 0–582–08489–X. — ISBN 0–582–08488–1 (pbk.)
    1. United States—History—Handbooks, manuals, etc. I. Waller,
David, 1963– . II. Title. III. Series.
    E174.C66   1997
    973—dc21   97–14206
                                                                CIP

Set by 35 in 9½/12 pt New Baskerville
Produced by Longman Singapore Publishers Pte Ltd
Printed in Singapore

Contents

List of maps

Preface and acknowledgements

This handbook attempts to provide a convenient reference work for both teachers and students of modern American history. It covers the period from the War of Independence to the present day, from the Boston Tea Party and the origins of the American Revolution to the presidential election of November 1996 and the politics of contemporary America in the middle 1990s.

It is a much condensed work, bringing together chronological, statistical and tabular information which is not to be found elsewhere within the confines of a single volume. The handbook covers not only political and diplomatic events but also the broader fields of social and economic history. It includes biographies of important individuals, a glossary of commonly used historical terms, and a topic bibliography. For those students with no background in American government and politics, many of the basic political terms encountered in textbooks on American history can be confusing. Hence the extensive glossary in this volume includes not just historical terms but a variety of American political terms with which historians need to be familiar. No book of this type can be entirely comprehensive, nor is it intended to substitute for textbooks and more detailed reading, but we have attempted to include those facts and figures which we believe are most useful for understanding courses in modern American history.

It is hoped that the volume has included essential material on all the major themes of modern American history. The authors would, however, welcome constructive ideas and suggestions for future editions of this book. For secretarial help, we are indebted as ever to the long labours of Linda Hollingworth. A particular debt is due to Dr Peter Thompson of St Cross College, Oxford, for his help in the preparation of the topic bibliography, and to Christa Starck of the Gail Borden Public Library in Elgin, Illinois, who greatly assisted us in the research for this volume.

Chris Cook
David Waller
20 June 1997

The publishers would like to thank HarperCollins Publishers Ltd for permission to reproduce Map 1. While every effort has been made to trace the owners of copyright material, in a few cases this has proved impossible and so we take this opportunity to offer our apologies to any copyright holders whose rights we may have unwittingly infringed.

Note on sources

The indispensable reference work for all aspects of American politics is Erik W. Austin, *Political Facts of the United States since 1789* (1986). This encyclopaedic work contains a mass of material on electoral statistics, Cabinet offices, diplomatic and military facts, and appointments of Supreme Court judges. Although not easy to use, it should be consulted by the more advanced student. For more recent facts and figures (as well as handy historical tables) the annual *World Almanac and Book of Facts* and the *Information Please Almanac* are the American equivalent of *Whitaker's Almanac*. For many of the economic and social statistics in this book, the definitive source to which all scholars must turn is the compilation of the US Department of Commerce, Bureau of the Census, *Historical Statistics of the United States* (1960, but updated at regular intervals). Students should remember, however, that in some areas (such as statistics on crime where laws vary from state to state) meaningful nationwide figures cannot easily be assembled. This Longman Handbook gives only a sample of the immense wealth of data available on American history and politics. For both student and teacher, the problem is one of too much material rather than too little.

Note on spelling

For American place-names, institutions, government departments, and also for direct quotations, American spellings have normally been followed (Pearl Harbor, Secretary of Defense, Department of Labor, etc.) In the main text, standard English spelling has been adopted.

List of abbreviations

AAA	Agricultural Adjustment Administration
ACLU	American Civil Liberties Union
ADA	Americans for Democratic Action
AFL	American Federation of Labor
CAB	Civil Aeronautics Board
CBO	Congressional Budget Office
CCC	Civilian Conservation Corps
CDF	Conservative Democratic Forum
CEA	Council of Economic Advisers
CIA	Central Intelligence Agency
CIO	Committee for (later Congress of) Industrial Organization(s)
COPE	Committee on Political Education
CORE	Congress of Racial Equality
CPPA	Conference for Progressive Political Action
CWA	Civil Works Administration
DNC	Democratic National Committee
DSG	Democratic Study Group
EPA	Environmental Protection Agency
ERA	Equal Rights Amendment
FBI	Federal Bureau of Investigation
FERA	Federal Emergency Relief Administration
FHA	Federal Housing Administration
FRB	Federal Reserve Board
GAO	General Accounting Office
HUAC	House Un-American Activities Committee
ICC	Interstate Commerce Commission
NAACP	National Association for the Advancement of Colored People
NAFTA	North American Free Trade Area
NAM	National Association of Manufacturers
NLB	National Labor Board
NLRB	National Labor Relations Board
NORAD	North American Air Defense Command
NOW	National Organization for Women
NRA	National Recovery Administration
NWLB	National War Labor Board
NWSA	National Woman Suffrage Association

NYA	National Youth Administration
OAS	Organization of American States
OMB	Office of Management and Budget
PAC	Political Action Committee
POUR	President's Organization for Unemployment Relief
PWA	Public Works Administration
RA	Resettlement Administration
REA	Rural Electrification Administration
RFC	Reconstruction Finance Corporation
SALT	Strategic Arms Limitation Talks
SCLA	Southern Christian Leadership Conference
SDI	Strategic Defense Initiative
SDS	Students for a Democratic Society
SEC	Securities and Exchange Commission
SNCC	Student Nonviolent Coordinating Committee
START	Strategic Arms Reduction Talks
STFU	Southern Tenant Farmers' Union
SWOC	Steel Workers' Organizing Committee
TERA	Temporary Emergency Relief Administration
TNEC	Temporary National Economic Committee
TVA	Tennessee Valley Authority
UAW	United Automobile Workers
UMW	United Mine Workers
USIA	United States Information Agency
USITC	United States International Trade Commission
USTC	United States Tariff Commission
USTR	United States Trade Representative (replaces STRC (Special Trade Representative))
WIB	War Industries Board
WNPC	Women's National Political Caucus
WPA	Works Progress Administration

SECTION ONE

Political history

Political chronology

1763
10 Feb. Peace of Paris signed: Britain gains Canada, Florida, Louisiana east of the Mississippi, Cape Breton, and islands of the St Lawrence. Proclamation establishing the Alleghenies as temporary boundary line, beyond which colonies could not expand.

1765
22 Mar. Stamp Act passed, imposing a stamp duty on legal transactions in America to pay for colonial defence.
7–25 Oct. Beginning of campaign in Britain and American colonies against the Stamp Act. 'Stamp Act Congress' held in New York.

1766
Petitioning movement of British merchants against the Stamp Act. Appointment of parliamentary inquiry into merchant grievances. Passing of Declaratory Act, confirming sovereign's right to tax the colonies.
18 Mar. Stamp Act repealed.

1767
New York Assembly formally refuses to enforce the Mutiny Act. Massachusetts grants indemnity for all offences committed during Stamp Act disturbances.
Townshend introduces duties on paper, paint, glass, lead and tea imported into America (passed 2 June) to pay for colonial defence and establish a civil list within the colonies.
Dec. First journey over Appalachians into Kentucky by Daniel Boone.

1768
Feb. Boston enters a non-importation agreement against the duties. Massachusetts House of Representatives petitions against taxation without representation and circularizes other colonies, urging common action against the import duties.
June Attacks upon customs officials and American Board of Customs forced to leave Boston.

1 Oct.   Troops sent to New England.

1769
1 May   Cabinet decides to abolish all Townshend duties except those on tea.

1770
5 Mar.   Boston 'Massacre': British soldiers kill five people in a mob attacking a customs house.
12 Apr.   Repeal of Townshend's Act.

1771
South Carolina assembly suspended for grant of £1,500 to the Supporters of the Bill of Rights Society in London.
Quarrels with assemblies of North Carolina and Georgia.
16 May   Battle of Alamance between militia and settlers on frontier.

1772
9 June   Revenue cutter *Gaspee* boarded and burnt.
2 Nov.   Committee of Correspondence, formed to publicize grievances and co-ordinate colonial resistance, elected by Boston town meeting.

1773
10 May   Tea Act passed. All duties on tea re-exported by East India Company to be remitted and direct export to America allowed.
16 Dec.   In 'Boston Tea Party' three shiploads of tea dumped in Boston harbour.

1774
Fuller's motion to repeal duty on tea defeated by 182 votes to 49.
Coercive measures taken against American colonies.
31 Mar.   Boston Port Act closes Boston to shipping until compensation is paid to East India Company and customs officers mistreated by the mob.
20 May   Massachusetts Government Act deprives colony of the right to elect councillors and gives the Governor power to appoint and dismiss all civil officers except judges of the Supreme Court and substitutes nominated jurors for elected ones and restricts town meetings.
20 May   Quebec Act provides for government of province of Quebec by an appointed Governor and Council. Toleration extended to Roman Catholics and provision made for payment of tithes by Roman Catholic communicants. French and English legal codes merged. Jurisdiction of Governor of Quebec extended along western edge of Pennsylvania to the Ohio and Mississippi Rivers.

5 Sept.–26 Oct. Continental Congress meets at Philadelphia. Congress decides on the 'Suffolk Resolves' for defiance of Coercive Acts, withholding of taxes until all privileges restored to Massachusetts, and defensive military preparations in the event of arrest of leaders. Considers and rejects a federal structure of government in North America controlling all aspects of administration but still subordinate to the British Parliament and Crown. 'Declaration of Rights' issued.

1775

22 Mar. Burke's conciliation proposals defeated.

30 Mar. New England Restraining Act forbids colonies of New England from trading with any nation other than Britain or its West Indies colonies.

19 Apr. Detachment of 700 British troops sent from Boston by General Gage to destroy stores of the Massachusetts militia at Concord. The force was opposed at Lexington, where the first shots of the war were fired, and harassed on the return march from Concord to Boston, suffering 273 casualties. Boston was besieged.

10 May Second Continental Congress meets at Philadelphia.

31 May American troops before Boston adopted by the Second Continental Congress as the Continental Army, and George Washington appointed Commander-in-Chief (15 June).

17 June After receiving reinforcements, Gage attacked the American entrenchments on Breed's Hill (Battle of Bunker Hill), suffering heavy losses in carrying them at the third attempt. Gage replaced by Howe.

23 Aug. George III declares American colonies to be in open rebellion.

Nov. Montreal in Canada taken by rebels, but an attack on Quebec failed in December. The following year Carleton, the British Governor, retook Montreal and forced the Americans back to Ticonderoga.

23 Dec. Decree of George III forbids all trade with colonies.

1776

9 Jan. *Common Sense* published by Thomas Paine. Rallies Americans to cause of independence.

Mar. British evacuate Boston following American capture of Dorchester Heights (4th–5th).

June Resolution for Independence moved (7th) (carried on 2 July). Charleston (South Carolina) beats off British attack (1st–28th).

2 July Howe arrived off New York from Halifax with 30,000 men, and landed on Staten Island.

4 July The American colonies declare independence. George III's statue in New York City pulled down (10th).

27 Aug. Washington defeated by British at Long Island.

Sept. British take New York City (15th). George Washington evacuates the city.

28 Oct. Heavy casualties inflicted on Washington's troops by British army in Battle of White Plains.

26 Dec. Battle of Trenton. Washington crossed the Delaware by night, and attacked a force of Hessians, taking 900 prisoners. As he withdrew he defeated the British at the Battle of Princeton (3 Jan. 1777).

1777

British plan to divide the rebel states by the line of the Hudson River, with Burgoyne advancing from Canada, in co-operation with St Leger from Lake Ontario and Howe from New York.

July Howe sailed from New York to Chesapeake Bay with 18,000 men, defeated the Americans at Brandywine Creek (11 Sept.) and occupied Philadelphia (27 Sept.).

5 July Burgoyne moved south with 8,200 men, and occupied Ticonderoga.

16 Aug. Colonel Baum was sent to seize stores, but was defeated at Bennington by colonial forces.

19 Sept. Burgoyne suffered heavy losses in a battle at Freeman's Farm. He was now confronted by a greatly superior force under Gates.

4 Oct. Howe defeated Washington's attempt to mount a surprise attack on camp at Germantown. Washington's army spent a hard winter at Valley Forge.

7 Oct. Attempting to break out, Burgoyne was defeated at Bemis Heights and began peace negotiations.

17 Oct. British surrender at Saratoga.

1778

6 Feb. Treaties of commerce and alliance between France and the United States.

18 June Clinton, who had succeeded Howe as Commander-in-Chief, began the evacuation of Philadelphia, which was successfully carried out, despite a defeat by Washington at Monmouth (28 June). Clinton now sent an army to overrun the Southern states, hoping for loyalist assistance. Savannah was occupied on 29 Dec. In the West Indies, the French captured Dominica (8 Sept.), but British forces took St Lucia (13 Nov.). At sea, an inconclusive engagement took place between Keppel and D'Orvilliers off Ushant (27 July). John Paul Jones successfully attacked British shipping in the Irish Sea.

10 July War between France and Britain begins.

1779

16 June Spain entered the war. Gibraltar was besieged June 1779–Feb. 1783. In the West Indies, D'Estaing took St Vincent in June and Grenada (4 July), and defeated Admiral Byron off Grenada (6 July).

Aug. A Franco-Spanish fleet entered the Channel, but withdrew.
Sept.–Oct. Assaults on Savannah by French and American troops beaten off.

1780
8 Jan. Rodney defeated a Spanish fleet and relieved Gibraltar.
Feb. Clinton landed with 12,000 men to attack Charleston, which fell 12 May. Clinton returned to New York, leaving the pacification of South Carolina to Cornwallis, who defeated Gates at Camden (16 Aug.).
Aug. Armed neutrality formed by Russia, Sweden and Denmark to resist British seizure of enemy goods in neutral ships. Later joined by Prussia, Austria, Portugal, the Netherlands and the Kingdom of the Two Sicilies.
7 Oct. British raiding force under Colonel Ferguson defeated at King's Mountain.
20 Dec. Britain declared war on Holland. Warren Hastings seized Dutch settlements of Negapatam and Trincomali, but an attempt on the Cape of Good Hope failed in 1781.

1781
17 Jan. British cavalry under Tarleton defeated by Morgan at Cowpens.
Feb. In the West Indies Rodney captured the Dutch islands of St Eustatius and St Martin. Later, in June, the French took Tobago, and St Eustatius in Oct.
1 Mar. The Continental Congress declares in force the Articles of Confederation between the United States.
15 Mar. Cornwallis defeated Greene at Guildford, but suffered heavy losses.
July–Aug. Franco-Spanish occupation of Minorca. Port Mahan fell 5 Feb. 1782.
Aug. Cornwallis established himself at Yorktown. He was besieged there by Washington and Rochambeau, and the French fleet under de Grasse, and forced to surrender on 19 Oct. Clinton's relieving force arrived too late on 24 Oct.

1782
Feb. French take St Kitts and Nevis.
12 Apr. Rodney's naval victory in the Battle of The Saints.
30 Nov. Preliminary peace between Britain and the United States.

1783
3 Sept. Treaty of Paris. Signed by Britain, France and the United States. Britain signed a separate treaty with Holland on 20 May 1784. Britain recognized the independence of the United States and guaranteed her fishing rights in the Newfoundland fisheries.

1784
7 May John Jay named Secretary for Foreign Affairs.

First American settlement established on north bank of Ohio River.

First anti-Christian book to be published in America – Ethan Allen's *Reason, the Only Oracle of Man*.

Breakaway state of Franklin created by 10,000 frontiersmen in the Watauga territory (forcibly reincorporated into North Carolina, 1788).

1785
11 Jan. Congress convenes in New York City (the temporary capital).

24 Feb. John Adams nominated as Minister to Britain. Henry Knox named as Secretary of War (Mar.).

17 Sept. Constitutional Convention approves three clauses protesting against slavery.

New York State makes slavery illegal.

First turnpike constructed (Little River Turnpike in Virginia).

1786
20 Feb. Challenge to Congress by New Jersey (which refuses to pay requisition).

26 Sept. Protesters led by Daniel Shays force Massachusetts State Supreme Court to adjourn.

20 Oct. Congress authorizes General Henry Knox to raise 1,340 troops to suppress Shays' rebellion.

Daniel Boone elected legislator of Kentucky territory.

1787
25 Jan. Shays leads 1,200 men in attack on arsenal at Springfield, Massachusetts.

4 Feb. Massachusetts militia quell Shays rebellion.

21 Feb. Congress endorses move to revise Articles of Confederation.

25 May–17 Sept. Washington presides over Constitutional Convention in Philadelphia which drafts US Constitution.

19 June Constitutional Convention votes 7–3 to use Virginia Plan as model for national government.

13 July Northwest Ordinance passed.

16 July Connecticut Compromise accepted by Congress (lower House to have proportional representation, equal representation in Senate).

27 Oct. First of Federalist Papers (see p. 322) published.

7 Dec. Delaware becomes first state to ratify the Constitution.

1788
21 June New Hampshire's ratification of the Constitution (the 9th state to do so) causes US Constitution to go into effect.

1789

1–6 Apr. First US Congress begins its session in New York City.
30 Apr. George Washington inaugurated as 1st President at Federal Hall in New York City.
26 Sept. John Jay becomes first Chief Justice of the United States.

1790

Philadelphia replaces New York as temporary capital.
29 May Rhode Island becomes 13th state to join the Union.

1791–94

Emergence of two main political parties/groups: the Federalists led by Alexander Hamilton and the Democratic-Republicans under Thomas Jefferson.

1791

25 Feb. Bank of the United States is chartered.
4 Mar. Vermont becomes 14th state to join the Union.
15 Dec. Bill of Rights (Amendments to Constitution) take effect.

1792

1 June Kentucky becomes 15th state.

1793

22 Apr. Washington issues neutrality proclamation after war breaks out between Britain and revolutionary France.

1794

22 Mar. Congress forbids slave trade to foreign ports.
27 Mar. Congress authorizes US Navy.
1 May First American trade union – Federal Society of Journeymen Cordwainers – established in Philadelphia.
July 'Whiskey Rebellion' by farmers, in protest at federal tax on whiskey, breaks out in western Pennsylvania. (Suppressed in mid-Nov.)
Foundation in Philadelphia of American Convention of Abolition Societies.

1795

29 Jan. Naturalization Act mandates five-year residency for citizenship.
8 May Post Office Department created by Congress.
24 June Jay Treaty ratification by Senate (completed 22 July).
Richard Allen ordained first black deacon in American Methodism.

1796
1 June   Tennessee admitted to Union as 16th state.
17 Sept. Washington's Farewell Address (he declines a further, third term as President).

1797
4 Mar.   John Adams inaugurated as 2nd President.

1798
8 Jan.   11th Amendment – no citizen of another state or country can sue any US state in the federal courts.
25 June   Aliens Act becomes law (authorizes President to expel aliens suspected of carrying out treasonable activities).
2 July   Prospect of war with France causes George Washington to be commissioned as Commanding General of US Army.
14 July   Sedition Act – provides for fines and jail sentences for those publishing false and malicious writing about the US President or government.
16 Nov.   Aliens and Sedition Acts declared unconstitutional by Thomas Jefferson's Kentucky Resolution (adopted by state legislature).
20 Nov.   French capture US schooner *Retaliation.*
24 Dec.   Virginia Resolution (by James Madison) also declares Aliens and Sedition laws unconstitutional.

1799
29 Mar.   New York State passes gradual Emancipation Act.
Sixth Congress convenes (the last to have a Federalist majority).
Slave rebellion in Southampton County, Virginia (2 whites killed).

1800
1 Nov.   President John Adams moves into White House. Later (21 Nov.) Congress meets for first time in Washington.

1801
4 Mar.   Inauguration of Thomas Jefferson as 3rd President (following crisis caused by tie in votes with Aaron Burr). This constitutional impasse removed by 1804 12th Amendment.

1801–05
War between US and North African pirates. The 'Tripoli War' ends with US forced to pay tribute.

1802
16 Mar.   West Point Military Academy set up by Act of Congress.

1803
24 Feb. In *Marbury v. Madison* Supreme Court declares Act of Congress unconstitutional – first such ruling (see p. 85).
1 Mar. Ohio created 17th state.
2 May Louisiana Purchase for $15 million from France.

1804
11 July Alexander Hamilton fatally wounded by Vice-President Aaron Burr in duel at Weehawken, New Jersey.
25 Sept. 12th Amendment proclaimed. Henceforth electors to vote separately for President and Vice-President.

1804–06
Exploration of Missouri River and Pacific Northwest by Lewis and Clark.

1805
26 Apr. Lewis and Clark reach mouth of Yellowstone River.
1 May Virginia state law requires all free future slaves to leave state.
25 May First employers' court action against a striking union (Federal Society of Journeymen Cordwainers).
4 July Final treaty with Indians for purchase of Cleveland.

1806
12 Dec. Thomas Jefferson appeals to Congress for ban on slave trade.

1807
1 Sept. Aaron Burr acquitted of treason (accused of plotting to build western empire).
22 Dec. Embargo Act bans all US trade with foreign countries in attempt to avoid conflict with Britain and France.

1808
1 Jan. Importation of slaves into the USA prohibited.

1809
4 Mar. Inauguration of James Madison as 4th President.

1810
Indian resistance to settlements in Ohio led by Tecumseh.
27 Oct. Madison proclaims annexation of West Florida from Spain.

1811
7 Nov. Conflict in Indiana Territory. General William Henry Harrison defeats Shawnee Prophet at Battle of Tippecanoe.

1812
14 Apr. Louisiana created a state.
19 June Maritime grievances caused the United States to declare war on Britain. A plan for a threefold attack on Canada failed, and British under General Brock forced the surrender of Detroit (16 Aug.).

1813
24 Apr. American expedition captured and burnt York (Toronto).
10 Sept. Americans under Commodore Perry won Battle of Lake Erie.
29 Sept. Americans advanced, recaptured Detroit and defeated General Proctor at the Battle of the Thames (5 Oct.).
18 Dec. British took Fort Niagara.

1814
July Americans advanced across the Niagara River, took Fort Erie, and won Battle of Chippewa (5 July). But after Battle of Lundy's Lane (25 July) they fell back on Fort Erie, which they later abandoned in Nov.
Aug. British veterans under Ross landed 40 miles from Washington, defeated the Americans at Bladensburg (24 Aug.), and captured and burnt parts of the capital.
11 Sept. American naval force won Battle of Plattsburg, halting a British invasion by way of Lake Champlain.
13 Sept. British attack on Baltimore repulsed.
15 Dec. Hartford Convention of delegates opposed to war.
24 Dec. War concluded by the Treaty of Ghent.

1815
8 Jan. Before news of the peace reached him, Pakenham was killed leading an unsuccessful British attack on New Orleans.
June Barbary pirates of North Africa defeated by US fleet under Capain Stephen Decatur.

1816
10 Apr. Second Bank of the United States chartered.
27 Apr. First protective tariff in USA.
11 Dec. Indiana created 19th state.

1817
4 Mar. Monroe becomes 5th President.
29 Apr. Rush-Bagot Agreement on disarmament of Great Lakes and Canadian border.
10 Dec. Mississippi created 20th state.
US acquires Florida from Spain in Seminole War (ratified by Adams-Onis Treaty with Spain, 22 Feb. 1819).

1818
20 Oct. Delineation of frontier with Canada; northern boundary of Louisiana Purchase.
3 Dec. Illinois created 21st state.

1819
2 Mar. Alabama created 22nd state.
6 Dec. Democratic-Republicans tighten grip (majority 156–27 in House, 35–7 in Senate).
Reconstruction of White House and Capitol completed.

1820
2 Mar. Missouri Compromise – Missouri admitted as slave state but slavery prohibited in rest of Louisiana Purchase north of 36°30′N.
24 Oct. Spain cedes Florida to USA.

1821
Settlement of Texas begins.
15 Mar. Maine became 23rd state.
10 Aug. Missouri created 24th state.

1822
4 May Congress votes money to open diplomatic missions in independent Latin American states.

1823
2 Dec. Promulgation of Monroe Doctrine excluding colonial settlements by non-American powers in western hemisphere. One of the key doctrines of American foreign policy.

1824
2 Mar. *Gibbons v. Ogden* judgment rules that only federal government can control inter-state trade.
25 May American Sunday School Union formed.
17 June Bureau of Indian Affairs established under War Department.
First recorded strike of women employees (weavers of Pawtucket, Rhode Island).
Workingman's Gazette, early labour paper, founded.
Illinois state proposal to establish slavery defeated.

1825
4 Mar. Inauguration of John Quincy Adams as 6th President (elected by House of Representatives following failure of any candidate to secure majority of electoral votes).
26 Oct. Completion of Erie Canal (linking New York with the West).

1826
24 Jan. Creek Indians of Georgia sign Treaty of Washington.
26 Apr. Treaty of friendship signed with Denmark.
First black (John Russworm) graduates from college (in Maine).

1827
28 Feb. Baltimore and Ohio railroad chartered.
16 Mar. *Freedom's Journal*, first black newspaper, published by John Russworm and Samuel Cornish.
4 July Slavery officially abolished in New York: 10,000 slaves freed.
Sam Houston elected Governor of Tennessee.
First anti-slavery novel, *Northwood*, published by Sarah Hale.

1828
Formation of Democratic Party.
19 Dec. South Carolina legislature resolves that the Tariff Act of May 1828 is unconstitutional and is null and void within the state.
22 Dec. Baltimore and Ohio railroad opened for passenger traffic.

1829
4 Mar. Andrew Jackson inaugurated as 7th President.

1830
April Joseph Smith organizes Mormon Church.
28 May Indian Removal Act passed: relocation of Cherokee Indians from Georgia to western Arkansas.

1831
13–23 Aug. Slave rebellion led by Nat Turner in Virginia. Some 57 whites killed. Turner executed.
17 Nov. Abolitionist periodical, *The Liberator*, founded by Garrison.

1832
6 Jan. Foundation of New England Anti-Slavery Society.
3 Mar. Supreme Court rules that federal government (not states) has jurisdiction over Indian territories (*Worcester v. Georgia*).
26 June Battle of Velasco (first bloodshed between Texans and Mexicans).
13 July Source of Mississippi River discovered by Henry Schoolcraft's expedition.
24 Nov. South Carolina state convention nullifies the Tariff Acts of 1828 and 1832.
5 Dec. President Jackson issues a proclamation against nullification and possible secession.
Oregon Trail becomes main route to the West.

1833

20 Feb. Congress reduces the tariff rates but passes a Force Act asserting the federal government's right to collect the duties.

Apr. American settlers agree to make Texas independent of Mexico.

May Oberlin becomes nation's first co-educational college.

1834

30 June Department of Indian Affairs established (to administer Indian lands west of the Mississippi River).

1 Aug. Slavery abolished throughout British Empire.

Methodists establish mission in Williamette Valley, Oregon.

1835

Aug. Distribution of 75,000 anti-slavery tracts by American Anti-Slavery Society incites slave-owners in South.

21 Oct. Pro-slavery mob attacks Female Anti-Slavery Society meeting in Boston.

Nov. Second Seminole War begins in Florida (ends 14 Aug. 1843). Chief Osceola leads Indian resistance.

16 Dec. Antimasonic Party nominates General William Henry Harrison for President.

1836

23 Feb.–6 Mar. The 'Siege of the Alamo'. Some 187 Texans and frontiersmen fight to the death in San Antonio against a vastly more numerous Mexican army.

2 Mar. Texas declares independence from Mexico (an independent state until 1845).

21 Apr. General Sam Houston defeats Mexicans under General Santa Anna in the Battle of San Jacinto.

15 June Arkansas becomes 25th state.

22 Oct. Sam Houston inaugurated as first President of the Republic of Texas.

First state child labour law (in Massachusetts) prohibits employment of children under the age of 15.

1837

First great depression in US – the 'panic of 1837'.

26 Jan. Michigan created 26th state.

3 Mar. Membership of Supreme Court increased to nine. Two associate judges added by Congress.

4 Mar. Inauguration of Martin Van Buren as 8th President.

7 Nov.   Abolitionist editor Elijah P. Lovejoy murdered by mob at Alton, Illinois.

1838
4 July   Iowa Territory established. Robert Lucas appointed first Governor.
3 Dec.   Joshua Giddings (Ohio Whig Representative) becomes first abolitionist in Congress.
'Mormon Wars' flare up as Mormons driven from Missouri to Illinois.

1839
Nauvoo, Illinois, settled by 10,000 Mormons driven from Missouri.

1840
4 July   Passage of Independent Treasury Act, allowing US government to bank its own funds.
First Jesuit missions organized north of Columbia River by Father de Smet.

1841
The Bidwell–Bartleson expedition to California – first overland migration to the Far West.
4 Mar.   William Henry Harrison becomes 9th President.
4 Apr.   John Tyler succeeds Harrison as 10th President.
9 Aug.   Signing of Webster-Ashburton Treaty (settles disputed boundary of Maine with Britain).
13 Aug.   Whig-controlled Congress repeals Independent Treasury Act.

1842
9 Aug.   Webster–Ashburton Treaty between USA and Canada ratified.

1843
First major overland migrants arrive in Oregon.

1844
12 Apr.   United States and Texas sign Annexation Treaty negotiated by John C. Calhoun.
3 July   Treaty of Wanghiya (between China and USA) opens up five Chinese ports for commerce. Legal rights granted to Americans living in China.
8 Aug.   Brigham Young to succeed Joseph Smith as Mormon head.
Blacks form Knights and Daughters of Tabor to end slavery by any means.

1845
3 Mar.   Florida becomes 27th US state.
4 Mar.   James K. Polk becomes 11th President.
29 Dec.   Texas becomes 28th US state.

1846
25 Apr.   Mexico attacks US troops on Rio Grande in Texas.
13 May   Congress declares war on Mexico.
15 June   Oregon frontier defined by Treaty of Washington. Boundary with Canada settled at 49th parallel.
5 Aug.   Treaty of Washington becomes effective.
28 Dec.   Iowa becomes 29th US state.

1847
10 Jan.   American forces capture Los Angeles, ending hostilities with Mexicans in California.
22–23 Feb.   Battle of Buena Vista, Mexico. US General Taylor defeats Mexican dictator Santa Anna.
9 Mar.   US amphibious expedition assaults and captures Vera Cruz, Mexico (29 Mar.).
24 July   Mormon settlers under Brigham Young reach Great Salt Lake and establish independent state of Deseret (now Utah).
13–14 Sept.   US General Winfield Scott captures Mexico City.

1848
24 Jan.   Gold discovered at Sutter's Mill, California, by James W. Marshall. Beginning of the gold rush of the '49ers'.
2 Feb.   Peace concluded with Mexico: Mexico cedes Arizona, New Mexico, California, Texas, Nevada, Utah and parts of Colorado and Wyoming by the Treaty of Guadeloupe-Hidalgo.
29 May   Wisconsin admitted as 30th state.
19–20 July   First women's rights convention held at Seneca Falls, New York.

1849
4 Mar.   Zachary Taylor becomes 12th President.

1850
19 Apr.   Clayton–Bulwer agreement on canal in Central America.
9 July   Death of Zachary Taylor: succeeded by Millard Fillmore as 13th President.
9 Sept.   California admitted as 31st (and free) state. Slave trade forbidden in District of Columbia (20th). The 'Compromise of 1850' between

slavery and anti-slavery forces. The Fugitive Slave Act orders federal government to capture runaway slaves.

1851
14 May   Opening of New York City to Lake Erie rail link.
5 June   *National Era* (anti-slavery paper) begins serialization of *Uncle Tom's Cabin.*
Young Men's Christian Association founded at Cleveland, Ohio.

1852
20 Mar.   Publication in Boston of Harriet Beecher Stowe's *Uncle Tom's Cabin.* Runaway publishing success.

1853
4 Mar.   Inauguration of Franklin Pierce as 14th President.

1854
28 Feb.   Foundation of Republican Party at Ripon, Wisconsin.
31 Mar.   First US commercial treaty with Japan: Commodore Matthew Perry forces opening of Japanese ports.
30 May   Kansas and Nebraska created Territories of USA. Kansas-Nebraska Act repeals Missouri Compromise.
29 June   Gadsden Purchase from Mexico (for $10 million) adds southern Arizona and New Mexico to US territory.

1855
Kansas is a centre of conflict between supporters and opponents of slavery.
28 Apr.   Massachusetts bans segregation in all schools.
3 Nov.   Anti-Chinese mob in Tacoma, Washington, drives Chinese out of town.
Frederick Douglass publishes *My Bondage, My Freedom.*

1856
6 June   Democrat convention at Cincinnati nominates James Buchanan for President, John C. Breckinridge for Vice-President.

1857
4 Mar.   Democrat James Buchanan becomes 15th President.
'Utah War' between Mormons and federal government.
James Birch operates first stage route across the West.

1858

12 May   Minnesota admitted as 32nd US state.

21 Aug.–15 Oct.   Lincoln–Douglas debates in Illinois senatorial race promote Lincoln to national prominence.

'Drake's folly' launches first oil bonanza. Rich mining discoveries at Pike's Peak and Comstock Lode.

1859

14 Feb.   Oregon created 33rd US state.

16 Oct.   John Brown's raid on Harper's Ferry, Virginia.

2 Dec.   Execution of John Brown after he is found guilty of inciting slave revolt.

1860

Pony Express established (ceases operations 1861).

6 Nov.   Republican Abraham Lincoln elected 16th President.

20 Dec.   Secession of South Carolina from the Union.

1861

Pacific Telegraph completed.

Secession of South Carolina followed by ten other states (Tennessee the last on 8 June 1861). For full list, see p. 58.

29 Jan.   Kansas created 34th US state.

8 Feb.   Congress of Montgomery. Formation of Confederation of eleven Southern states under President Jefferson Davis (elected provisional president, 9 Feb.).

4 Mar.   Inauguration of Abraham Lincoln as 16th President of the United States.

12–13 Apr.   Confederates take Fort Sumter (South Carolina): outbreak of the Civil War (see p. 240).

21 July   Confederate victory at first Battle of Bull Run (Manassas), Virginia.

10 Aug.   Battle of Wilson's Creek (Missouri).

1862

6–16 Feb.   Grant captures Fort Henry and Fort Donelson, Tennessee.

7–8 Mar.   Battle of Pea Ridge (Arkansas).

9 Mar.   Gunboat duel in Hampton Roads (Virginia).

6–7 Apr.   Battle of Shiloh (Tennessee).

25 Apr.   New Orleans captured by Admiral Farragut for the Union.

20 May   Homestead Act. Legislation provides for cheap land for settlement of the West.

31 May   Battle of Seven Pines (Virginia).

May–June   'Stonewall' Jackson's Shenandoah Valley campaign in Virginia.

7 July   Land Grant Act provides for sale of public land to benefit agricultural education.

29–30 Aug.   Second Battle of Bull Run (Second Manassas).

2 Sept.   Lincoln's declaration on slavery. All slaves free from 1 Jan. 1863.

17 Sept.   Confederates defeated at Antietam (Maryland).

13 Dec.   Battle of Fredericksburg (Virginia).

31 Dec.   Battle of Stones River, Tennessee (concluded 2 Jan. 1863).

1863

1 Jan.   Emancipation Proclamation issued by Abraham Lincoln.

Mar.   Beginning of Grant's final campaign against Vicksburg (Mississippi).

2–4 May   Confederate victory at Chancellorsville (Virginia).

June   Union consolidates hold on Mississippi River.

20 June   West Virginia created 35th US State.

1–3 July   Gettysburg defeat for Confederates. Lee's army turned back by General Meade (Pennsylvania).

4 July   Confederates defeated at Vicksburg.

9 July   Surrender of Port Hudson.

13–16 July   Draft riots in New York City: 1,000 dead.

19–20 Sept.   Battle of Chickamauga (Georgia).

24–25 Nov.   Defeat of Confederates at Chattanooga (Tennessee).

1864

Mar.–May   Red River Campaign (Mississippi and Louisiana).

5–7 May   Battle of the Wilderness (Virginia).

8–19 May   Battles at Spotsylvania (Virginia).

3 June   Battle of Cold Harbor (Virginia).

20–28 July   Battles around Atlanta (Georgia).

5 Aug.   Naval Battle of Mobile Bay (Alabama).

2 Sept.   Atlanta captured following General Sherman's march through Georgia.

31 Oct.   Nevada created 36th US State.

Nov.–Dec.   Savannah Campaign (Sherman's march to the sea) (Georgia).

29 Nov.   Sand Creek massacre of Cheyenne and Arapaho Indians by Chivington's Colorado Volunteers.

30 Nov.   Battle of Franklin (Tennessee).

15–16 Dec.   Battle of Nashville (Tennessee).

22 Dec.   Savannah surrenders to Union army.

1865

3 Feb.   Abortive peace conference at Hampton Roads, Virginia.

19 Mar.   Battle of Bentonville (North Carolina).

2 Apr.   Confederates evacuate Richmond and Petersburg (Virginia).

9 Apr. Lee capitulates to Grant at Appomattox Court House (Virginia).
14 Apr. Assassination of Lincoln (dies 15 April). Succeeded by Vice-President Andrew Johnson as 17th President.
26 Apr. Capitulation of last Confederate army at Durham, North Carolina, when Johnston surrenders to Sherman.
Oct. US demands withdrawal of French troops from Mexico.
18 Dec. 13th Amendment to the Constitution (slavery abolished).
Black Codes passed by Southern states.
24 Dec. Ku Klux Klan secretly formed in Tennessee.

1865–67
Sioux War.

1866
6 Apr. First post of the Grand Army of the Republic formed.
Congress takes control of Reconstruction, backing freedmen's rights.
Freedmen's Bureau Bill vetoed by Johnson (19 Feb.; passed over president's veto 10 July). Civil Rights Bill passed over his veto.
16 June Fourteenth Amendment (on civil rights) passed by Congress.
July Race riots in the South; worst outbreak in New Orleans kills 48 blacks.
20 Aug. National Labor Union organized.
21 Dec. Sioux destroy detachment of 82nd US Cavalry in Fetterman Massacre.
Nov. Congressional elections reduce Johnson's supporters in Congress.
Radical measures to reconstruct the South.
First cattle drive from Texas to Kansas.
25 Nov. Beginning of impeachment proceedings against President Johnson.

1867
1 Mar. Nebraska created 37th state.
2 Mar. First Reconstruction Act passed over Johnson's veto.
30 Mar. Alaska bought by USA from Russia for $7.2 million.
4 Dec. Organization of 'The Grange' pressure group to protect farmers' interests.
Birth of Abilene, first 'cow-town' in Kansas.
Tenure of Office Act passed (over Johnson's veto).

1868
24 Feb. Impeachment of President Johnson (126–47 vote in House). After Senate trial, vital vote is one short of two-thirds needed for conviction.
28 July Ratification of 14th Amendment to Constitution (see p. 59).
3 Nov. General Grant (Republican) elected as 18th President.

'Ohio Idea' (calling for redemption of federal bonds with Greenbacks) proposed by the Democrats, becomes a campaign issue.

1869
27 Feb.   15th Amendment proposed by Congress.
4 Mar.   Inauguration of General Ulysses S. Grant as 18th President.
10 May   Completion of first transcontinental railway. The golden spike driven into the ground at Promontory Point, Utah, links Union Pacific and Central Pacific.
24 Sept.   'Black Friday' in New York as financiers attempt to corner gold.
10 Dec.   Territory of Wyoming passes first woman suffrage law.
Knights of Labor formed in Philadelphia.
Attempt to annex Santo Domingo failed.
Massachusetts legislature establishes first state Board of Health.

1870
25 Feb.   First black in US Congress (Senator Hiram P. Revels of Mississippi).
30 Mar.   15th Amendment to Constitution passed (on suffrage).
31 May   First Enforcement Act passed to put down Ku Klux Klan.
Last four Confederate states restored to Union (Virginia, 26 Jan.; Mississippi, 23 Feb.; Texas, 30 Mar. and Georgia, 15 July).
End of Reconstruction governments in most Southern states.

1871
8 May   Treaty of Washington with Great Britain ends 'Alabama claims' (see p. 300).
8 July   Tweed Ring exposed in New York ('Boss' William Tweed convicted in 1873).
8–9 Oct.   Chicago fire destroys much of city: 300 killed, 100,000 homeless.

1872
22 May   Political rights restored to most Confederates by Amnesty Act.
4 Sept.   Credit Mobilier scandal exposed in New York press.
9 July   Horace Greeley nominated by Liberal Republicans.
5 Nov.   Grant wins presidential election despite Greeley.
Congress founds first national park – Yellowstone in Wyoming.

1873
Andrew Carnegie concentrates business interests in steel manufacturing.
18 Sept.   'Panic of 1873' triggered by failure of Jay Cooke's banking firm.

1874

Gold Rush begins in the Black Hills of Dakota.

Invention of barbed wire by J.F. Glidden.

18–20 Nov. Formation of Women's Christian Temperance Union.

1875

14 Jan. Resumption Act provides for return to gold standard in 1879.

1 Mar. Civil Rights Act gives equal rights to blacks in public accommodation and jury service (Act invalidated by Supreme Court, 1883).

1 May Grant Administration rocked by Whisky Ring scandals which indict 239.

Formation of Greenback Party.

1 Sept. Leaders of Irish secret society, the Molly Maguires (see p. 340) hanged for murder of mine officials and police.

1876

2 Mar. Impeachment and resignation on bribery charges of Secretary of War William W. Bellknap. The Senate later votes to acquit.

25 June Battle of the Little Big Horn in Montana. Massacre of General George A. Custer's troops of the 7th Cavalry by Sioux Indians led by Chief Crazy Horse and Chief Sitting Bull.

1 Aug. Colorado becomes 38th US State.

7 Nov. Constitutional crisis resulted from disputed Hayes–Tilden presidential election (Hayes eventually awarded Presidency, February 1877). *Tom Sawyer* published by Mark Twain.

1877

5 Mar. Rutherford Hayes inaugurated as 19th President.

10–24 Apr. Reconstruction governments ended in southern states: emergence of the 'Solid South'.

14 July National railroad strike begins. President Hayes sends in troops (16 July).

1878

17 Jan. US (along with Germany and Britain) signs commercial treaty with Samoa.

22 Feb. Greenback Labor Party organized.

28 Feb. Bland–Allison Act passed (bases monetary system on gold and silver. Silver at 16:1 ratio).

Sept. Desert Land Act passed.

1879

Henry George publishes *Progress and Poverty*.

Organization of Christian Science Church.

First Woolworth store opened (in Utica, New York).

1 Jan.   Resumption of redemption of greenbacks in gold by Treasury.
11 Mar.   Congress passes bill to restrict immigration of Chinese labourers;
vetoed by President Hayes.
19–21 Oct.   Electric light invented by Thomas A. Edison at Menlo Park,
New Jersey.

1880
Beginnings of 'New Immigration' – Eastern and Southern European
immigrants arrive in the States.
Mar.   Organization of Salvation Army.
1 Mar.   Supreme Court rules (in *Strauder v. West Virginia*) that 14th
Amendment renders exclusion of blacks from jury duty unconstitutional.
Apr.   National Farmers' Alliance organized.
8 June   James A. Garfield nominated by Republicans for President on
36th ballot.
2 Nov.   James A. Garfield elected President.

1881
19 Feb.   Kansas is first state to prohibit sale of alcohol.
4 Mar.   Republican James A. Garfield inaugurated as 20th President.
2 July   Garfield shot in Washington DC (dies later, 19 Sept.).
19 Sept.   Vice-President Chester Arthur becomes 21st President on death
of Garfield (sworn in 20th).
17 Nov.   Federation of Organized Trades and Labor Unions of the U.S.
is established by Samuel Gompers.
Tuskegee Institute for Negroes founded by Booker T. Washington.
Publication of *A Century of Dishonor* by Helen Hunt Jackson (its subject
is the mistreatment of Indians).

1882
2 Jan.   Standard Oil Trust created by John D. Rockefeller. Standard Oil
controls 90% of US oil refining.
6 May   Congress prohibits immigration of Chinese labourers. Chinese
Exclusion Act passed over President Arthur's veto.

1883
16 Jan.   Pendleton Act reforms civil service, creating basis of modern
system.
24 May   Opening of Brooklyn Bridge.
18 Nov.   US and Canadian railroads set up standard time zones.
Completion of Southern Pacific, Santa Fé and Northern Pacific railroads.

1884
4 Nov.   Grover Cleveland (Democrat) defeats James G. Blaine in presidential election.

Traditional Indian religious practices made criminal offence by Department of the Interior.

1885
4 Mar.   Grover Cleveland (Democrat) inaugurated as 22nd President. Cattle boom at peak.

1886
4 May   Haymarket Riot in Chicago at anarchist-labour demonstration. Seven police killed.
4 Sept.   Final surrender of Indian leader Geronimo in Apache Indian War in South-West.
25 Oct.   *Wabash* case nullifies state regulation of interstate railroads.
8 Dec.   American Federation of Labor founded at Columbus, Ohio, by 25 craft unions.
Severe winter decimates cattle herds.

1887
4 Feb.   Regulation of railroads by Interstate Commerce Act (Interstate Commerce Commission created).
8 Feb.   Dawes Severalty Act breaks up tribal reservations, providing for individual and family holdings.
11 Feb.   Cleveland vetoes Dependent Pension Bill.

1888
11–14 Mar.   Eastern US devastated by great blizzard. 400 deaths.
6 Nov.   Benjamin Harrison (Republican) defeats Cleveland in presidential election dominated by tariffs, despite Cleveland winning popular vote.
Publication of *Looking Backward* by Edward Bellamy.

1889
22 Feb.   North Dakota, South Dakota, Montana and Washington created states.
4 Mar.   Republican Benjamin Harrison inaugurated as 23rd President.
22 Apr.   Oklahoma land rush begins.
14 June   US (with Britain and Germany) establishes condominium over Samoa.
2 Oct.   First Pan-American Conference held in Washington.
2 Nov.   North Dakota and South Dakota admitted to the Union as 39th and 40th states.
8 Nov.   Montana admitted to the Union as 41st state.
11 Nov.   Washington admitted to the Union as 42nd state.

1890
2 July   Sherman Anti-Trust Act prohibits monopolies in industry.
3 July   Idaho becomes 43rd state.
10 July   Wyoming becomes 44th state, and is first to permit women to vote.
14 July   Sherman Silver Purchase Act regulates silver coinage.
1 Oct.   McKinley Tariff. Protective rates raised further.
29 Dec.   Battle of Wounded Knee: last major conflict with Indians. 200 Sioux Indians massacred. 'Closure' of American frontier.
'Grandfather clauses' introduced in Southern states to restrict black suffrage.
Mormon Church bans polygamy.

1891
3 Mar.   Office of Superintendent of Immigration created by Congress to deal with massive influx of immigrants.
19 May   Populist Party founded by farmers and labour activists.
22 Sept.   Additional 900,000 acres of Oklahoma Indian land opened for white settlement.
31 Dec.   Opening of Ellis Island as New York immigration centre.
How the Other Half Lives published by Jacob Riis (indictment of urban slums).

1892
6 July   Massacre at Homestead, Pennsylvania, when strikers at Carnegie Steel Company fire on blacklegs.
8 Nov.   Cleveland re-elected President. Election reveals growing strength of Populists.

1893
Onset of four-year depression following financial panic which bankrupts 15,000 businesses.
4 Mar.   Inauguration of Grover Cleveland as 24th President.
1 May   World's Columbian Exposition in Chicago celebrates 400th anniversary of European discovery of the Americas.
1 Nov.   Sherman Silver Purchase Act repealed by Cleveland.
Completion of Great Northern Railroad.
Anti-Saloon League organized.
Seminal essay by Frederick Jackson Turner, 'The Significance of the Frontier in American History'.

1894
Apr.   Mid-West unemployed (Coxey's Army) march on Washington led by Jacob S. Coxey. Coxey arrested (29th).

21 June–20 July   Pullman strike. Cleveland uses federal troops to restore order.

27 Aug.   Wilson–Gorman Tariff fails to reduce protective tariffs and includes provision for income tax.

1895

Feb.   Revolt in Cuba against Spanish rule.

20 May   Income tax declared unconstitutional by Supreme Court.

War threatened between US and Britain over Venezuelan boundary dispute. Olney Note issued by US Secretary of State (20 July). (Dispute settled Oct. 1899.)

1896

4 Jan.   Utah becomes 45th US state.

7 July   'Cross of Gold' speech by William Jennings Bryan at Chicago Democratic National Convention.

18 May   *Plessy v. Ferguson* case. Supreme Court legitimizes racial segregation – the 'separate but equal' doctrine.

12 Aug.   Beginning of Klondike gold rush to Alaska.

3 Nov.   William McKinley (Republican) defeats Bryan in bitter election contest.

1897

4 Mar.   William McKinley (Republican) becomes 25th President.

7 July   US protective tariff increased by Dingley Bill.

1898

15 Feb.   US battleship *Maine* blown up in Havana, Cuba – 260 killed.

24 Apr.   War breaks out with Spain (fought in Cuba and Philippines).

1 May   US Navy destroys Spanish fleet in Philippines.

20 June   Guam taken by US forces.

7 July   Hawaii annexed by US.

25 July–12 Aug.   Puerto Rico taken by US.

10 Dec.   Treaty of Paris with Spain. Spain cedes Cuba, Guam and Puerto Rico. The Philippines sold to US for $20 million.

Samoan Islands divided between US and Germany.

1899

4 Feb.   Beginning of Philippine insurrection and guerrilla war led by Emilio Aguinaldo.

6 Sept.   Open Door Policy set out by US: China to become an international market but retain independence.

Publication of *School and Society* (in support of progressive education) by John Dewey.

US claims Wake Island.

1900

14 Mar. Gold Standard Act passed by Congress.

12 Apr. Civil government in Puerto Rico established by Foraker Act.

20 June Boxer Uprising in China (US forces help suppress it).

6 Nov. Republican William McKinley re-elected President, defeating Bryan. Campaign issue dominated by the Philippines.

1901

25 Feb. United States Steel becomes first billion dollar corporation.

2 Mar. Platt amendment makes Cuba an American protectorate.

23 May Capture of Filipino guerrilla leader Aguinaldo.

6 Sept. William McKinley shot in Buffalo by an anarchist, Leon Czolgosz (dies 14 Sept).

14 Sept. Vice-President Theodore Roosevelt becomes (youngest ever) 26th President on death of McKinley.

18 Nov. Hay–Pauncefote Treaty (over Panama Canal) with Britain.

1902

10 Mar. President Roosevelt begins 'trust-busting' against J.P. Morgan's Northern Securities Company.

7 Apr. Texas Oil Company (Texaco) founded.

2 June Oregon first to adopt state-wide initiative and referendum law.

17 June Newlands Reclamation Act facilitates irrigation of desert lands in West.

28 June USA pays $40,000 to France for rights to Panama Canal. Treaty for its construction signed with Colombia (Jan. 1903).

1 July Philippine Government Act passed providing for rule by US Presidential Commission.

Maryland first state to adopt workmen's compensation law.

1903

22 Jan. Hay–Herrán Pact concerning Panama Canal territory.

14 Feb. Department of Commerce and Labor created.

19 Feb. Anti-Trust Law re-enforced.

3 Mar. Immigration Bill passed banning 'undesirables'.

23 May Wisconsin adopts first direct primary election law.

20 Oct. Great Britain and US settle Alaska frontier.

17 Dec. First airplane flight by Orville and Wilbur Wright at Kitty Hawk.

1904

23 Feb. Hay–Bunau–Varilla Treaty ratified, giving US control of Panama Canal Zone for $10 million.

14 Mar. Supreme Court orders dissolution of Northern Securities Company. First success for President Roosevelt's campaign to regulate big business.

Nov.   Theodore Roosevelt wins presidential election (8th). 'Roosevelt Corollary' to Monroe Doctrine announced. Start of the Russo-Japanese War.
6 Dec.   Muckraking *History of Standard Oil* published by Ida Tarbell.

1905
5 Sept.   Treaty of Portsmouth (New Hampshire) signed between Russia and Japan.

1906
18 Apr.   Most of San Francisco destroyed by earthquake: hundreds dead.
30 June   Pure Food and Drug Act passed (Meat Inspection Act passed the same day).
Construction of Panama Canal begins.

1907
26 Feb.   US Army given charge of building Panama Canal.
13 Mar.   Economic panic begins following collapse of Knickerbocker Trust Company.
14 Mar.   Immigration Commission established by Congress.
16 Nov.   Oklahoma admitted to the Union.

1908
30 May   National Monetary Commission created by Aldrich-Vreeland Act.
3 Nov.   Republican William Howard Taft elected 27th President.
Roosevelt appoints National Conservation Commission.

1909
4 Mar.   Republican Taft inaugurated President.
5 Aug.   Payne–Aldrich Tariff.

1910
19 Mar.   Revolt by Progressives in Congress against 'Cannonism', dictatorial rule of Speaker Joe Cannon.
18 June   Mann–Elkins Act reforms railroad regulation.
Aug.   Split of Taft and Roosevelt.
8 Nov.   Mid-term Congressional elections won by Democrats.
20 Nov.   Mexican Revolution begins.

1911
15 May   Standard Oil Company dissolved by Supreme Court in antitrust action.

1912
6 Jan. New Mexico created 47th state.
14 Feb. Arizona created 48th state.
6 Nov. Democrat Woodrow Wilson elected 28th President after 'Bull Moose' campaign of Theodore Roosevelt.

1913
4 Mar. Woodrow Wilson inaugurated.
25 Feb. Federal income tax introduced (16th Amendment).
31 May 17th Amendment to Constitution (concerning popular election of Senators).
3 Oct. Underwood Tariff reduces rates.
23 Dec. Federal Reserve System created.
Policy of 'Watchful Waiting' over counter-revolution led by Huerta in Mexico.

1914
14–15 Apr. US fleet shells (and seizes) Veracruz (Mexico).
5 Aug. US makes formal proclamation of neutrality in war between European powers.
15 Aug. Opening of Panama Canal to shipping.
15 Oct. Clayton Anti-Trust Act strengthens Federal anti-monopoly powers.

1915
23 Jan. Lansing becomes Secretary of State.
24 Jan. First large US loan to Allies.
7 May Sinking of *Lusitania* by German submarines: 128 American passengers die.
16 Sept. Haiti becomes a US protectorate.

1916
15 Mar. US troops invade Mexico in pursuit of revolutionary leader General Pancho Villa and remain until 19 Feb. 1917.
17 July Rural Credits Act aids farmers.
7 Nov. Woodrow Wilson re-elected Democratic President. Jeannette Rankin (Montana) becomes first woman member of House of Representatives. Jones Act extends local self-government powers in the Philippines.
29 Nov. US Marines land in Dominican Republic and remain until 1924.
18 Dec. Wilson sends 'peace note' to all belligerents calling on them to end war and take steps to preserve future peace.
Federal Farm Loan Act.

1917
17 Jan.   US pays Denmark $25 million for Virgin Islands.
3 Feb.   US breaks off diplomatic relations with Germany in protest against sinking of American shipping.
5 Feb.   Immigration Act excluding Asian labourers from US passed, despite presidential veto attempt.
1 Mar.   Zimmermann Telegram suggesting German–Mexican alliance against US made public in Washington.
2 Mar.   Jones Act declares Puerto Rico a US territory and its inhabitants American citizens.
6 Apr.   US declares war on Germany.
26 June   First of 2 million US troops land in France.
3 Nov.   US troops go into action in France for first time.
7 Dec.   US declares war on Austria-Hungary.
18 Dec.   18th (Prohibition) Amendment submitted to the states.

1918
8 Jan.   President Wilson announces Fourteen Points to Congress as basis of peace terms and post-war settlement.

1919
29 Jan.   18th Amendment to Constitution prohibiting sale, manufacture and transportation of alcoholic drink from 16 Jan. 1920 (i.e. prohibition) ratified by 36th state.
2 Oct.   President Wilson crippled by stroke.
19 Nov.   Senate refuses to ratify Versailles Treaty and US membership of League of Nations by 55 votes to 39.

1919–20
Mass arrests and deportations of left-wing and trade union activists.

1920
26 Aug.   19th Amendment to Constitution gives women the vote.
2 Nov.   Republican Warren Harding defeats Democrat James Cox in presidential election.

1921
13 Jan.   Census Bureau announces US an urban society with over half of population living in towns.
4 Mar.   Harding inaugurated as 29th President.
19 May   Immigration into US limited to 357,000 a year with quotas for nationalities.
Aug.   Wave of Ku Klux Klan (see p. 336) terrorist activity sweeps through the Southern and Mid-West states.

1922
6 Feb. US signs Washington Treaty with Britain, France, Italy and Japan limiting size of navies.

1923
20 Jan. US withdraws occupation forces from Germany.
2 Aug. Harding dies. Calvin Coolidge sworn in as 30th President on 3 Aug.
15 Sept. Oklahoma placed under martial law because of extent of Ku Klux Klan activities.
25 Oct. Teapot Dome scandal investigation begins into corruption in Harding's Administration.

1924
9 Aug. London Conference accepts US General Charles Dawes' plan for German war reparations payments. Germany to have $200 million international loan, two-year moratorium on payments, and submit to financial controls.
4 Nov. Coolidge wins presidential election.

1926
10 May US Marines land in Nicaragua to quell insurrection and leave on 5 June.

1927
23 Aug. Execution of anarchists Sacco and Vanzetti for murder allegedly committed in 1920 arouses world-wide protests.

1928
27 Aug. US and France sign Kellogg-Briand Pact outlawing war; 62 other states eventually sign.
6 Nov. Republican Herbert Hoover defeats Democrat Alfred Smith in presidential election.

1929
4 Mar. Hoover sworn in as 31st President.
6–31 Aug. Hague Conference accepts US businessman Owen Young's plan for future German war reparations payments. Germany to have $300 million international loan, reparations to be reduced, financial controls imposed by 1924 Dawes Plan to be removed, and payments to be completed in 1988.
24 Oct. 'Black Thursday'. Wall Street Crash starts as 13 million shares change hands, beginning panic selling which lasts till the end of October. Shares lose $30,000 million in paper value over three weeks. Leads to Depression which spreads from US to Europe.

1930
10 Feb.   158 arrests in Chicago for violation of Prohibition by producing estimated 7 million gallons of whiskey worth $50 million.
17 June   Hawley–Smoot Act raises tariff levels to new heights.
10 Dec.   Congress passes legislation to provide $116 million public works scheme to alleviate unemployment.

1931
20 June   Hoover announces 'moratorium' on war debts payments to US, effectively abandoning German war reparations.
Sept.–Oct.   Bank panic forces closure of 827 banks following run on funds by customers.

1932
2 Feb.   Reconstruction Finance Corporation set up to alleviate Depression. Lends $2 billion to banks, business and agriculture.
29 May   Thousand-strong unemployed veteran 'Bonus Army' march arrives in Washington seeking relief. It is joined by supporters through the summer and rises to 17,000.
28 July   Federal troops and tanks led by General Douglas MacArthur break up and disperse unemployed demonstrators in Washington.
8 Nov.   Democrat Franklin Roosevelt defeats Hoover in election.

1933
6 Feb.   Adoption of 20th Amendment (see p. 60).
4 Mar.   Roosevelt sworn in as 32nd President.
6 Mar.   Roosevelt declares Bank Holiday until 9 Mar. to prevent run on banks. Only financially solvent banks allowed to re-open.
9 Mar.   100 days of 'New Deal' legislation to provide relief to banks, industry, agriculture and the unemployed begins. Results in over $15 billion expenditure by 1940.
12 Mar.   Roosevelt broadcasts first of Sunday radio 'fireside chats'.
31 Mar.   Reforestation Unemployment Act creates Civilian Conservation Corps to reduce unemployment through a reforestation programme.
12 May   Agricultural Adjustment Act restricts production of some crops and finances farmers for not producing.
12 May   Federal Emergency Relief Act passed.
18 May   Tennessee Valley Act passed, establishing Tennessee Valley Authority to create work by extending rural electrification.
16 June   National Industrial Recovery Act creates the National Recovery Administration and the Public Works Administration.
5 Aug.   National Labor Board established under Senator Robert Wagner to arbitrate in collective bargaining disputes.

8 Nov.   Civil Works Administration established with initial $400 million funding to create 4 million jobs.

5 Dec.   Prohibition on manufacture and sale of alcohol repealed by 21st Amendment to Constitution.

1934

Agriculture devastated in Mid-Western states by drought and inadequate conservation of land.

31 Jan.   Farm Mortgage Refinancing Act passed to assist farmers.

28 June   Federal Farm Bankruptcy Act calls a moratorium on farm mortgage foreclosures.

1935

27 May   Sections of National Industrial Recovery Act declared unconstitutional by Supreme Court.

5 July   Wagner-Connery Act establishes National Labor Relations Board with authority to encourage collective bargaining.

14 Aug.   Unemployment and old-age insurance instituted by Social Security Act.

8 Sept.   Louisiana Governor Huey Long assassinated in State Capitol building.

9 Nov.   Committee for Industrial Organization formed as eventual breakaway from American Federation of Labor. Organizes occupations of car and steel works to encourage unionization in new industrial sectors.

1936

6 Jan.   Sections of Agricultural Adjustment Act declared unconstitutional by Supreme Court.

30 July   US signs London Naval Treaty with Britain and France to limit naval armaments.

3 Nov.   Roosevelt defeats Landon to win presidential re-election.

1937

22 July   Senate overturns Roosevelt's attempt to alter Supreme Court balance in his favour by appointment of additional liberal judges.

5 Oct.   Roosevelt calls for international sanctions against aggressive powers.

12 Dec.   Japanese aircraft bomb and sink US gunboat *Panjay* carrying Chinese refugees on Yangtse River. Japan apologizes.

1938

28 Jan.   Roosevelt calls on Congress to vote funds for expansion of Army and Navy.

26 May   House of Representatives Committee to Investigate Un-American Activities formed.

25 June   Minimum wage of 40c an hour and maximum working week of 40 hours guaranteed by 1940 under Wages and Hours Law. Child labour under age 16 banned.

1939

1 July   Federal Works Agency established to co-ordinate New Deal activities.

2 Aug.   Hatch Act outlaws political activity of federal employees below policy level.

1 Sept.   Roosevelt declares in radio talk that US will remain neutral in war.

3 Oct.   US and 20 members of Pan-American Conference sign Declaration of Panama establishing a 300-mile neutrality zone round American continent.

4 Nov.   Neutrality Act amended at Roosevelt's insistence to allow 'cash and carry' arms sales to belligerents, effectively favouring Britain.

1940

May   US fleet moved to Pearl Harbor. Japanese forces begin to occupy French Indo-China (Sept.).

30 July   Declaration of Havana by US and 20 American republics bans transfer of European colonies on American continent to other European powers.

3 Sept.   US gives Britain 50 destroyers in exchange for bases in Newfoundland and the West Indies.

16 Sept.   US introduces first peacetime conscription measure to draft 900,000 recruits a year.

5 Nov.   Roosevelt wins 3rd presidential term by defeating Republican Wendell Willkie.

1941

20 Jan.   Roosevelt inaugurated to 3rd term.

11 Mar.   Roosevelt authorized to supply war materials to Britain by Lend-Lease Act.

14 June   All German and Italian assets in US frozen.

July   Negotiations between US government and Japan propose neutral area in Indo-China; US freezes Japanese assets. Japanese propose withdrawal from Indo-China; America presents counter-demands (Nov.).

9–12 Aug.   Meeting between Roosevelt and Churchill off Newfoundland produces Atlantic Charter (q.v.) setting out post-war aims.

18 Aug.   Roosevelt abolishes limitations on size of armed forces.

26 Nov.   Japanese task force puts to sea in readiness for attack on Pearl Harbor.

5 Dec. Tokyo orders departure of diplomatic staff from Washington.
7 Dec. Japanese mount surprise attack on US naval base at Pearl Harbor.
8 Dec. Congress approves Roosevelt's declaration of war against Japan.
11 Dec. Germany and Italy declare war on US.
22 Dec. Large-scale Japanese landings in the Philippines.

1942
Jan. Emergency Price Control Act empowers fixing of maximum prices and rents.
2 Jan. Manila falls to Japanese; much of South-East Asia in Japanese hands.
16 Jan. Creation of War Production Board.
26 Jan. First US troops for European theatre arrive in Northern Ireland.
4–8 May Battle of the Coral Sea forestalls Japanese invasion of Australia through Port Moresby in New Guinea.
6 May Surrender of last American and Filipino forces at Corregidor.
2 June Battle of Midway; major defeat for Japanese navy.
Aug. Battle for Guadalcanal opens after US landing.

1943
1–7 Feb. Japanese withdraw from Guadalcanal.
Nov. Americans land on Makin and Tarawa in Gilbert Islands; beginning of island-hopping campaign.
Dec. American landing in New Britain.

1944
Feb. Americans land in Marshall Islands.
6 June D-Day landings in Normandy.
15 June Americans invade Saipan, Mariana Islands.
19–20 June Battle of the Philippine Sea – Japanese carrier forces receive crippling defeat and retire to Okinawa.
July Americans retake Saipan (9 July) and Guam (26 July).
Sept.–Oct. US marines take Peleliu Island in Palau Group.
20 Oct. American forces land in Philippines.
23–26 Oct. Battle of Leyte Gulf destroys much of remaining Japanese navy.
7 Nov. Roosevelt re-elected for 4th term (defeats Dewey).

1945
3 Feb. Americans capture Manila.
19 Feb. Marines land on Iwo Jima.
Feb.–Aug. · Large-scale incendiary raids on Tokyo begin massive air assault on Japanese cities.

7 Mar.   American forces take Lashio in northern Burma, opening the 'Burma Road' to China.

1 Apr.   Americans land in Okinawa.

12 Apr.   Roosevelt dies. Harry Truman sworn in as 33rd President.

8 May   VE Day. End of war in Europe.

2 June   Okinawa campaign completed.

26 June   Fifty nations sign United Nations Charter in San Francisco.

16 July   Atom bomb exploded near Alamogordo, New Mexico.

17 July   Potsdam Conference between Truman, Stalin and Churchill (later Attlee) reaches decision on division of Germany and demand for Japan's unconditional surrender.

6 Aug.   Atom bomb dropped on Hiroshima.

9 Aug.   Atom bomb dropped on Nagasaki.

14 Aug.   VJ Day. Japan acknowledges defeat.

2 Sept.   Japan formally surrenders on *USS Missouri* in Tokyo.

1946

11 Apr.   McMahon Act declares government monopoly over all US atomic energy activities.

4 July   US grants Philippines independence.

1 Aug.   Atomic Energy Act restricts exchange of nuclear information with other nations.

16 Oct.   UN General Assembly opens in New York.

1947

12 Mar.   Truman signs Greek-Turkish Aid Bill, promising the two states $400 million aid to resist Soviet aggression and internal communist subversion. Becomes known as the 'Truman Doctrine'.

5 June   Secretary of State George Marshall proposes Marshall Plan to assist European economic recovery.

23 June   Taft–Hartley Act outlawing trade union closed shop and allowing government to impose 'cooling-off' period before strike passed by Congress despite presidential veto.

26 July   Defense Department formed to co-ordinate military organization.

1948

3 Apr.   Marshall's European Recovery Program enacted. By 1952 Europe receives $17,000 million in aid.

24 June   Berlin airlift begins, US and Britain fly in 2 million tons of supplies to counter Soviet rail and road blockade. Ends following negotiations, 12 May 1949.

2 Nov.   Truman defeats Republican candidate Thomas Dewey in presidential election.

1949

20 Jan.   Truman inaugurated to 2nd term as president.

4 Apr.   US signs North Atlantic Treaty in Washington with eleven other states to create NATO alliance.

14 Oct.   Eleven Communist Party leaders jailed for advocating overthrow of government.

26 Oct.   Minimum Wage Bill (raises minimum wage from 40c to 75c).

1950

21 Jan.   Alger Hiss, a former State Department official, jailed for perjury after denying membership of a communist spy organization.

31 Jan.   Truman orders work to proceed on development of hydrogen bomb.

25 May   US, UK and France conclude Tripartite Agreement to reduce Middle East tension by guaranteeing existing borders and limiting arms sales.

1 July   US troops arrive as part of United Nations force to assist South Korea, invaded by North Korea on 25 June.

1 Aug.   Guam becomes a United States Territory.

28 Aug.   Truman takes control of railways to avert a strike. Returned to private owners on 23 May 1952.

26 Sept.   US troops recapture South Korean capital, Seoul.

7 Oct.   US troops cross 38th Parallel into North Korea and advance (by 20 Nov.) to Manchurian border on Yalu River.

29 Nov.   US troops forced to retreat in Korea by heavy Chinese attack.

11 Dec.   Supreme Court rules that 5th Amendment to the Constitution protects an individual from being forced to incriminate him or herself.

19 Dec.   US General Dwight Eisenhower appointed Supreme Commander of NATO forces in Europe.

1951

3 Jan.   22nd Amendment to the Constitution limits Presidents to two terms in office.

4 Jan.   Seoul abandoned by US forces.

14 Mar.   Seoul recaptured by US troops.

11 Apr.   General Douglas MacArthur dismissed by Truman from command in Korea and all military offices for defying policy by advocating attack on Communist China.

10 Oct.   Truman signs Mutual Security Act, authorizing over $7 billion expenditure overseas on economic, military and technical aid.

1952

8 Apr.   Truman takes control of steel works to avert strike; action ruled unconstitutional by Supreme Court.

25 July   Puerto Rico becomes a self-governing commonwealth.
1 Nov.   First hydrogen bomb exploded at Eniwetok atoll, Marshall Islands.
4 Nov.   Republican Dwight Eisenhower defeats Democrat Adlai Stevenson in presidential election.

1953
20 Jan.   Eisenhower inaugurated as 34th President.
20 Apr.   US Communist Party ordered to register with Justice Department as an organization controlled by the USSR.
19 June   Julius and Ethel Rosenberg executed as spies for passing atomic secrets to USSR.
27 July   Armistice signed at Panmunjom ends fighting in Korea. 54,000 US servicemen died in the war.

1954
12 Jan.   Secretary of State John Foster Dulles announces doctrine of 'massive retaliation', warning USSR that aggression will be met with nuclear attack.
8 Mar.   US mutual defence agreement with Japan allows gradual re-arming of Japan.
22 Apr.   Senate hearings into Senator Joseph McCarthy's claims of communist subversion in Army begin. They continue until 17 June.
17 May   Supreme Court outlaws racial segregation in schools (see p. 86).
24 May   Supreme Court declares Communist Party membership valid grounds for deportation of aliens.
8 Sept.   Manila Treaty creates South East Asia Treaty Organization (SEATO) of US and seven other states for military and economic co-operation.
2 Dec.   US signs Mutual Security Pact with Taiwan, guaranteeing protection from Chinese attack. In effect until 1978.
2 Dec.   Senate vote of censure against McCarthy effectively ends his witch-hunt campaign.

1955
12 Feb.   Eisenhower despatches troops to South Vietnam as military advisers.
16 Mar.   Eisenhower announces that atomic weapons would be used in event of war. US reported to have 4,000 bombs stockpiled.
18–23 July   US attends summit meeting with Britain, France and USSR. Independence of East and West Germany recognized; Eisenhower proposes 'open skies' aerial photography plan as move towards disarmament.
15 Aug.   US signs Austrian State Treaty with Britain, France and USSR, restoring Austrian independence within 1937 borders.

1 Dec. Black bus boycott led by Reverend Martin Luther King begins in Montgomery, Alabama, in protest against racial discrimination.

5 Dec. American Federation of Labor and Congress of Industrial Organizations merge under leadership of George Meany.

1956

6 Nov. Eisenhower defeats Stevenson in presidential election.

13 Nov. Supreme Court outlaws racial segregation on buses.

1957

5 Jan. Eisenhower Doctrine proposes military and economic aid to Middle East states threatened internally or externally by communism. Congress votes $200 million.

20 Jan. Eisenhower inaugurated to 2nd term as President.

24 Sept. Eisenhower despatches 1,000 paratroops to protect black high-school students asserting their rights to non-segregated education in Little Rock, Arkansas.

1958

15 July US troops intervene in Lebanon Civil War under Eisenhower Doctrine, following appeal from Lebanon president. Withdraw 25 Oct.

23 Aug. US military preparations provoked by fears that Chinese shelling of offshore Nationalist island of Quemoy is a prelude to invasion.

1959

3 Jan. Alaska becomes 49th state.

21 Aug. Hawaii becomes 50th state.

15–27 Sept. Eisenhower meets Soviet Prime Minister Nikita Khrushchev at Camp David and both agree on need for 'peaceful co-existence'.

1 Dec. US signs Antarctica Treaty with eleven other states guaranteeing the area's neutrality.

1960

19 Jan. US and Japan sign mutual defence pact. Comes into effect 23 June.

1 May American U–2 spy plane shot down over USSR and pilot captured.

9 May US announces suspension of U–2 flights.

16 May Summit conference with USSR in Paris terminated when Eisenhower refuses to apologize to Khrushchev over U–2 incident.

11 July American RB–47 reconnaissance bomber shot down over USSR.

9 Nov. Democrat John Kennedy narrowly defeats Republican Richard Nixon in presidential election.

1961

3 Jan. US breaks off diplomatic relations with Cuba over nationalization of American property without compensation.

20 Jan. Kennedy inaugurated as 35th President.

1 Mar. Kennedy sets up Peace Corps as part of overseas aid programme.

17 Apr. 1600-strong invasion of Cuba at Bay of Pigs by CIA-trained Cuban exiles with Kennedy's backing. Crushed by 20 April.

3–4 June Kennedy and Khrushchev discuss German unification at unsuccessful summit conference in Vienna.

6 Oct. Kennedy declares that a 'prudent family' should possess a fall-out shelter to protect itself in event of nuclear war.

5 Dec. Kennedy announces that five out of seven army recruits are rejected on physical grounds and calls for public to take up exercise and become 'athletes' rather than 'spectators'.

11 Dec. US despatches helicopters and crews to assist South Vietnam. 3,500 US troops in area.

1962

12 Jan. State Department announces that Communist Party members will be denied passports.

12 May US troops deployed in Thailand to counter communist threat. They withdraw on 27 July.

16 June Defense Secretary Robert McNamara announces 'flexible response' to replace 'massive retaliation' strategy.

27 June Kennedy promises Taiwan military assistance in the event of Chinese attack.

22–28 Oct. Cuban Missile Crisis. Kennedy announces aerial photography reveals Soviet missile sites in Cuba. Places Cuba under naval and air blockade to prevent delivery of missiles. Khrushchev removes missiles in return for US promise not to invade Cuba.

20 Nov. Kennedy signs order prohibiting racial discrimination in housing built with federal funds.

18 Dec. Nassau Agreement between Kennedy and UK Prime Minister Macmillan to provide Britain with Polaris nuclear missiles for submarines.

1963

5 Apr. Hot Line connected between White House and Kremlin.

17 June Supreme Court rules religious ceremonies not essential in schools.

25 June Kennedy announces on European tour that US 'will risk its cities to defend yours'.

5 Aug. Nuclear weapons tests in atmosphere, space and under water banned by treaty between US, UK and USSR.

28 Aug. Martin Luther King leads 200,000-strong civil rights 'freedom march' in Washington.

7 Oct. White House announces aid to Vietnam will continue and that war could be won by end of 1965.

22 Nov.   Kennedy assassinated in Dallas, Texas, by Lee Harvey Oswald. Vice-President Lyndon Johnson sworn in as 36th President.

1964

2 July   Civil Rights Act bans racial discrimination in services provision and by trade unions and businesses carrying on inter-state commerce.

5 Aug.   First US bombing of North Vietnam.

7 Aug.   Congress grants Johnson sweeping military powers under Gulf of Tonkin Resolution, following alleged North Vietnamese attacks on US destroyers (2–4 Aug.).

30 Aug.   Johnson signs anti-poverty Economic Opportunity Policy, providing almost $1 billion for community action programmes.

27 Sept.   Warren Commission, appointed to investigate Kennedy assassination, declares there was no conspiracy and that Oswald acted alone.

3 Nov.   Johnson defeats Republican Barry Goldwater in election.

1965

20 Jan.   Johnson is inaugurated President.

18 Feb.   Defense Secretary McNamara announces deterrent strategy of 'mutually assured destruction'.

8 Mar.   US combat troops land in Vietnam bringing numbers involved to 74,000.

28 Apr.   400 US Marines land in Dominican Republic to prevent left-wing takeover. The force eventually rises to 24,000.

15 June   US troops in first action against Viet Cong.

28 July   Johnson announces numbers of US troops in Vietnam will be increased from 74,000 to 125,000.

30 July   Congress passes Medicare programme, providing federal medical insurance for over-65s.

6 Aug.   Government takes powers under Voting Rights Act to compel local authorities to register black voters and to remove obstacles to their voting.

11 Aug.   Black riots begin in Watts, Los Angeles, and continue until 16 Aug. 35 die.

17 Oct.   Demonstrations throughout US against involvement in Vietnam.

19 Oct.   House Committee on Un-American Activities begins investigation into Ku Klux Klan.

27 Nov.   25,000 demonstrate in Washington against Vietnam War.

1966

8 Feb.   Declaration of Honolulu by Johnson and South Vietnam Premier Ky promises economic and social reforms in Vietnam.

2 Mar.   Defense Secretary Robert McNamara announces US forces in Vietnam will be increased to 235,000.

11 June   US forces in Vietnam to rise to 285,000.

1 July   Medicare comes into operation.

8 Nov.   Republican Edward Brooke becomes first black ever elected to Senate.

1967

27 Jan.   Space Treaty with UK and USSR outlaws use of nuclear weapons in space.

23–25 June   Summit meeting between Johnson and Soviet Prime Minister Kosygin in Glassboro, New Jersey.

22 July   Announcement of intention to deploy 525,000 US troops in Vietnam by end of 1968.

23 July   Black riots in Detroit. Troops deployed as disturbances continue until 30 July. 40 die and over 2,000 injured.

27 July   Puerto Rico votes against independence and to remain a US commonwealth territory.

21 Oct.   Major anti-Vietnam War demonstration in Washington.

1968

23 Jan.   North Korea seizes crew of *USS Pueblo* and accuses them of spying. They are released on 22 Dec.

30 Jan.   Viet Cong open Tet Offensive. Although a military failure for the communists, the attack has a dramatic effect on US commitment to war in Vietnam.

29 Feb.   National Advisory Committee on Civil Disorders (Kerner Commission) Report condemns white racism in US and calls for aid to black communities.

16 Mar.   US troops massacre 450 inhabitants in Vietnamese village of My Lai. News does not break until November. Lt. William Calley given life imprisonment for atrocity on 29 March 1971 but sentence reduced.

31 Mar.   Johnson announces end to bombing of North Vietnam and that he will not run for second term as President.

4 Apr.   Martin Luther King assassinated in Memphis, Tennessee. Riots in over 100 cities follow.

2 May   Black 'Poor People's March' on Washington begins. Culminates in 3,000-strong camp at 'Resurrection City'.

13 May   Preliminary Vietnam peace talks open in Paris.

5 June   Senator Robert Kennedy shot in Los Angeles while campaigning for Democratic presidential nomination. Dies on 6 June.

1 July   US signs Nuclear Non-Proliferation Treaty with Britain and USSR.

26 Aug.   Anti-Vietnam War demonstrations at Democratic convention in Chicago quelled by police and troops. Disturbances continue until 30 Aug.

8 Nov.   Republican Richard Nixon defeats Democrat Hubert Humphrey in presidential election.

1969

20 Jan. Nixon inaugurated as 37th President.
25 Jan. Full Vietnam peace talks begin in Paris.
Mar. US troops in Vietnam reach their highest level at 541,000.
15 Oct. Mass demonstrations against Vietnam War throughout US.
3 Nov. Nixon announces intention to withdraw US forces and to 'Vietnamize' the war.
25 Nov. US renounces use of biological weapons.

1970

16 Apr. Strategic Arms Limitations Talks (SALT) open between US and USSR in Vienna.
21 Apr. Nixon announces 150,000 US troop reduction in Vietnam over next year.
30 Apr. US troops deployed in Cambodia.
4 May National Guard kills four anti-war students demonstrating at Kent State University, Ohio.

1971

20 Apr. Supreme Court upholds 'busing' as a means of achieving racial balance in schools.
2 May Beginning of three-day anti-Vietnam War protest in Washington. Over 13,000 arrests.
3 June Publication of leaked 'Pentagon Papers', disclosing hidden background to Vietnam War. Supreme Court refuses to prevent publication, 30 June.
10 June US lifts 21-year trade embargo on China.
5 July 26th Amendment to Constitution reduces voting age to 18.
11 Aug. Law enforcing educational desegregation in eleven Southern states comes into effect.
15 Aug. Nixon introduces anti-inflation wages and prices freeze; suspends convertibility of dollar into gold.
25 Oct. US signs Seabed Treaty with USSR, UK and other states, banning nuclear weapons on the ocean floor.

1972

21–25 Feb. Nixon reverses US policy by visiting Communist China.
6 Apr. US resumes bombing of North Vietnam following communist offensive.
15 May Alabama Governor George Wallace, in the past an uncompromising segregationalist, wounded and crippled in assassination attempt.
22–30 May Nixon and Brezhnev agree to limit atomic weapon production at Moscow summit. Senate ratifies agreement on 3 Aug.

17 June Five men arrested burgling the Democratic National Committee offices at Watergate building, Washington. On June 22 Nixon denies White House involvement.

7 Nov. Nixon wins landslide victory over Democrat George McGovern in presidential election.

1973

8–30 Jan. Watergate burglary trial. Two of the seven convicted had been 'Committee to Re-elect the President' officials, and one a White House consultant.

28 Jan. Ceasefire ends US involvement in Vietnam War. Final combat troops leave 29 Mar.

7 Feb. Senate forms a committee to investigate the Watergate affair.

27 Feb. Indians protesting against government treatment mount siege of Wounded Knee. Two Indians die before it ends on 8 May.

30 Apr. White House advisers H.R. Haldeman and John Ehrlichman and staff member John Dean resign over participation in Watergate cover-up.

11 May 'Pentagon Papers' case against Daniel Elsberg dismissed because government used burglary to obtain evidence.

16–24 June Nixon and Brezhnev summit meeting in US reaches agreement on co-operation to prevent nuclear war and on future arms negotiations.

1 July Congress orders end to US bombing of Cambodia and military action in area by 15 Aug.

16 July Revelation that Nixon has taped his White House conversations since 1970, eventually showing his active involvement in Watergate cover-up.

10 Oct. Vice-President Spiro Agnew forced to resign after disclosure of income tax evasion.

17 Oct. Arab states ban oil supplies to US in protest against support for Israel. Ends 1974.

23 Oct. Nixon ordered to surrender White House tapes to Senate Watergate investigation under threat of impeachment.

7 Nov. Congress votes to limit presidential powers to wage war.

6 Dec. Gerald Ford sworn in as Vice-President.

1974

1 Jan. Three former cabinet members and Nixon's two leading White House aides are convicted for their part in covering up Watergate events.

10 Jan. Defense Secretary James Schlesinger announces 'limited strategic strike options' as new nuclear doctrine.

7 May Ford declares Vietnam War era is over a week after Saigon falls to communists.

3 July US signs Threshold Test Ban Treaty with USSR, placing limits on underground nuclear testing.

24 July Supreme Court orders Nixon to release his tape recorded conversations.

9 Aug. Nixon resigns under threat of impeachment proceedings for involvement in Watergate. Ford sworn in as 38th President.

8 Sept. Ford grants Nixon full pardon.

16 Sept. Ford announces amnesty for Vietnam War draft evaders and deserters.

1975

1 Aug. US signs Helsinki Treaty with USSR guaranteeing European post-war boundaries and recognizing human rights.

1976

26 Apr. Senate Committee on Central Intelligence Agency demands stronger control over and greater accountability of intelligence services following concern over activities.

1 Nov. Democrat Jimmy Carter defeats Ford in presidential election.

1977

20 Jan. Carter inaugurated as 39th President.

7 Sept. Carter signs Panama Canal Zone Treaty, agreeing to evacuate Canal Zone by the year 2000.

1978

6 June Proposition 13 in California state referendum limits local taxes, triggering a campaign nationally to reduce federal and state taxation.

5–17 Sept. Carter mediates at Camp David negotiations between Egyptian President Sadat and Israeli Prime Minister Begin, culminating in outline of Middle East peace treaty. Treaty signed at White House, 26 March 1979; effective 25 April 1979.

1979

1 Jan. US establishes full diplomatic relations with China and severs links with Nationalist government on Taiwan.

8 Feb. US withdraws support from President Somoza of Nicaragua, ensuring his downfall to Sandinista revolution.

12 Feb. Carter appeals for voluntary conservation to limit effects of growing energy crisis.

28 Mar. Serious atomic reactor accident at Three Mile Island, Pennsylvania, provokes loss of public confidence in nuclear power.

13 June $100 million awarded to Sioux Indians as compensation for land taken from them in 1877.

27 Sept. Division of Department of Health, Education and Welfare into Departments of Education and Health and Human Services.

23 Oct.   Congress grants Carter powers to introduce petrol rationing because of world oil crisis.

4 Nov.   Iranian students occupy US Embassy in Tehran and seize 52 American hostages.

4 Nov.   US establishes formal relations with German Democratic Republic.

1980
24–25 Apr.   Unsuccessful helicopter attempt to rescue Tehran Embassy hostages – eight US citizens dead.

4 Nov.   Republican Ronald Reagan gains landslide presidential election victory over Carter.

21 Dec.   Iran demands $10,000 million payment for release of hostages.

1981
20 Jan.   US Embassy hostages released from Tehran as Reagan is sworn in as 40th President.

30 Mar.   Reagan wounded in assassination attempt in Washington.

13 Aug.   Reagan's New Economic Programme projects 25% income tax reductions in 1981–84.

1982
June   Resignation of Alexander Haig as Secretary of State. Unemployment at 10.8%, a post-1945 record. Siberian pipeline sanctions lifted. Democrat mid-term gains.

1983
23 Oct.   241 US Marine members of peace-keeping force killed by suicide bombers in Beirut.

25 Oct.   US troops invade Grenada with forces of six Caribbean states to put down alleged left-wing threat. Suffer 42 dead in fighting with Grenadian army and Cuban construction workers.

1984
28 Feb.   Senator Gary Hart of Colorado wins New Hampshire primary.

6 June   Former Vice-President Walter Mondale wins Democratic nomination.

12 July   Geraldine Ferraro first woman Vice-Presidential candidate.

6 Nov.   Landslide re-election victory for Ronald Reagan.

1985
20 Jan.   Reagan inaugurated to 2nd term as President.

1 May   US bans all trade with Nicaragua.

19–21 Nov.   Reagan and Gorbachev summit in Geneva agrees on future annual meetings but fails to resolve differences over 'Star Wars' as obstacle to arms control.

1986

7 Jan. Reagan orders US citizens to leave Libya and bans trade in retaliation for alleged Libyan involvement in international terrorism.

18 Feb. Reagan announces $15 million military aid to anti-government guerrillas in Angola.

20 Mar. House of Representatives rejects Reagan's $100 million aid package to anti-government Contra guerrillas in Nicaragua. Finally approves on 25 June and Reagan signs Bill on 18 Oct.

24 Mar. US task force, asserting sailing rights in Gulf of Sidra, attacked by Libyan missile ships. US sinks two ships and bombs coastal radar installation.

14 Apr. American F–111 bombers strike Tripoli and Benghazi following alleged Libyan links with international terrorism.

18 June House of Representatives votes for trade embargo on South Africa and withdrawal by US companies.

27 June International Court rules US support of Contras in Nicaragua illegal.

15 July US troops deployed in Bolivia to assist in operations against cocaine producers.

26 Sept. Reagan vetoes South African sanctions proposal by House of Representatives.

2 Oct. US Senate defies presidential veto and imposes trade sanctions on South Africa.

10–11 Oct. Reagan and Gorbachev meet in Reykjavik, Iceland. Blame each other for failure to achieve arms control agreement.

13 Nov. Reagan admits US arms sales to Iran, opening what becomes known as the Iran–Contra scandal.

25 Nov. Further revelations about arms sales to Iran force resignations of National Security Adviser Admiral John Poindexter and Marine Colonel Oliver North.

2 Dec. Reagan appoints special prosecutor to investigate Iran–Contra scandal. As investigation develops, details emerge of plan for proceeds of arms sales to Iran to be diverted to aid Contra forces in Nicaragua.

1987

Feb. Report of Tower Commission on Iran–Contra affair.

3 Mar. Reagan says arms for Iran had been intended to help in release of hostages held in Middle East.

15 July Admiral Poindexter says Reagan was unaware of plan to divert Iran arms sales proceeds to aid Contras.

12 Aug. Reagan accepts responsibility for Iran–Contra affair but denies knowledge of diversion of funds.

19 Oct. 'Black Monday': massive slump in share prices on Wall Street.

24 Nov. US reaches agreement with USSR on scrapping of intermediate range nuclear missiles.

8–11 Dec. Reagan and Gorbachev summit meeting in Washington. Intermediate Range Missiles Treaty signed; agreement on further arms reductions proposals and for a meeting in 1988.

1988

16 Mar. Poindexter and North indicted on Iran–Contra charges.

29 May Reagan and Gorbachev meet in Moscow and agree on further intermediate range missile reductions.

3 July USS *Vincennes* shoots down Iranian airbus over Gulf of Iran, killing 290 passengers.

8 Nov. George Bush defeats Democrat Michael Dukakis in presidential election.

14 Dec. US declares willingness to talk with Palestine Liberation Organization following Yasser Arafat's 7 Dec. acceptance of Israel's right to exist. Discussions in Tunis take place on 16 Dec.

1989

4 Jan. US Navy jets shoot down two Libyan aircraft over Mediterranean.

20 Jan. George Bush sworn in as 41st President.

15 Mar. Veterans' Administration is made a Cabinet department.

7 Nov. Democrats' striking success in mid-term elections. Douglas Wilder (Democrat) elected Governor of Virginia (nation's first black Governor since the Reconstruction Era). First elected black mayor of New York City (David Dinkins).

18 Nov. Pennsylvania becomes first state to restrict abortions (Supreme Court gave states this right in July).

19 Nov. Increase in minimum wage (from $3.35 an hour to $4.25 by 1991).

20 Dec. US troops invade Panama. Noriega regime overthrown. (Noriega seeks asylum in Vatican nuncio's mission.)

1990

7 Aug. US forces embark for Saudi Arabia to repel Iraqis from Kuwait (Operation Desert Shield).

15 Nov. President Bush signs Bill designed to reduce federal budget deficits by $500 billion over five years. Upper personal income tax rate to rise from 28% to 31%.

1991

Jan.–Feb. Defeat of Iraqi forces and liberation of Kuwait (Operation Desert Storm) in '100-hour war' (see p. 246).

9 July   President Bush cancels the sanctions set up against the Republic of South Africa in 1986.

10 July   Defense Base Closure and Realignment Commission proposals to reduce military bases accepted (start of post-Cold War rundown).

1992

Apr.–May   Rioting and arson in south-central Los Angeles (following acquittal of those police accused of beating Rodney King). Death toll estimated at 52.

May   27th Amendment (concerning Congressional pay rises) finally becomes part of Constitution (when Michigan becomes 38th state to approve).

15 July   Governor Bill Clinton of Arkansas nominated as candidate for presidency (Senator Al Gore of Tennessee for Vice-President – 16 July). The populist Ross Perot, a Texan billionaire, temporarily withdraws from the presidential race (17 July).

3 Nov.   Bill Clinton elected 42nd President, defeating Bush. Independent candidate H. Ross Perot polls 19%. Record number of women elected to Senate. Carol Moseley Braun of Illinois becomes first black woman to serve in Senate.

24 Nov.   The last American soldier leaves the military base in Subic Bay and in this way the US military presence (there since 1898) ends in the Philippines.

9 Dec.   UN military force, led by US troops, arrives in Somalia.

17 Dec.   US, Canada and Mexico sign the North American Free Trade Agreement (NAFTA) treaty.

1993

20 Jan.   Inauguration of Bill Clinton as 42nd President.

22 Jan.   Executive order of Clinton overturns restrictions on abortion imposed under Reagan and Bush.

25 Jan.   Hillary Clinton appointed to head Task Force on National Health Care Reform.

26 Feb.   Bombing of World Trade Center, New York City, kills six people.

28 Feb.   Four federal agents killed in botched raid on Branch Davidian site in Waco, Texas. Beginning of 51-day siege and storming of compound.

12 Mar.   Janet Reno becomes first woman US Attorney General.

19 Apr.   FBI agents' final assault on Branch Davidian ranch at Waco, Texas – 80 dead.

13 May   Formal abandonment of Strategic Defense Initiative ('Star Wars' programme).

26 June   US rocket attack on Iraq in retaliation for earlier attempt on the life of George Bush.

19 July Clinton appears to remove ban on gays and lesbians serving in armed forces.

20 July Suicide of Vincent Foster, Deputy White House counsel and close friend of President Clinton.

26 July Disaster areas now proclaimed in nine states after worst Mississippi floods in living memory – 'The Great Flood of 1993'.

6 Aug. Tax-raising budget breaks election pledges.

29 Sept. Health-care reform package unveiled – the 1993 American Health Security Act.

4 Nov. Democrat David Dinkins narrowly defeated as Mayor of New York by Republican Rudolph Giuliani.

24 Nov. Following successful passage through the House of Representatives, the Senate also endorses the Brady Bill, which creates a compulsory five-day waiting period for the purchase of fire-arms.

1994

1 Jan. North American Free Trade Agreement came into force (endorsed earlier, on 18 November 1993, by Congress).

3 Feb. The nineteen-year old economic embargo against Vietnam lifted.

25 Mar. Last US troops leave Somalia.

30 May Dan Rostenkowski, Chairman of House Ways and Means Committee, indicted on fraud and corruption charges.

15 June Four-day tour of North Korea by ex-President Jimmy Carter. Threat of US sanctions avoided.

July Special counsel Kenneth Starr appointed to probe Whitewater allegations.

18 Aug. State of emergency in Florida in anticipation of influx of Cuban refugees. President Clinton ends 30-year policy of right to asylum for Cuban refugees (19th).

26 Sept. US sanctions lifted against Haiti (US troops had earlier (19th) landed in mission to restore democracy).

9 Nov. Sweeping Republican gains in mid-term elections. Republicans gain control of Senate and (for first time for 40 years) the House of Representatives. Triumph of Newt Gingrich and the 'Contract with America'.

6 Dec. Orange County (California) files for bankruptcy.

11 Dec. Miami Summit pledges creation of Free Trade Area of the Americas to end trade barriers by 2005.

1995

4 Jan. Senator Bob Dole (Kansas) becomes Majority Leader. Newt Gingrich becomes first Republican Speaker since 1954.

2 Mar. Republican amendments to balance budget rejected by Senate.

7 Mar.   Gerry Adams, Sinn Fein leader, received at White House.

19 Apr.   Oklahoma bombing by right-wing anti-government militia leaves 168 dead. Arrest of Timothy James McVeigh (found guilty 2 June 1997).

2 May   Agreement signed with Cuba regulating immigration policies.

11 July   Establishment of full diplomatic links with Vietnam.

17 Aug.   Special prosecutor indicts business associates of President Clinton over Whitewater affair.

5 Sept.   Ross Perot announces formation of the Reform Party.

26 Oct.   Senate Legal Affairs Committee resumes investigation into the Whitewater affair.

14 Nov.   Government 'shut-down' after budget deadlock between President and Congress.

21 Nov.   Dayton Peace Accords signed. US commits 20,000 troops to Bosnia.

1996

7 Jan.   Longest-ever government shut-down ended by compromise budget proposals.

21 Feb.   In primary elections, Republican Pat Buchanan wins New Hampshire (followed by victory for millionaire Steve Forbes in Arizona, 27 Feb.).

6 Mar.   Senator Bob Dole wins vital primaries, effectively securing Republican Party presidential nomination.

20 Mar.   US Navy task force sent to Taiwan in stand-off with China.

July   Bomb blast aboard TWA flight 800 over Long Island. Over 220 dead. Bomb blast at Centennial Olympic Games at Atlanta. Two die, over 100 injured.

Aug.   Welfare Reform Bill signed by Clinton. End of the 60-year old 'safety-net' for those in poverty. Resignation of Dick Morris, presidential campaign manager, in sex scandal, overshadows Chicago Democratic Convention (29th).

3 Sept.   Missile strike launched to punish Iraqi action over Kurds.

14 Oct.   Dow Jones passes 6,000 mark to hit new high.

Nov.   Presidential election results in comfortable victory for incumbent Bill Clinton (with 49% of the vote and 379 electoral votes). Bob Dole (Republican) took 42% of the vote and 159 electoral votes. Ross Perot's Reform Party polled only 8.4% of the vote. Turnout dropped to its lowest in post-war history (at 49.1%). Republicans retained control of both houses of Congress in a 'celebration of incumbency'. Presidential election followed by retirement of Warren Christopher as Secretary of State.

5 Dec.   Madeleine Albright named as first woman Secretary of State. Anthony Lake nominated new CIA Director and Republican William Cohen named as Defense Secretary.

Helms–Burton Bill (on trade with Cuba) becomes law.

1997

7 Jan.   Newt Gingrich narrowly re-elected Speaker despite allegations of corruption against him.

13 Jan.   Sexual harassment case against Bill Clinton, brought by Paula Jones, reaches Supreme Court.

20 Jan.   Bill Clinton inaugurated for second term, the first Democrat since Roosevelt in January 1937 to achieve this feat.

The Constitution

The making of the Constitution

Continental Congress

The First Continental Congress was a meeting of the delegates of 12 of the British colonies in North America. It met in Philadelphia in September 1774 to consider resistance to the Intolerable Acts (q.v.). The Congress narrowly failed to adopt Joseph Galloway's Plan of Union for an imperial federation among them with a colonial legislature, but did establish a Continental Association to boycott economic relations with Great Britain. The Second Continental Congress, which assembled in May 1775, organized the military defence of the colonies in the War of Independence (q.v.) and passed the Declaration of Independence (q.v.). It acted as the effective American government during the war and under the Articles of Confederation (q.v.).

Presidents of Congress: 1774–89

Name	State	Elected
Peyton Randolph	Virginia	5 Sept. 1774
Henry Middleton	South Carolina	22 Oct. 1774
Peyton Randolph	Virginia	10 May 1775
John Hancock	Massachusetts	24 May 1775
Henry Laurens	South Carolina	1 Nov. 1777
John Jay	New York	10 Dec. 1778
Samuel Huntington	Connecticut	28 Sept. 1779
Thomas McKean	Delaware	10 July 1781
John Hanson	Maryland	5 Nov. 1781
Elias Boudinot	New Jersey	4 Nov. 1782
Thomas Mifflin	Pennsylvania	3 Nov. 1783
Richard Henry Lee	Virginia	30 Nov. 1784
John Hancock	Massachusetts	23 Nov. 1785
Nathaniel Gorham	Massachusetts	6 June 1786
Arthur St Clair	Pennsylvania	2 Feb. 1787
Cyrus Griffin	Virginia	22 Jan. 1788

Meeting place (and dates) of Continental Congress and National Congress of the Articles of the Confederation

Philadelphia, Pennsylvania:	5 Sept. 1774 to 26 Oct. 1774
	10 May 1775 to 12 Dec. 1776
Baltimore, Maryland:	20 Dec. 1776 to 4 Mar. 1777
Philadelphia, Pennsylvania:	5 Mar. 1777 to 18 Sept. 1777
Lancaster, Pennsylvania:	27 Sept. 1777 (one day only)
York, Pennsylvania:	30 Sept. 1777 to 27 June 1778
Philadelphia, Pennsylvania:	2 July 1778 to 21 June 1783
Princeton, New Jersey:	30 June 1783 to 4 Nov. 1783
Annapolis, Maryland:	26 Nov. 1783 to 3 June 1784
Trenton, New Jersey:	1 Nov. 1784 to 24 Dec. 1784
New York City, New York:	11 Jan. 1785 to 4 Nov. 1785
	7 Nov. 1785 to 3 Nov. 1786
	6 Nov. 1786 to 30 Oct. 1787
	5 Nov. 1787 to 21 Oct. 1788
	3 Nov. 1788 to 2 Mar. 1789

Declaration of Independence

Declaration of the Continental Congress (q.v.) of 4 July 1776 that the American colonies were now, of right, free states independent of the British Crown. Drafted largely by Thomas Jefferson, the Declaration is famous for the natural rights philosophy (derived from John Locke and set out in the preamble) that all men are created equal and as such are equally entitled to 'life, liberty and the pursuit of happiness'. The independence of the United States should, however, more properly be dated from the adoption by Congress two days earlier of Richard Henry Lee's motion that the 'United Colonies are, and of right ought to be, free and independent states'.

Articles of Confederation

The first system of government among the original thirteen American states. The Articles of Confederation were drafted by a Committee of Thirteen appointed by the Continental Congress (q.v.) in 1776, but were not ratified by all the states until 1781. They provided for a limited national legislature without any central executive or judiciary. However, disputes between the states rendered the new government powerless and the Articles were replaced in 1788 by the present US Constitution which provided for a much more powerful federal government.

Summary of the Constitution (as it applies to President and Congress)

(For the full text of the Constitution, see Appendix I p. 411.)

The Constitution of 1787 established a federal republic. By 1945 there were 48 states of the union and the capital District of Columbia. Alaska and Hawaii became states in 1959, bringing the total to 50.

The President is head of state and government. He is elected by an electoral college chosen by popular vote, and his term is four years. His executive power is exercised through a Cabinet of departmental heads, whom he appoints with the consent of the Senate. The Constitution has had 27 amendments, beginning with the 10-point Bill of Rights in December 1791 (see Appendix II, p. 421).

The federal government has authority over national taxation, dealings with foreign powers and other national issues. Each state has its own elected Governor and its own domestic legislative authority.

The Congress consists of a House of Representatives and a Senate. Representatives are elected every second year by adult suffrage, qualified in some states on grounds of residence. Seats are distributed per state according to census population. Since 1964 the population of the congressional districts has been approximately equal.

Senators, two from each state, are elected for a six-year term by popular vote; one-third are up for election every two years.

All legislation may originate in either House except for finance bills, which may originate only in the House of Representatives. The Senate may amend or reject any legislation from the House of Representatives. The Senate can also give or withhold its consent to formal treaties with foreign powers (but not to working agreements, which do not have the status of formal treaties).

Both Houses work by committee. A bill passing through all committee stages and full debate in one House must then go through the same procedure in the other.

Date of ratification (or date of admission to the union)

Delaware	7 Dec.	1787
Pennsylvania	12 Dec.	1787
New Jersey	18 Dec.	1787
Georgia	2 Jan.	1788
Connecticut	9 Jan.	1788
Massachusetts	6 Feb.	1788
Maryland	28 Apr.	1788
South Carolina	23 May	1788
New Hampshire	21 June	1788
Virginia	26 June	1788
New York	26 July	1788

North Carolina	21 Nov.	1789
Rhode Island	29 May	1790
Vermont	4 Mar.	1791
Kentucky	1 June	1792
Tennessee	1 June	1796
Ohio	1 Mar.	1803
Louisiana	30 Apr.	1812
Indiana	11 Dec.	1816
Mississippi	10 Dec.	1817
Illinois	3 Dec.	1818
Alabama	14 Dec.	1819
Maine	15 Mar.	1820
Missouri	10 Aug.	1821
Arkansas	15 June	1836
Michigan	26 Jan.	1837
Florida	3 Mar.	1845
Texas	29 Dec.	1845
Iowa	28 Dec.	1846
Wisconsin	29 May	1848
California	9 Sept.	1850
Minnesota	11 May	1858
Oregon	14 Feb.	1859
Kansas	29 Jan.	1861
West Virginia	20 June	1863
Nevada	31 Oct.	1864
Nebraska	1 Mar.	1867
Colorado	1 Aug.	1876
North Dakota	2 Nov.	1889
South Dakota	2 Nov.	1889
Montana	8 Nov.	1889
Washington	11 Nov.	1889
Idaho	3 July	1890
Wyoming	10 July	1890
Utah	4 Jan.	1896
Oklahoma	16 Nov.	1907
New Mexico	6 Jan.	1912
Arizona	14 Feb.	1912
Alaska	3 Jan.	1959
Hawaii	11 Aug.	1959

Date of secession from the Union

Eleven states joined the Confederate States of America (see p. 312), beginning with South Carolina on 20 December 1860 and concluding with Tennessee on 8 June 1861. The states, with dates of secession and re-admission, are set out below:

State	Seceded from Union	Readmitted to Union
South Carolina	20 Dec. 1860	9 July 1868
Mississippi	9 Jan. 1861	23 Feb. 1870
Florida	10 Jan. 1861	25 June 1868
Alabama	11 Jan. 1861	13 July 1868
Georgia	19 Jan. 1861	15 July 1870
Louisiana	26 Jan. 1861	9 July 1868
Texas	2 Mar. 1861	30 Mar. 1870
Virginia	17 Apr. 1861	26 Jan. 1870
Arkansas	6 May 1861	22 June 1868
North Carolina	20 May 1861	4 July 1868
Tennessee	8 June 1861	24 July 1866

Constitutional amendments

Article V of the Constitution provided that the original document might be amended, with the exception that no state without its own consent can be deprived of equal representation in the Senate. Since ratification in 1789 there have been 27 amendments. All but the Twenty-first Amendment of 1933 were measures passed by Congress and then ratified by at least three-quarters of the legislatures of the several states; the Twenty-first, which abolished national prohibition, was ratified by state conventions established for the purpose, following the adoption of the amendment by Congress. (In theory there are two other mechanisms of amendment, which have never been employed to date.) Only one amendment has ever been repealed – the Eighteenth of 1919 establishing Prohibition – although others have been superseded. In law, amendments come into effect when they have been certified by the Archivist of the United States as having been ratified.

Amendments 1 to 10

Known as the Bill of Rights, these were proposed by James Madison, a member of the Constitutional Convention of 1787, and ratified on 15 December 1791. They provide the essential protection of the rights of the states and of the individual citizen against the federal government. The First Amendment specifically forbids the establishment of religion and the abridgement of free speech, free assembly and the right to petition. The Second guarantees the right to possess and bear arms. The

Fourth to Eighth Amendments regulate the use of search warrants, criminal trials and common law suits; and the Fifth specifically allows one to decline to give evidence against oneself (hence the expression 'to plead [or take] the Fifth'). The Ninth Amendment provides that the enumeration of certain rights in the Constitution shall not be taken to mean that the citizens do not possess others which are not explicitly stated therein; and the Tenth provides that any powers not delegated to the federal government by the Constitution are reserved to the states or to the people. For full text, see Appendix II p. 421.

Amendment 11: Lawsuits against the states

Ratified 7 February 1795
Federal courts have no authority to hear legal actions brought against individual states by citizens of another state or of a foreign country.

Amendment 12: The election of the President and Vice-President

Ratified 27 July 1804
The method of election is amended to provide for separate ballots for the President and the Vice-President. (Originally the candidate receiving the second highest number of votes in the Electoral College became Vice-President.)

Amendment 13: The abolition of slavery

Ratified 6 December 1865
Slavery, and 'involuntary servitude' except as a punishment for a duly convicted criminal, are abolished.

Amendment 14: Civil rights

Ratified 9 July 1868
All persons born in the United States, and naturalized immigrants, are citizens of the US as a whole and of their own state of residence; no state may deny to citizens of the United States their citizenship rights, nor deprive any person of life, liberty or property without 'due process of law'; and each state must afford any person under its jurisdiction 'the equal protection of the laws'.

Amendment 15: The right to vote

Ratified 3 February 1870
Neither the federal government nor any state may deny the right to vote to any citizen on account of his race.

Amendment 16: Income tax

Ratified 3 February 1913

The US Congress may levy a national income tax without regard to its apportionment among the states according to population. (Article 1, Section 9 of the Constitution required direct taxes to be levied in proportion to the population of each state.)

Amendment 17: Election of Senators

Ratified 8 April 1913

United States Senators are to be directly elected by the voters of each state, rather than chosen by the state legislatures as previously.

Amendment 18: Prohibition of alcoholic liquor

Ratified 16 January 1919; repealed 5 December 1933

The manufacture and sale of intoxicating liquors for the purposes of beverage to be prohibited one year after ratification of the amendment.

Amendment 19: Votes for women

Ratified 18 August 1920

Neither the federal government nor any state may deny the right to vote to any citizen on account of sex.

Amendment 20: Terms of office

Ratified 23 January 1933

Congressional sessions are to begin on 3 January of each and every year and the terms of office of the President and Vice-President shall begin at noon on 20 January following their election.

Amendment 21: Repeal of Prohibition

Ratified 5 December 1933

The Eighteenth Amendment to the Constitution is repealed; the importation of intoxicating liquor into any state which has legislated Prohibition within its own territory is itself prohibited.

Amendment 22: Limit on presidential terms

Ratified 27 February 1951

No person may be elected more than twice to the office of President; but a person who succeeds to the term of office to which another was elected may serve out up to two years of the predecessor's term and be twice eligible for election.

Amendment 23: Suffrage in Washington, DC

Ratified 29 March 1961
The District of Columbia shall be entitled to choose electors to the Electoral College, thus allowing the voters of Washington to vote for President and Vice-President.

Amendment 24: The right to vote

Ratified 23 January 1964
Neither the federal government nor any state may deny to any citizen the right to vote in federal elections on account of failure to pay a poll tax or other tax.

Amendment 25: Succession to the Presidency

Ratified 10 February 1967
The President may appoint a Vice-President, subject to the confirmation of Congress, whenever there is a vacancy in that office; and the Vice-President shall serve as acting President whenever the President deems himself, or is deemed to be, incapable of discharging his powers and duties.

Amendment 26: The age of majority

Ratified 1 July 1971
Neither the federal government nor any state may deny the right to vote to any citizen aged 18 or over on account of age.

Amendment 27: Congressional pay

Ratified 7 May 1992
Any vote made by Congress to increase the remuneration of its members shall not take effect until after the subsequent election for the House of Representatives.

The Executive

The President

The Chief Executive of the United States. Article II of the Constitution vests the complete executive power in the President. The President is elected to office every four years (election years coincide with leap years) by the Electoral College and is eligible to be elected twice to a four-year term of office (*see* Vice-President). He (all Presidents to date have been male) is assisted in the discharge of his duties by officers of the Cabinet, whom he appoints and who are responsible for the direction of departments of state. The powers of the President stem firstly from the provisions of the Constitution and secondly from custom. The foremost power of the President is his conduct of foreign policy and defence of the United States. He is Commander-in-Chief of the armed forces, he determines the recognition by the United States of foreign states and governments and, with the approval of the Senate, he has the power to make treaties and agreements with foreign powers. In his role of chief administrator, the President exercises extensive powers of appointment and removal of government officials. He directs and supervises the operations of the executive branch, assisted in this by the Executive Office of the President within the White House, to which he appoints his personal advisers. He directs the creation of the annual budget of the United States (*see* OMB) and is required to see 'that the laws are faithfully executed'. As principal legislator, the President initiates many legislative proposals, delivers regular and special messages to Congress regarding matters of state, summons Congress into special session, wields a veto over legislation and influences the course of legislation in Congress through his relations with its leading officials. In practice, the President has usually been at the head of a major political party, through which he can dispense patronage, influence the substance of party policy, and give leadership to the party's members in Congress. As Chief of State, the President maintains relations with other heads of state and performs numerous ceremonial duties within the United States.

Presidents of the United States

The terms are for four years; only President F.D. Roosevelt has served more than two terms.

President	Party	Served
George Washington	Federalist	1789–97
John Adams	Federalist	1797–1801
Thomas Jefferson	Republican	1801–09
James Madison	Republican	1809–17
James Monroe	Republican	1817–25
John Quincy Adams	Republican	1825–29
Andrew Jackson	Democrat	1829–37
Martin Van Buren	Democrat	1837–41
William H. Harrison (died in office)	Whig	1841
John Tyler	Whig	1841–45
James K. Polk	Democrat	1845–49
Zachary Taylor (died in office)	Whig	1849–50
Millard Fillmore	Whig	1850–53
Franklin Pierce	Democrat	1853–57
James Buchanan	Democrat	1857–61
Abraham Lincoln (assassinated)	Republican	1861–65
Andrew Johnson	Democrat	1865–69
Ulysses S. Grant	Republican	1869–77
Rutherford B. Hayes	Republican	1877–81
James A. Garfield (assassinated)	Republican	1881
Chester A. Arthur	Republican	1881–85
Grover Cleveland	Democrat	1885–89
Benjamin Harrison	Republican	1889–93
Grover Cleveland	Democrat	1893–97
William McKinley (assassinated)	Republican	1897–1901
Theodore Roosevelt	Republican	1901–09
William Howard Taft	Republican	1909–13
Woodrow Wilson	Democrat	1913–21
Warren G. Harding (died in office)	Republican	1921–23
Calvin Coolidge	Republican	1923–29
Herbert C. Hoover	Republican	1929–33
Franklin D. Roosevelt (died in office)	Democrat	1933–45
Harry S. Truman	Democrat	1945–53
Dwight D. Eisenhower	Republican	1953–61
John F. Kennedy (assassinated)	Democrat	1961–63
Lyndon B. Johnson	Democrat	1963–69
Richard M. Nixon (resigned)	Republican	1969–74
Gerald R. Ford	Republican	1974–77

President	Party	Served
James Carter	Democrat	1977–81
Ronald Reagan	Republican	1981–89
George Bush	Republican	1989–93
Bill Clinton	Democrat	1993–

The Vice-President

The popularly elected officer who presides over the Senate and who is designated to assume the office of the President in case of the death, disability, resignation or removal from office of the incumbent. The Vice-President is elected on the same ballot as the President; however, if no candidate receives a majority of the electoral vote, it falls to the Senate to elect the Vice-President from the two front-runners. The Vice-President is considered to be a member of the executive rather than the legislative branch of government. Vice-Presidents are generally considered to be powerless because they depend entirely upon the President for their influence, and because Presidents are reluctant to countenance the growth of power of possible rivals. They are also frustrated by the method of their selection as candidates; more importance is attached to their enhancement of the presidential 'ticket' than to competence in office.

Vice-Presidents of the United States

Vice-President	Party	Served
John Adams	Federalist	1789–97
Thomas Jefferson	Dem-Rep.	1797–1801
Aaron Burr	Anti-Fed.	1801–05
George Clinton	Dem-Rep.	1805–12
Elbridge Gerry	Dem-Rep.	1813–14
Daniel D. Tompkins	Dem-Rep.	1817–25
John C. Calhoun	Dem-Rep.	1825–32
Martin Van Buren	Democrat	1833–37
Richard M. Johnson	Democrat	1837–41
John Tyler	Whig	1841*
George M. Dallas	Democrat	1845–49
Millard Fillmore	Whig	1849–50
William R. King	Democrat	1853
John C. Breckinridge	Democrat	1857–61

Vice-President	Party	Served
Hannibal Hamlin	Republican	1861–65
Andrew Johnson	Democrat	1865
Schuyler Colfax	Republican	1869–73
Henry Wilson	Republican	1873–75
William A. Wheeler	Republican	1877–81
Chester A. Arthur	Republican	1881
Thomas A. Hendricks	Democrat	1885
Levi P. Morton	Republican	1889–93
Adlai E. Stevenson	Democrat	1893–97
Garret A. Hobart	Republican	1897–99
Theodore Roosevelt	Republican	1901
Charles W. Fairbanks	Republican	1905–09
James S. Sherman	Republican	1909–12
Thomas R. Marshall	Democrat	1913–21
Calvin Coolidge	Republican	1921–23
Charles G. Dawes	Republican	1925–29
Charles Curtis	Republican	1929–33
John N. Garner	Democrat	1933–41
Henry A. Wallace	Democrat	1941–45
Harry S. Truman	Democrat	1945
Alben W. Barkley	Democrat	1949–53
Richard M. Nixon	Republican	1953–61
Lyndon B. Johnson	Democrat	1961–63
Hubert H. Humphrey	Democrat	1965–69
Spiro T. Agnew	Republican	1969–73
Gerald R. Ford	Republican	1973–74
Nelson A. Rockefeller	Republican	1974–77
Walter F. Mondale	Democrat	1977–81
George Bush	Republican	1981–89
Dan Quayle	Republican	1989–93
Al Gore	Democrat	1993–

* Vice-Presidency unoccupied for four years when Tyler became President on death of President Harrison.

The growth of Cabinet government*

Chronology of key events

1789   Department of Foreign Affairs created by Act of Congress (27 July). Name changed to Department of State (15 Sept.).

* For a note on the Cabinet and Departments, see p. 308 and p. 316 respectively.

War (and Navy) Department organized (7 Aug.).

Treasury Department organized (2 Sept.).

Post Office Department established as a branch of the Treasury (22 Sept.).

Office of Attorney General created (24 Sept.).

1798   Separate Navy Department created (30 Apr.).

1829   Postmaster-General became member of the Cabinet (9 Mar.).

1849   Department of the Interior created (3 Mar.).

1862   Department of Agriculture created (under a non-Cabinet Commissioner) (15 May).

1870   Department of Justice created (22 June).

1889   Commissioner of Department of Agriculture becomes Secretary of Agriculture (office now in Cabinet).

1903   Department of Commerce and Labor created (14 Feb.).

1913   Department of Commerce and Labor split into separate departments of Commerce and Labor (each with a Secretary of Cabinet rank).

1947   Department of Defense created (26 July), originally known as National Military Establishment. Secretary of Defense is member of Cabinet (but not the three Secretaries of the individual armed forces).

1953   Department of Health, Education and Welfare created (11 Apr.).

1965   Creation of Department of Housing and Urban Development (9 Sept.) with Robert C. Weaver as first Secretary.

1966   Department of Transportation created by Act of Congress (15 Oct.).

1970   Under Postal Reorganization Act, US Postal Service created as independent federal agency. Postmaster-General no longer in Cabinet.

1977   Department of Energy created by federal law (4 Aug.).

1979   Division of Department of Health, Education and Welfare into two separate Departments of Education, and Health and Human Services, both with a Secretary of Cabinet rank (27 Sept.). New departments became operational on 4 May 1980.

1989   The Veterans Administration (established 1930) elevated to Cabinet status by federal law (15 Mar.).

Selected holders of Cabinet office

These lists omit those offices that are less likely to be of significance for the general student, e.g., Transportation, Energy and Attorneys General.

Secretaries of State See p. 229

Secretaries of State See p. 229

Secretaries of the Treasury

Alexander Hamilton	1789
Oliver Wolcott	1795
Oliver Wolcott	1797
Samuel Dexter	1801
Samuel Dexter	1801
Albert Gallatin	1801
Albert Gallatin	1809
George W. Campbell	1814
Alexander J. Dallas	1814
William H. Crawford	1816
William H. Crawford	1817
Richard Rush	1825
Samuel D. Ingham	1829
Louis McLane	1831
William J. Duane	1833
Roger B. Taney	1833
Levi Woodbury	1834
Levi Woodbury	1837
Thomas Ewing	1841
Thomas Ewing	1841
Walter Forward	1841
John C. Spencer	1843
George M. Bibb	1844
Robert J. Walker	1846
William M. Meredith	1849
Thomas Corwin	1850
James Guthrie	1853
Howell Cobb	1857
Philip F. Thomas	1860
John A. Dix	1861
Salmon P. Chase	1861
William P. Fessenden	1864
Hugh McCulloch	1865
Hugh McCulloch	1865
George S. Boutwell	1869
William A. Richardson	1873
Benjamin H. Bristow	1874
Lot M. Morrill	1875
John Sherman	1877
William Windom	1881
Charles J. Folger	1881

Walter Q. Gresham	1884
Hugh McCulloch	1884
Daniel Manning	1885
Charles S. Fairchild	1887
William Windom	1889
Charles Foster	1891
John G. Carlisle	1893
Lyman J. Gage	1897
Lyman J. Gage	1901
Leslie M. Shaw	1902
George B. Cortelyou	1907
Franklin MacVeagh	1909
William G. McAdoo	1913
Carter Glass	1918
David F. Houston	1920
Andrew W. Mellon	1921
Andrew W. Mellon	1923
Andrew W. Mellon	1929
Ogden L. Mills	1932
William H. Woodin	1933
Henry Morgenthau, Jr.	1934
Fred M. Vinson	1945
John W. Snyder	1946
George M. Humphrey	1953
Robert B. Anderson	1957
C. Douglas Dillon	1961
C. Douglas Dillon	1963
Henry H. Fowler	1965
Joseph W. Barr	1968
David M. Kennedy	1969
John B. Connally	1971
George P. Shultz	1972
William E. Simon	1974
William E. Simon	1974
W. Michael Blumenthal	1977
G. William Miller	1979
Donald T. Regan	1981
James Baker 3rd	1985
Nicholas F. Brady	1988
Nicholas F. Brady	1989
Lloyd Bentsen	1993
Robert E. Rubin	1995

Secretaries of Defense

James V. Forrestal	1947
Louis A. Johnson	1949
George C. Marshall	1950
Robert A. Lovett	1951
Charles E. Wilson	1953
Neil H. McElroy	1957
Thomas S. Gates Jr	1959
Robert S. McNamara	1961
Robert S. McNamara	1963
Clark M. Clifford	1968
Melvin R. Laird	1969
Elliot L. Richardson	1973
James R. Schlesinger	1973
James R. Schlesinger	1974
Donald H. Rumsfeld	1975
Harold Brown	1977
Caspar W. Weinberger	1981
Frank C. Carlucci	1987
Richard B. Cheney	1989
Les Aspin	1993
William J. Perry	1994
William S. Cohen	1997

Secretaries of War

Henry Knox	1789
Timothy Pickering	1795
James McHenry	1796
James McHenry	1797
Samuel Dexter	1800
Henry Dearborn	1801
William Eustis	1809
John Armstrong	1813
James Monroe	1814
William H. Crawford	1815
John C. Calhoun	1817
James Barbour	1825
Peter B. Porter	1828
John H. Eaton	1829
Lewis Cass	1831
Benjamin F. Butler	1837
Joel R. Poinsett	1837
John Bell	1841

John Bell	1841
John C. Spencer	1841
James M. Porter	1843
William Wilkins	1844
William L. Marcy	1845
George W. Crawford	1849
Charles M. Conrad	1850
Jefferson Davis	1853
John B. Floyd	1857
Joseph Holt	1861
Simon Cameron	1861
Edwin M. Stanton	1862
Edwin M. Stanton	1865
John M. Schofield	1868
John A. Rawlins	1869
William T. Sherman	1869
William W. Belknap	1869
Alphonso Taft	1876
James D. Cameron	1876
George W. McCrary	1877
Alexander Ramsey	1879
Robert T. Lincoln	1881
Robert T. Lincoln	1881
William C. Endicott	1885
Redfield Proctor	1889
Stephen B. Elkins	1891
Daniel S. Lamont	1893
Russell A. Alger	1897
Elihu Root	1899
Elihu Root	1901
William H. Taft	1904
Luke E. Wright	1908
Jacob M. Dickinson	1909
Henry L. Stimson	1911
Lindley M. Garrison	1913
Newton D. Baker	1916
John W. Weeks	1921
John W. Weeks	1923
Dwight F. Davis	1925
James W. Good	1929
Patrick J. Hurley	1929
George H. Dern	1933
Harry H. Woodring	1937
Henry L. Stimson	1940

Robert P. Patterson   1945
Kenneth C. Royall   1947

Secretaries of the Interior

Thomas Ewing   1849
Thomas M.T. McKennan   1850
Alex H.H. Stuart   1850
Robert McClelland   1853
Jacob Thompson   1857
Caleb B. Smith   1861
John P. Usher   1863
John P. Usher   1865
James Harlan   1865
Orville H. Browning   1866
Jacob D. Cox   1869
Columbus Delano   1870
Zachariah Chandler   1875
Carl Schurz   1877
Samuel J. Kirkwood   1881
Henry M. Teller   1882
Lucius Q.C. Lamar   1885
William F. Vilas   1888
John W. Noble   1889
Hoke Smith   1893
David R. Francis   1896
Cornelius N. Bliss   1897
Ethan A. Hitchcock   1898
Ethan A. Hitchcock   1901
James R. Garfield   1907
Richard A. Ballinger   1909
Walter L. Fisher   1911
Franklin K. Lane   1913
John B. Payne   1920
Albert B. Fall   1921
Hubert Work   1923
Hubert Work   1923
Roy O. West   1929
Ray Lyman Wilbur   1929
Harold L. Ickes   1933
Harold L. Ickes   1945
Julius A. Krug   1946
Oscar L. Chapman   1949
Douglas McKay   1953

Fred A. Seaton	1956
Stewart L. Udall	1961
Stewart L. Udall	1963
Walter J. Hickel	1969
Rogers C.B. Morton	1971
Rogers C.B. Morton	1971
Stanley K. Hathaway	1975
Thomas S. Kleppe	1975
Cecil D. Andrus	1977
James G. Watt	1981
William P. Clark	1983
Donald P. Hodel	1985
Manuel Lujan	1989
Bruce Babbitt	1993

Secretaries of Agriculture

Norman J. Colman	1889
Jeremiah M. Rusk	1889
J. Sterling Morton	1893
James Wilson	1897
James Wilson	1901
James Wilson	1909
David F. Houston	1913
Edwin T. Meredith	1920
Henry C. Wallace	1921
Henry C. Wallace	1923
Howard M. Gore	1924
William M. Jardine	1925
Arthur M. Hyde	1929
Henry A. Wallace	1933
Claude R. Wickard	1940
Clinton P. Anderson	1945
Charles F. Brannan	1948
Ezra Taft Benson	1953
Orville L. Freeman	1961
Orville L. Freeman	1963
Clifford M. Hardin	1969
Earl L. Butz	1971
Earl L. Butz	1974
John A. Knebel	1976
Bob Bergland	1977
John R. Block	1981
Richard E. Lyng	1986

Clayton K. Yeutter	1989
Edward Madigan	1991
Mike Espy	1993
Dan Glickman	1995

Secretaries of Commerce and Labor

George B. Cortelyou	1903
Victor H. Metcalf	1904
Oscar S. Straus	1906
Charles Nagel	1909

In 1913 the Office was divided into Commerce and Labor.

Secretaries of Commerce

William C. Redfield	1913
Joshua W. Alexander	1919
Herbert C. Hoover	1921
Herbert C. Hoover	1923
William F. Whiting	1928
Robert P. Lamont	1929
Roy D. Chapin	1932
Daniel C. Roper	1933
Harry L. Hopkins	1939
Jesse Jones	1940
Henry A. Wallace	1945
Henry A. Wallace	1945
W. Averell Harriman	1947
Charles Sawyer	1948
Sinclair Weeks	1953
Lewis L. Strauss	1958
Frederick H. Mueller	1959
Luther H. Hodges	1961
Luther H. Hodges	1963
John T. Connor	1965
Alex B. Trowbridge	1967
Cyrus R. Smith	1968
Maurice H. Stans	1969
Peter G. Peterson	1972
Frederick B. Dent	1973
Frederick B. Dent	1974
Rogers C.B. Morton	1975
Elliot L. Richardson	1975
Juanita M. Kreps	1977
Philip M. Klutznick	1979

Malcolm Baldrige	1981
C. William Verity Jr	1987
Robert A. Mosbacher	1989
Barbara H. Franklin	1992
Ronald H. Brown	1993
Mickey Kantor	1996
William H. Daley	1997

Secretaries of Labor

William B. Wilson	1913
James J. Davis	1921
James J. Davis	1923
James J. Davis	1929
William N. Doak	1930
Frances Perkins	1933
L.B. Schwellenbach	1945
Maurice J. Tobin	1949
Martin P. Durkin	1953
James P. Mitchell	1953
Arthur J. Goldberg	1961
W. Willard Wirtz	1962
W. Willard Wirtz	1963
George P. Shultz	1969
James D. Hodgson	1970
Peter J. Brennan	1973
Peter J. Brennan	1974
John T. Dunlop	1975
W.J. Usery Jr	1976
F. Ray Marshall	1977
Raymond J. Donovan	1981
William E. Brock	1985
Ann D. McLaughlin	1987
Elizabeth Hanford Dole	1989
Lynn Martin	1991
Robert B. Reich	1993
Alexis M. Herman	1997

Secretaries of Housing and Urban Development

Robert C. Weaver	1966
Robert C. Wood	1969
George W. Romney	1969
James T. Lynn	1973
James T. Lynn	1974
Carla Anderson Hills	1975

Patricia Roberts Harris	1977
Moon Landrieu	1979
Samuel R. Pierce Jr	1981
Jack F. Kemp	1989
Henry G. Cisneros	1993
Andrew M. Cuomo	1997

Secretaries of Health, Education and Welfare

Oveta Culp Hobby	1953
Marion B. Folsom	1955
Arthur S. Flemming	1958
Abraham A. Ribicoff	1961
Anthony J. Celebrezze	1962
Anthony J. Celebrezze	1963
John W. Gardner	1965
Wilbur J. Cohen	1968
Robert H. Finch	1969
Elliot L. Richardson	1970
Caspar W. Weinberger	1973
Caspar W. Weinberger	1974
Forrest D. Mathews	1975
Joseph A. Califano Jr	1977
Patricia Roberts Harris	1979

In 1979 the Office was divided into two separate departments, Education, and Health and Human Services.

Secretaries of Education

Shirley Hüfstedler	1979
Terrel Bell	1981
William J. Bennett	1985
Lauro F. Cavazos	1986
Lauro F. Cavazos	1989
Lamar Alexander	1991
Richard W. Riley	1993

Secretaries of Health and Human Services

Patricia Roberts Harris	1979
Richard S. Schweiker	1981
Margaret M. Heckler	1983
Otis R. Bowen	1985
Louis W. Sullivan	1989
Donna E. Shalala	1993

The Legislature

Congress

The legislature of the United States which is composed of two chambers, namely the Senate of two members from each state and the House of Representatives with 435 members elected by district. Members of both chambers are elected by popular vote, Senators for six years with one-third standing for election every two years, and members of the House (usually referred to as Congressmen) for two years.

The Senate

The name of the upper House of Congress and also of 49 of the state legislatures. Representation in the Senate is based upon the principle of state equality and the Constitution specifies that no state may be deprived of its equal representation in the Senate without its consent. At present the Senate comprises 100 Senators from 50 states; most states' senates have less than 50 members. The Seventeenth Amendment of 1913 provided that US Senators should be popularly elected (previously they had been chosen by the state legislatures) for a term of six years. The Vice-President is the presiding officer of the Senate; in state legislatures the lieutenant or deputy governor normally presides. In the absence of the presiding officer a president *pro tempore*, elected from the membership, assumes that role. The Senate has the sole power to try cases of impeachment and the conclusion of treaties and appointments to certain offices by the President may only be done by and with the advice and consent of the Senate.

The House of Representatives

The lower House of the bicameral Congress, in which representation is based upon population. The House was intended to be the popular chamber of Congress, and was made larger and more responsive to the public will than the Senate, which was to represent the states. Each state of the Union is guaranteed at least one representative. Since 1910 the House has had a permanent membership of 435. The ratio of population to representatives has been steadily increasing – it now stands at over 500,000 per representative. The Constitution vests certain powers exclusively in the House. Among them are: (1) the power of impeachment; (2) the initiation of revenue bills; (3) the election of a President if no candidate obtains a majority of votes in the Electoral College; (4) the determination of its own rules of procedure; and (5) the discipline of its members. The American voter is usually inclined to regard the Representative as his or her most direct contact with government.

Apportionment of states, 1900

State		State		State	
Alabama	9	Maryland	6	Oregon	2
Arkansas	7	Massachusetts	14	Pennsylvania	32
California	8	Michigan	12	Rhode Island	2
Colorado	3	Minnesota	9	South Carolina	7
Connecticut	5	Mississippi	8	South Dakota	2
Delaware	1	Missouri	16	Tennessee	10
Florida	3	Montana	1	Texas	16
Georgia	11	Nebraska	6	Utah	1
Idaho	1	Nevada	1	Vermont	2
Illinois	25	New Hampshire	2	Virginia	10
Indiana	13	New Jersey	10	Washington	3
Iowa	11	New York	37	West Virginia	5
Kansas	8	North Carolina	10	Wisconsin	11
Kentucky	11	North Dakota	2	Wyoming	1
Louisiana	7	Ohio	21		386
Maine	4				

Apportionment of states, 1996

State		State		State	
Alabama	7	Indiana	10	Nebraska	3
Alaska	1	Iowa	5	Nevada	2
Arizona	6	Kansas	4	New Hampshire	2
Arkansas	4	Kentucky	6	New Jersey	13
California	52	Louisiana	7	New Mexico	3
Colorado	6	Maine	2	New York	31
Connecticut	6	Maryland	8	North Carolina	12
Delaware	1	Massachusetts	10	North Dakota	1
Florida	23	Michigan	16	Ohio	19
Georgia	11	Minnesota	8	Oklahoma	6
Hawaii	2	Mississippi	5	Oregon	5
Idaho	2	Missouri	9	Pennsylvania	21
Illinois	20	Montana	1	Rhode Island	2

South Carolina	6	Utah	3	West Virginia	3
South Dakota	1	Vermont	1	Wisconsin	9
Tennessee	9	Virginia	11	Wyoming	1
Texas	30	Washington	9		435

Composition of Congress (since 1945)

The Senate

			Senate		
Congress	Years	Number of Senators	Democrats	Republicans	Others
79th	1945–47	96	57	38	1
80th	1947–49	96	45	51	
81st	1949–51	96	54	42	
82nd	1951–53	96	48	47	1
83rd	1953–55	96	46	48	2
84th	1955–57	96	48	47	1
85th	1957–59	96	49	47	
86th	1959–61	98	64	34	
87th	1961–63	100	64	36	
88th	1963–65	100	67	33	
89th	1965–67	100	68	32	
90th	1967–69	100	64	36	
91st	1969–71	100	58	42	
92nd	1971–73	100	54	44	2
93rd	1973–75	100	56	42	2
94th	1975–77	100	61	37	2
95th	1977–79	100	61	38	1
96th	1979–81	100	58	41	1
97th	1981–83	100	46	53	1
98th	1983–85	100	46	54	
99th	1985–87	100	47	53	
100th	1987–89	100	55	45	
101st	1989–91	100	55	45	
102nd	1991–93	100	56	44	
103rd	1993–95	100	57	43	
104th	1995–97	100	48	52	
105th	1997–	100	45	55	

The House of Representatives

Congress	Number of Representatives	House of Representatives		
		Democrats	Republicans	Others
89th	435	295	140	
90th	435	248	187	
91st	435	243	192	
92nd	435	255	180	
93rd	435	242	192	1
94th	435	291	144	
95th	435	292	143	
96th	435	277	158	
97th	435	242	192	1
98th	435	269	166	
99th	435	253	182	
100th	435	258	177	
101st	435	260	175	
102nd	435	267	167	1
103rd	435	258	176	1
104th	435	199	233	1 [1 vacancy]
105th	435	204	230	1

Speakers of the House of Representatives (since 1945)

Sam Rayburn	Democrat	1940–47
Joseph W. Martin Jr	Republican	1947–49
Sam Rayburn	Democrat	1949–53
Joseph W. Martin Jr	Republican	1953–55
Sam Rayburn	Democrat	1955–61
John W. McCormack	Democrat	1962–71
Carl Albert	Democrat	1971–77
Thomas P. O'Neill Jr	Democrat	1977–87
James Wright	Democrat	1987–89
Thomas S. Foley	Democrat	1989–95
Newt Gingrich	Republican	1995–

Majority Leaders: the US Senate (since 1945)

Wallace H. White	Republican	1944–47
Alben W. Barkley	Democrat	1947–49
Kenneth S. Wherry	Republican	1949–51
Henry Styles Bridges	Republican	1951–53
Lyndon B. Johnson	Democrat	1953–55
William F. Knowland	Republican	1955–59
Everett M. Dirksen	Republican	1959–69
Hugh D. Scott	Republican	1969–77
Howard H. Baker Jr	Republican	1977–81
Robert C. Byrd	Democrat	1981–87
Robert J. Dole	Republican	1987–96
Trent Lott	Republican	1996–

The Judicature

The Supreme Court

The highest court of appeal in the United States and in most states. The membership of the US Supreme Court comprises the Chief Justice of the United States and several associate justices whose number is determined by Congress (it has been eight since 1869); cases are decided by majority vote. The Supreme Court is the only judicial body whose existence is specifically established by the US Constitution, Congress having the power to set up other federal courts. Its jurisdiction as an appeal court is also determined by Congress, but the Supreme Court may nonetheless determine which specific cases it will hear through a mechanism known as writ of *certiorari*. Its decisions can be and have been of enormous importance on American political life, as they may involve the determination of the legality of legislation through the Court's power definitively to interpret the Constitution.

The Chief Justice

The highest judicial officer of the United States, or of a particular state. The President, with the consent of the Senate, appoints the Chief Justice of the United States for life. He presides over sessions of the United States Supreme Court and acts as the administrative head of the system of federal courts. In fact, the position of the Chief Justice carries no greater power in the Supreme Court than that of 'first among equals' but it is indisputably a position of greater prestige.

Chief Justices of the Supreme Court

John Jay	1789–95
John Rutledge*	1795
Oliver Ellsworth	1796–99
John Marshall	1801–35
Roger B. Taney	1836–64
Salmon P. Chase	1864–73

* Acting Chief Justice, rejected by Senate.

Morrison R. Waite	1874–88
Melville W. Fuller	1888–1910
Edward D. White	1910–21
William H. Taft	1921–30
Charles E. Hughes	1930–41
Harlan F. Stone	1941–46
Fred M. Vinson	1946–53
Earl Warren	1953–69
Warren E. Burger	1969–86
William H. Rehnquist	1986–

Supreme Court Justices *(Chief Justices in italic)*

John Jay	1789–95
James Wilson	1789–98
John Rutledge	1790–91
William Cushing	1790–1810
John Blair	1790–96
James Iredell	1790–99
Thomas Johnson	1792–93
William Paterson	1793–1806
John Rutledge	1795
Samuel Chase	1796–1811
Oliver Ellsworth	1796–1800
Bushrod Washington	1799–1829
Alfred Moore	1800–04
John Marshall	1801–35
William Johnson	1804–34
Brockholst Livingston	1807–23
Thomas Todd	1807–26
Gabriel Duval	1811–35
Joseph Story	1812–45
Smith Thompson	1823–43
Robert Trimble	1826–28
John McLean	1830–61
Henry Baldwin	1830–44
James M. Wayne	1835–67
Roger B. Taney	1836–64
Philip P. Barbour	1836–41
John Catron	1837–65
John McKinley	1838–52
Peter V. Daniel	1842–60
Samuel Nelson	1845–72

Levi Woodbury	1845–51
Robert C. Grier	1846–70
Benjamin R. Curtis	1851–57
John A. Campbell	1853–61
Nathan Clifford	1858–81
Noah H. Swayne	1862–81
Samuel F. Miller	1862–90
David Davis	1862–77
Stephen J. Field	1863–97
Salmon P. Chase	1864–73
William Strong	1870–80
Joseph P. Bradley	1870–92
Ward Hunt	1873–82
Morrison R. Waite	1874–88
John M. Harlan	1877–1911
William B. Woods	1881–87
Stanley Matthews	1881–89
Horace Gray	1882–1902
Samuel Blatchford	1882–93
Lucius Q.C. Lamar	1888–93
Melville W. Fuller	1888–1910
David J. Brewer	1890–1910
Henry B. Brown	1891–1906
George Shiras, Jr	1892–1903
Howell E. Jackson	1893–95
Edward D. White	1894–1910
Rufus W. Peckham	1896–1909
Joseph McKenna	1898–1925
Oliver W. Holmes	1902–32
William R. Day	1903–22
William H. Moody	1906–10
Horace H. Lurton	1910–14
Charles E. Hughes	1910–16
Edward D. White	1910–21
Willis Van Devanter	1911–37
Joseph R. Lamar	1911–16
Mahlon Pitney	1912–22
James C. McReynolds	1914–41
Louis D. Brandeis	1916–39
John H. Clarke	1916–22
William H. Taft	1921–30
George Sutherland	1922–38
Pierce Butler	1923–39

Edward T. Sanford	1923–30
Harlan F. Stone	1925–41
Charles E. Hughes	1930–41
Owen J. Roberts	1930–45
Benjamin N. Cardozo	1932–38
Hugo L. Black	1937–71
Stanley F. Reed	1938–57
Felix Frankfurter	1939–62
William O. Douglas	1939–75
Frank Murphy	1940–49
Harlan F. Stone	1941–46
James F. Byrnes	1941–42
Robert H. Jackson	1941–54
Wiley B. Rutledge	1943–49
Harold H. Burton	1945–58
Frederick M. Vinson	1946–53
Tom C. Clark	1949–67
Sherman Minton	1949–56
Earl Warren	1953–69
John Marshall Harlan	1955–71
William J. Brennan, Jr	1956–90
Charles E. Whittaker	1957–62
Potter Stewart	1958–81
Byron R. White	1962–93
Arthur J. Goldberg	1962–65
Abe Fortas	1965–70
Thurgood Marshall	1967–91
Warren E. Burger	1969–86
Harry A. Blackmun	1970–94
Lewis F. Powell, Jr	1971–87
William H. Rehnquist	1971–86
John Paul Stevens	1975–
Sandra Day O'Connor	1981–
Antonin Scalia	1986–
Anthony Kennedy	1988–
David Souter	1990–
Clarence Thomas	1991–
Ruth Bader Ginsburg	1993–
Stephen Breyer	1994–

Sources: Paul S. Boyer *et al.*, *The Enduring Vision*, 3rd edn (1996); Erik W. Austin and Jerome M. Chubb, *Political Facts of the United States since 1789* (1986).

Major decisions of the Supreme Court

1803 Marbury v. Madison

The Supreme Court asserts the right of judicial review, i.e., it has the power (not specifically granted in the Constitution) to determine whether an Act of Congress, or other government action, infringes the Constitution of the United States.

1819 McCulloch v. Maryland

The federal government is independent of the sovereignty of the several states, deriving its own authority from the Constitution (which is superior to state law); and Acts of Congress on matters not specifically stated by the Constitution to be within the power of the Congress are nonetheless valid if they are 'necessary and proper' to the execution of powers which are so granted.

1824 Gibbons v. Ogden

The Congress has the power under the Constitution to regulate commerce between the different states, and state laws which affect commercial activities are inferior to federal law if they are found to be in conflict.

1833 Barron v. Baltimore

The Bill of Rights applies only against the federal government and not, *prima facie*, against the states.

1857 Dred Scott v. Sandford

The plaintiff (the sometime slave Scott), being a black American, cannot be a citizen of the United States, and therefore has no standing to sue for his freedom in the federal courts; and the Missouri Compromise of 1820 is unconstitutional, because the Congress does not have the power to prevent citizens from carrying their own property (e.g., slaves) anywhere within the Territories of the United States, since under the Fifth Amendment this would amount to deprivation without due process of law.

1896 Plessy v. Ferguson

It is not a violation of the Fourteenth Amendment's 'equal protection' clause for states to allow separate provision of public facilities for members of different races provided that those facilities are of an equal standard. (Thus segregation may be legal.)

1911 Standard Oil Co. v. United States

The Sherman Act of 1890, outlawing 'combinations in restraint of trade', can only be applied against those which can be judged to be 'unreasonable' combinations. (This allowed legal protection to certain categories of business company.)

1925 Gitlow v. New York

The constitutional protections of the Bill of Rights (specifically in this case the First Amendment) are, by the 'due process' clause of the Fourteenth Amendment, 'incorporated' and effectively made applicable to the states as well as to the federal government.

1937 National Labor Relations Board v. Jones & Laughlin Steel Corporation

The power of the Congress under the Constitution to regulate interstate commerce includes the power to regulate all activities *within* states which may have a bearing upon commercial transactions between them. (Thus the Congress may regulate industrial relations.)

1954 Brown v. Board of Education of Topeka, Kansas

Segregation within schools on the grounds of race is inherently unequal and thus unconstitutional because it violates the 'equal protection' clause of the Fourteenth Amendment. (Thus *Plessy v. Ferguson* is overturned.)

1962 Baker et al. v. Carr

Federal courts have the authority to review the apportionment of legislative electoral districts, in order to ensure that each person's vote is of equal weight to any other's as required by the 'equal protection' clause of the Fourteenth Amendment.

1963 Gideon v. Wainwright

Defendants in state as well as federal criminal trials are protected by the 'due process' clause of the Fourteenth Amendment. (Thus attorneys must be available to those charged with serious crimes, to be provided at public expense to indigent defendants.)

1964 New York Times v. Sullivan

The First Amendment protection of press freedom preserves newspapers from libel suits unless it can be proved that their reporting is actually malicious rather than merely factually incorrect.

1965 Griswold v. Connecticut

States may not ban the use of contraceptives by married couples, because this would infringe the 'right to privacy' inherent in the First and Ninth Amendments.

1966 Miranda v. Arizona

Criminal suspects must be advised by law enforcement officials of their constitutional protections during criminal proceedings, e.g., the right to remain silent.

1972 Furman v. Georgia

Capital punishment as it is regularly imposed by state courts is unconstitutional because its application violates the Eighth Amendment against cruel and unusual punishment, and the 'due process' clause of the Fourteenth.

1973 Roe v. Wade

State laws banning abortion during the first six months of pregnancy are unconstitutional because they violate a 'right to privacy' arising from the Fourteenth Amendment.

1974 United States v. Nixon

President Nixon's claim of 'executive privilege' to withhold certain evidence from judicial investigation in a pending criminal proceeding is not justified by the concept of the separation of powers within the federal government.

1976 Gregg v. Georgia

The death penalty as a punishment for first-degree murder is not, in and of itself, a violation of the Eighth Amendment.

1978 Regents of the University of California v. Bakke

The use of 'racial quotas' to determine admission to an educational institution may be a violation of the 'equal protection' clause of the Fourteenth Amendment and of the Civil Rights Act of 1964, if there is no legacy of discrimination at that institution which reasonably requires affirmative action in order to be corrected.

1986 Bowers v. Hardwick

The constitutionally protected 'right to privacy' does not extend to sexual activity. (Thus a law of the state of Georgia outlawing sodomy was not unconstitutional.)

1995 US Term Limits, Inc. v. Thorton

Attempts by the states to limit by law the number of terms which any citizen might serve in the US Congress are unconstitutional, because they add to the number of qualifications for federal office-holding contained in the Constitution.

Political parties

Democratic Party

One of the oldest political organizations in the world – and often described as the oldest formal political party – the modern Democratic Party emerged during the Presidency of Andrew Jackson (1829–37). Its ideological forebear was the Republican Party of President Thomas Jefferson (1801–09) which had developed in opposition to the *Federalists*; the first Republicans stood for the continuation of the Union, albeit under a federal government which deferred to the rights of the individual states. By the end of the first decade of the nineteenth century their party had developed a national electoral organization, whose candidates contested elections in the several states under the same label and on similar platforms; during the 'Era of Good Feelings' associated with the Presidency of James Monroe (1817–25) the Republicans were the dominant political force in the country and their Federalist opponents faded away. Nevertheless by the 1820s the party itself had begun to divide between those who favoured stronger government – dominant in the former Federalist stronghold of New England – and the more populist factions associated with the expanding South and West. During the Presidency of John Quincy Adams (1825–29) the former established themselves as the *National-Republicans*. Adams's opponents under General Andrew Jackson of Tennessee, a hero of the War of 1812 against Great Britain, took the name *Democratic-Republican*, later shortened to Democratic Party.

Jackson's election in 1828 is regarded as having inaugurated an important period of democratic political reform and national expansion, in which the United States established itself as the continental power. The President's sometimes autocratic personal style led his opponents to form themselves into the *Whig Party*. The Democratic Party remained the dominant political force in the United States, leading the country into war with Mexico in 1848 under President James Polk (1845–49). By the next decade, as the United States was riven by disputes about the expansion of slavery into the new Western Territories acquired from Mexico, the Democratic Party, with its traditional defence of states' rights, became a voice for the concerns of the slave-holding South, which feared the federal government would attempt to forbid slavery throughout the Union. President James Buchanan (1857–61) attempted to maintain some semblance of a national party, but the victory of the new Republican Party candidate Abraham Lincoln in the election of 1860 impelled the Southern Democrats to lead their states out of the Union and to create the Confederate States of America in February 1861.

The defeat of the Confederacy in the American Civil War (1861–65) led to a period of Republican hegemony and, in the South, to the era of Reconstruction (1865–77) when that region was placed under the direct rule of Congress and then Republican state governments. The end of the war, however, had led also to the re-establishment of the national Democratic Party, which enjoyed some success in congressional elections by appealing to the Northern masses and especially to the rising number of working-class immigrants. In 1877 the Democrats accepted a Republican President chosen in a disputed election in return for their own control of the South. The so-called 'Solid South' now emerged as the bastion of conservative Democrats; the region persisted as the Democratic stronghold until the 1980s.

At the national level, the Democrats regained the Presidency in 1884 under Grover Cleveland. Although the party was seemingly more amenable to the interests of the working class and immigrants than the Republicans, it did not represent any radical alternative to the pro-business conservative politics of the Gilded Age. The emergence of the *People's Party* in the 1890s indicated a widespread discontent. The Democrats strategically adopted much of the Populist platform, but their joint defeat in the 1896 election inaugurated an era of Republican political dominance which lasted until the Great Depression.

Divisions within the Republican Party between *Progressives* and conservatives during the second decade of the twentieth century allowed the election of the progressive Democratic President Woodrow Wilson (1913–21). Wilson's reforming Administration, however, was undermined by US participation in World War I, which was unpopular despite the United States' emergence as the world's leading power as a result. The Democratic Party of the 1920s was a potential vehicle for the excluded minorities of American society, but the prosperity of the decade ensured continued Republican rule; and the Democrats themselves were divided between a Northern wing representing Catholic immigrants and white ethnic minorities and a racist, nativist Solid South. It took the emergency of the Great Depression, beginning in 1929, to forge a new Democratic Party under President Franklin Roosevelt (1933–45).

The Democratic Party of Roosevelt's New Deal represented a new coalition of political forces which, for the next generation, established itself as a majority in the United States. Consolidated by Roosevelt's subsequent electoral victories in 1936 and 1940, the New Deal party was composed of Southern conservatives, urban dwellers, ethnic and racial minorities, the industrial working class and intellectual professionals. This coalition was electorally dominant, especially at congressional and state levels, through to the late 1960s. Roosevelt's death in office in 1945 elevated his Vice-President Harry Truman, who unexpectedly won re-election in 1948 despite a nation-wide conservative swing and the division of his own party over civil rights (*see* States' Rights Democratic Party). Through most of the Eisenhower years (1953–61) the Democrats retained control of the Congress but pursued a moderate ambition of retaining rather than extending the New Deal.

The landslide election of Southern Democrat Lyndon Johnson in 1964, on the back of national mourning for the assassinated President Kennedy, and the inauguration of President Johnson's own Great Society programme seemed to indicate a new dawn for American liberalism. However, the war in Vietnam and policy failures at home split the Democratic Party. Despite federal support for the Civil Rights Movement, the New Deal coalition was in disarray by 1968 as racial minorities, the young and the so-called 'New Left' sought more radical change and the more socially conservative working class feared it. A disastrous national convention in Chicago in 1968, marred by rioting and police brutality, consigned the Democrats to defeat, especially when the Southern wing of the party split off once more on the civil rights issue to form the *American Independent Party*.

The collapse of the Nixon Presidency in the Watergate scandal and the subsequent election in 1976 of Southerner Jimmy Carter, former Governor of Georgia, did not, however, lead to a new Democratic majority in the United States. The Carter Presidency was marred by economic recession and by various foreign policy errors which Republicans claimed weakened America's ability to offer global leadership. During the conservative Reagan and Bush years (1981–93) the Democratic Party attempted to rebuild itself as an electoral force. Solid control of the US House of Representatives in particular had not been replicated at the presidential level and critics on the party's right wing charged that its identification with inefficient 'big government' had become a liability. The creation of the Democratic Leadership Council (DLC) in 1984 to lead the party back to a more socially and fiscally conservative stance was seen by many to bear fruit in 1992 with the election to the Presidency of former DLC chairman Bill Clinton of Arkansas. However, in the 1990s the Democratic Party continued to be an uneasy coalition of 'progressive conservatives', traditional liberals and racial minorities.

Republican Party

A consequence of the great nineteenth-century contest over slavery, the modern Republican Party was established in 1854 from among various political groups opposed to the Kansas-Nebraska Act. This Act had been passed in the same year by Congress to organize the civil government of the Mid-Western territories of Kansas and Nebraska. Anti-slavery activists in the North charged that it would allow settlers in those territories legitimately to import their own slaves. The Republicans attracted to their standard the remnants of previous anti-slavery or nativist parties such as the *American Party* and the *Free Soil Party* and also those former *Whigs* who were opposed to the extension of slavery.

The Republican Party of the 1850s stood not only for the limitation (if not abolition) of slavery, but also, more broadly, for the political independence of the white working-class man and for the emerging capitalist society of the North. It ran its first presidential candidate in 1856 without success, but in 1860, against a divided Democratic Party (*see* Southern Democratic Party *and* Constitutional Union Party) its nominee, Abraham Lincoln of Illinois, prevailed. Lincoln's election led to the secession of 13 Southern states in 1860–61 and the subsequent American Civil War (1861–65). Throughout the war constitutional politics continued: Lincoln was subject to re-election in 1864 and the Democratic Party in the North, although a weakened force, presented a candidate against him. The President's assassination in 1865, however, led to the elevation of his Vice-President Andrew Johnson of Tennessee, a Democrat whom Lincoln had selected in order to be able to present the Republicans as a national party.

The era of Reconstruction (1865–77), when the federal government sought to re-establish civil government in the South, saw the creation of Republican state governments which drew their support from lower-class whites and from free blacks, whom the Republican Administration and radical Congress had emancipated in 1865. Ultimately, however, Reconstruction was inconclusive: the new Republican President, General Ulysses Grant (1867–77), failed to offer consistent federal support for black civil rights and his Administration was marred by such political corruption that the party suffered its first split with the creation of the *Liberal Republicans* in 1872. Although the Republicans won the next election, they conceded the South to the Democrats by the so-called Compromise of 1877.

The radicals' vision of creating a democratic party committed to political (if not social) equality for all Americans faded away in the last two decades of the nineteenth century and the Republican party in government became dominated by industrial interests. The so-called 'trusts' (monopolies) exercised control over the political process, often by bribery, and both Democrats and Republicans were wedded to pro-business conservative politics. The triumphant election of former Governor of Ohio William McKinley in 1896 may have marked the beginning of a period of Republican dominance that was to last a generation, but the party itself had now become identified almost exclusively with nativist Protestantism and white, rural Americans and with the economic interests of industrial capitalism.

The Progressive movement of the turn of the century nonetheless found its most successful champion in President Theodore Roosevelt (1901–09), whose second Administration pursued a platform of economic and political reform to curb the excesses of capitalism. However, conservative elements within the party ultimately refused to support Roosevelt, who vainly attempted to secure the Presidency in 1912 with his own *Progressive Party*, and the Republican Party which emerged from World War I was dominated by a *laissez-faire* approach to the economy and by isolationism in international affairs. The prosperity of the decade ensured the election of Republican candidates in 1920 (Harding), 1924 (Coolidge) and 1928 (Hoover). President Hoover himself was perhaps the epitome of a technocratic modernizer whose own vision of Republicanism was forward-looking, but his attachment to the ideal of limited government ultimately offered no answer to the disaster of the Great Depression.

Throughout the New Deal era the Republican Party continued its opposition to an activist federal government (which it claimed was unconstitutional), but with little success. However, although the New Deal Democratic Party dominated presidential and state politics, the Republicans had – particularly after 1938 – been able to limit President Roosevelt's domestic reforms by their alliance in Congress with the conservative Southern Democrats. Congress came under the Republicans' control in 1946 as the national mood swung against the Democratic establishment and was to remain Republican until 1954. Riding a wave of discontent at political corruption and particularly fear at the expansion of Soviet communism, the party also won the 1952 presidential election under war hero General Dwight Eisenhower, who seemed to represent a new, more pragmatic Republicanism which accepted the role of government established by the New Deal.

The Republican Party which ruled throughout the 1950s was a coalition of its traditional native Protestant and rural elements and the now greatly expanded professional middle classes. It fully endorsed the corporatism of Big Business, but had largely abandoned its pre-war isolationism in the face of the Soviet challenge. However, the party was also divided between a more liberal, elitist wing (often associated with East Coast politics) and the 'new' more economically and socially conservative Republicanism of the Far West and the 'Sun Belt' South. Its presidential challenger in 1964, the near-libertarian Barry Goldwater of

Arizona, was overwhelmed by Lyndon Johnson, but the Republicans won the Presidency again in 1968 and 1972 under Eisenhower's former Vice-President, Richard Nixon (1969–74), a pragmatist who proved able to hold together the two wings of the party.

The Watergate scandal which brought down President Nixon in 1974 also led to the decimation of liberal Republicanism as the party turned against the supposedly establishment politics of Washington, DC. The chief beneficiary of this was to be the former California Governor, Ronald Reagan, who defeated Democratic incumbent Jimmy Carter in 1980. The Reagan years represented the consolidation of the 'New Right' at the presidential level, as the Republicans sought to expand the American military to confront the Soviet Union abroad and to restrict the federal government's role at home, especially its social programmes, by large tax reductions.

The New Right's success was limited by the Democrats' control of Congress, but by the later 1980s the electoral politics of the United States was undergoing profound change. Despite the election of a Democratic President in 1992, the South had now largely abandoned the Democratic Party to vote Republican instead. The Republican capture of the US House of Representatives in 1994 for the first time in 40 years also represented new divisions within the electorate, as white men and women came clearly to prefer the Republicans and Democrats respectively. But the Republican Party itself was riven by divisions between its liberal elements which favoured limited government interference in both economy and society and its social conservative wing with an anti-abortion, anti-immigrant and anti-gay agenda. These divisions contributed to its defeat in 1996. By the late 1990s popular sentiment remained decidedly alienated from both mainstream political parties.

Chronology of key party conventions (Democrats since 1832, Republicans since 1856)

1832	Democrats	First Democratic convention. Delegates from 23 states meet in Baltimore to nominate Andrew Jackson for a second term. Convention adopts rule requiring two-thirds delegate majority to nominate candidates.
1835	Democrats	First credentials dispute arises when rival Pennsylvania delegations appear in Baltimore. Convention seats both groups and nominates Martin Van Buren.
1840	Democrats	Democrats appoint a committee 'to prepare resolutions declaratory of the principles of the

party' and adopt their first platform, a document of less than 1,000 words. Martin Van Buren wins the nomination.

1844	Democrats	After nine ballots, delegates nominate former Tennessee Governor James K. Polk, the first 'dark horse' to emerge from a convention. The platform calls for 'reannexation' of Texas and 'reoccupation' of Oregon.
1848	Democrats	Delegates vote to create a National Committee to run party affairs until the next convention.
1852	Democrats	Deadlocked convention. A little-known former New Hampshire Congressman, Franklin Pierce, prevails on the 49th roll call.
1856	Democrats	Convention meets in Cincinnati (first time outside Baltimore). Delegates from 31 states nominate James Buchanan of Pennsylvania on the 17th ballot.
1856	Republicans	The Republicans hold their first national nominating convention in Philadelphia to select a presidential ticket. The party selects John C. Frémont as its presidential nominee.
1860	Democrats	Stephen A. Douglas of Illinois wins the nomination following the party's most tumultuous convention. Delegates from nine states bolt the Charleston, SC convention over the platform's progressive stand on slavery.
1864	Republicans	Abraham Lincoln is renominated for the Presidency; the Republican Party briefly renames itself the Union Party. The convention adopts a platform calling for a constitutional amendment outlawing slavery. Some Southern states denied voting rights at the convention. South Carolina is denied representation entirely.
1864	Democrats	Union war hero General George B. McClellan wins the nomination on the first ballot after split among delegates over Lincoln's conduct of the war.
1868	Republicans	Ulysses S. Grant is given 100 per cent of the vote on the first ballot, the first time in Grand Old Party history.
1868	Democrats	Delegates go 22 ballots before a bandwagon develops and the convention chairman, Horace Seymour of New York, is nominated.

1872	Democrats	Delegates meet for a total of only six hours and ratify the candidate – Horace Greeley – and platform adopted by the short-lived Liberal Republican Party one month earlier.
1876	Democrats	Democrats meet in St Louis, marking the first time a convention is held west of the Mississippi. The party nominates incumbent Governor Samuel J. Tilden of New York.
1880	Republicans	After 36 ballots, the all-time record for the Republican Party, James Garfield receives the nomination for President over former President Grant and Maine Senator James G. Blaine.
1884	Democrats	For the first time, the territories and the District of Columbia are granted voting rights. Delegates nominate Grover Cleveland despite opposition from Tammany Hall.
1888	Republicans	Frederick Douglass receives one vote on the fourth ballot, becoming the first black to receive a vote in presidential balloting at a national convention.
1896	Democrats	Proceedings dominated by silver controversy. William Jennings Bryan declares 'You shall not press down upon the brow of labor this crown of thorns, you shall not crucify mankind upon a cross of gold'. Bryan wins nomination on fifth ballot.
1898	Democrats	First major party convention in a western state (Denver).
1904	Democrats	Vice-Presidential candidate Henry G. Davis, aged 80, becomes the oldest candidate ever put on a major party ticket.
1904	Republicans	Theodore Roosevelt becomes the first Vice-President to receive the nomination after succeeding a President who died in office (William McKinley).
1912	Republicans	Republicans renominate presidential ticket for the first time (President William H. Taft and Vice-President James S. Sherman).
1912	Democrats	New Jersey Governor Woodrow Wilson wins the nomination on the 46th ballot – the most roll calls since 1860. The platform calls for a single-term Presidency and extension of primaries to all states.

1920	Democrats	With the passage of suffrage, 93 women delegates and 206 alternates meet in San Francisco – the first time a convention is held west of the Rockies.
1920	Republicans	Women serve as delegates to the Grand Old Party convention for the first time in significant numbers.
1924	Republicans	Republican convention is the first to be broadcast over national radio.
1924	Democrats	Longest convention in American history. A split between urban and rural delegates forces 103 roll calls before delegates settle on John W. Davis of West Virginia. Radio coverage begins.
1928	Democrats	Democrats nominate Alfred E. Smith of New York – the first Roman Catholic to run on a major party ticket.
1932	Democrats	Franklin D. Roosevelt nominated on fourth ballot. He pledges 'a new deal for the American people'.
1940	Republicans	Republicans hold first televised convention.
1940	Democrats	Television coverage of conventions begins as Roosevelt is nominated for his unprecedented third term.
1944	Republicans	Thomas E. Dewey is the first Grand Old Party presidential candidate to accept the nomination in person at the convention.
1944	Democrats	Democrat platform argues for a United Nations, and supports a constitutional amendment on equal rights for women.
1948	Democrats	Harry Truman wins the nomination on the first ballot, but the delegates first disagree, and then divide, over a platform plank calling for full civil rights. Dissident 'Dixiecrats' bolt the proceedings, later staging their own convention.
1948	Republicans	Dewey becomes the first defeated GOP presidential candidate to be renominated.
1952	Democrats	Third ballot nomination of Illinois Governor Adlai E. Stevenson.
1956	Democrats	First time since 1888 that the Democrat convention is held before the Republican one.
1960	Democrats	Los Angeles hosts its first political convention. Delegates nominate John F. Kennedy. Kennedy is the first Senator nominated by a major party

since 1920, and the first Catholic to run since 1928. Kennedy declares that the United States is 'on the edge of a new frontier'.

1960	Republicans	Richard M. Nixon becomes the first Vice-President to be nominated to the Presidency at the end of his eight-year term.
1964	Democrat	A record 5,260 delegates and alternates meet in Atlantic City to nominate Lyndon Johnson. Johnson takes the unprecedented step of announcing in person his choice for Vice-President – Senator Hubert Humphrey.
1964	Republicans	Senator Margaret Chase Smith from Maine, the first woman elected to both the House and Senate, is the first woman to be placed in nomination for the Presidency by a major political party.
1968	Democrats	Anti-war protesters fill the streets of Chicago. Vice-President Humphrey wins a first-ballot nomination. The Reverend Channing E. Phillips of Washington DC. – the first black to be nominated for President at a Democratic convention – garners 67.5 votes on the only roll call.
1972	Democrats	With new party rules in force, a record number of women, minorities and youth go to Miami Beach as delegates. Senator George McGovern of South Dakota is nominated on the first ballot.
1976	Democrats	Delegates nominate former Georgia Governor Jimmy Carter on the first ballot. For the first time, a woman, Representative Lindy Boggs of Louisiana, chairs the convention.
1984	Democrats	Vice-President choice, Geraldine Ferraro, becomes the first woman placed on the ticket by a major political party. Reflecting the growing diversity in the Party, Reverend Jesse Jackson, who ran for the Democratic presidential nomination, receives 465.5 delegate roll-call votes (3rd behind Mondale and Gary Hart).
1992	Democrats	Convention brought to order by Democratic National Committee (DNC) Chair Ronald H. Brown, the first African-American chairman of a major political party. Arkansas Governor Bill Clinton and Senator Al Gore are nominated for President and Vice-President, ushering in a new generation of political leadership.

Other parties

Outline Chronology[1]

Dates indicate the beginning of national organization or period of established influence; in certain cases candidates had run under these names at earlier dates. Some parties, whose influence was effectively confined to single states, have not been included. Please note that no distinction is made as to whether the word 'party' was part of the organization's formal title or not.

1823	People's Party
1824	National Republican Party
1826	Antimasonic Party
1828	Workingmen's Party (Pennsylvania)
1835	Locofoco (Equal Rights) Party
1840	Liberty Party
1848	Free Soil Party
1849	American (Know Nothing) Party
1860	Constitutional Union Party
	Southern Democratic Party
1864	Independent Republican Party
1869	Prohibition Party
1872	Liberal Republican Party
	National Labor and Reform Party
	Straight-Out Democratic Party
1876	National (Greenback) Party
1877	Socialist Labor Party
	United Labor Party
	Workingmen's Party (California)
1884	Anti-Monopoly Party
	Equal Rights Party
1887	Union Labor Party
1892	People's Party
1896	National Democratic Party
	National Party
	Silver Republican Party
1898	Social Democratic Party
1901	Socialist Party
1904	National Liberty Party
1908	Independence Party
1912	Progressive Party

[1] By far the most indispensable source on American third parties is Earl R. Kruschke, *Encyclopaedia of Third Parties in the United States* (1991). Their history is discussed in J. David Gillespie, *Politics at the Periphery: Third Parties in Two-Party America* (1993).

1915	Nonpartisan League
1916	National Women's Party
1918	Farmer-Labor Party
1919–21	Communist Party of the USA
1924	Progressive Party
1932	Jobless Party
	Liberty Party
1934	Wisconsin Progressives Party
1936	American Labor Party
	Christian Party
	Union Party
1938	National Progressives of America
	Socialist Workers Party
1944	Liberal Party of New York
	South Carolina Progressive Democratic Party
1947	Christian Nationalist Party
	Independent Progressive Party
1948	American Vegetarian Party
	Progressive Party
	States' Rights Democratic Party (Dixiecrats)
1952	Constitution Party
	Poor Man's Party
1958	National States' Rights Party
1959	American Beat Party
	American Nazi Party
	Workers World Party
1960	Afro-American Party
	Tax Cut Party
1962	Conservative Party of New York
	Progressive Labor Party
1963	Freedom Now Party
	Universal Party
1964	Mississippi Freedom Democratic Party
1965	Lowndes County Freedom Organization (Black Panther Party)
1966	Black Panther Party for Self-Defense (California)
1967	Peace and Freedom Party
	National Socialist White People's Party
1968	American Independent Party
	Freedom and Peace Party
	Loyal Democrats of Mississippi
	National Democratic Party of Alabama
1969	United Citizens' Party (South Carolina)
1970	La Raza Unida Party
	National Socialist Party of America

	People's Peace Prosperity Party
1971	Libertarian Party
	People's Party
1972	American Party
1974	Liberty Union Party
1979	New Alliance Party
1980	Citizens' Party
	National Unity Campaign
1988	Internationalist Workers Party
1992	New Party
	Taxpayers Party
1995	Reform Party

Third party strength in US presidential elections

Since 1832, the following are the only occasions when third party (or independent) candidates have together polled more than 5 per cent of the popular vote:

Date	Party	Percentage of vote
1832	Antimasonic	7.78
1848	Free Soil	10.12
1856	American (Know Nothing)	21.53
1860	Southern Democrat	18.09
	Constitutional Union	12.61
1892	Populist	8.50
1912	Progressive	27.39
	Socialist	5.99
1924	Progressive (and Socialist)	16.56
1968	American Independent	13.53
1980	National Unity	6.61
1992	Independent (Ross Perot)	18.86
1996	Reform Party (Ross Perot)	8.40

Source: Gillespie, 295–7

American Independent Party

Founded by George C. Wallace (1919–) of Alabama, independent presidential candidate in 1968. It was primarily composed of Southern and Western right-wing Democrats opposed to their party's stance on civil rights. Wallace, Democratic Governor of Alabama, 1963–67, was an arch-segregationist who made populist appeals to often working-class voters

dissatisfied with the liberal Great Society, with the radical anti-war movement, and with the federal government's increased authority over the
states. In 1964 Wallace had campaigned for his party's presidential
nomination and had run well in several Northern primaries, indicating
that his conservative message was not confined to the South. Four years
later he ran again as an independent, rapidly creating his own popular
organization across all 50 states, which he himself named the American
Independent Party (AIP). Having no hope of an outright victory himself,
he aimed to deny a majority to either the Democrats or the Republicans
in the hope that their candidates, Hubert Humphrey and Richard Nixon,
might treat with him after the election. Wallace had the support of a
quarter of the electorate in September 1968, but was undermined by
his extremist vice-presidential nominee, General Curtis LeMay (former
head of the Strategic Air Command), and by Nixon's 'Southern Strategy' in which the Republicans ran in the South on a platform similar to
Wallace's. At the election the AIP candidates polled nearly 10 million
votes and carried four Southern states; Wallace denied a popular majority to either Nixon or Humphrey, but it is probable that he in fact
helped the former by dividing the Democratic vote in the South. After
1968 Wallace himself returned to the fold of the Democratic Party,
seeking its nomination again in 1972, in which campaign he was seriously injured in a would-be assassination. Deprived of its leading light,
the AIP soon faded into insignificance and suffered splits, although its
presidential candidate in 1972 polled 1.4% of the national vote. Subsequent tickets did not achieve significant results.

American Labor Party

Leftist political party founded in 1936 by New York trade unionists David
Dubinsky of the International Ladies Garment Workers and Sidney
Hillman of the Amalgamated Clothing Workers. The American Labor
Party was active in New York City in the 'fusion' campaigns against the
Democratic Party's Tammany Hall machine, supporting the election of
Republican mayor Fiorello La Guardia, and sought to rally union support for the New Deal of Democratic President Franklin Roosevelt (who
was bitterly opposed by Tammany regulars). The party succeeded in
electing a representative to the US Congress in 1948 but came under
the influence of communists during the Cold War, which caused it to
split and led to its effective disappearance by the mid-1950s.

American Nazi Party

The creation of McCarthyite anti-communist George Lincoln Rockwell
(1918–67), the party was founded in 1959 and based in Arlington,

Virginia. The name was chosen specifically to ensure maximum publicity (though the party never had more than a few thousand members), but Rockwell was also a committed supporter of Adolf Hitler's views and claimed that 'Jewish Communism' was undermining the United States. In 1967 he was assassinated by a disgruntled supporter and the American Nazi Party split into various successor factions, such as the *National Socialist White People's Party* (NSWPP) led by Matt Koehl, which sought to create not a mass party but a revolutionary cadre which would prepare for the Aryan New Order (which name it adopted in 1982), the *National Socialist Party of America* (NSPA), established in 1970 by members expelled from the NSWPP (and which included at one time John Hinckley, the attempted assassin of President Reagan), and the *White Patriot Party*, which demanded an independent nation for whites in the South. In 1978 the NSPA won its First Amendment right in federal court to march through the Jewish suburb of Skokie, Chicago.

American (Know Nothing) Party

Organized from numerous nativist secret societies in 1849 and strongest in the Southern states and on the Eastern seaboard of the United States; popularly known as the 'Know-Nothings', supposedly from its members' standard response to inquisitions about the party's organization or membership but actually coined pejoratively by newspaper editor Horace Greeley. The American Party was a reaction to concerns about the social and political effects of immigration, especially of European Catholics; one of its main tenets was the need to keep government in the hands of 'true' (i.e., native-born Anglo-Saxon) Americans, to which end it proposed a 21-year residence qualification for naturalization. The party attracted mainly Protestants and for a few years was spectacularly successful, controlling perhaps a quarter of the US House of Representatives in 1855–57 and several state legislatures. However, it was divided over the issue of slavery and split after the 1856 presidential election, the anti-slavery elements being absorbed into the Republican Party.

Antimasonic Party

The first national 'third party' in United States history, the Antimasonic Party was founded in 1826 in the state of New York by a number of dissident Freemasons who recanted their former secretive practices. Explicitly populist in its rhetoric and political ambitions, the party had no established programme but instead opposed the forces of the establishment, especially at this time the Jacksonian Democrats. The Antimasons, claiming that the political elite wished to undermine the basis of popular government in the United States, attracted the support largely of the poor and those swept up by the contemporary religious revival, the Second Great Awakening. By 1828–30 the party was competitive in several Northern states and controlled a tenth of the US House of Representatives. In 1831 in Baltimore, Maryland, it held the first national convention in American history for nominating a presidential candidate; its nominee, William Wirt, captured nearly 8% of the popular vote in 1832. However, thereafter the Antimasons were largely supplanted by the opposition *Whig Party*.

Black Panther Party

The forebear of the party was created in 1965 when the militant civil rights organization, the Student Nonviolent Coordinating Committee (SNCC), established the Lowndes County Freedom Organization in the state of Alabama in order to register its majority black population for the purposes of voting. Lowndes County was one of the poorest and most segregated in the country and the organization, whose symbol was a black panther, worked without federal help and in the face of armed white resistance. The example of militant black self-help inspired the radicals, Huey Newton and Bobby Seale, to set up the *Black Panther Party for Self-Defense* in Oakland, California. With a programme which was a mixture of black nationalism and Marxism-Leninism, the Black Panthers were a relatively small but tightly organized party whose local 'chapters' established independent schools, newspapers and legal and medical services in black communities across the United States and which aggressively resisted the police and 'white' authorities. Its leftist philosophy was always more important, however, than black nationalism, and it was prepared to seek allies among white radicals; in the early 1970s it participated in local electoral politics, but by the 1980s police and FBI action against its leadership had effectively eliminated the party.

Bull Moose Party   *See* Progressive Party

Citizens Party

A short-lived populist party of environmentalists and consumers' rights activists, the Citizens Party was founded in 1980 by the ecologist Barry Commoner. Its manifesto was effectively democratic socialist: it sought the nationalization of major industries, citizen representation on boards of directors, an end to nuclear power, a reduction in military spending and support for the civil rights of minorities. Strongest in the Northern state of Vermont, the party ran Commoner for president in 1980 but largely disappeared after 1984, many of its activists abandoning formal electoral politics and joining the Green movement.

Communist Party of the USA

When the Russian Revolution of 1917 split the international socialist movement, Marxist-Leninists in the United States left the *Socialist Party* in 1919 and established two rival communist parties (the Communist Party of America and the Communist Labor Party), which merged two years later to form the Workers Party. In 1929 it was renamed the Communist Party of the United States of America (CPUSA). Organized as a Leninist party operating on 'democratic centralist' principles, the CPUSA was throughout its history often subordinate to, if not controlled by, the Communist Party in the Soviet Union. It drew its greatest strength from among trades union and labour activists in the major urban centres and from the industrial working class, especially among East European immigrant communities. Several labour unions were under CPUSA control in the 1930s. It also appealed to black Americans and nominated a black vice-presidential candidate as early as 1932. The height of the party's electoral fortunes was in the period 1935–48 when it often pragmatically supported the New Deal Democratic Party of Franklin Roosevelt (after demonizing him as a fascist) and, in foreign affairs, joined other anti-fascist organizations in the Popular Front against Nazi Germany. It loudly demanded American entry in the war after Hitler's 1941 attack on Russia, and in 1948 campaigned heavily for the *Progressive* candidate, Henry Wallace, who favoured accommodation with the Soviets. However, the onset of the Cold War made it the target of oppressive government activity, especially as the CPUSA had rigidly followed the Stalinist line from Moscow. The Smith Act of 1940 had made illegal membership of any political party dedicated to the revolutionary overthrow of the US government; a decade later the Internal Security (or McCarran) Act required communists to register party membership with the US Department of Justice. Senator Joseph McCarthy of Wisconsin's Senate investigations into supposed communists in the federal government and the hearings of the House Un-American Activities Committee (HUAC) effectively destroyed the party, despite McCarthy's later political fall. The social and cultural revolution of the 1960s failed to produce any mass support for the CPUSA; many of the younger members of the so-called 'New Left' rejected its hardline Stalinist legacy for being as anti-democratic as capitalism. The party's political significance was effectively ended by the collapse of the Soviet Union in 1991.

Constitutional Union Party

Short-lived political party which fought the presidential election of 1860 on the platform of preserving the federal Union against the potential secession of the Southern states over the issue of slavery. Its candidate,

John Bell, polled nearly 13% of the popular vote and carried the states of Tennessee, Kentucky and Virginia. Constitutional Unionists had been elected to the US Congress during the preceding decade but the party organized nationally only in this year, drawing its support from wealthier former *Whigs* and *Know-Nothings*. Its platform ignored all other issues and the party collapsed following the election of Republican (unionist) Abraham Lincoln.

Dixiecrats   *See* States' Rights Democratic Party

Farmer-Labor Party

Radical co-operative party organized in the state of Minnesota in the inter-war period, the Farmer-Labor Party emerged as an organized entity in 1924. Its political programme was explicitly social democratic – it advocated the nationalization of banks, industry and public utilities, the establishment of a universal state welfare system, and the redistribution of wealth as part of a progressive programme to supersede capitalism; and it appealed to the class-interest of both farmers and workers. A mass membership party in the European manner, it enjoyed electoral success in the state legislature and the US Congress and thrice elected Floyd Olson as Governor in the 1930s. Although its rhetoric was often radical, the Farmer-Labor leaders were happy to co-operate with Franklin Roosevelt's New Deal and when their own support waned in the later 1930s, the party merged with state Democrats in 1944 to create the still extant Democratic-Farmer-Labor Party.

Federalists

The original Federalists of American history were those statesmen who favoured the ratification and adoption of the US Constitution drawn up by the Philadelphia Convention in 1787. Their opponents were the Antifederalists. In 1788 the former triumphed when New Hampshire became the ninth state to ratify and the Constitution came into effect. Thereafter the term was used to describe those who, in the era before formal parties, favoured a greater concentration of power in the national government and a stronger Union. Their opponents, as supporters of the rights of the separate states, took the name 'Republican'. The leading statesmen associated with each respectively were Alexander Hamilton (sometime US Secretary of the Treasury) and Thomas Jefferson and James Madison (third and fourth Presidents). The Federalists wanted an active federal government which would encourage the development of industry; their opponents feared that they represented an upper-class cabal which was unduly pro-British in foreign affairs and unsympathetic towards popular political rights. The contest between the two led to the creation of the first national electoral organizations, but after the Republican presidential triumph in 1800 the Federalists lost much of their support; within a decade they had become unable to fight elections on a national level.

Free Soil Party

Formed in 1848 from Barnburner Democrats (*see* glossary, p. 303), the old *Liberty Party* and anti-slavery *Whigs*, with the aim of preventing the extension of slavery into the Territories of the United States. It supported the Wilmot Proviso of 1846, a congressional measure restricting slavery's expansion, in preference to seeking immediate abolition. The party nominated former Democratic President Martin Van Buren as its candidate in 1848, when he took just over 10% of the popular vote but failed to carry any state. The Freesoilers' support was concentrated in the North and overtures to Democrats in this region to build an anti-slavery coalition alienated its more abolitionist wing. By the mid-1850s the party's supporters had been absorbed by the Republican Party.

Greenback Party   *See* National Party

Know-Nothings   *See* American Party

La Raza Unida Party

Radical Hispanic political party. Established in the early 1970s, it grew out of the most politicized elements of the Chicano (Mexican-American) consciousness movement. Organized largely in the major urban centres of the South-West, it seeks to provide for Hispanics an electoral alternative to the Democratic Party and to organize working-class Mexican-Americans to better their own economic and social interests.

Liberal Republican Party

Members of the Republican Party who refused to support the re-election of President Grant in 1872 in protest at the inefficiency and corruption of his Administration. Disillusion at the way in which industrial and commercial interests were coming to dominate their party had motivated certain Mid-Western Republicans to establish a separate identity some two years earlier in the hope of correcting the administration's course; but the new party was organized on a national basis only for this election. Their candidate, the newspaper editor Horace Greeley, who was also adopted by the Democrats, was easily defeated by Grant and Liberal Republicanism disappeared as a result.

Libertarian Party

Extremist party of near-anarchist tendencies, which opposes all forms of government regulation (both social and economic) and supports an isolationist foreign policy. It was founded in 1971, but has significant popular support only in the Western states and in Alaska. The party claimed some 200,000 registered voters in the early 1990s.

Liberty Party

Anti-slavery party founded in 1840 by New York abolitionists opposed to the extremer (direct action) position of Henry Lloyd Garrison. The Liberty Party preferred moral suasion, believing that the Constitution did not allow the federal government to abolish slavery. It nominated James G. Birney in the presidential election of that year. In the 1844 election Birney took enough votes from the Whig candidate, Henry Clay, to throw the state of New York to the Democrat James Polk and so ensure the latter's election. The Liberty Party was absorbed into the *Free Soil Party* four years later.

Locofoco (Equal Rights) Party

Originally a grouping in the Democratic Party in New York in the 1830s, the Locofocos supported political reform and legislation (such as recognition of trades unions) to benefit the working classes. In October 1835 they separated from the mainstream Democrats after a meeting at the party's headquarters, Tammany Hall in New York City, during which candles were lighted with matches known as 'locofocos'. The faction then reformed itself as an independent organization, the Equal Rights Party, but within 18 months the majority had been subsumed once more into the Democratic Party, which however did co-opt some of its pro-labour platform, thus strengthening the party among the urban working class.

Mississippi Freedom Democratic Party

A breakaway movement from the national Democratic Party in the state of Mississippi, organized by the Student Nonviolent Coordinating Committee (SNCC) to mobilize the disenfranchised black majority, the MFDP under Fannie Lou Hamer sought to challenge the right of the all-white party delegation to be seated at the 1964 Democratic national convention, on the grounds that the regular Democratic Party in Mississippi was racist and excluded blacks. President Lyndon Johnson and the party's establishment tried to obstruct the MFDP by offering it a partial representation of two seats at the convention, which was rejected. The failure of the MFDP (despite the fact that the regular white Democratic Party in the state was inclining towards Johnson's Republican opponent Barry Goldwater) turned many black radicals towards direct action for civil rights.

National (Greenback) Party

The most significant independent party to emerge in the two decades after the Civil War, the National Party had its origin in the economic distress of American farmers, who were suffering from overproduction and from exorbitant rates for rail freight being charged by the railway cartels. Recession in the 1870s (especially the Panic of 1873) pushed farmers' commercial organizations, the so-called Grangers, to organize politically. Their economic solution was the free circulation of paper currency (known as 'greenbacks', hence the party's popular name), which they hoped would provide an inflationary stimulus and lessen the burden of agricultural debt. By the early 1880s the party was competitive in a number of Mid-Western and Northern states, although its presidential candidates never achieved above 2% of the popular vote (the best showing being by James Weaver of Iowa in 1880 who organized in nearly every state, which even mainstream parties did not do at this date). The Greenbackers' later manifesto demanded the state regulation of workplace health and safety, a progressive income tax and votes for women, all of which were assumed by its effective successor, the *People's Party* in the 1890s.

National Republican Party

That part of the first (Jeffersonian) Republican Party which in the 1820s was associated with President John Quincy Adams (1825–29). Adams's faction endorsed the concept of a more activist federal government and was out of sympathy with the populist majority of the contemporary Democratic-Republican Party associated with General Andrew Jackson, which favoured states' rights. In the 1828 presidential election (won by Jackson) Adams stood as a National Republican candidate. Having been defeated, the Nationalists disappeared by the time of the next presidential contest and the mainstream party shortened its name to 'Democratic'.

National Unity Campaign

The campaign organization of former Republican Congressman John Anderson who in 1980, having failed to win his own party's nomination, made an independent bid for the Presidency. A liberal Republican himself, Anderson was alarmed by his party's move towards the New Right, with its adoption of Californian Governor Ronald Reagan as candidate. Anderson sought to unite progressive Republicans and Democrats; his manifesto advocated gun control, environmental taxes, Social Security reform and defence cuts. In the election Anderson polled 5.7 million votes (6.6% of the total), running best in the East and Far West and among upper-income professionals. Although his policies were closer to the ideals of the liberal wing of the Democratic Party, Ronald Reagan's margin of victory over incumbent President Carter was such that Anderson's candidacy probably did not affect the outcome.

National Women's Party

Formed in 1916 from the Congressional Union for Woman Suffrage, the National Women's Party (NWP) revived the programme of the Equal Rights Party of the 1880s which had campaigned for votes for women in federal elections (certain states allowed female suffrage in local ballots). The party's leadership was inspired by the example of the British Suffragette movement and its adoption of a strategy of direct action alienated it from the larger, moderate National American Suffrage Association. Its campaigns successfully persuaded a number of states to allow women to vote for President, before the Nineteenth Amendment to the Constitution in 1920 forbade sex discrimination. Having achieved this objective, the party largely dissolved as a mass organization, although a remnant continued in support of the Equal Rights Amendment.

People's Party (Populists)

Founded in Cincinnati in 1891 and on a national basis the following year. Known also as the Populists, the party drew its support from the discontent of Mid-Western and Southern farmers and from those sections of society who were economically and politically disadvantaged by the growing power of industrial corporations in the United States. Its platform in the presidential election of 1892 proposed the abolition of national banks, the free coinage of silver (which would help Western silver mining interests and might induce inflation in the economy, to the advantage of indebted farmers), laws against non-native landowning, a progressive income tax and state control of the railways. The national party had been preceded by various populist parties which had enjoyed some electoral success at the state level; with the establishment of a national organization the Populists attempted to unite the two formally separate social groups of native farmers and the industrial, urban working class which included many immigrants. In 1896, however, the

People's Party was forced to throw its lot in with the Democrats, who had nominated as their presidential candidate the Nebraskan populist William Jennings Bryan. Despite a vigorous campaign, Bryan was defeated by the Republican William McKinley, whose victory established his party as the dominant one in the United States. The majority of supporters of the People's Party was then rapidly absorbed into the Democratic Party and it lost its independent representation in the US Congress.

Progressive Party

For a description of the historical movement which gave rise to the first Progressive Party, see p. 350.

The Bull Moose Party. In 1912 former President Theodore Roosevelt (1901–09) sought to contest the Republican presidential nomination. Although 'TR' had effectively anointed his own successor, William Howard Taft (1909–13), he had become increasingly disillusioned with the latter's more conservative policies and wished to regain office himself. Roosevelt ran well ahead of Taft in the party's state primary elections, but at this date a majority of delegates were effectively selected by the party bosses, who were for Taft, and when the incumbent secured the nomination at the party's convention the Roosevelt forces withdrew to form their own Progressive Party. At its convention in Chicago in August, TR was nominated for President on a platform reminiscent of the activist federal government of his own second Administration. In particular it stood for votes for women, the direct election of US Senators, an income tax and regulation of working conditions. Roosevelt pledged himself to campaign 'as fit as a bull moose', whence was derived the popular name of the party. TR's national status as an ex-president was a serious challenge to the Taft Republicans and to the Democrats who had nominated Woodrow Wilson; both concentrated their attacks on the Progressives. In the popular election Roosevelt (who survived an assassination attempt during the campaign) won over 27% of the vote – the best third-party share in history – and took 88 electoral votes (compared with 8 for Taft). However, he succeeded only in splitting the Republican vote and ensuring the election of Wilson. There was moderate success in the congressional election (the Progressives won one seat in the US Senate and nine in the House), but the party's national organization was fragile and much depended upon TR's leadership. He declined to run again in 1916 and the Bull Moosers then broke apart, losing their representation in Congress after 1918.

La Follette Progressives. The second Progressive Party was established in 1924 by followers of the former Republican Wisconsin Governor and US Senator, Robert 'Fighting Bob' La Follette. La Follette had sought his party's presidential nomination successively from 1912 to 1924; in that year he was finally nominated by the Conference for Progressive Political Action (CPPA), a grouping of liberal progressive activists, on a platform which called for the nationalization of the railways, strict regulation of monopolies and direct presidential elections. La Follette's left-wing manifesto attracted the support of the *Farmer-Labor Party* and the *Socialist Party*, which supported him for President; in a number of states he was on the ballot as the Socialist candidate. Against enormous odds – a respected incumbent President, the Republican Calvin Coolidge, and only weak support from many Progressive forces which considered his effort doomed – La Follette nonetheless won almost 17% of the popular vote and carried his home state. His 4.8 million votes were the greatest number obtained by a third-party candidate up to that date. However, following La Follette's death the next year, the CPPA dissolved, its appeal undermined by rising prosperity.

The Wisconsin Progressive Party. The progressive tradition of the upper Mid-West continued under the leadership of Robert La Follette's sons, Philip and Robert, Jr, who, after their father's death, served as Republican Governor of Wisconsin (1930–32) and Republican US Senator (1925–34) respectively. With the advent of Democratic President Franklin Roosevelt's New Deal, however, the younger La Follettes found themselves increasingly alienated from the more conservative Republican Party and in 1934, with the President's support, they founded the Wisconsin Progressive Party. Through the 1930s these progressives, who were closely associated with the *Farmer-Labor Party* in neighbouring Minnesota, enjoyed electoral success: Philip was re-elected as Governor and Robert as US Senator in 1934 and most of the state's representatives in the US House were Progressives. The La Follette administration in Wisconsin implemented a reform programme, including large-scale public works to help the jobless and the first state unemployment insurance system, which provided a model for similar measures at the national level under President Roosevelt. However, as the national political mood became more conservative at the end of the decade and during World War II, the Party faltered and after 1946 most of its supporters defected to the Democrats and the Republicans.

The (Wallace) Progressive Party. In 1946 the former US Vice-President and Secretary of Commerce Henry Wallace, who had been dismissed by President Truman for being too conciliatory towards Soviet communism, established the Progressive Citizens of America. Two years later in July 1948 the group formed itself into a new Progressive Party in order to contest that year's presidential election. The party's platform stood for friendship with Russia abroad (essentially a continuation of the US position during the War) and, at home, for an 'American Commonwealth' akin to the ideals of the British Labour government elected in

1945. The Progressives' national organization was heavily dependent upon the support of the *Communist Party of the USA* and their candidate Wallace was severely criticized as a dupe of Moscow, especially when his party condemned the anti-communist activities of the US government. The CPUSA's prominent role in the Progressive campaign alienated other leftist forces, which now rallied to the Democratic Party; in 1948 President Truman himself ran on a progressive platform which included federal support for civil rights and national health insurance. Wallace polled over a million votes but failed to carry any state and the Progressive Party did not survive beyond the 1952 contest, when its candidate took less than 150,000 votes.

Prohibition Party

The third oldest national party in the United States, the Prohibitionists first organized in 1869 to campaign for the prohibition of the manufacture and sale of alcoholic beverages. A product of nineteenth-century moral fundamentalism, the party latterly co-operated with the Democrats and Republicans to ensure the passage of the Eighteenth Amendment to the Constitution in 1919 which established national Prohibition. The law, however, was a disaster, being widely flouted and encouraging organized crime, and Prohibition was repealed in 1932. The party, which had elected representatives to the US Congress, is now insignificant and otherwise indistinguishable from other Protestant fundamentalist movements. In 1872, however, the party had been the first in the United States to demand votes for women.

Reform Party

Founded in 1995 by Texas billionaire Ross Perot as the vehicle for his presidential ambitions, the Reform Party developed out of Perot's existing organization, United We Stand America. Perot had run for the Presidency as an independent in 1992, spending $60 million of his own money and winning nearly 19% of the popular vote, but failing to carry any individual state. The party, which claimed over 1.3 million members, held a national convention in August 1996 at which Perot defeated former Democratic Governor Richard Lamm of Colorado for its presidential nomination. Perot managed only 8.4% of the vote in November 1996 (less than half his 1992 tally).

Socialist Labor Party

The national Workingmen's Party, founded in 1876, was reconstituted a year later as the Socialist Labor Party (SLP). Today it is the fourth oldest party in the United States. A Marxist party, it explicitly rejected the amendments to Marx's doctrines made by the Russian leader Lenin and sought to build socialism through syndicalist action – the fostering of revolutionary trades unions. The SLP was associated in the industrial sphere with the radical Industrial Workers of the World ('Wobblies'), but was severely weakened in 1899 by the defection of the faction which was to establish the *Socialist Party*. The SLP continued to contest presidential elections until 1976.

Socialist Party

Founded in 1901, the Socialist Party was more moderate than its Marxist predecessor the *Socialist Labor Party*. It attracted wide support from different ethnic groups, including native-born Americans, and not only from among the German, Italian and Jewish immigrants with whom labour activism in the United States is usually associated. The Socialist Party was particularly strong in urban areas and the rural Western states where the Populist movement had been a force in the 1890s. The party's presidential candidate was the trade unionist Eugene Debs, who received 6% of the popular vote in both 1904 and 1912. The height of its electoral fortunes was in 1910 when it returned a representative to the US Congress (Victor Bergen of Milwaukee, Wisconsin), and in 1912 there were over 50 elected Socialist mayors in America, but the party declined rapidly after the 'Red Scare' of 1919–20.

Socialist Workers Party

Founded in 1938 by Trotskyists who had been expelled from the *Communist Party of the USA*, the Socialist Workers Party (SWP) was a founding member of the Fourth International of Trotskyist communist parties. It drew some support from anti-Stalinist intellectuals and the trade union movement, particularly the Teamsters Union which it effectively controlled in the 1930s, but was damaged by the federal government's war on extremist organizations in the 1940s and 1950s – the SWP's leadership was the first to be prosecuted under the Smith Act of 1940. In the 1960s, however, it profoundly influenced the New Left; its Young Socialist Alliance mobilized many university students and membership rose as high as 10,000 by the early 1970s. The party remained critical of the USSR and supportive of 'progressive' regimes (e.g., Cuba); and, although membership has since declined greatly, it continues to offer presidential and congressional candidates.

Southern Democratic Party

Party formed in 1860 by the secession of Southern Democrats from the national Democratic Party over the issue of slavery. Dissatisfied that the national party at its convention that year would not support amending the Constitution to protect slavery, delegates from the Deep South withdrew and formed a secessionist party, nominating John Breckinridge for President. As the first major party to offer explicit support for slavery, the secessionists carried the South and a good many Northern Democratic votes at the presidential election of 1860, winning some 18% of the popular poll. The election of the Republican Abraham Lincoln, however, extinguished the party.

States' Rights Democratic Party (Dixiecrats)

A secession from the national Democratic Party in 1948, the Dixiecrats were those conservative Southern Democrats who were dismayed by the liberal platform adopted by the national party at its presidential nominating convention. Incumbent President Truman supported national health insurance, federal aid for education, increased welfare spending and, particularly, vigorous federal action on civil rights – such as a federal anti-lynching law, the abolition of poll taxes for voting and the outlawing of racial discrimination in employment and inter-state travel. Southern delegates withdrew, claiming that such measures interfered with the states' constitutional right of self-government, and a secessionist party was hastily organized, drawing the support of the entire leadership of the Democratic Party in the Deep South. Governor Strom Thurmond of South Carolina was nominated for President. The party's platform eschewed explicitly racist appeals but did endorse segregation and the separate development of the races. Thurmond won over a million votes (about 2.5% of the popular total) and carried four states, but the Democratic establishment outside the Deep South remained loyal to Truman and the party was unable to nominate any leading candidate to contest the 1952 election, effectively marking its demise.

Whig Party

A political party which had its origins among the opponents of Democratic President Andrew Jackson (1829–37). It included the remnants of the *National Republican Party* and the *Antimasonic Party*. The Whigs, who named themselves after the opponents of the supposedly autocratic British monarch George III, supported the ideal of a limited Presidency, in which the chief official would leave the formulation of legislation entirely to the Congress and would act simply as an executive. They also believed, however, in contrast to the Democrats, that the federal government should be active in stimulating the economic and social development of the country; and their leading member, Senator Henry Clay of Kentucky, was an advocate of the 'American System' of a protective tariff and government-sponsored transportation improvements which he had been proposing since the 1820s. The Whig Party derived its support from across the United States, especially from among social conservatives and native-born Protestants and the urban professional classes; in the Western states it attracted yeoman farmers who would benefit from internal improvements and in the South, plantation owners. The Whigs successfully elected to the Presidency Generals William Henry Harrison in 1840 and Zachary Taylor in 1848, but both died in office (Harrison after only one month) without distinction. In the 1850s the party, which had always stood for a strong Union of states, was progressively undermined by the division between the North and South over the expansion of slavery. After 1855 the Whigs were fatally divided between their Northern and Southern supporters; the latter tended to join the Southern-dominated Democratic Party while the former were absorbed by the new anti-slavery Republican Party.

Workingmen's Party

Founded in California in the wake of industrial unrest in 1877, the Workingmen's Party opposed the continued immigration of Chinese labourers into the state. Cheap Chinese labour had been in demand since the Gold Rush of 1849 and by 1880 there were to be 75,000 in California, equivalent to more than one-tenth of the population. White labour leaders denounced the Chinese as the tools of an exploiting capitalist class; the party's leader, Dennis Kearney, was himself the son of an Irish immigrant but he capitalized upon white racist sentiment. Although the Workingmen were shortlived as an organized political party within the state, breaking up after limited electoral successes in 1879 (including electing the Mayor of San Francisco), their opposition to Asian immigration gained national appeal and in 1882 the US Congress was to prohibit any further Chinese immigration for a decade.

Elections

Presidential election results, 1789–1996

Introductory Note: The following table is derived from the *Historical Abstract of US Statistics*. It excludes a variety of minor party candidates polling only a small proportion of the total vote. It should be noted that, prior to the 1804 election, each elector voted for two candidates for President; the one receiving the highest number of votes, if a majority, was declared elected President, the next highest, Vice-President. This provision was modified by adoption of the Twelfth Amendment which was ratified on 25 September 1804.

Year	Presidential candidate	Political party	Vote cast, electoral	Vote cast, popular
1789	George Washington		69	
	John Adams		34	
	John Jay		9	
	R.H. Harrison		6	
	John Rutledge		6	
	Others (7)		14	
	(Not voted)		12	
1792	George Washington	Federalist	132	
	John Adams	Federalist	77	
	George Clinton	Democratic-Republican	50	
	Thomas Jefferson		4	
	Aaron Burr		1	
1796	John Adams	Federalist	71	
	Thomas Jefferson	Democratic-Republican	68	
	Thomas Pinckney	Federalist	59	
	Aaron Burr	Antifederalist	30	
	Samuel Adams	Democratic-Republican	15	
	Oliver Ellsworth	Federalist	11	
	Others		22	
1800	Thomas Jefferson	Democratic-Republican	73	
	Aaron Burr	Democratic-Republican	73	
	John Adams	Federalist	65	
	C.C. Pinckney	Federalist	64	

Year	Presidential candidate	Political party	Vote cast, electoral	Vote cast, popular
1800	John Jay	Federalist	1	
1804	Thomas Jefferson	Democratic-Republican	162	
	C.C. Pinckney	Federalist	14	
1808	James Madison	Democratic-Republican	122	
	C.C. Pinckney	Federalist	47	
	George Clinton	Independent-Republican	6	
	(Not voted)		1	
1812	James Madison	Democratic-Republican	128	
	De Witt Clinton	Fusion	89	
	(Not voted)		1	
1816	James Monroe	Republican	183	
	Rufus King	Federalist	34	
	(Not voted)		4	
1820	James Monroe	Republican	231	
	John Q. Adams	Independent-Republican	1	
	(Not voted)		3	
1824	John Q. Adams		84	108,740
	Andrew Jackson	No distinct party	99	153,544
	Henry Clay	designations	37	47,136
	W.H. Crawford		41	46,618
1828	Andrew Jackson	Democratic	178	647,286
	John Q. Adams	National Republican	83	508,064
1832	Andrew Jackson	Democratic	219	687,502
	Henry Clay	National Republican	49	530,189
	William Wirt	Antimasonic	7	
	John Floyd	Nullifiers	11	
	(Not voted)		2	
1836	Martin Van Buren	Democratic	170	765,483
	William H. Harrison	Whig	73	
	Hugh White	Whig	26	739,795
	Daniel Webster	Whig	14	
	W.P. Mangum	Anti-Jackson	11	
1840	William H. Harrison	Whig	234	1,274,624
	Martin Van Buren	Democratic	60	1,127,781
1844	James K. Polk	Democratic	170	1,338,464
	Henry Clay	Whig	105	1,300,097
	James G. Birney	Liberty		62,300

Year	Presidential candidate	Political party	Vote cast, electoral	Vote cast, popular
1848	Zachary Taylor	Whig	163	1,360,967
	Lewis Cass	Democratic	127	1,222,342
	Martin Van Buren	Free Soil		291,263
1852	Franklin Pierce	Democratic	254	1,601,117
	Winfield Scott	Whig	42	1,385,453
	John P. Hale	Free Soil		155,825
1856	James Buchanan	Democratic	174	1,832,955
	John C. Frémont	Republican	114	1,339,932
	Millard Fillmore	American	8	871,731
1860	Abraham Lincoln	Republican	180	1,865,593
	J.C. Breckinridge	Democratic (S)	72	848,356
	Stephen A. Douglas	Democratic	12	1,382,713
	John Bell	Constitutional Union	39	592,906
1864	Abraham Lincoln	Republican	212	2,206,938
	George B. McClellan	Democratic	21	1,803,787
	(Not voted)		81	
1868	Ulysses S. Grant	Republican	214	3,013,421
	Horatio Seymour	Democratic	80	2,706,829
	(Not voted)		23	
1872	Ulysses S. Grant	Republican	286	3,596,745
	Horace Greeley	Democratic	*	2,843,446
	Charles O'Connor	Straight Democratic		29,489
	Thomas A. Hendricks	Democratic	42	
	B. Gratz Brown	Democratic	18	
	Charles J. Jenkins	Democratic	2	
	David Davis	Democratic	1	
	(Not voted)		17	
1876	Rutherford B. Hayes	Republican	185	4,036,572
	Samuel J. Tilden	Democratic	184	4,284,020
	Peter Cooper	Greenback		81,737
1880	James A. Garfield	Republican	214	4,453,295
	Winfield S. Hancock	Democratic	155	4,414,082
	James B. Weaver	Greenback-Labor		308,578
	Neal Dow	Prohibition		10,305
1884	Grover Cleveland	Democratic	219	4,879,507
	James G. Blaine	Republican	182	4,850,298
	Benjamin F. Butler	Greenback-Labor		175,370
	John P. St John	Prohibition		150,369

* Died after polling day.

Year	Presidential candidate	Political party	Vote cast, electoral	Vote cast, popular
1888	Benjamin Harrison	Republican	233	5,447,129
	Grover Cleveland	Democratic	168	5,537,857
	Clinton B. Fisk	Prohibition		249,506
	Anson J. Streeter	Union Labor		146,935
1892	Grover Cleveland	Democratic	277	5,555,426
	Benjamin Harrison	Republican	145	5,182,690
	James B. Weaver	People's	22	1,029,846
	John Bidwell	Prohibition		264,133
1896	William McKinley	Republican	271	7,102,246
	William J. Bryan	Democratic	176	6,492,559
	John M. Palmer	National Democratic		133,148
	Joshua Levering	Prohibition		132,007
1900	William McKinley	Republican	292	7,218,491
	William J. Bryan	Democratic	155	6,356,734
	John C. Wooley	Prohibition		208,914
1904	Theodore Roosevelt	Republican	336	7,628,461
	Alton B. Parker	Democratic	140	5,084,223
	Eugene V. Debs	Socialist		402,283
	Silas C. Swallow	Prohibition		258,536
	Thomas E. Watson	People's		117,183
1908	William H. Taft	Republican	321	7,675,320
	William J. Bryan	Democratic	162	6,412,294
	Eugene V. Debs	Socialist		420,793
	Eugene W. Chafin	Prohibition		253,840
1912	Woodrow Wilson	Democratic	435	6,296,547
	Theodore Roosevelt	Progressive	88	4,118,571
	William H. Taft	Republican	8	3,436,720
	Eugene V. Debs	Socialist		900,672
	Eugene W. Chafin	Prohibition		206,275
1916	Woodrow Wilson	Democratic	277	9,127,695
	Charles E. Hughes	Republican	254	8,533,507
	A.L. Benson	Socialist		585,113
	J. Frank Hanly	Prohibition		220,506
1920	Warren G. Harding	Republican	404	16,143,407
	James M. Cox	Democratic	127	9,130,328
	Eugene V. Debs	Socialist		919,799
	P.P. Christensen	Farmer-Labor		265,411
	Aaron S. Watkins	Prohibition		189,408
1924	Calvin Coolidge	Republican	382	15,718,211
	John W. Davis	Democratic	136	8,385,283
	Robert M. LaFollette	Progressive	13	4,831,289

Year	Presidential candidate	Political party	Vote cast, electoral	Vote cast, popular
1928	Herbert C. Hoover	Republican	444	21,391,993
	Alfred E. Smith	Democratic	87	15,016,169
	Norman Thomas	Socialist		267,835
1932	Franklin D. Roosevelt	Democratic	472	22,829,501
	Herbert C. Hoover	Republican	59	15,760,684
	Norman Thomas	Socialist		884,649
	William Z. Foster	Communist		103,253
1936	Franklin D. Roosevelt	Democratic	523	27,757,333
	Alfred M. Landon	Republican	8	16,684,231
	William Lemke	Union		892,267
	Norman Thomas	Socialist		187,833
1940	Franklin D. Roosevelt	Democratic	449	27,313,041
	Wendell L. Willkie	Republican	82	22,348,480
	Norman Thomas	Socialist		116,410
1944	Franklin D. Roosevelt	Democratic	432	25,612,610
	Thomas E. Dewey	Republican	99	22,017,617
1948	Harry S. Truman	Democratic	303	24,179,345
	Thomas E. Dewey	Republican	189	21,991,291
	Strom Thurmond	States' Rights Democratic	39	1,176,125
	Henry Wallace	Progressive		1,157,326
	Norman Thomas	Socialist		139,572
	Claude A. Watson	Prohibition		103,900
1952	Dwight D. Eisenhower	Republican	442	33,936,234
	Adlai E. Stevenson	Democratic	89	27,314,992
	Vincent Hallinan	Progressive		140,023
1956	Dwight D. Eisenhower	Republican	457	35,590,472
	Adlai E. Stevenson	Democratic	73	26,022,752
	Walter Jones	(not a candidate)	1	
	T. Coleman Andrews	Independent States' Rights		111,178
1960	John F. Kennedy	Democratic	303	34,226,731
	Richard M. Nixon	Republican	219	34,108,157
	Harry F. Byrd	(not a candidate)	15	
1964	Lyndon B. Johnson	Democratic	486	43,129,484
	Barry M. Goldwater	Republican	52	27,178,188
1968	Richard M. Nixon	Republican	301	31,785,480
	Hubert Humphrey	Democratic	191	31,275,166
	George C. Wallace	American Independent	46	9,906,473

Year	Presidential candidate	Political party	Vote cast, electoral	Vote cast, popular
1972	Richard M. Nixon	Republican	520	47,169,911
	George McGovern	Democratic	17	29,170,383
	John G. Schmitz	American		1,099,482
1976	Jimmy Carter	Democratic	297	40,830,763
	Gerald R. Ford	Republican	240	39,147,973
	Eugene J. McCarthy	Independent		756,631
	Roger MacBride	Libertarian		173,011
	Lester Maddox	American Independent		170,531
	Thomas J. Anderson	American		160,773
1980	Ronald Reagan	Republican	489	43,899,248
	Jimmy Carter	Democratic	49	36,481,435
	John B. Anderson	Independent		5,719,437
	Ed Clark	Libertarian		921,299
	Barry Commoner	Citizens		234,294
1984	Ronald Reagan	Republican	525	54,455,075
	Walter F. Mondale	Democratic	13	37,577,185
	David Bergland	Libertarian		228,314
1988	George Bush	Republican	426	48,886,097
	Michael Dukakis	Democratic	111	41,809,074
	Ron Paul	Libertarian		432,179
	Lenora B. Fulani	New Alliance		217,219
1992	William J. Clinton	Democratic	370	44,908,254
	George Bush	Republican	168	38,102,343
	Ross Perot	Independent		19,741,065
	Andre V. Marrou	Libertarian		291,627
	James 'Bo' Gritz	Populist		107,014
1996	William J. Clinton	Democratic	379	45,238,951
	Robert Dole	Republican	159	37,607,011
	Ross Perot	Reform		7,807,588
	Ralph Nader	Green		575,985
	Harry Browne	Libertarian		464,076
	Howard Phillips	US Taxpayers		177,195
	John Hagelin	Natural Law		109,238

The Electoral College

The Electoral College is the body which under the Constitution chooses the President and the Vice-President of the United States. It is described in Article II, Section 1 of the Constitution, as varied by the Twelfth and Twenty-Fourth Amendments. The members of the body, known as 'electors', are chosen from each of the several states and the District of Columbia; each state is entitled to the same number of electors as it has members of Congress (i.e., Representatives and Senators) and the District is allowed three electors, this being equivalent to the representation it would enjoy in the Congress if it were a state. At the presidential election every four years in November, the people of each state do not vote directly for the presidential and vice-presidential candidates but for the state's electors; each party running candidates in the election nominates in each state a slate of electors (usually party activists). The presidential ticket which wins the popular vote in each state – in a first-past-the-post system – is entitled to that state's entire number of electors (thus if the Democratic candidates beat the Republicans by one vote in California, they are entitled to *all* 54 electors; the entitlement is not divided proportionately). The electors are pledged to vote for their party's candidates in the Electoral College and they meet in their respective state capitals the following month to cast ballots for the President and Vice-President. These ballots are then transmitted to Washington, DC where, in a special ceremony in January, they are counted before the Congress. The candidates receiving a majority of the votes of the entire College (i.e., 270) are deemed elected; constitutionally speaking, it is only at this point that the President and Vice-President are chosen. The College never meets as a national body; nor are the electors *legally* obliged to vote for the candidates for whom they are chosen, but because convention dictates that they do, the outcome of the election is a foregone conclusion from the moment that the popular vote has been counted in each state the preceding November. However, if no candidate receives a majority of Electoral College votes, the House of Representatives, according to Article II of the Constitution, must choose the President, and the Senate the Vice-President. There was speculation in 1992 that this might in fact happen, because there were three leading candidates for President, but although Ross Perot won over 19 million popular votes, he did not secure a plurality in any state and so was not entitled to any electors. The existence of the Electoral College means that it is technically possible for a person to be elected President without winning the largest share of the popular vote, though this has not happened since 1888; and it also tends to militate against the establishment of third parties in presidential politics.

Electoral College votes, 1996

Alabama	9	Louisiana	9	Ohio	21
Alaska	3	Maine	4	Oklahoma	8
Arizona	8	Maryland	10	Oregon	7
Arkansas	6	Massachusetts	12	Pennsylvania	23
California	54	Michigan	18	Rhode Island	4
Colorado	8	Minnesota	10	South Carolina	8
Connecticut	8	Mississippi	7	South Dakota	3
Delaware	3	Missouri	11	Tennessee	11
D/Columbia	3	Montana	3	Texas	32
Florida	25	Nebraska	5	Utah	5
Georgia	13	Nevada	4	Vermont	3
Hawaii	4	New Hampshire	4	Virginia	13
Idaho	4	New Jersey	15	Washington	11
Illinois	22	New Mexico	5	West Virginia	5
Indiana	12	New York	33	Wisconsin	11
Iowa	7	North Carolina	14	Wyoming	3
Kansas	6	North Dakota	3	Total: 538	
Kentucky	8				

Presidents securing minority of popular vote, 1824–1996

1824	John Quincy Adams	(Republican)	29.8
1844	James K. Polk	(Democratic)	49.3
1848	Zachary Taylor	(Whig)	47.3
1856	James Buchanan	(Democratic)	45.3
1860	Abraham Lincoln	(Republican)	39.9
1876	Rutherford B. Hayes	(Republican)	47.9
1880	James A. Garfield	(Republican)	48.3
1884	Grover Cleveland	(Democratic)	48.8
1888	Benjamin Harrison	(Republican)	47.8
1892	Grover Cleveland	(Democratic)	46.0
1912	Woodrow Wilson	(Democratic)	41.8
1916	Woodrow Wilson	(Democratic)	49.3
1948	Harry S. Truman	(Democratic)	49.5
1960	John F. Kennedy	(Democratic)	49.7
1968	Richard M. Nixon	(Republican)	43.4
1992	William J. Clinton	(Democratic)	43.2
1996	William J. Clinton	(Democratic)	49.0

Turnout in presidential elections since 1945[1]

1948	51.1
1952	61.6
1956	59.3
1960	62.8
1964	61.9
1968	60.9
1972	55.2
1976	53.5
1980	54.0
1984	53.1
1988	50.2
1992	55.9
1996	49.1

[1] The enfranchisement of the 18–21-year olds is partly responsible for the fall in turnout in 1972.

Source: Federal Election Commission.

SECTION TWO

Social and religious history

Public health and social welfare

Chronology of key events

1793	Yellow fever epidemic in Philadelphia followed by sanitation and water improvements.
1798	Marine Hospital Service established for disabled merchant seamen (not effectively organized until 1870).
1819	Passenger Act includes regulations over health of immigrants.
1824	County Poor House Act of New York provides for workhouses and almshouses.
1832	New York cholera epidemic leads to improvements in supply of clean water.
1840	First state to aid blind (Indiana), followed by Boston for mentally retarded (1848).
1843	Foundation of New York Association for Improving the Conditions of the Poor. Beginnings of visits to homes by social workers.
1855	Earliest permanent health boards created (in Louisiana and in Providence, Rhode Island).
1863	Massachusetts creates unified Board of Charities.
1864	Columbia Institute for Deaf and Dumb (now Gallaudet College) founded by Congress.
1866	Permanent health board created in New York City.
1869	Permanent health board created in Massachusetts.
1870	Marine Hospital Service effectively organized. Gradually evolves into US Public Health Service.
1872	Founding of American Public Health Association.
1873	First Charity Organization Society branch founded (in Germantown, Pennsylvania).
1879	National Board of Health created.
1907	Food and Drug Administration created to handle problems of food hygiene, food manufacturing processes, etc.
1910	Start of medical department at Harvard, MIT, Johns Hopkins, etc.
1912	Children's Bureau organized.
1915	Rockefeller Foundation established to support a variety of major health programmes.

1917   Supreme Court upholds state compensation laws for accidents at work.

1920   Office of Vocational Rehabilitation formed.

1921   Maternity and Infancy Act. Subsequently many states establish child welfare divisions.

1932   Wisconsin becomes the first state to pass unemployment insurance law.

1933   Establishment of Home Owners Loan Corporation (HOLC), emergency refinancing agency to tackle problem of foreclosure leading to loss of homes.

1934   National Housing Act. Creates Federal Housing Authority (FHA).

1935   Social Security Act marks birth of modern American welfare state. Social Security Administration established. Effectively the start of social security in the United States. The 1935 Act secures federal old age pensions, survivors' benefits, unemployment insurance and specific aid for the aged, blind, dependent children, etc. Provides basis of social security until 1996.

1939   Federal Security Agency set up (incorporates Social Security Administration and other agencies).

1946   Employment Act. Responsibility of maintaining full employment given to federal government.

1949   Housing Act. Federal funds allocated to local authorities to acquire slum property and build houses.

1953   Department of Health, Education and Welfare (HEW) established (11 April). All functions of old Federal Security Agency transferred to the HEW. Oveta Culp Hobby becomes the first Secretary.

1954   Housing Act marks birth of urban regeneration.

1960   Beginning of a decade of reforms, including the 'War on Poverty' and the Medicaid program.

1961–62 Housing Acts.

1964   Civil Rights Act (see p. 144) helps black Americans to take more advantage of benefits. Economic Opportunity Act offers a variety of youth programmes (e.g., Job Corps), the VISTA programme, small business loans and community action programmes to fight local poverty.

1965   New Department of Housing and Urban Development (HUD) created with cabinet status. Major amendment of 1935 Social Security Act provides extensions for medical protection.

1966   Demonstration Cities Act places emphasis on rehabilitation of existing housing in 'model cities' programme.

1968   Housing and Urban Development Act. HUD is given power to provide financing for homes and rental housing for lower-income families. Interest subsidies introduced.

1974   Housing and Community Development Act. Initiative shifted to localities.

1980   Department of Health, Education and Welfare divided into two Separate Cabinet departments of Education, and Health and Human Services (4 May).

1993   Hillary Clinton's radical health-care reform plan put to Congress. Subsequently fails (29 Sept.).

1995   Social Security Administration, previously part of the Department of Health and Human Services, becomes an independent agency (31 Mar.).

1996   Welfare Reform Bill, signed by President Clinton, ends 60 years of 'safety net' welfare payments to children and poor mothers. It is the first serious legislative measure to challenge the 'unconditional war on poverty' launched by Lyndon Johnson in 1964.

Key statistics

The growing cost of national health expenditure, 1960–94

	Total (in billion $)	Total as % of GDP
1960	27.1	5.3
1965	41.6	5.9
1970	74.3	7.4
1975	132.6	8.4
1980	251.1	9.3
1985	434.5	10.8
1990	696.6	12.6
1994	949.4	13.7

Growth of public assistance, 1940–80[1]

Year	$ Total[1]
1940	1,020,115,000
1945	990,700,000
1950	2,372,200,000
1955	2,525,600,000
1960	3,276,700,000
1965	4,025,900,000
1970	8,864,400,000
1975	16,312,600,000
1980	21,463,955,000

[1] Includes old age, blind, aid to families with dependent children, etc.
Source: Social Security Administration

The Medicare programme (totals in $)

1970	7,099,000,000
1975	15,588,000,000
1980	35,700,000,000
1985	71,385,000,000
1990	112,091,000,000
1994	169,246,000,000

Food stamp programme

	Numbers of participants
1965	425,000
1970	4,340,000
1975	17,064,000
1980	21,071,000
1985	19,900,000
1990	20,100,000
1993	27,000,000

Average monthly benefits rose from $6.38 in 1965 to $21.42 in 1975 and $34.35 in 1980.
Source: Department of Agriculture

Social welfare expenditures

Combined federal, state and local government expenditures for social welfare programmes are shown in millions of dollars (add 000,000).

	1950	1960	1965	1970	1975	1980	1985	1990
TOTAL	23,508	52,293	77,175	145,856	290,047	493,354	732,000	1,050,000
Social insurance	4,947	19,307	28,123	54,691	23,013	229,552	370,000	514,000
Public Aid	2,496	4,101	6,283	16,488	41,326	72,385	98,000	147,000
Health & medical programmes	2,063	4,464	6,246	9,907	17,707	28,119	39,000	62,000
Veterans' programmes	6,866	5,479	6,031	9,078	17,019	21,465	27,000	31,000
Education	6,674	17,626	28,108	50,845	80,863	170,588	239,000	258,000
Housing	15	177	318	701	3,172	7,209	13,000	19,000
Other social welfare	448	1,139	2,066	4,145	6,947	14,036	14,000	18,000

Source: Social Security Bulletin

Education

Chronology of key events since 1776

1779	Reorganization of College of William and Mary (founded 1693, the only college in the South).
1784	University of the State of New York organized (reorganized, 1787) (a centralized school system).
1785	Charter for state university granted by Georgia. Followed by North Carolina (1789), Vermont (1791) and Tennessee (1794). Land Ordinance reserves lot (Section Sixteen) in each township in Western Territory 'for maintenance of public schools'.
1789	Massachusetts law established district school system (made compulsory in 1827).
1805	Free Public School Society founded in New York.
1812	New York appoints Gideon Hawley first state superintendent of schools.
1827	Society for the Promotion of Public Schools of Philadelphia founded.
1833	Oberlin (Ohio) becomes first college to have women students.
1836	Mount Holyoke founded, the first permanent women's college.
1857	Cooper Union founded in New York with objective of 'the advancement of science and art'.
1861	First US Doctorate of Philosophy awarded (at Yale).
1867	Office of Education established. Howard University established to provide higher education for black Americans.
1876	Johns Hopkins founded at Baltimore – the first entirely graduate college.
1896	*Plessy v. Ferguson* decision undermines efforts to improve Afro-American education. Sets legal precedent for segregation.
1900	Association of American Universities formed.
1902	Public junior college movement started.
1910	Appearance of first junior high school (at Berkeley, California).
1917	Smith–Hughes Act promotes vocational education.
1920	First developments in pre-school and nursery education.
1923	Nebraska law against teaching foreign languages in private elementary schools declared illegal.
1933	Federal government sponsors National Survey of Secondary Education.

1938   Gaines decision by US Supreme Court (first of several important decisions for racial integration) followed by Sipuel (1948), Sweatt (1950) and McLaurin (1950).

1940   *Alston v. Norfolk School Board* decision in favour of equal pay for white and black teachers in public schools.

1944   Servicemen's Readjustment (G.I. Bill of Rights) provides financial assistance to veterans for education, housing, etc. (22 June).

1946   National School Lunch Act. Fulbright Act for educational exchanges with foreign countries (followed by Smith-Mundt Act, 1948 and Fulbright–Hays Act, 1961).

1949   Report of President's Commission on Higher Education. Foundation of Southern Regional Education Program. Establishment of State University of New York as pioneer in state-wide higher education.

1954   *Brown v. Board of Education of Topeka* rules that segregated education by race is illegal.

1958   Report of President's Committee on Education Beyond High School. National Defense Education Act promotes teaching of science, mathematics, modern languages, etc.

1963   Vocational Education Act passed.

1964   Civil Rights Act provides for withholding of federal money from public school districts where racial discrimination exists.

1965   Higher Eduction Act aids teacher education and library services. Elementary and Secondary Education Act passed in response to increased pressure for federal aid to education.

1967   Education Professions Development Act.

1970–71   Supreme Court decisions in favour of speedier desegregation.

1972   Title XI of the Educational Amendments Act requires higher education institutes to establish 'affirmative action' programmes for women.

1975   Public Law 94–142 extended educational opportunities for disabled children and adults and required that they be educated in the same classes as others as far as possible.

1973   *Tinker v. Des Moines Independent Community School District.* Supreme Court rules that school children enjoy their right to constitutionally protected free speech whilst at school.

1981   Elementary and Secondary Education Act revised as the Educational Consolidation and Improvement Act.

1983   The federal National Commission on Excellence in Education issued its report, 'A Nation At Risk', criticising standards of secondary education.

1994   Goals 2000: Educate America Act established a series of National Education Goals to improve educational attainment and help the States to raise standards (31 March).

Key statistics

Total elementary and secondary school enrolment, 1890–1993 (to nearest 000)

1890	14,479,000
1900	16,855,000
1910	19,372,000
1920	23,278,000
1930	28,329,000
1940	28,045,000
1950	28,491,000
1960	42,181,000
1970	51,272,000
1980	46,318,000
1990	45,669,000
1993	47,913,000

High School graduates
Totals

1870	16,000
1900	95,000
1920	311,000
1930	667,000
1950	1,199,700
1970	2,937,000
1980	3,043,000
1994	2,517,000

As percentage of 17 year olds, 1870–1956

1870	2.0
1880	2.5
1890	3.5
1900	6.4
1910	8.8
1920	16.8
1930	29.0
1940	50.8
1956	62.3

College enrolment, 1960–93 (in millions)

Year	College Total	Male	Female
1960	3.5	2.3	1.2
1970	7.4	4.4	3.0
1975	9.7	5.3	4.4
1980	11.4	5.4	6.0
1985	12.5	5.9	6.6
1990	13.6	6.2	7.4
1993	13.9	6.3	7.6

College graduates (bachelors degrees or equivalent)

1900	27,400
1920	48,600
1940	186,500
1960	392,400
1970	827,000
1980	999,500
1990	1,095,000

Source: Department of Education: National Center for Education Statistics

Slavery and Abolition (to 1865)

Chronology of key events

1775   Formation of Pennsylvania Society for Promoting the Abolition of Slavery (April). Benjamin Rush and Benjamin Franklin among its presidents.

1776   Plan for African colonization proposed by Jefferson. Continental Congress calls for an end to importation of slaves.

1780   Gradual abolition act passed by Pennsylvania.

1783   Slave trade prohibited in Maryland (and abolished by judicial decision in Massachusetts).

1784   Bills for gradual abolition passed in Rhode Island and Connecticut.

1785   New York Society for the Promoting of the Manumission of Slaves formed (with John Jay as its first president).

1786   First slaves begin to escape north by 'underground railroad'.

1787   Northwest Ordinance. Slavery excluded from all land north of the Ohio River in Northwest Territory.

1788   Delaware forms abolition society (followed by Maryland, 1789; Rhode Island and Connecticut, 1790; Virginia, 1791; and New Jersey, 1792).

1793   Federal Fugitive Slave Law passed. Cotton gin invented by Eli Whitney.

1794   First convention of abolition societies.

1799   New York adopts bill for gradual abolition of slavery.

1800   Suppression of planned slave revolt by Gabriel Prosser in Virginia.

1803   South Carolina opens slave trade from Caribbean and South America.

1804   Bill for gradual abolition of slavery passed in New Jersey. Movement of free blacks restricted by law in Ohio.

1805   All slaves emancipated after 1 May required by law to leave Virginia.

1807   Import of slaves from Africa banned by Congress (effective from 1 January 1808).

1816   Establishment of American Colonization Society, founded in Washington to form colony in Liberia.

1820   The Missouri Compromise. Agrees Missouri to be admitted to Union as a slave state, but slavery to be prohibited in future states north of the 36°30' parallel.

1822   Negro colony of Liberia established at Monrovia by the American Colonization Society. By 1831, 1,400 had returned to Africa. Insurrection attempt by Denmark Vesey discovered at Charleston, South Carolina.

1827   First black newspaper, the *Freedom's Journal*, begins publication. Final emancipation of all slaves in New York (under 1817 Law).

1829   Militant resistance by blacks to slavery argued by free black David Walker in *Walker's Appeal, in Four Articles.*

1831   Publication of *The Liberator* in Boston by William Lloyd Garrison. Nat Turner's Rebellion (August). Killing of 57 whites in Southampton County, Virginia. Turner (see p. 162), a slave preacher, captured and subsequently hanged in Jerusalem, Virginia.

1832   New England Anti-Slavery Society formed by militant Garrison supporters (6 Jan.). Becomes Massachusetts Anti-Slavery Society. Appearance of Garrison's *Thoughts on African Civilisation.*

1833   Formation of National Anti-Slavery Society in Philadelphia (6 Dec.). American Anti-Slavery Society activated by William Lloyd Garrison. British government compensates West Indies slave-owners on abolition of slavery.

1835   New York Anti-Slavery Society organized (21 Oct.). Oberlin becomes first college to admit black students.

1837   Murder of newspaper editor, Elijah Lovejoy, in Alton, Illinois, provides martyr for anti-slavery cause.

1838   Escape of Frederick Douglass (see p. 267) from slavery in Maryland.

1839   Liberty Party (see p. 108) organized by Gerrit Smith, Myron Holley and others, aims to bring slavery question into political debate. *American Slavery As It Is* published by Theodore Dwight Weld.

1840   James G. Birney runs as presidential candidate of Liberty Party.

1844   Birney polls 632,000 votes in presidential election, but Liberty Party subsequently splits. Many become Free-Soilers. Split in Methodist Church over slavery.

1845   House of Representatives rescinds 'gag rule'.

1846   Defeat in Senate of Wilmot's Proviso (see p. 365), proposing ban on slavery in territory acquired from Mexico.

1847   Liberia declares itself an independent country. Abolitionist newspaper, *North Star*, begun in Rochester (NY) by Frederick Douglass and Martin Delany.

1848   Establishment of Free Soil Party (see p. 107).

1850   The Compromise of 1850 (see p. 18).

1851   Split of Frederick Douglass and William Lloyd Garrison over tactics.

1852   Publication of *Uncle Tom's Cabin* by Harriet Beecher Stowe, a highly popular sentimental novel on the wrongs of slavery. Successor to Free Soilers, Free Democratic Party, polls 150,000 votes in presidential election.

1854   Kansas–Nebraska Act. The provision of the Missouri Compromise, prohibiting slavery north of the 36°30' line, is repealed. Popular sovereignty allowed in Kansas and Nebraska. Results in birth of Republican Party to oppose extension of slavery in the West.

1855   Racial segregation abolished in Massachusetts schools. *My Bondage and My Freedom* published by Frederick Douglass.

1856   Five pro-slavers murdered by abolitionist John Brown at Pottawatomie. Formal organization of Republican Party (see p. 92).

1857   Critical ruling in *Dred Scott v. Sanford* case (see p. 85) effectively renders Missouri Compromise unconstitutional (Congress has no power to exclude slavery from the territories). Proslavery constitution (Lecompton) for Kansas. Never accepted.

1859   Abortive planned slave insurrection led by John Brown on the arsenal at Harper's Ferry. Brown accompanied by 16 whites and five blacks (Oct.).

1861   Provisional government of seceding states formed (the Confederacy, see pp. 57 and 312).

1865   Abolition of slavery formally made effective (18 Dec.).

The final abolition of slavery by state, 1777–1858

1777   Vermont
1780   Maine, Massachusetts
1783   New Hampshire
1803   Ohio
1816   Indiana
1818   Illinois
1827   New York
1837   Michigan
1842   Rhode Island
1846   Iowa, New Jersey
1848   Connecticut, Wisconsin (and also Washington Territory and Oregon Territory)
1850   Pennsylvania, California
1858   Minnesota

Growth of the slave population

1790	697,624
1810	1,191,362
1830	2,009,043
1850	3,204,313
1860	3,953,760

Source: Statesman's Year Book, 1910

Black American history (since 1865)

Civil Rights Movement

Movement to secure access for American blacks to the voting and citizenship rights which had been guaranteed them by the Fourteenth and Fifteenth Amendments to the Constitution of 1868 and 1870. The National Association for the Advancement of Colored People (*see* NAACP) was formed in 1909 to press for legal amelioration but little progress was made for 50 years, largely because the Supreme Court had, in 1883 and 1896, decided that the right of the states to make their own laws (even laws segregating white and black citizens and effectively preventing the latter from voting) could not be overriden by the federal government. However, in 1954 (in the ruling *Brown v. Board of Education of Topeka, Kansas*), the Court declared segregated education to be unconstitutional and three years later federal troops were used at Little Rock (q.v.) in Arkansas to force the admittance of black students to an all-white school. From the later 1950s civil disobedience became widespread; a campaign of boycotts and demonstrations led by Dr Martin Luther King (1929–68) of Atlanta, Georgia eventually resulted in *federal* legislation to enforce civil rights for blacks, especially the Voting Rights Act of 1964. However, riots in Harlem, New York (July 1964) and Watts, Los Angeles (August 1965) revealed dissatisfaction with the pace of reform and encouraged the growth of black militancy, especially after the assassination of King in April 1968. In the 1970s and 1980s many blacks felt their progress towards full equality, especially in employment and education, was not enhanced by unsympathetic Republican Administrations.

Chronology of key events

1868   Fourteenth Amendment passed (see p. 59).

1869   Ebenezer D. Bassett becomes first US black diplomat on appointment as Minister-Resident to Haiti.

1870   Fifteenth Amendment passed (see p. 59). Hiram Revels, first black elected to US Senate for Mississippi. Jefferson Long from Georgia, first black elected to US House of Representatives.

1881	Tennessee adopts new segregation laws – beginning of the 'Jim Crow' era (see p. 334).
1883	Supreme Court ruling over rights of states to make laws, even if discriminating against blacks.
1896	Supreme Court ruling reinforces 1883 judgement.
1898	Riots in Wilmington (see p. 163).
1906	Riots and mob violence in Atlanta (see p. 163).
1908	Riots in Springfield (see p. 163).
1909	Foundation of National Association for the Advancement of Colored People (NAACP) for the promotion of civil rights through peaceful means, especially via the courts.
1911	National Urban League founded to campaign for equal conditions and opportunities for black workers in employment, etc.
1915	Victories for NAACP in Supreme Court rulings (*Guinn v. United States*) and in 1917 (*Buchanan v. Warley*) which declare 'grandfather clause' unconstitutional and outlaw Jim Crow housing regulations.
1917	Houston Incident (see p. 163).
1919	Race riots in Chicago (see pp. 163–4).
1921	Race riots in Tulsa County, Oklahoma (see p. 164).
1930	Black Muslims (Nation of Islam) founded in Detroit by Wali Farad, with belief in black nationalism, self-defence against violence and the formation of a separate black state.
1931	Verdict in Scottsboro case (April).
1938	Integration of Missouri Law School ordered, followed later by Oklahoma and Texas.
1942	Congress of Racial Equality (CORE) formed with pacifist objectives and non-violent protest.
1943	Race riot in Detroit. Federal troops deployed.
1944	Election to Congress of black leader, Adam Clayton Powell. *Smith v. Allwright* ruling bans all-white primary.
1954	Supreme Court ruling in *Brown v. Board of Education of Topeka, Kansas* declares segregated education unconstitutional and unequal.
1957	Foundation of Southern Christian Leadership Conference (SCLC). Led by Martin Luther King, it advocates non-violent methods of protest. Federal troops sent to Little Rock, Arkansas.
1960	Student Nonviolent Coordinating Committee (SNCC) formed. A black and white non-violent student protest committee which made much use of sit-ins. Ends hegemony of NAACP.
1961	Attacks on Freedom Riders (q.v.) as they travelled by bus to Birmingham, Alabama (May).
1963	Civil rights mass march culminates in a peaceful demonstration of 250,000 people in Washington (28 Aug.).

1964   Riots in Harlem, New York (July). Civil Rights Act and Voting Rights Act become law (aids black registration in deep South).

1965   Watts Riots, Los Angeles (Aug.), triggered by arrest of a black motorist. Rioting leaves 34 dead, 1,000 injured and over 3,700 people arrested.

1966   Black Panthers founded by Huey Newton and Bobby Seale in Oakland, San Francisco. The ten-point Black Panther programme called for full employment, land, bread, housing, education, clothing, justice and peace, an end to police brutality and the murdering of black people. Robert C. Weaver appointed first black Cabinet Minister (Secretary of the Department of Housing and Urban Development). Riots in over a dozen cities leave eleven dead (June–Sept.).

1967   Thurgood Marshall appointed first black Associate Justice of US Supreme Court (2 Oct.). Black Panther leader Huey Newton shot by police while being arrested; he is tried and jailed. Rioting in Newark, New Jersey (July). Worst rioting since Watts, after arrest of black cab driver, leaves 26 dead and 1,400 injured. Rioting in Detroit. These riots leave 43 dead, over 2,000 injured. Federal troops deployed to put down civil disorder on first occasion since 1943. Appointment of Kerner Commission in wake of Newark and Detroit rioting.

1968   Assassination of Martin Luther King (April). Violence sweeps 125 cities across America. Week of unrest leaves 46 dead and damage of $67 million. Eldridge Cleaver, Panther leader, arrested then released. He fled the country in face of re-arrest.

1969   FBI intensify campaign against Panthers. Twenty-seven Black Panthers killed by police and 749 arrested and jailed.

1972   Barbara Jordan (of Texas) becomes first black woman to chair a state legislature.

1980   Rioting in Liberty City section of Miami (May). Triggered after all-white jury acquits four former Miami police officers of the fatal beating of black insurance executive. Riots leave 18 dead, with 1,100 arrests and damage of $200 million.

1988   Rioting in Overtown section of Miami after black motorcyclist shot and killed by police (Jan.).

1989   Barbara Harris, first woman black Episcopal bishop appointed.

1990   L. Douglas Wilder elected in Virginia as first black elected Governor of a state. First black Mayor of New York, David Dinkin, takes office.

1992   Rioting erupts in Los Angeles (April–May) after acquittal of four white police officers in the case of Rodney King. Death toll put at 58, with 4,000 injuries and 11,900 arrests.

Key statistics

Lynching of blacks in United States, 1882–1935

1882	49	1900	106	1918	60
1883	53	1901	105	1919	76
1884	51	1902	85	1920	53
1885	74	1903	84	1921	59
1886	74	1904	76	1922	51
1887	70	1905	57	1923	29
1888	69	1906	62	1924	16
1889	94	1907	58	1925	17
1890	85	1908	89	1926	23
1891	113	1909	69	1927	16
1892	161	1910	67	1928	10
1893	118	1911	60	1929	7
1894	134	1912	61	1930	20
1895	113	1913	51	1931	12
1896	78	1914	51	1932	6
1897	123	1915	56	1933	24
1898	101	1916	50	1934	15
1899	85	1917	36	1935	18

Source: US Bureau of the Census, *Statistical Abstract of the United States: 1996*

Life expectancy of blacks (figures for whites in parenthesis)

1920	45.3 (54.9)
1930	48.1 (61.4)
1940	53.1 (64.2)
1950	60.8 (69.1)
1960	63.6 (70.6)
1970	65.3 (71.7)
1980	69.5 (74.4)
1990	71.2 (76.1)
1994	71.8 (76.4)

Source: National Center for Health Statistics

Non-white illiteracy rates, 1870–1952 (figures in parenthesis for total of all races)[1]

1870	79.9 (20.0)
1880	70.0 (17.0)
1890	56.8 (13.3)
1900	44.5 (10.7)
1910	30.5 (7.7)
1920	23.0 (6.0)
1930	16.4 (4.3)
1940	11.5 (2.9)
1952	10.2 (2.5)

[1] Over 10 years old until 1940; 14 years old for 1952.

Highest proportion of black residents (in 25 largest US cities, 1960 census)[1]

	% (1960)	% (1990)
Washington	53.9	65.8
Atlanta	38.3	67.1
New Orleans	37.2	61.9
Memphis	37.0	54.8
Baltimore	34.8	59.2
Detroit	28.9	75.7
Cleveland	28.6	46.6
St Louis	28.6	47.5
Philadelphia	26.4	39.9
Chicago	22.9	39.1
Houston	22.9	28.1
Cincinnati	21.6	37.9

[1] Only New York (14%) had more than one million black residents. Numerically it was followed by Chicago (812,637) and Philadelphia (529,240).

Source: Statistics derived from The World Almanac, 1968

Black poverty in contemporary America[1]

Year	Percentages below poverty level			
	All races	White	Black	Hispanic origin
1960	22.2	17.8	na	na
1965	17.3	13.3	na	na
1970	12.6	9.9	33.5	na
1975	12.3	9.7	31.3	26.9
1980	13.0	10.2	32.5	25.7
1990	13.5	10.7	31.9	28.1
1993	15.1	12.2	33.1	30.6

[1] Poverty is defined as the proportion of the population whose income falls below the government's official poverty level (which itself is adjusted annually for inflation).

The black population of America

Year	Numbers (in 000s)	% total of population
1790	757	19.3
1810	1,378	19.0
1820	1,772	18.4
1840	2,874	16.8
1860	4,442	14.1
1870	4,880	12.7
1880	6,581	13.1
1890	7,489	11.9
1900	8,834	11.6
1920	10,463	9.9
1930	11,891	9.7
1940	12,866	9.8
1950	15,045	9.9
1960	18,872	10.5
1970	22,581	11.1
1980	26,683	11.8
1985	28,569	12.0
1990	29,986	12.1
1994	32,672	12.5

The American Indians

Chronology of key events (including major treaties)

1763	Attempt to separate tribes and pioneers by Royal Proclamation Line. Rebellion against British expansion in Great Lakes led by Pontiac (Pontiac's War). Pontiac himself was killed in 1769 by an Illinois Indian.
1778	First US treaty with an Indian tribe (the Delaware).
1779	Beginnings of smallpox epidemic among the tribes.
1782	Gnanenhutten massacre (a Delaware village on Tuscarawas River, Ohio) of peaceful Christian Indians.
1784	Second Treaty of Fort Stanwix with the Iroquois.
1785	Treaty of Hopewell with the Cherokee, who cede lands in North Carolina, Tennessee and Kentucky.
1790	Treaty of New York City with Creek Indians. Start of conflict in Ohio River Valley with Indians.
1791	Treaty of the Holsten River with the Cherokee.
1794	Battle of the Fallen Timbers (north-west Ohio) (20 Aug.). Victory paves way for the frontier enforcement of Jay's Treaty (see p. 231).
1795	Treaty of Greenville. Indians cede much of southern and eastern Ohio.
1798	Treaty of Tellico. Cherokees cede land in Tennessee.
1803	Treaty of Vincennes. Indians cede lands in central and south-east Illinois.
1808	Treaty of Fort Clark. Osage cede land between Arkansas and Missouri Rivers.
1809–10	Indian resistance to Western settlement led by Shawnee Chief Tecumseh who sought to organize a tribal confederacy. Tecumseh died in Battle of the Thames (5 Oct. 1813).
1811	Indian defeat at Battle of Tippecanoe.
1813	Battle of the Thames (5 Oct.).
1814	Treaty of Fort Jackson. Creeks cede lands in Georgia and Alabama.
1816	Treaty of St Louis. Indians cede land in Illinois (between Illinois and Mississippi Rivers) and in south-west Wisconsin.

1818   Chickasaw Indians cede land between Tennessee and Mississippi Rivers in Treaty of Old Town.

1819   Indian Civilisation Fund established by Congress. Treaty of Saginaw. Chippewa cede land in Michigan.

1820   Choctaw Indians cede land in west-central Mississippi under Treaty of Doak's Stand.

1821   Treaty of Chicago. Land ceded by Ottawa, Chippewa and Potawatomi Indians in southern Michigan and northern Indiana.

1823   Treaty of St Louis. Osage and Kansa Indians cede large tracts of land.

1824   Office of Indian Affairs organized by War Department.

1830   Indian Removal Act signed by Andrew Jackson. Leads to removal of 100,000 Indians, mainly Cherokee and Seminole, from Georgia to western Arkansas (see Trail of Tears, p. 360).

1831   Treaty of Prairie du Chien with Indian tribes. Verdict in *Cherokee Nation v. Georgia*. Supreme Court ruled that it lacked the jurisdiction to protect Cherokee territory from predations by the State of Georgia because it was a 'domestic dependent nation' rather than a foreign state.

1832   Black Hawk War fought in Illinois and Wisconsin.
        Treaty of Fort Armstrong (the 'Black Hawk Purchase').
        Worcester v. Georgia decision. Supreme Court ruled that Georgian state law had no authority over the Cherokees, but the US government refused to enforce this.

1834   Enactment of Indian Trade and Intercourse Act.

1835   Outbreak of Second Seminole War (lasts until 1842).

1837   Smallpox outbreak decimates tribes along the Missouri.

1842   Indian lands in Iowa ceded in Treaty of Sauk and Fox Agency.

1846   Acquisition of Oregon, followed by rapid movement of pioneers west along Oregon and California trails (1847–49).

1849   Office of Indian Affairs transferred to Department of the Interior.

1851   Treaty of Traverse des Sioux and Treaty of Fort Laramie (provisions of Fort Laramie altered by Senate, not ratified by Indians).

1853   Treaty of Table Rock with Rogue River Indians ceding land in Oregon.

1862   Homestead Act opens up vacant lands to white settlement. Sante Sioux War in Minnesota.

1863–68 Navajo Indians forced out to the Bosque Redondo.

1864   Sand Creek Massacre (Nov.). Some 450 sleeping Cheyennes and Arapahoes killed by Colonel John M. Chivington's 3rd Colorado Volunteers.

1865	Beginning of Sioux War (lasts till 1867).
1866	Fetterman Massacre in which detachment of 82nd US Cavalry wiped out by Sioux.
1867	Establishment of Board of Indian Commissioners.
1868	Sioux victory under leadership of Red Cloud.
1870	First appropriation by Congress of money specifically for Indian education.
1871	Treaty system ended by Congress.
1872–73	Oregon witnesses Modoc War.
1874	Red River War occurs in Texas.
1875	Start of Sioux War.
1876	Defeat of Custer. 'Custer's Last Stand'. See p. 266.
1877	Nez Perce War (on borders of Washington, Oregon and Idaho).
1879	Founding of National Indian Association. Carlisle Indian School set up by Richard Pratt.
1881	Publication of *A Century of Dishonour* by Helen Hunt Jackson, cataloguing ill-treatment of Indians by whites.
1882	Foundation of Indian Rights Association.
1883	Start of Lake Mohonk Conferences.
1884	Traditional Indian religious practices made criminal offence by Department of the Interior.
1886	Apache Wars ended by surrender of Geronimo.
1887	Tribal reservations broken up into family and individual holdings by Dawes Act.
1889	Spread of 'Ghost Dance' teachings by Paiute Indian Wovoka (1854–1932) who saw himself as an Indian messiah.
1890	Massacre of 200 Sioux at Wounded Knee, South Dakota by eight troops of the 7th US Cavalry commanded by Colonel James W. Forsyth. Marks end of all Indian resistance in Dakota.
1903	Outcome of *Lone Wolf v. Hitchcock* case.
1907	Dawes Act amended by passage of Burke Act. Oklahoma statehood (merges Oklahoma and Indian Territory).
1910	Revival of the 'Sun Dance' after suppression of 'Ghost Dance'.
1911	Foundation of Society of American Indians.
1918	Incorporation in Oklahoma of Native American Church.
1923	Investigation of Indian Affairs by Committee of One Hundred.
1924	Passage of American Indian Citizenship Act, declaring all native Americans US citizens and giving them right to vote in national elections.
1926	Foundation of National Council of American Indians.
1928	Publication of Meriam Report.
1934	Johnson–O'Malley Act provides major impetus towards public school enrolment.
1935	Establishment of Indian Arts and Crafts Board.

1944	Foundation of National Congress of American Indians.
1946	Indian Claims Act makes possible claims against US government before a special tribunal (Indian Claims Commission).
1952	Passage of Public Law 280.
1953	Liquor regulations for Indians revised by Congress.
1961	Self-determination demand from American Indian Chicago Conference. Establishment of National Indian Youth Council.
1964	Foundation at Santa Fe of Institute of American Indian Arts.
1968	Indian Bill of Rights passed by Congress. Foundation of American Indian Movement (AIM).
1969	Militant Indian activists occupy former federal prison on Alcatraz Island, San Francisco Bay.
1970	Publication of Dee Brown's *Bury My Heart at Wounded Knee.*
1971	Settlement of Alaska Native Claims issue by Congress.
1972	Headquarters of Bureau of Indian Affairs (BIA) in Washington occupied by Indian militants.
1973	Militant Indians occupy village of Wounded Knee on Pine Ridge Reservation, South Dakota, in 67-day confrontation.
1975	Passage of Indian Self-determination and Educational Assistance Act. Boldt decision in *United States v. State of Washington.*
1978	Passage of American Indian Religious Freedom Act.
1980	Settlement of Penobscot/Passamaquoddy claims.
1988	Indian Gaming Act. Huge cultural effect on some reservations.
1990	Total Indian population given by census at 1,959,000.

The Women's Movement

Chronology of key events

1800   Women vote in local elections for first time (at Elizabethtown, New Jersey).

1821   Emma Willard founds Troy Female Seminary (New York), the first college-level school for women.

1824   Strike by women workers at Pawtucket weaving mill, Rhode Island (first recorded industrial action by women).

1835   Admission of women to Oberlin College, Ohio (subsequently first degrees awarded to women in 1841).

1836   Publication of Sarah Grimke's *Equality of the Sexes and the Condition of Women*.

1836–37 Foundation of Georgia Female College at Macon and Mt Holyoke Female Seminary in Massachusetts, the first permanent women's colleges.

1845   Female Labor Reform Association formed. Fights both slavery and exploitation of women workers.

1848   New York state legislature gives women the right to own property in their own name. Seneca Falls, New York, hosts first women's rights convention (19–20 July).

1861   Women win right to vote in school board elections in Kansas.

1862   Wisconsin legislature passes eight-hour day law for women and children.

1865   American Woman Suffrage Association founded in Boston by Lucy Stone and Julia Ward Howe.

1869   Wyoming territorial legislature enacts first law giving women the right to vote and hold office. The National American Woman Suffrage Association founded. Daughters of St Crispin founded.

1870   First occasion women vote in territorial election in Utah. (Right lost in 1887.)

1872   Victoria Woodhull becomes first woman to run for President of the United States.

1874   Foundation of National Woman's Christian Temperance Union in Cleveland, Ohio.

1883   Frances E. Willard founds World's Woman's Christian Temperance Union, the first international organization for women.

1886	Working Women's Society founded.
1887	Susanna Madora Salter elected in Argonia, Kansas, as first-ever woman Mayor.
1890	Equal voting rights for women granted in Wyoming constitution. Formation of National American Woman Suffrage Association (NAWSA).
1893	Colorado permits women to vote.
1895	Colored Women's League of Washington founded by Mary Church Terrell.
1896	Utah reinstates women's suffrage. Constitutional amendment gives women the vote in Idaho.
1900	Carrie Chapman Catt takes on leadership of NAWSA.
1903	Women's National Trade Union League founded (with Mary Morton Kehew as president).
1904	Leadership of NAWSA passes to Anna Howard Shaw.
1906	Death of Susan B. Anthony, leader of the women's movement.
1910	Mann Act outlaws inter-state transport of women for immoral purposes. Women granted the vote in Washington State.
1911	Votes for women won in California.
1912	Women win vote in Oregon, Kansas and Arizona. Massachusetts passes first minimum wage act for women and children. National Woman's Party founded. Women's suffrage supported by Roosevelt's Progessive Party.
1913	Illinois grants women the vote – first victory east of the Mississippi. Alaskan Territory gives women the vote.
1914	Montana and Nevada adopt women's suffrage.
1915	First vote in the House on women's suffrage ends in defeat.
1916	Jeannette Rankin elected to Congress as first woman (representing Montana). Margaret Sanger (organizer of National Birth Control League) jailed for attempting to open clinic in Brooklyn, New York. Republican platform adopts suffrage for first time.
1917	Women's suffrage granted in Arkansas, Nebraska, North Dakota, New York and Rhode Island. House sets up Women's Suffrage Committee.
1918	Michigan, Oklahoma, South Dakota and Texas grant women the vote. Department of Labor establishes Woman-in-Industry Service as first agency for women. In 1920 it became the Women's Bureau. Senate defeats women's suffrage amendment.
1919	First Feminist Congress organized by Crystal Eastman. Suffrage amendment finally passes (4 June).
1920	Nineteenth Amendment to US Constitution giving women the right to vote for first time in national elections is ratified (Aug.). American Civil Liberties Union established.

1922	Rebecca Latimer Felton (Democrat, Georgia) appointed first woman Senator (attending sessions on only two days).
1924	Nellie Taylor Ross becomes first woman to be elected state Governor (in Wyoming).
1932	Hattie Wyatt Carraway becomes first woman to be elected to US Senate (Jan.). Re-elected 1932 and 1938.
1933	Frances Perkins becomes Secretary of Labor (first woman Cabinet minister).
1953	Oveta Culp Hobby appointed Secretary of Health, Education and Welfare.
1956	Women ordained by Methodists and Presbyterians.
1962	New-wave feminism launched with publication of Betty Friedan's *The Feminine Mystique*.
1964	Civil Rights Act bans jobs discrimination against women.
1966	Major new pressure group formed for women's liberation when Betty Friedan founds National Organization for Women (NOW).
1971	Formation of Women's National Political Caucus (WNPC).
1972	Congress approves equal rights for women constitutional amendment by overwhelming majority. Sent for ratification to states (subsequently fails in 1982).
1973	Abortion debate ignited when repeal of abortion laws in 46 states is ordered by Supreme Court in *Roe v. Wade* landmark judgment. Caucus of Labor Union Women (CLUW) formed. Hawaii eliminates pregnancy as disqualification for unemployment benefit.
1974	Landmark Supreme Court ruling that women must be paid equal wages by employers for performing same work as men (June). First woman ordained Episcopal priest in United States (Betty Bone Schiess).
1975	Women in Illinois win equal employment-related death benefits.
1976	*Craig v. Boren* case. Supreme Court struck down a state law setting different alcoholic drinking ages for men and women.
1979	*Orr v. Orr* case. Supreme Court declared unconstitutional any law allowing women but not men to receive alimony.
1980	First women graduate officers emerge from US military academies.
1981	Sandra Day O'Connor sworn in as first woman justice of US Supreme Court.
1982	Defeat of 1972 Equal Rights Amendment after ratification by only 35 states.
1983	Cabinet appointments include Mary Heckler (Health and Human Services), Elizabeth Dole (Transportation) and Ann McLaughlin (Labor).

1984	Democrat Geraldine A. Ferraro becomes first woman to run for Vice-President (with Walter Mondale as presidential candidate).
1987	Equal pay laws now enacted in 40 states.
1989	First woman black Episcopal bishop appointed (Barbara Harris).
1991	Women's Health Equity Act passed.
1993	Series of major appointments includes Janet Reno as Attorney General, Hazel O'Leary as Secretary of Energy and Donna Shalala as Secretary of Health and Human Services. In addition, Ruth Bader Ginsberg is second woman to be appointed to the Supreme Court.
1994	Freedom of Access to Clinic Entrances Law.
1996	Nomination of Madeleine Albright as first woman Secretary of State.

Growth of women's suffrage (prior to passing of the Nineteenth Amendment)

1869	(Territory of) Wyoming
1890	Wyoming (when becomes a state)
1893	Colorado
1896	Utah and Idaho
1910	Washington State
1911	California
1912	Arizona, Kansas and Oregon
1913	Illinois; (Territory of) Alaska
1914	Nevada and Montana
1917	New York
1918	Michigan, Oklahoma, South Dakota

Key statistics

Divorce rates (selected years)[1]

1920	1.6^2
1946	4.3
1951	2.5
1961	2.3
1971	3.7
1980	5.2
1990	4.7^2
1993	4.6

[1] Rate per thousand of the population.
[2] The absolute total in 1920 was 170,505; in 1990 it was 1,175,000.
Source: Statesman's Yearbook, various dates

Legal abortions (since the *Roe v. Wade* judgment)

1973	615,831
1975	854,853
1977	1,079,430[1]
1979	1,251,921
1992	1,528,930

[1] The first year the annual figure reached one million.
Sources: US Department of Health and Human Services;
Statesman's Yearbook (1973–)

Religion

Chronology of key events

1777   New York becomes first state to enfranchise Jews completely.

1784   'Christmas Conference' held at Baltimore, Maryland heralds beginning of Methodist church in America and period of rapid expansion.

1789   Protestant Episcopal Church founded. John Carroll becomes first Roman Catholic Bishop of Baltimore.

1791   Ratification of the Bill of Rights. Article I regarding freedom of religion states that 'Congress shall make no law respecting an establishment of religion'.

1804   Church of Christ (Disciples) emerges among evangelical Presbyterians in Kentucky and later (1809) in Pennsylvania.

1808   Roman Catholic see of Baltimore raised to metropolitan rank. Four suffragan dioceses created (Boston, New York, Philadelphia and Bardstown (Kentucky)).

1819   Unitarian Christianity preached by William Ellery Channing.

1822   First Roman Catholic newspaper founded at Charleston, *United States Catholic Miscellany*.

1827   Origin of Mormons (see p. 341). Joseph Smith receives revelation of *The Book of Mormon*.

1832   Church of Christ (Disciples) organized.

1833   Massachusetts disestablished Congregationalism, the end of last remnant of 'establishment'.

1844   Divisions in Methodist ranks over slavery cause three-way split into Methodist Episcopal Church, Methodist Episcopal Church South and the anti-slavery Wesleyan Methodist Connection (founded 1843). Anti-Catholic riots in Philadelphia.

1845   Split in Baptist Churches, largely over slavery. Birth of Southern Baptist Convention.

1847   *Christian Nurture* published by Horace Bushnell. Salt Lake City founded by Mormons (see p. 341).

1850   Methodism is largest Protestant denomination. Immigration makes Roman Catholicism largest single religious group in America. Jewish population estimated at 50,000.

1873	The liberal Union of American Hebrew Congregations organized by Rabbi Isaac Mayer Wise.
1875	Founder of Christian Science, Mary Baker Eddy, publishes *Science and Health with a Key to the Scriptures*. John McCloskey, Archbishop of New York, becomes first American cardinal. Hebrew Union College organized.
1877	New Hampshire becomes last state to enfranchise Jews.
1880	Rise of Afro-American Baptists reflected in formation of National Baptist Convention of America.
1884	Third Plenary Council of Baltimore gives major impetus to Catholic educational efforts.
1889	Central Conference of American Rabbis organized.
1901	Emergence of Pentecostalism, at first in Topeka (Kansas).
1907	Northern Baptist Convention formed. The same year sees split of National Baptist Convention of America with majority faction becoming National Baptist Convention, USA (Inc). Publication of *Christianity and the Social Crisis* by Walter Rauschenbusch marks rethinking of Christian ethics. Followed by his *Christianity and the Social Order* (1912) and *A Theology for the Social Gospel* (1917).
1908	Search for Christian unity reflected in foundation of Federal Council of Churches of Christ. Methodist Social Creed adopted as its statement of social principles.
1909	First publication of best-selling *Scofield Reference Bible*.
1918	Merger forms United Lutheran Church.
1930	American Lutheran Church formed.
1932	Northern Baptists split over beliefs (and again in 1947).
1939	Methodist divisions began to heal. Merger of Methodist Episcopal Church, Methodist Episcopal Church South and Methodist Protestant Church.
1950	National Council of Churches succeeds earlier Federal Council of Churches of Christ. Northern Baptist Convention becomes American Baptist Convention.
1956	Ordination of women by Methodists and Presbyterians.
1957	United Church of Christ formed from merger of Congregational Christian with Evangelical and Reformed Churches.
1962	Consultation on Church Unity (COCU) convened, attempting to unite nine major denominations.
1962–65	Major changes to Catholic Church following Second Vatican Council.
1963	School prayers banned in ruling by Supreme Court.
1968	Union of the Methodist churches which merged in 1939 with the Evangelical United Brethren to form the United Methodist Church.

1973	American Baptist Churches in the USA formed from American Baptist Convention.
1974	First woman ordained Episcopal priest in United States (Betty Bone Schiess).
1980	'Washington for Jesus' rally demonstrates strength of fundamentalist revival.
1989	First woman black Episcopal bishop appointed (Barbara Harris).

Church membership

Methodist

1790	58,000
1830	478,000
1860	1,661,000
1891	3,511,000
1914	5,394,000
1950	8,936,000
1995	13,500,000

Protestant Episcopal

1927	1,789,000
1957	3,163,000
1995	2,500,000

Roman Catholics

1789	35,000
1830	318,000
1860	3,103,000
1891	8,297,000
1900	12,041,000
1914	16,068,000
1930	45,640,000
1974	48,465,000
1995	59,858,000

Southern Baptist

1845	352,000
1860	650,000
1891	1,282,000
1914	2,589,000
1950	7,080,000
1995	15,359,000

Presbyterian

1826	127,000
1860	292,000
1891	790,000
1914	1,428,000
1950	2,364,000
1995	3,998,000

Temperance and Prohibition

Background

Temperance had been an important movement throughout the nine-teenth century and it was given new impetus during the Progressive Era by a belief in the politically and socially corrupting effects of alcohol abuse. In 1917 Congress passed the Eighteenth Amendment to the US Constitution prohibiting alcohol production and consumption and it was ratified by the states in 1920. Prohibition was widely flouted throughout the 1920s and the supply of drink became a criminal enterprise on a massive scale. The Democratic Party's platform in the election of 1928 promised repeal. Following President Roosevelt's election in 1932 the Twenty-First Amendment was passed to this effect and was ratified in 1933.

Chronology of key events

1784   Publication by Benjamin Rush of *An Inquiry into the Effects of Spiritous Liquors on the Human Mind and Body.*

1808   Billy J. Clark founds first temperance society at Moreau, Saratoga County, New York.

1813   Agitation by pastor Lyman Beecher leads to formation of Connecticut Society for the Reformation of Morals (May). Similar anti-intemperance campaign in Massachusetts.

1826   Formation of American Society for the Promotion of Temperance (Feb.).

1836   Dissension in temperance ranks (e.g., over total abstinence).

1841   Revival of temperance led by Washington Temperance Society with emotional 'experience meetings'.

1845   New York State law prohibits sale of intoxicants (repealed in 1847).

1846   Maine prohibits retail sale of intoxicants (followed in 1851 by complete prohibition). Example of Maine followed by 13 states, but nine of these repeal laws or declare them unconstitutional.

1869   Formation in Chicago, by delegates from 20 states, of Prohibition Party (Sept.) (see. p. 113).

1872   First presidential nominee (James Black) of Prohibition Party contests election.

1874	Women's Christian Temperance Union founded.
1880	State of Kansas became first to go 'dry'.
1892	Prohibition presidential candidate John Bidwell receives 265,000 votes (peak of support for Prohibition).
1893	Formation of non-partisan Anti-Saloon League to campaign for government control of liquor.
1914	Thirteen states completely dry as a result of state laws.
1919	Passage of Eighteenth Amendment (ratified 29 Jan.) and subsequent Volstead Act introduces era of Prohibition. Widespread flouting of alcohol ban in 'speakeasies'.
1932	Democratic National Convention calls for repeal of Eighteenth Amendment.
1933	Repeal of Prohibition in Twenty-First Amendment (ratification takes less than a year).

Postscript: After 1933, the strength of the temperance movement steadily declined. Now no state-wide prohibition law exists in the United States.

Popular protest and public order

Chronology of riots, rebellions and public disorder

1786–87 Shays's Rebellion, when farmers from western Massachusetts rose in protest against tax system and harsh foreclosure laws. Put down by state troops commanded by General Benjamin Lincoln.

1794 Whiskey Rebellion, an uprising on the Pennsylvania frontier, against excise tax imposed by Federalist government in Philadelphia.

1799 Uprising in eastern Pennsylvania in protest against federal taxes. Led by auctioneer John Fries.

1800 Gabriel uprising in Virginia. A black slave rising in which 1,000 slaves in Henrico County marched on Richmond.

1822 Abortive Denmark Vesey slave uprising in South Carolina aimed at wiping out white population of Charleston. Vesey, and the other conspirators, were arrested and later executed.

1831 Nat Turner's insurrection based on Southampton County, Virginia (begins 21 Aug.). Most significant of the slave revolts. Its defeat led to a white reign of terror and more stringent slavery laws.

1836 Lovejoy riots, in Alton, Illinois, against Elijah P. Lovejoy, an abolitionist clergyman. Lovejoy was murdered and his printing presses destroyed.

1842 Dorr's Rebellion in Rhode Island. A radical, democratic movement for universal male suffrage and abolition of the 1662 colonial charter.

1859 Insurrection led by John Brown (see p. 262).

1861–65 Draft riots in New York.

1875 Clinton, Mississippi, riot. One of the worst disturbances in Mississippi during the Reconstruction era. Many blacks were killed. President Grant refuses to use the Army.

1876 Ellenton Riot. The incident, in Aiken County, was the bloodiest event in South Carolina during Reconstruction. Two whites and up to 100 blacks were killed.

1877 Riots against Chinese immigrant labour organized by Workingmen's Party in San Francisco. Violent disturbances during nation-wide railroad strike.

1883   Cincinnati, Ohio riots. Rioters storm jail. Violence leaves 45 dead and 138 injured.

1886   Haymarket Riot (4 May). Part of the militant movement for an eight-hour working day. A bomb caused seven deaths and 70 injuries.

1892   Coeur d'Alene riots resulting from strike in lead and silver mines of northern Idaho. State troops intervene and martial law proclaimed.

1898   Wilmington mob violence. During a campaign to prevent black citizens exercising their right to vote, a white mob attacked the black community in Wilmington, North Carolina (Nov.), killing over 30 people and burning down the offices of a black newspaper.

1906   Riots in Atlanta. As part of a campaign to deny black people the vote in Atlanta, Georgia, white mobs attacked black areas on 1 September 1906. In clashes which spread over several days, the attackers suffered heavier casualties than black people who armed to defend themselves. However, legislation to exclude black citizens from the electoral roll followed soon after.

1908   Riots in Springfield. White mobs attacked black areas in this Illinois city on 14–15 August following the accusation that a black man had raped a white woman. Eight black people were killed and over 2,000 fled the city. No whites were arrested for the deaths.

1914   Ludlow Massacre (Colorado). The location of one of the most bitter episodes in any labour conflict. During a strike of coal-miners against John D. Rockefeller on 20 April 1914, National Guardsmen fired on the families of the strikers, setting fire to their tented camp and killing 17 women and children.

1916   Massacre in Everett, Washington State, of members of the radical left-wing union, the Industrial Workers of the World (IWW), who travelled to the city to support striking lumber workers in May 1916. As 250 IWW members arrived by ferry, they were met with an unprovoked armed attack from a sheriff and his deputies. Five died, six were missing and 27 passengers were injured.

1917   Houston Incident. Members of the black 24th Infantry Regiment attacked the town of Houston, Texas, on 26 August following rumours that a black woman arrested by white police had died. The soldiers, who had suffered abuse and police violence in the city, killed 17 whites during the attack.

1919   Race riots in Chicago. On 17 July a black teenager accidentally swam in front of a white beach on Lake Michigan. The teenager was stoned and drowned, provoking bitter race riots in Chicago. Lasting 13 days, the riots left 15 whites and 23 blacks dead and over 1,000 families homeless.

1921   The bloodiest race riot in US history occurs in Tulsa, Oklahoma, leaving 79 dead in its wake.

1922   'Herrin Massacre' in Illinois, when the Southern Illinois Coal Company attempted to use strike-breakers to resume production. Two strikers were killed by company guards. In the Herrin Massacre which followed, striking miners killed 19 strike breakers.

1932   Bonus Marches. Veterans march on Washington for cash payments of bonus certificates. Two veterans and two police were killed.

1935   Harlem riots. A black ghetto in New York City, the scene in March of attacks on white-owned property following reports that a black youth had been killed by a shop-owner. Over 200 stores were destroyed in looting. A commission of inquiry blamed racial discrimination and poverty for the events.

1937   Memorial Day Massacre (South Chicago) when police fire on steel workers during demonstration, killing four and injuring 84.

1943   Federal troops deployed in race riot in Detroit. One of worst racial outbreaks to date.

1957   President Eisenhower despatches 1,000 paratroops to enforce school integration after disturbances at Little Rock, Arkansas.

1965   Watts Riot (see p. 144).

1966   Riots by blacks in over a dozen cities leave eleven dead (June–Sept.).

1967   Riots in Detroit and Newark (see p. 144).

1968   Report of National Advisory Commission on Civil Disorders (Mar.). Violence sweeps across the country after the assassination of Martin Luther King (April) (see p. 144).

1970   Kent State disturbances (anti-Vietnam protests) (see p. 334).

1971   Attica Prison revolt (the worst in US history).

1974   Patty Hearst, 19-year-old granddaughter of newspaper magnate William Randolph Hearst, is kidnapped in Berkeley, California by members of the Symbionese Liberation Army.

1975   Eleven people are killed and 70 injured when a bomb explodes in a baggage-claim area at La Guardia Airport, New York (29 Dec.).

1979   An anti-Ku Klux Klan rally organized in a black housing project in Greensboro, North Carolina, by the Communist Workers Party on 3 November 1979 was fired on by a nine-car convoy of Klan and Nazi Party members. Within 90 seconds five CWP members and supporters had been killed and seven wounded. Two all-white juries acquitted the attackers.

1980   Widespread rioting in Liberty City section of Miami (see p. 144).

1988   Renewed outbreak of violence in Miami (see p. 144).

1991   Worst violence in Washington since 1968. Shooting of a Hispanic man by police triggers major disturbance in the Hispanic Mount Pleasant section.

1992   Race riots in Los Angeles cause 58 deaths (see p. 144).

1993   Seven dead, 1,000 injured (some seriously) in car bomb explosion in World Trade Center, New York (26 Feb.). FBI assault on Branch Davidian compound at Waco leaves 80 dead.

1995   Oklahoma bombing by extremist anti-government militia causes carnage. Timothy James McVeigh later found guilty.

1996   Terrorist bombing in early hours of 27 July of Centennial Olympic Park, Atlanta, Georgia leaves two dead and over 100 injured.

Chronology of assassinations and attempted assassinations

1835   Unsuccessful attempt in Washington on the life of President Andrew Jackson by deranged Richard Lawrence (30 Jan.).

1865   Assassination in Washington of President Abraham Lincoln by John Wilkes Booth (14 Apr.).

1881   Assassination of President James A. Garfield at Union Railroad Station, Washington, by Charles J. Guiteau (2 July). Garfield died later on 19 September.

1901   Assassination of President William McKinley at Buffalo by young anarchist, Leon F. Czolgosz (9 June).

1912   Attempted assassination of former President Theodore Roosevelt, during a campaign speech in Milwaukee, by John N. Schrank (14 Oct.).

1933   Attempted assassination of President-elect Franklin D. Roosevelt in Miami, Florida by Giuseppe Zangara (15 Feb.). Mayor Anton J. Cermak of Chicago, seated beside Roosevelt, was killed.

1935   Huey P. Long, Senator from Louisiana, assassinated in Baton Rouge (8 Sept.) by Carl A. Weiss.

1950   Attempt to assassinate Harry Truman when two Puerto Ricans attempt to shoot their way into Blair House, the President's temporary residence. Attack foiled (1 Nov.).

1963   Assassination of President John F. Kennedy in Dallas, Texas (22 Nov.). The subsequent Warren Commission found Lee Harvey Oswald the sole assassin, but controversy still continues. Murder the same year of civil rights leader Medgar W. Evers.

1965   Assassination of black militant leader Malcolm X in New York (21 Feb.) by unknown assailant.

1968   Assassination of civil rights leader Martin Luther King in Memphis (4 Apr.) by James Earl Ray. Followed by widespread riots across major cities of America (see p. 144).

1968   Assassination in Los Angeles, California, of presidential candidate Senator Robert F. Kennedy by Sirhan Sirhan (5 June).

1972   Unsuccessful attempt to kill presidential candidate George Wallace of Alabama at Laurel, Maryland. Wallace badly wounded.

1974   Unsuccessful attempted assassination of Richard Nixon at Baltimore.

1975   Two unsuccessful attempts on life of Gerald Ford at Sacramento on 5 Sept. and at San Francisco on 20 Sept.

1978   Fatal shootings of San Francisco mayor George Moscone and member of the Board of Supervisors Harvey Milk, a gay rights activist, by fellow Supervisor Dan White (27 Nov.)

1981   Attempt on life of Ronald Reagan by John Hinckley at Washington (30 Mar.). Reagan wounded.

1993   Kuwaiti Intelligence foiled a suspected Iraqi plot to assassinate former President George Bush during a visit to Kuwait (April).

Pacifism and the Anti-War Movement

Chronology of key events

1815   David Low Dodge forms first local peace society in New York.

1828   Foundation of nation-wide American Peace Society under leadership of William Ladd.

1846   League of Universal Brotherhood, opposed to support for war for any purpose, founded by Elihu Burritt.

1866   Universal Peace Union, founded by Philadelphia merchant, Alfred Love, stresses arbitration of international disputes. Also involved in internal labour disputes.

1899   Boston-centred American Anti-Imperialist League vociferously opposed Spanish–American War. Bryan, the Democratic presidential nominee in 1900, also opposes Philippine annexation. Bryan defeated.

1900–14   Peace movement flourishes. Carnegie Endowment for World Peace sponsored by Andrew Carnegie.

1914   World War I in Europe sees new US organizations aiming to prevent US entry into the conflict (e.g., American Union Against Militarism, Emergency Peace Federation, Women's Peace Party). War gives birth to predecessor of American Civil Liberties Union (aids conscientious objectors to conscription). Early peace advocated by People's Council of America for Democracy and Terms of Peace.

1920–30   Disenchantment mounts with objectives and conduct of World War I. Series of Neutrality Acts passed by Congress.

1941   Treachery of Japanese attack on Pearl Harbor ensures America is almost totally united in war effort.

1957   Re-emergence of peace movement after Korean War (see p. 245) and McCarthyism (see p. 339).

1958   Liberals and pacifists form SANE (National Committee for a Sane Nuclear Policy). Following years see birth of Student Peace Union, Women Strike for Peace and the Committee for Nonviolent Action.

1963   Fruits of Anti-War Movement seen in limited nuclear test ban treaty with Soviet Union.

1965   Era of anti-Vietnam protests. Students for a Democratic Society call national demonstration in Washington (Apr.) attended by 20,000.

1967   Anti-war marches in New York City and San Francisco attract 500,000 participants. Draft resistance movement widespread on college campuses.

1968   Support for anti-war presidential contender Senator Eugene McCarthy in Wisconsin primary leads Lyndon Johnson to withdraw.

1969   Largest anti-war demonstration in US history at Washington (15 Nov.).

1970   Nation-wide student strike against US invasion of Cambodia closes campuses.

1973   Moves to end Vietnam War begin to defuse Anti-War Movement.

1990–1   US participation in the Gulf War provokes protests against the use of military force against Iraq and Iraqi forces in Kuwait. Rallies were held in Washington by the radical National Coalition to Stop US Intervention in the Middle East (19 Jan. 1991) and by the Campaign for Peace in the Middle East (26 Jan. 1991).

The environment

Chronology of key events

1864 Yosemite Valley, California, reserved as a state park. Publication by Marsh of *Man and Nature*.

1872 Efforts of J. Sterling Morton result in 10 April being designated Arbor Day. Establishment of Yellowstone National Park (Wyoming–Idaho–Montana).

1874 First zoological garden in US (at Philadelphia).

1875 Founding of American Forestry Association.

1876 Founding of Appalachian Mountain Club.

1877–81 As Secretary of the Interior, Carl Schurz urges establishment of federal forest reservations and scientific care of forests.

1890 Origin of Sequoia and Yosemite National Parks (both California). National Zoological Park created by Congress in Washington DC.

1891 Forest Reserve Act signed. Allows 13 million acres to be set aside by President Harrison as forest reservations. An additional 21 million acres later set aside by Grover Cleveland. Provisions for disposal of public lands tightened.

1892 Sierra Club founded.

1898 Appointment of professional forester Gifford Pinchot as head of Division of Forestry, with great influence on Roosevelt, heralds 'Roosevelt–Pinchot' era.

1899 Origin of Mount Rainier National Park, Washington.

1901 Creation of the Bureau of Forestry.

1902 Reclamation Act (also known as the Newlands Act). Revolving fund established to finance irrigation projects. Achieves particular success in the West.

1905 Foundation of National Audubon Society. Bureau of Forestry becomes US Forest Service headed by Gifford Pinchot.

1906 Antiquities Act sets aside federal land to preserve national monuments.

1907 Establishment of Inland Waterways Commission.

1908 White House Conference debates status of US resources. National Conservation Commission established under Gifford Pinchot. Country Life Commission appointed.

1909	Meeting of North American Conservation Commission.
1910	Withdrawal Act. All coal, oil, gas, etc., lands preserved in public domain.
1911	American Game Protective and Propagation Association founded. Weeks Act empowers government to protect watersheds in Appalachians and White Mountains.
1916	National Park Service Act passed.
1918	Save-the-Redwoods League founded. Migratory Bird Treaty Act with Canada, restricting hunting of migratory species, becomes law.
1920	Mineral Leasing Act regulates mining on federal lands. Federal Water Power Act passed.
1922	Izaak Walton League founded.
1933	Start of 'golden age' period of 'New Deal' conservation activity with formation of Soil Erosion Service, Civilian Conservation Corps (CCC) and the Tennessee Valley Authority (TVA).
1936	Soil Conservation and Domestic Allotment Act passed. Farm production restricted by making benefit payments to farmers in return for them planting soil-building crops on part of their land. Soil Conservation Service established.
1948	Catastrophic smog in Donora, Pennsylvania; 20 deaths (Oct). Major impetus given to the need for air pollution control. Establishment of Conservation Foundation.
1952	Resources For The Future established.
1956	Ten-year improvement program (Mission 66) for the National Park Service launched.
1958	Outdoor Recreation Resources Review Commission appointed by Congress.
1962	White House Conference on Conservation convened by President Kennedy.
1963	Clean Air Act becomes law. Provides federal funds for co-ordinated attack on air pollution. Establishment of Bureau of Outdoor Recreation (part of Department of the Interior).
1964	Wilderness Act establishes National Wilderness Protection Scheme.
1966	National Historic Preservation Act passed.
1969	National Environmental Policy Act, a key measure in protecting environmental quality. Establishes Council of Environmental Quality.
1970	Establishment of Environmental Protection Agency (EPA) (2 Dec.). Water Quality Improvement Act becomes law.
1972	Establishment of Consumer Product Safety Commission (27 Oct.).

1979   A major nuclear accident at Three Mile Island, near Harrisburg, Pennsylvania; thousands of gallons of radioactive water and a plume of radioactive gas released. Temporary evacuation of population puts effective end to nuclear power station construction in United States.

1980   Foundation of pro-environment Citizens' Party (see p. 104).

1989   Massive spillage from oil tanker *Exxon Valdez* off Alaska contaminates large area of coastline.

1992   US participates in 'Earth Summit', organized by UN Conference on Environment and Development in Brazil.

1997   US hosts '2nd Earth Summit'.

The Gay and Lesbian Movement

Chronology of key events

1950   Marxist Harry Hay forms International Bachelor's Fraternal Orders for Peace and Social Dignity in Los Angeles.

1951   International Bachelor's group re-named Mattachine Society.

1955   Daughters of Bilitis formed under leadership of Del Martin and Phyllis Lyon in San Francisco.

1961   Sodomy still illegal in all 50 states.

1965   Harassment of gays in San Francisco becomes major issue.

1969   Police raid on Stonewall Inn in Christopher Street, New York (June), marks birth of more militant gay activism. Gay Liberation Front formed. Foundation of gay-embracing Metropolitan Community Church in Los Angeles by Troy Perry, a young minister. Gay Activists Alliance formed (Dec.).

1970   First gay pride march in New York.

1976   Supreme Court ruling that states have the right to enforce laws banning homosexual acts.

1978   Assassination of George Moscone, pro-gay Mayor, and murder of Harvey Milk, first openly gay official in San Francisco.

1981   AIDS virus first identified in USA.

1984   HIV I retrovirus isolated (HIV II discovered in 1985).

1986   Gay rights bill passed by New York City Council. Supreme Court decision in Michael Hardwick case upholds Georgia anti-sodomy law.

1987   AIDS Coalition to Unleash Power founded by Larry Kramer.

1991   State of Hawaii sued by three same-sex couples for denying them marriage licences.

1993   Supreme Court of Hawaii holds that refusal to grant same-sex marriage licences may violate law against sexual discrimination. Clinton anounces circumstances in which gay men can serve in the armed forces (19 July). The 'Don't Ask, Don't Tell' policy.

1996   Defense of Marriage Act approved by House of Representatives (12 July). The movement is a response to pressure for same-sex marriages.

The AIDS epidemic

	Deaths from AIDS	New AIDS cases
1985	6,961	8,160
1988	21,019	30,716
1990	31,339	41,761
1992	40,072	45,961
1994	44,052	61,301
Total 1985–94	284,249	

Source: National Center for Health Statistics

SECTION THREE

Economic history

Population

Growth of population

Figures represent the resident population, excluding members of the armed forces overseas. From 1960, Alaska and Hawaii are included in totals.

1790	3,929,214
1800	5,308,483
1810	7,239,881
1820	9,638,453
1830	12,866,020
1840	17,069,453
1850	23,191,876
1860	31,443,321
1870	39,818,449
1880	50,155,783
1890	62,947,714
1900	75,994,575
1910	91,972,266
1920	105,710,620
1930	122,775,046
1940	131,669,275
1950	150,697,361
1960	179,323,175
1970	203,302,031
1980	226,542,203
1990	248,709,873
1996	261,000,000 (estimated)

Decennial increase in population (as a percentage)

1790–1800	35.1		1850–60	35.6
1800–10	36.4		1860–70	26.6
1810–20	33.1		1870–80	26.0
1820–30	33.5		1880–90	25.5
1830–40	32.7		1890–1900	20.7
1840–50	35.9		1900–10	21.0

1910–20	14.9	1950–60	18.5
1920–30	16.1	1960–70	13.4
1930–40	7.2	1970–80	11.4
1940–50	14.5	1980–90	9.8

Source: US Bureau of the Census, *Statistical Abstract of the United States: 1996*

Population of the states, 1790[1] (in rank order of population)

Virginia	747,610
Pennsylvania	434,373[2]
North Carolina	393,751
Massachusetts	378,707
New York	340,120
South Carolina	249,073
Connecticut	237,946
New Jersey	184,139
New Hampshire	141,885
Maine	96,540
Vermont	85,425
Georgia	82,548
Kentucky	73,677
Rhode Island	68,825
Delaware	59,096
Tennessee	35,691

[1] *Source:* 1790 Census (Bureau of the Census).
[2] Also includes what is now West Virginia.

Growth of major towns from 1790 (figures rounded)

New York

1790	49,000
1850	696,000
1900	3,437,000
1950	7,892,000
1980	7,071,000
1990	7,323,000

Chicago

1850	30,000
1900	1,699,000
1950	3,621,000
1980	3,005,000
1990	2,784,000

Washington

1850	40,000
1900	279,000
1950	802,000
1980	638,000
1990	607,000

Boston

1790	18,000
1850	137,000
1900	561,000
1950	801,000
1980	563,000
1990	574,000

Los Angeles

1850	1,600
1900	102,000
1950	1,970,000
1980	2,967,000
1990	3,486,000

Houston (Texas)

1850	2,000
1900	45,000
1950	596,000
1980	1,594,000
1990	1,631,000

Philadelphia

1790	28,500
1850	121,000
1900	1,294,000
1950	2,072,000
1980	1,688,000
1990	1,586,000

Urbanization

Urbanization, 1900

Population	Number of cities	Population
200,000 (or more)	19	11,795,809
100,000–200,000	19	2,412,538
50,000–100,000	40	2,709,338
25,000–50,000	82	2,800,627
25,000 (or more) – total	160	19,724,312

Source: Statesman's Yearbook, 1910

Population of metropolitan areas (1990)

Rank	Metropolitan area	Population[1]
1	New York City	18,087,000
2	Los Angeles	14,532,000
3	Chicago	8,066,000
4	San Francisco	6,253,000
5	Philadelphia	5,899,000
6	Detroit	4,665,000
7	Boston	4,172,000
8	Washington	3,924,000
9	Dallas–Forth Worth	3,885,000
10	Houston	3,711,000

Birth rates and key statistics

The declining birth rate

Year	Births	Rate*
1910	2,777,000	30.1
1920	2,950,000	27.7
1930	2,618,000	21.3
1940	2,559,000	19.4
1950	3,632,000	24.1
1960	4,258,000	23.7
1970	3,731,000	18.4
1980	3,612,000	15.9
1990	4,179,000	16.7
1993	4,039,000	15.7

* Rate per thousand of the population. Births to nearest thousand.

Rise of illegitimate births 1940–93

Year	Totals (in 000s)	% of all births
1940	89,500	3.5
1950	141,600	3.9
1955	183,400	4.5
1960	224,300	5.3
1965	291,200	7.7
1970	398,700	10.7
1975	447,900	14.2
1980	665,800	18.4
1985	828,200	22.0
1990	1,165,400	28.0
1993	1,240,000	31.0

Sources: World Almanac, 1968, 1983. Information Please Almanac, 1996

Average life expectancy at birth

Year	Total population	Male	Female
1900	47.3	46.3	48.3
1910	50.0	48.4	51.8
1920	54.1	53.6	54.6
1930	59.7	58.1	61.6
1940	62.9	60.8	65.2
1950	68.2	65.6	71.1
1960	69.7	66.6	73.1
1970	70.8	67.1	74.7
1980	73.8	70.0	77.7
1994	76.0	73.0	79.0

Source: National Center for Health Statistics, US Department of Health and Human Services

Death rates and causes of death

The long-term decline in the death rate was only rarely interrupted (as in the 1918 influenza epidemic when it rose to 18.1). Death rates in the table below are per 1,000 population.

Death rates (since 1900)

1900	17.2
1910	14.7
1920	13.0
1930	11.3
1940	10.8
1950	9.6
1960	9.5
1970	9.5
1980	8.9
1990	8.6

Sources: Department of Commerce, Bureau of the Census and Department of Health and Human Services, National Center for Health Statistics

Causes of death*

	1900–04	1920–24	1950	1980	1990
Infant mortality	na	76.7	29.2	12.5	9.2
Typhoid fever	26.7	7.3	0.1	0.0	0.0
Diphtheria	32.7	13.7	0.3	0.0	0.0
Cancer	67.7	86.9	139.8	182.5	203.2
Heart/cardiovascular	359.5	369.9	510.8	434.5	368.3
Tuberculosis	184.7	96.7	22.5	0.8	0.7

* Cause of death per 100,000.

Source: National Center for Health Statistics, Department of Health and Human Services

Immigration

Immigration restriction: Chronology of key events

1876   Supreme Court rules that federal government has responsibility for immigration regulation. Pressure by California Workingmen's Party, under Denis Kearney, to bar Chinese.

1882   Earliest attempt to restrict immigration, with the passing of the Chinese Exclusion Act, prohibiting Chinese immigration for ten years.

1885   Law passed (after pressure from Knights of Labor) prohibiting import of workers under contract (so-called 'pauper labor').

1900   First steps to restrict Japanese immigration (after large immigration in 1890s). American Protective Association campaigns for tighter immigration control against Catholics.

1902   Chinese Exclusion Act made permanent.

1908   Further steps to restrict Japanese immigration.

1916   Racialist theory propounded by Madison Grant in his *Passing of the Great Race*.

1917   Literacy test imposed on all immigrants.

1921   Quota system applied. A limit of 3% of the population, determined by the 1910 census, was placed on immigration by any national group, with an absolute upper limit of 357,000.

1922   Immigration falls to 309,556 (compared to over 800,000 in previous year).

1924   The Johnson–Reed Act of 1924 severely reduced the numbers that could be admitted, to only 2% of the 1890 census, drastically reducing immigration from eastern Europe and Italy.

1948   Restrictions were relaxed to allow displaced persons to enter.

1952   McCurran–Walter Act passed, regularizing the procedure and relaxing the quota system; as a result, more Asian immigrants were admitted.

1965   Mounting criticism that the quota system discriminated on racial grounds resulted in the 1965 Act removing the national origins quota system from 1968 onwards.

1990   Three-year immigration programme, the Visa Lottery Program, begun.

Immigration statistics

Sources of Immigration, 1820–1930

Europe	32,121,210
Asia	1,058,331
Americas	4,241,429
Total (all areas)	37,762,012

Major European countries (figures rounded to nearest 000)

Austria	3,659,000
Germany	5,908,000
England	2,619,000
Ireland	4,579,000
Italy	4,651,000
Sweden	1,213,000
Russia	3,341,000

Immigration since 1901: decennial totals (in 000s)

Period	Number (in 000s) %	Rate[1]
1901–10	8,795	10.4
1911–20	5,736	5.7
1921–30	4,107	3.5
1931–40	528	0.4
1941–50	1,035	0.7
1951–60	2,515	1.5
1961–70	3,322	1.7
1971–80	4,493	2.1
1981–90	7,338	3.1

[1] Annual Rate per thousand of the population.
Source: US Immigration and Naturalization Service, *Statistical Yearbook,* annual

The new immigration (since 1970)

Immigration by area (in 000s)

Continent of birth	1971–80 (total)	1981–90 (total)
All countries	4,493	7,338
Europe	801	706
Asia	1,634	2,817
North America	1,645	3,125
South America	284	456
Africa	91	192

Immigration by individual country (list includes countries with over 100,000 emigrants in either 1971–80 or 1981–90) (in 000s)

Country of origin	1971–80	1981–90
Cambodia	8.4	116.6
Canada	114.8	119.2
China	202.5	388.8
Colombia	77.6	124.4
Cuba	276.8	159.2
Dominican Republic	148.0	251.8
El Salvador	34.4	214.6
Haiti	58.7	140.2
India	176.8	261.9
Iran	46.2	154.8
Italy	130.1	32.9
Jamaica	142.0	213.8
Korea	272.0	338.8
Laos	22.6	145.6
Mexico	637.2	1,653.3
Philippines	360.2	495.3
Portugal	104.5	40.0
United Kingdom	123.5	142.1
Vietnam	179.7	401.4

Source: World Almanac, 1995

Percentage of the US population foreign-born, 1900–94

1900	13.6
1910	14.7
1920	13.2
1930	11.6
1940	8.8
1950	6.9
1960	5.4
1970	4.8
1980	6.2
1990	7.9
1994	8.7

Source: Statesman's Yearbook, various dates

Government income and expenditure

Federal income and expenditure ($ millions)

Year	Net receipts	Net outlays	Surplus (+) or deficit (−)
1789–91	4	4	—
1800	11	11	—
1810	9	8	+1
1820	18	18	—
1830	25	15	+10
1840	20	24	−4
1850	44	40	+4
1860	56	63	−7
1865	334	1,298	−964
1870	411	310	+101
1880	334	268	+66
1890	403	318	+85
1900	567	521	+46
1910	675	694	−19
1915	683	746	−63
1918	3,645	12,677	−9,032
1929	3,862	3,127	+734
1933	1,997	4,598	−2,602
1939	4,979	8,841	−3,862
1945	44,362	98,303	−53,941
1950	36,422	39,544	−3,122
1960	92,492	92,223	+269
1965	116,833	118,430	−1,596
1970	193,743	196,588	−2,845
1975	280,997	326,105	−45,108
1980	520,050	579,011	−58,961
1985	734,057	946,391	−212,334
1990	1,031,321	1,252,705	−221,384
1994	1,257,745	1,460,914	−203,169

Growth of public debt ($ billion)

Year	Debt	Percentage of federal outlays
1870	2.4	—
1880	2.0	—
1890	1.1	—
1900	1.2	—
1910	1.1	—
1920	24.2	—
1930	16.1	—
1940	43.0	10.5
1945	258.7	4.1
1950	256.1	13.4
1955	272.8	9.4
1960	284.1	10.0
1965	313.8	9.6
1970	370.1	9.9
1975	533.2	9.8
1980	907.7	12.7
1985	1823.1	18.9
1990	3233.3	21.1
1994	4692.8	20.3

Source: Bureau of the Public Debt, Department of the Treasury

Prices and inflation

Warren and Pearson Price Index, 1776–1890*

(all commodities: 1910–14 = 100)

Year	Index	Year	Index	Year	Index
1776	86	1813	162	1845	83
1777	123	1814	182	1846	83
1778	140	1815	170	1847	90
1779	226	1816	151	1848	82
1780	225	1817	151	1849	82
1781	216	1818	147	1850	84
1785	92	1819	125	1851	83
1786	90	1820	106	1852	88
1787	90	1821	102	1853	97
1789	86	1822	106	1854	108
1790	90	1823	103	1855	110
1791	85	1824	98	1856	105
1793	102	1825	103	1857	111
1794	108	1826	99	1858	93
1795	131	1827	98	1859	95
1796	146	1828	97	1860	93
1797	131	1829	96	1861	89
1798	122	1830	91	1862	104
1799	126	1831	94	1863	133
1800	129	1832	95	1864	193
1801	142	1833	95	1865	185
1802	117	1834	90	1866	174
1803	118	1835	100	1867	162
1804	126	1836	114	1868	158
1805	141	1837	115	1869	151
1806	134	1838	110	1870	135
1807	130	1839	112	1871	130
1808	115	1840	95	1872	136
1809	130	1841	92	1873	133
1810	131	1842	82	1874	126
1811	126	1843	75	1875	118
1812	131	1844	77	1876	110

1877	106	1882	108	1887	85
1878	91	1883	101	1888	86
1879	90	1884	93	1889	81
1880	100	1885	85	1890	82
1881	103	1886	82		

* No figures available for 1782, 1783, 1784 and 1792.
Source: US Bureau of the Census, *Statistical Abstract of the United States: 1996*

Consumer prices (all items), 1945–95 (Index 100 = 1982–84)

1945	18.0
1950	24.1
1955	26.8
1960	29.6
1965	31.5
1967	33.4
1970	38.8
1975	53.8
1980	82.4
1985	107.6
1990	130.7
1995	152.4

Source: Department of Labor, Bureau of Labor Statistics

Banking and finance

Chronology of key events

1781   Bank of North America founded by Robert Morris.

1791   First Bank of the United States is founded (25 Feb.). Succeeded by Second Bank in 1816. First Bank is the official bank of the government.

1792   System of bimetallism established by Coinage Act.

1804   Farmers' Bank of Maryland becomes first to pay interest on deposits.

1809   Farmers' Exchange Bank of Gloucester, Rhode Island, becomes first bank to fail.

1811–15   'Banking Mania'. Number of state banks soars from 88 to 208. Numerous banks default.

1816   Foundation of Second Bank of the United States (1816–36).

1837   Overspeculation and bank collapses in 'Panic of 1837'.

1840   Enactment of Independent Treasury Bill creates system to provide depositories for federal funds. Temporarily abolished,1841–46.

1863   National Bank Act lays foundation for establishment of National Banking System. Number of banks totals 1,532. This system in place until 1913 Federal Reserve Act (see p. 192).

1875   Resumption Act makes greenbacks redeemable in gold. Effectively puts America on the gold standard.

1878   Attempts to restore bimetallic standard with Bland–Alison Act.

1890   Sherman Silver Purchase Act – a victory for advocates of use of silver. Treasury required to purchase and coin 4,500,000 ounces of silver per month.

1893   'Panic of '93' results in nearly 500 bank failures.

1896   Stock Exchange (Dow Jones Index) born on 26 May.

1900   Gold Standard Act.

1907   'Bankers' Panic' as depositors rush to convert their deposits into cash. Banks compelled to suspend payments and restrict withdrawals.

1908   National Monetary Commission headed by Senator Nelson Aldrich created by Aldrich–Vreeland Act to examine banking and currency systems. Its proposals become Federal Reserve Act (see p. 192).

1913	Federal Reserve Act passed. It established twelve districts in each of which a Federal Reserve Bank was created with major benefits – e.g., cheap credit, greater control of money supply, discouragement of speculation. Acts as 'lender of last resort' to other banks. Number of banks in 1913 totals 26,664.
1916	New tax measures include doubling of income tax (to 2%), raising of surtax, introduction of federal estate tax, etc.
1917	War Loan Act and War Revenue Bill. Further increases in taxation (income tax to 4%, surtax maximum to 63%).
1919	Revenue Act further raises tax burden. Income tax (for those earning $4,000) increased to 12%. Maximum rate of tax for those in highest income bracket reaches 77%.
1920	Dow Jones Index at 40.94. Start of 1920s boom in stocks and shares, becoming increasingly speculative.
1929	Dow Jones Index peaks at 381. Stock market crash on Wall Street is followed by 9,106 bank failures in four years.
1932	Dow plunges to low of 41.44 (an 85% fall since 1929 peak) (Mar.). Bank Moratorium. Reconstruction Finance Corporation created.
1933	Federal Deposit Insurance Corporation (FDIC) established.
1972	1,000 level breached by Dow Jones Index.
1983	1,100 breached by Dow Jones Index.
1987	Crash of '87 – 'Black Monday'. Dow falls 508 points (22.61%).
1997	Dow Jones lists record highs (above 6,600) (Jan.). Breaks 7,500 barrier (June).

Banking statistics

Number of state banks, 1811–65

1811	88
1815	208
1820	307
1830	329
1840	901
1850	824
1860	1,562
1865	1,643

Assets or liabilities of US banks, 1866–1957

1866	1,673
1880	3,399
1890	6,358

1900	11,388
1910	22,922
1920	53,094
1930	74,290
1940	79,729
1950	179,165
1957	242,629

Source: US Bureau of the Census, *Statistical Abstract of the United States: 1996*

The wealth of America

Gross National Product (1952–85) for major states ($ billion)

Country	1952	1960	1970	1975	1985
United States	350	506	1,011	1,509	3,635
Japan	16	39	195	495	1,158
West Germany	32	71	185	409	613
France	29	60	148	305	489
United Kingdom	44	72	121	215	426
USSR	113	201	390	666	2,063

Sources: Various

Gross National Product (since 1929) for US (in $ billion)

1929	103
1933	56
1938	85
1946	210
1950	286
1960	506
1970	1,011
1980	2,708
1985	3,635
1990	5,546
1994	6,727

Source: Statesman's Yearbook, various dates

Personal consumption expenditure in US (in $ billion)

1929	77.5
1933	45.9
1970	646.5
1980	1,748.1
1990	3,761.2
1993	4,378.2

The Labour Movement

Chronology of key events

1780s Short-lived craft groups begin to emerge.

1792 First emergence of more permanent protective organizations (e.g., Philadelphia shoemakers).

1794 Foundation of Typographical Society of New York.

1806 'Conspiracy' decision against Philadelphia cordwainers (and in 1809–10 against New York cordwainers).

1813 'Waltham' system (highly paternalistic) introduced by Francis Cabot Lowell at Waltham, Massachusetts.

1824 First recorded strike of women workers (at Pawtucket, Rhode Island).

1827 Formation in Philadelphia of first city central trade council (the Mechanics Union of Trade Associations) by fifteen unions. A decade later thirteen other cities had followed example of Philadelphia.

1828 First Workingmens' Party formed (Philadelphia). Followed by New York and Boston. These have only short-lived independent existences.

1834 First use of federal troops in a labour dispute (Jan.) when Andrew Jackson orders intervention against striking Irish workers on the Chesapeake and Ohio Canal in Maryland. Emergence of National Trades Union led by Ely Moore (a New York printer who was labour's first Congressman, 1834–39).

1836 First major victory for 10-hour day (in Philadelphia Navy Yard).

1837 'Panic of 1837' severely damages union aspirations.

1840 Campaign for 10-hour day wins victory when labourers on federal public works given this right by Martin Van Buren (legislation then passed in seven states, but with legal loopholes).

1842 Landmark legal judgment, *Commonwealth v. Hunt.* Legality of unions and right to strike for a closed shop recognized by Massachusetts Chief Justice, Lemuel Shaw.

1852 National Typographical Union founded. Heralds number of new unions in 1850s (stonecutters, machinists, etc.).

1863 Start of railroad unions (locomotive engineers) (see p. 220).

1866	National Labor Union established in Baltimore under leadership of Sylvis and Trevellick.
1867	Order of the Knights of St Crispin founded (shoemakers union).
1868	Hours of federal employees limited to eight hours a day.
1869	Foundation of Knights of Labor by Uriah S. Stephens. Membership grows rapidly only after 1876. Its secret nature abandoned in 1881.
1872	National Labor Reform Party emerges from National Labor Union.
1873	Union membership falls in 'Panic of 1873'.
1876	Ten Irish miners ('Molly Maguires') hanged after violence and murder in bitter Pennsylvania confrontation.
1877	Socialist Labor Party (originally founded as Marxist Workingmen's Party in 1876) organized. Nation-wide rail strike: 26 dead in Pittsburgh and nine in Martinsburg. Reorganization of Cigarmakers Union under Gompers and Strasser.
1878	Foundation of National Greenback Labor Party at Toledo, Ohio.
1881	Federation of Organized Trades and Labor Unions established in Pittsburgh (15 Nov.). Disbands in 1886 when American Federation of Labor organized.
1883	House of Representatives establishes Standing Committee on Labor.
1884	Data-gathering federal Bureau of Labor set up.
1885	Passing of Foran Act, aimed at cutting off contract labour from entering US.
1886	American Federation of Labor organized at Columbus, Ohio. Initial membership is 200,000. Agitation for an 8-hour working day leads to seven deaths in Chicago (Haymarket riot, 4 May). Four anarchists later hanged.
1887	Oregon is the first state officially to designate a labor day holiday.
1888	Bureau of Labor becomes Department of Labor, independent but of non-Cabinet status.
1890	United Mine Workers (UMW) founded.
1892	Homestead battle between strikers at Carnegie steel works and mill guards. Violence also at Coeur d'Alene lead and silver mines (see p. 163).
1893	Foundation of American Railway Union (conducts successful strike in 1894 against the Great Northern Railroad).
1894	The Pullman railroad strike. Riots and violence as federal troops ordered to intervene.
1895	US Supreme Court upholds use of injunctions in Pullman strike (*In re Debs*). Socialist Labor Party sets up Socialist Trade

and Labor Alliance. Manufacturers form National Association of Manufacturers.

1897   Defectors from Socialist Labor Party set up the Social Democracy.

1900   Organization of International Ladies Garment Workers Union (ILGWU).

1901   Foundation of Socialist Party of America.

1902   Maryland becomes first state to pass workmen's compensation laws. Federal government intervenes in anthracite dispute on workers behalf.

1903   Department of Commerce and Labor established (of Cabinet rank).

1904   Membership of American Federation of Labor (AFL) reaches 1,750,000.

1905   Formation of Industrial Workers of the World (IWW) – known as the 'Wobblies' (see p. 333).

1908   Supreme Court declares union actions illegal in 1902 Danbury Hatter's case.

1909   Montana passes workmen's compensation laws.

1910   New York State passes workmen's compensation laws.

1911   Improved factory laws follow horrific 'Triangle Fire' in New York in which 140 women workers die.

1912–13 Wage increases won by textile workers in Paterson and Lawrence after strikes organized by 'Wobblies'.

1913   Department of Labor established as tenth executive department (4 Mar.). Newlands Act provides for Board of Mediation and Conciliation in railroad disputes.

1915   La Follette Seaman's Act. Conditions for seamen in merchant marine regulated and improved. Attacked by shipowners for putting up costs.

1916   Adamson Act provides for 8-hour day for railroad workers on inter-state railroads.

1918   War Labor Board established.

1919   National Labor Party formed. Number of organized workers reaches 4.25 million (declines in the 1920s). Failure of AFL strike against US Steel Corporation.

1922   Herrin massacre in Williamson County, Illinois (see p. 164).

1924   La Follette polls 4.8 million votes in presidential election.

1929   Onset of depression causes further decline in union membership.

1932   Wisconsin becomes first state to adopt unemployment insurance law. Enactment of Norris–LaGuardia Act. The anti-union 'yellow-dog' contracts outlawed by Congress. Use of injunctions against labour unions in strikes outlawed.

1933   Establishment under New Deal programme of National Recovery Administration (NRA), Civilian Conservation Corps,

Federal Emergency Relief Administration, National Industry Recovery Association (NIRA), etc. The NRA administers codes of competition, fixes minimum prices and wages, maximum hours, etc.

1935   Wagner Act creates National Labor Relations Board to administer laws on labour–management relations in inter-state commerce. Split at AFL convention leads to creation of Committee for Industrial Organization (CIO).

1936   Walsh–Healey Government Contracts Act aims to enforce fair labour standard for those contractors accepting government work.

1937   Violence in bitter steel industry strikes. Two Republic Steel strikers killed at Massillon, Ohio. Ten killed by South Chicago police in Memorial Day massacre (see p. 164).

1938   Committee of Industrial Organization renamed Congress of Industrial Organizations. Chairman is John L. Lewis. Fair Labor Standards Act establishes 40-hour week, ends child labour and fixes minimum wages in, for example, inter-state commerce (sometimes called Wages and Hours Act).

1941   Capitulation of Little Steel sees entire steel industry organized. Ford capitulates to unions.

1942   National War Labor Board created.

1945–46 Outbreak of strikes (e.g., in mines and railroads) as rising cost of living reduces workers' standard of living.

1947   Taft–Hartley Act passed (over President Truman's veto). Aims to redress balance between union power and rights of management. Called by unions 'slave labour act'. It modified the pro-labour Wagner Act of 1935.

1953   'No-raiding' agreement between AFL and CIO heralds closer co-operation and improved relations under new leadership of George Meany and Walter Reuther.

1955   Merger of the AFL and CIO into new federation, the AFL–CIO with Meany as President and Reuther heading industrial union department. Combined membership of 16 million.

1957   Expulsion of the Teamsters Union from AFL–CIO for corrupt practices.

1959   Landgrum–Griffin Act curbs abuses by labour union officers and extends prohibition of secondary boycotts. Marks most important federal legislation since 1947 Taft–Hartley Act.

Key statistics

Patterns of trade union membership (since 1930)

Year	Members (000s)	% of labour force
1930	3,401	11.6
1935	3,584	13.2
1940	8,717	26.9
1945	14,322	35.5
1950	14,267	31.5
1955	16,802	33.2
1960	17,049	31.4
1965	17,299	28.4
1970	19,381	27.3
1975	19,611	25.5
1980	19,843	21.9
1985	16,996	18.0
1990	16,740	16.1
1994	16,748	15.5

Source: Bureau of Labor Statistics

Average weekly hours worked by production workers

1966	38.6
1970	37.1
1980	35.3
1990	34.5
1994	34.7

Strikes, 1916–65

Year	Strikes	Workers involved	Man-days idle
1916	3,789	1,599,917	
1917	4,450	1,227,254	
1918	3,353	1,239,989	
1919	3,630	4,160,348	
1920	3,411	1,463,054	
1921	2,385	1,099,247	
1922	1,112	1,612,562	
1923	1,553	756,584	
1924	1,249	654,641	
1925	1,301	428,416	
1926	1,035	329,592	
1927	707	329,939	26,218,628
1928	604	314,210	12,631,863
1929	921	288,572	5,351,540
1930	637	182,975	3,316,808
1931	810	341,817	6,893,244
1932	841	324,210	10,502,033
1933	1,695	1,168,272	16,872,128
1934	1,856	1,466,695	19,591,949
1935	2,014	1,117,213	15,456,337
1936	2,172	788,648	13,901,956
1937	4,470	1,860,621	28,424,857
1938	2,772	688,376	9,148,273
1946	4,985	4,600,000	116,000,000
1947	3,693	2,170,000	34,600,000
1948	3,419	1,960,000	34,100,000
1949	3,606	3,030,000	50,500,000
1950	4,843	2,410,000	38,800,000
1954	3,468	1,530,000	22,600,000
1955	4,320	2,650,000	28,200,000
1956	3,825	1,900,000	33,100,000
1957	3,673	1,390,000	16,500,000
1958	3,694	2,060,000	23,900,000
1959	3,708	1,880,000	69,000,000
1960	3,333	1,320,000	19,100,000
1961	3,367	1,450,000	16,300,000
1962	3,614	1,230,000	18,600,000
1964	3,655	1,640,000	22,900,000
1965	4,511	1,545,200	23,297,000

The decline of industrial militancy, 1970–94 (disputes involving 1,000 workers or more)

	Number of stoppages[1]	Workers involved[1] (000)	Work days idle[1] (000)
1970	381	2,468	52,761
1971	298	2,516	35,538
1972	250	975	16,764
1973	317	1,400	16,260
1974	424	1,796	31,809
1975	235	965	17,563
1976	231	1,519	23,962
1977	298	1,212	21,258
1978	219	1,006	23,774
1979	235	1,021	20,409
1980	187	795	20,844
1981	145	729	16,906
1982	96	656	9,061
1983	81	909	17,461
1984	62	376	8,499
1985	54	324	7,079
1986	69	533	11,861
1987	46	174	4,481
1988	40	118	4,364
1989	51	452	16,996
1990	44	185	5,926
1991	40	392	4,584
1992	35	364	3,989
1993	35	184	3,981
1994	45	322	5,020

[1] The numbers of stoppages and workers involved relate to stoppages that began in the year. Days of idleness include all stoppages in effect. Workers are counted more than once if they were involved in more than one stoppage during the year.

Source: US Department of Labor (Bureau of Labor Statistics)

Employment and unemployment

Size of labour force*

Year	Number (000s)
1830	3,932
1840	5,420
1850	7,697
1860	10,533
1870	12,925
1880	17,392
1890	23,318
1900	29,073
1910	37,371
1920	42,434
1930	48,830
1940	52,789
1950	60,054
1960	69,877
1970	82,049
1980	106,085
1985	116,500
1990	125,840
1995	132,304

* Prior to 1945, table includes persons aged 14 and over.
After 1945, aged 16 and over.
Source: Department of Labor

Increase in non-farm occupations

Year	Percentage of labour force
1830	29.5
1840	31.4
1850	36.6
1860	41.1
1870	47.0
1880	50.6
1890	57.4
1900	62.5
1910	69.0
1920	73.0
1930	78.6
1940	82.6
1950	88.4
1960	94.0
1970	96.9
1980	97.8
1990	98.4

The rise of working women as a percentage of total working population

Year	Number (000s)	Percentage total working population[1]
1900	5,319	18.3
1910	7,445	19.9
1920	8,637	20.4
1930	10,752	22.0
1940	12,845	24.3
1950	18,408	29.0
1960	23,268	32.5
1970	31,580	37.2
1980	45,611	42.0
1990	56,554	45.3
1995	60,944	46.1

[1] Includes all those over ten years old.

Source: 1996 Information Please Almanac

Unemployment rates (at four-year intervals since 1916)

1916	4.8
1920	5.2
1924	5.0
1928	4.2
1932	23.6
1936	16.9
1940	14.6
1944	1.2
1948	3.8
1952	3.0
1956	4.1
1960	5.5
1964	5.2
1968	3.6
1972	5.6
1976	7.7
1980	7.1
1984	7.5
1988	5.5
1992	7.4
1994	6.1

Source: Department of Labor, Bureau of Labor Statistics

Federal-state unemployment insurance, 1940–85

Year	Average weekly benefit ($)	Average weekly beneficiaries
1945	18.77	464,996
1950	20.76	1,304,991
1955	25.04	1,099,466
1960	32.87	1,640,429
1965	37.19	1,131,025
1970	50.34	1,516,500
1975	70.23	3,371,246
1980	98.87	2,739,773
1985	127.94	2,295,267

Source: Department of Labor

Workers' compensation

Year	Total benefits ($ million)
1940	256
1945	408
1950	615
1955	916
1960	1,295
1965	1,614
1970	3,031
1975	6,598
1980	13,562
1985	22,200
1990	38,200
1993	42,900

Source: Social Security Administration

Industry and trade

Industrial regulation and trusts: Chronology of key events (to 1946)

1879   Establishment of Standard Oil Company, the prototype of subsequent trusts.

1882   Standard Oil Company becomes Standard Oil Trust and its monopoly organization is revealed.

1884   American Cotton Oil Trust set up.

1885   National Linseed Oil Trust established.

1887   Distillers and Cattle Feeders Trust (the 'whiskey' trust) set up.

1890   Passing of Sherman Anti-Trust Act (2 July).

1895   Decision of Supreme Court in *United States v. E.C. Knight Company* (concerning monopoly in sugar refining) seriously undermines 1890 Sherman Act.

1901   Foundation of $1 billion US Steel Corporation.

1904   Decision of Supreme Court in Northern Securities Company case (14 Mar.) begins trust-busting movement.

1911   Supreme Court decisions against Standard Oil Company and also American Tobacco Company for acting in 'unreasonable' restraint of trade.

1912   Woodrow Wilson's 'New Freedom' campaign pledges to restore free competition in trade and industry.

1914   Clayton Anti-Trust Act condemns interlocking directorates, local price discrimination, etc. A major move against trusts. Separate Federal Trade Commission Act broadly outlaws unfair methods of competition in commerce.

1918   Webb–Pomerene Act (and in 1920 the Merchant Marine Act) reflect less hostile attitude to trusts.

1920   US Supreme Court does not dissolve US Steel Corporation (although it controls over half of nation's steel). Inaugurates period of mergers and combinations in 1920s.

1933   Great Depression leads to National Industrial Recovery Act. Trade associations permitted to control prices, draw up codes of fair competition, etc.

1935   *Schechter v. United States* ruling (May) in Supreme Court ends this new freedom.

1938   Temporary National Economic Committee (under Senator Joseph O'Mahoney) produces report urging need to curb trusts.

1945   Judgment given against Aluminium Company of America (Alcoa) in case which had begun in 1937.

1946   Anti-Trust Division takes action against Du Pont Company, Pullman Company, etc.

Tariffs and trade: Chronology

1807   Embargo Act. An attempt by Jefferson to secure the recognition of American commercial rights. An extreme measure which stopped all American foreign trade.

1809   Nonintercourse Act, applied an embargo against Britain and France. There was a provision that trade would be re-opened if either Britain or France repealed restrictions against US shipping.

1810   Macon's Bill re-opens trade with Britain and France.

1833   Compromise Tariff worked out by Clay and Calhoun.

1841   Walker Act heralds tariff reductions (further reductions in 1857).

1861   First of the Morrill tariffs (2 Mar.), precipitated by the 1857 financial panic.

1890   McKinley Tariff Act raises duties on manufactured goods to an average of nearly 50%; but also empowers the President to vary tariffs upon imports (such as sugar) from Latin American countries which reduced duties against US goods.

1909   Payne–Aldrich Tariff Act reduces rates and greatly expands the 'free list' of necessary items of consumption (such as many foodstuffs).

1913   Underwood–Simmons Tariff Act, a major shift in the direction of freer trade and a real attempt to fulfil Democratic election pledges, reduces duties on nearly 1,000 items.

1916   US Tariff Commission (USTC) established as a fact-finding body.

1921   Anti-Dumping Act requires the Secretary of the Treasury to levy special duties against foreign competitors found to be selling goods below market prices in US.

1922   Fordney–McCumber Act. The President is authorized upon the recommendation of the USTC to vary prevailing tariffs by 50% in order to equalize production costs between US and foreign companies.

1930   Smoot–Hawley Act (June) sets a new high for restrictive legislation; was last case of Congress specifying the actual tariff rates in the legislation. Attracts much criticism.

1934   Reciprocal Trade Agreements Act authorizes the President to negotiate tariff reductions with other nations which will reduce their own barriers to US exports.

1939–45 Destruction of European economies by war and the need for renewed international monetary co-operation leads to changes in US policy.

1944   Bretton Woods Agreement (July) to establish the International Monetary Fund (IMF) and the International Bank for Reconstruction and Development (World Bank). Exchange rates of foreign currencies against the US dollar and the dollar price of gold are fixed.

1947   United States initiates the Marshall Plan (June) to offer financial aid for European economic reconstruction. GATT (General Agreement on Tariffs and Trade) formulated in Geneva (Aug.).

1948   Havana Charter (Mar.) proposes creating an International Trade Organization (ITO) to manage world trade. The US Congress declines to ratify it.

1957   European Economic Community (EEC) established.

1962   Office of Special Trade Representative (STR) for trade negotiations established. Trade Expansion Act creates 'trade adjustment assistance' – government financial aid to US companies affected by imports – to allow for retraining and relocation of workforces.

1964   United Nations Conference on Trade and Development (UNCTAD) convenes in Geneva to address issues of trade policy relating to less-developed countries.

1974   Trade Act establishes the US International Trade Commission (USITC) as the successor to the Tariff Commission; and grants the executive branch power to negotiate agreements with foreign countries on non-tariff barriers to trade. Section 151 establishes a 'fast-track' procedure requiring Congress to vote upon such agreements within 90 days of submission.

1980   Office of the US Trade Representative (USTR) established as the successor to the Special Trade Representative. The official has Cabinet-level and ambassadorial rank.

1984   Trade and Tariff Act empowers the US government to embark upon negotiations with foreign countries to establish free-trade areas.

1988   Section 301 of the Omnibus Trade and Competitiveness Act enables US negotiators to threaten special surcharges against a country's exports to the US if that country does not address its 'unfair' trade practices (as defined by the US).

1993   NAFTA (North American Free Trade Agreement) establishes a common market between Mexico, Canada and the United States.

1995   WTO (World Trade Organization) formed as the successor to
        the GATT.

Source: I.M. Destler, *American Trade Politics* (2nd edn, 1992)

The Balance of Trade, 1900–57 ($ 000)

(+ = excess of exports over imports; − = excess of imports over exports.)

	Exports	Imports	+/−
1900	1,499	930	+570
1901	1,605	926	+680
1902	1,480	984	+496
1903	1,511	1,095	+416
1904	1,592	1,118	+474
1905	1,660	1,199	+461
1906	1,848	1,367	+481
1907	1,989	1,592	+397
1908	1,991	1,387	+604
1909	1,810	1,400	+410
1910	1,919	1,646	+273
1911	2,137	1,647	+490
1912	2,323	1,749	+577
1913	2,615	1,923	+692
1914	2,532	1,991	+541
1915	2,966	1,875	+1,091
1916	5,709	3,110	+2,599
1917	6,690	3,558	+3,131
1918	6,443	3,165	+3,278
1919	8,528	4,070	+4,457
1920	8,664	5,784	+2,880
1921	4,560	3,264	+1,297
1922	3,931	3,459	+473
1923	4,269	4,189	+79
1924	4,763	4,004	+759
1925	5,272	4,419	+852
1926	5,017	4,714	+303
1927	5,142	4,447	+695
1928	5,776	4,328	+1,448
1929	5,411	4,755	+686
1930	4,013	3,500	+514
1931	2,918	2,731	+186
1932	2,434	1,706	+729
1933	2,061	1,703	+358
1934	2,202	2,944	−742

	Exports	Imports	+/−
1935	2,304	4,143	−1,839
1936	2,495	3,750	−1,254
1937	3,407	4,807	−1,400
1938	3,107	4,170	−1,063
1939	3,192	5,978	−2,786
1940	4,030	7,433	−3,403
1941	5,153	4,375	+778
1942	8,081	3,113	+4,968
1943	13,028	3,511	+9,517
1944	15,345	4,066	+11,279
1945	10,097	4,280	+5,816
1946	9,996	5,533	+4,464
1947	14,674	7,904	+6,770
1948	12,967	9,176	+3,791
1949	12,160	7,467	+4,693
1950	10,816	9,125	+1,691
1951	15,672	11,152	+4,520
1952	15,262	11,525	+3,737
1953	15,827	11,015	+4,812
1954	15,136	10,333	+4,803
1955	15,563	11,562	+4,001
1956	19,124	12,877	+6,247
1957	20,989	13,409	+7,580

Source: US Bureau of the Census, *Statistical Abstract of the United States: 1996*

Key statistics

Exports and Imports, 1960–94

Year	Exports ($ million)	Imports ($ million)
1960	19,659	15,073
1965	26,742	21,520
1970	42,681	40,356
1975	107,652	98,503
1980	220,626	244,871
1985	213,133	345,276
1990	394,030	495,042
1994	512,627	663,256

Source: Department of Commerce

Principal trading partners of America (1994)

Country	Imports ($ million)
Canada	128,406
Japan	119,156
Mexico	49,494
China	38,787
Germany	31,744
Taiwan	26,706
United Kingdom	25,058
South Korea	19,629

Country	Exports ($ million)
Canada	114,439
Japan	53,488
Mexico	50,844
United Kingdom	26,900
Germany	19,229
South Korea	18,025
Taiwan	17,109
France	13,619

Percentage share of world manufacturing exports 1913–80: major countries

Country	1913	1929	1937	1950	1960	1970	1980
USA	12.6	20.7	19.6	29.1	17.9	15.3	11.5
UK	29.9	23.6	22.4	25.0	12.7	8.6	6.8
Japan	2.4	3.9	7.2	3.3	5.3	9.3	10.4
Germany[1]	26.4	21.0	22.4	7.1	14.8	15.8	13.9
Italy	3.6	3.7	3.6	3.8	3.9	5.7	5.5
France	12.9	11.2	6.4	10.2	7.4	6.9	6.9

[1] West Germany only after 1945.

Sources: H. Tyszynski, 'World Trade in Manufactured Commodities, 1899–1950', The Manchester School, 19 (1951), pp. 278–86; Cambridge Economic Policy Review (1979); National Institute Economic Review

Production of petroleum, 1860–1950[1]

1860	500
1870	5,261
1880	26,286
1890	45,824
1900	63,621
1910	209,557
1920	442,929
1930	898,011
1940	1,353,214
1950	1,973,574

[1] Quantities in thousands of 42-gallon barrels. Production hit 1 million 42-gallon barrels for the first time in 1929. It passed 2 million for the first time in 1948.

Output of crude oil 1950–84: selected countries (million metric tons)

	1950	1960	1975	1984
USA	285.2	384.1	411.4	487.0
Canada	3.8	27.5	70.0	82.0
Mexico	10.3	14.1	41.4	150.0
Venezuela	78.2	148.7	122.1	95.0
Iraq	6.7	47.5	111.0	58.5
Iran	32.3	52.1	266.7	105.0
Saudi Arabia	26.6	61.1	352.1	235.0
Kuwait	17.3	81.7	104.8	58.0
Nigeria	—	1.0	88.0	68.0
China	—	5.0	77.0	110.0
Indonesia	6.5	20.6	65.5	70.5

Iron Ore Production, 1860–1950[1]

1860	2,873
1870	3,832
1880	7,120
1890	16,036
1900	27,300
1910	57,015
1920	67,604
1930[2]	58,409
1940	73,696
1950	98,045

[1] In thousands of long tons.
[2] 1929 total (the highest for the 1920s) was 73,028.

Output of Steel, 1910–90[1]

1910	26.5
1918	45.2
1930	41.4
1940	60.8
1950	96.4
1960	99.3
1970	131.5
1975	116.6
1980	111.8
1985	88.3
1990	98.9

[1] Figures in net tons of 2,000 lb.

Output of coal and lignite, 1910–85: selected countries (in million metric tons)

	1910	1920	1940	1950	1960	1975	1985
United States[1]	470	521	466	468	377	643	828
United Kingdom	264	230	224	220	197	124	91
USSR	27	11	133	261	509	701	716
Japan	16	29	57	49	51	20	17
Germany	247	250	267	188	240	214	207
(E. Germany after 1945)				140	228	245	278

[1] Short tons.
Sources: B.R. Mitchell, *European Historical Statistics, 1750–1970* (1975), pp. 365–8; J. Paxton (ed.), *The Statesman's Yearbook, 1985–86* (1985)

Generation of Electricity (billion kW)

1970	1,532
1975	1,918
1980	2,286
1985	2,470
1990	2,808
1993	2,883

Changing source of energy (figures are percentages)

Source of energy	1970	1975	1980	1985	1990	1993
Coal	46.0	44.6	51.0	57.2	55.5	56.9
Nuclear	1.4	9.0	11.0	15.5	20.5	21.2
Oil	12.0	15.1	10.8	4.1	4.2	3.5
Gas	24.3	15.6	15.1	11.8	9.4	9.0
Hydro	16.2	15.6	12.1	11.4	10.4	9.2

Source: US Federal Power Commission

Agriculture (since 1862)

Chronology of key events

1862   Department of Agriculture created by Congress. Homestead Act passed, providing free title grant to 160 acres of land for those resident for five years.

1867   Agricultural leaders organize 'Patrons of Husbandry' (National Grange) under Oliver Hudson Kelley (see Grangers, p. 327).

1887   Hatch Act provides federal assistance for state agricultural experiment stations.

1889   Commissioner of Agriculture granted Cabinet rank.

1890   Militant Farmers Alliance wins political victories. Leads to Populist (q.v.) movement.

1894   Carey Act encourages irrigation of desert lands in West. Its lack of provision for inter-state co-operation renders it a failure.

1900   Numbers in agricultural employment fall to 37% of workforce (from 60% in 1860).

1902   Foundation of National Farmers' Union by Newt Gresham.

1905   Introduction of internal combustion engine tractor revolutionizes farming.

1913   Rural Credits Commission appointed under chairmanship of Duncan U. Fletcher.

1914   Smith–Lever Act provides federal funds for agricultural extension work.

1916   Federal Farm Loan Act provides first long-term farm credits. Twelve Federal Farm Loan Banks created, lending money secured by land mortgage.

1917   Smith–Hughes Act provides for federal aid for vocational and agricultural teaching in public schools. Exigencies of World War I lead to Food Control Program, Food Administration, Lever Act, etc.

1920   American Farm Bureau Federation organized in Chicago.

1929   Agricultural Marketing Act creates Federal Farm Board.

1933   Agricultural Adjustment Act (AAA), the key initial farm relief measure of the New Deal. Under the Act, production is restricted by paying farmers to reduce crop acreage. Act declared unconstitutional. Replaced by 1936 Act.

1934   Frazier–Lemke Bankruptcy Act delays foreclosure of farm mort-gages (declared unconstitutional and replaced with modified Act in 1935).

1936   Soil Conservation and Domestic Allotment Act replaces 1933 AAA. Superseded itself by 1938 Act.

1937   Bankhead–Jones Farm Tenant Act aims to improve position of share-croppers. Farm Security Administration to lend money to tenants who wished to purchase land.

1938   Second Agricultural Adjustment Act supersedes 1936 legisla-tion.

1939   The distress caused by the Dust Bowl (in Oklahoma, etc.) and plight of migrant labourers and share-croppers highlighted by John Steinbeck's *Grapes of Wrath*.

1949   Brennan Plan, proposal of Agriculture Secretary Brennan in 1949, to amend the nature of government support to farmers by subsidizing them directly instead of maintaining price sup-ports for their products.

1955   Formation in Iowa of National Farmers' Organization in protest at low farm prices.

1956   Agricultural Act creates 'soil bank' by taking land out of production.

1960s   Emergence of United Farm Workers' Union to campaign on behalf of farm workers.

1964   Food Stamp Act passed.

1965   Food and Agriculture Act repeals soil bank programme of 1956.

1966   President's Commission on Rural Poverty established.

1970   Agriculture Act places limits on payments for price support to any one company or person.

1990   Numbers employed in farm occupations fall to 2.4% of workforce (compared to 11.6% in 1950).

1993   Death of César Chavez, founder of UFWU (23 April).

Key statistics

The agricultural workforce

Year	Farm workers	Percentage of labour force
1850	4,902	63.7
1870	6,850	53.0
1900	10,888	37.5
1920	11,390	27.0
1930	10,321	21.2
1940	8,995	17.4
1950	6,858	11.6
1960	4,132	6.1
1970	2,881	3.6
1980	2,818	2.7
1990	2,864	2.4
1993	2,988	2.5

Total farm cash income ($ million)

Year	Total cash income
1920	12,600
1925	11,021
1930	9,055
1935	7,693
1940	9,105
1945	22,405
1950	28,744
1955	29,719
1960	34,950
1965	41,828
1970	54,226
1975	89,707
1980	141,355
1985	161,200
1990	198,500

Size of acreage of average farm[1]

1940	174
1950	215
1960	302
1970	390
1980	445
1994	471

[1] Since 1940, the number of farms has steadily declined, but the survivors have grown larger.

Transport

Early canals and roads

Canals: Chronology

1786–1808   Construction of Patowmack Company's works canal at Great Falls, Maryland.

1793–1804   Construction of Middlesex Canal (linking Boston with the Merrimac River).

1790s   Santee and Cooper Canal connects Santee and Cooper Rivers above Charleston, South Carolina.

1795   Construction of Western Inland Lock Navigation Company canal at Little Falls, New York.

1817–25   Major Erie Canal project, a landmark in US canal construction. The 'Erie School' of canal builders includes Bates, Geddes, Jervis, Roberts and White.

1826–34   Construction of Pennsylvania and Main Line Canal.

1827–29   Construction of Lehigh Canal (the work of Josiah White).

1828–50   Construction of Chesapeake and Ohio (C&O) Canal.

1836–43   Construction of Whitewater Canal.

Roads: Chronology of major developments

1775   Daniel Boone begins to cut trail into Kentucky, the 'Wilderness Road'.

1792–94   Macadamized 60-mile toll road constructed by Philadelphia and Lancaster Turn Pike Company (the Lancaster Turnpike).

1802   Enabling Act (granting statehood to Ohio) provides for an East–West Road. This eventually becomes the National (or Cumberland) Road.

1806   Decision reached to expand Cumberland Road into national toll road to the Mississippi at St Louis. Many political obstacles delayed progress and project never really materialized.

1821   Effective start of Santa Fé Trail, pioneered by William Becknell. It was an important route until 1880.

1841   Oregon Trail route completed. Trail ran from St Joseph (Montana) to Williamette Valley in Oregon.

1846	Expulsion of Mormons from Nauvoo, Illinois, leads to opening of Mormon Trail.
1848	Discovery of gold in California provides huge influx of travellers along the Oregon–California Trail.

Railroads

Chronology of major developments

1827	Baltimore and Ohio railroad chartered (28 Feb.). Generally accepted as start of modern railroad development.
1830	First passengers carried on Baltimore and Ohio (from Baltimore to Ellicott's Mills, Maryland) (24 May).
1831	Opening of first sections of Mohawk and Hudson (Albany–Schenectady), Camden and Amboy, and the Philadelphia, Germantown and Norristown railroads.
1840	Over 2,800 miles of railroad in operation.
1849–50	Michigan Central Railroad conspiracy. Participants jailed in 1851.
1850	Open railroad mileage passes 9,000 miles.
1851	Illinois Central line chartered.
1852	Chicago reached by Michigan Central and Michigan Southern lines.
1853	Railroad era commences in Texas with opening of Buffalo Bayou, Brazos and Colorado.
1854	Chicago and Rock Island railroad reaches the Mississippi.
1856	Opening of Sacramento Valley railroad in new state of California. First railroad bridge crosses Mississippi.
1861–65	Vital role of railways in Civil War – first major war in which railways are so important.
1862	President Lincoln signs bill authorizing transcontinental railroad via the central, 'overland' route (Missouri River to California) (1 July).
1863	Brotherhood of Locomotive Engineers founded (one of 'Big Five').
1868	Order of Railway Conductors founded (one of 'Big Five').
1869	Union Pacific and Central Pacific construction workers meet at Promontory, Utah. Famous ceremony of the 'golden spike' (10 May).
1870s	Beginning of Granger laws on railroad rates.
1873	Brotherhood of Locomotive Firemen and Enginemen founded (one of 'Big Five').
1877	*Munn v. Illinois*; Supreme Court rules states can fix interstate rates.

1880	Start of decade of greatest growth of railway mileage (7,000 miles per year).
1881	Second transcontinental route completed with meeting at Deming, New Mexico, of the Southern Pacific (building from the East) and the Atchison, Topeka and Santa Fé (building from the West).
1883	Northern Pacific becomes first railroad to reach the Pacific Northwest. Brotherhood of Railroad Trainmen founded (one of 'Big Five'). Standardization of railroad time zones (Nov.).
1886	*Wabash, St Louis and Pacific Railroad Company v. Illinois*; judgment in 1877 Munn case reversed.
1887	Passing of Interstate Commerce Act creates Interstate Commerce Commission (ICC).
1893	Third route to Pacific Northwest completed by Great Northern.
1894	Landmark Pullman strike. Switchmen's Union of North America founded (one of 'Big Five').
1898	Erdman Act creates railroad mediation machinery.
1903	Elkins Act strengthens ICC. Ends practice of railroad rebates.
1905	Union Pacific route to southern California completed.
1906	Hepburn Act. Gives ICC power to fix specific maximum rates. Amends 1887 Act.
1909	Opening of Western Pacific, last of the transcontinental connections.
1910	Mann–Elkins Act. ICC has power to freeze rates at 1890s level. Further strengthens regulation of railroads.
1913	Newlands Act for railroad mediation.
1916	Railroad route mileage reaches peak (254,000 miles). Absolute track peak (sidings, marshalling yards, etc.), is 430,000 miles in 1930.
1917	Railroad Administration established to control and operate all rail transport for duration of the war (Dec.).
1920	Esch–Cummins Transportation Act passed. Railroads returned to private management. Consolidation encouraged. US Railroad Labor Board established.
1922	First nation-wide strike on US railroads fails (but leads to 1926 Railway Labor Act).
1934	Railroad Retirement Act (June) promotes pensions for employees. Act declared unconstitutional in March 1935. New legislation introduced in 1936 and 1937. First diesel locomotives introduced into passenger service.
1946	Harry Truman counters nation-wide strike by seizing railroads under war powers.
1958	Transportation Act relaxes regulatory requirements.

1960	Number of companies has declined to 600 (compared to 1,400 in 1916).
1967	Seaboard Coast Line formed from merger of Atlantic Coast Line and Seaboard Air Line.
1968	Creation of Penn Central railroad (merger of New York Central, the Pennsylvania and the New York, New Haven and Hartford).
1969	Decline of railroads and weakened bargaining power causes four unions to merge into United Transportation Union (1 July). Locomotive engineers remain outside. Railroad share of public transit passengers declines to 20%. High-speed Metroliner service begins between New York and Washington.
1970	Penn Central forced into bankruptcy. National Railroad Passenger Corporation (Amtrak) formed under the Rail Passenger Service Act (31 Oct.). It takes over passenger services of 22 leading railroads.
1971	Amtrak created by the Rail Passenger Service Act of 1970 (1 May).
1996	Approval of $4 billion merger of the Union Pacific and Southern Pacific railroads, creating the largest railroad in the Western World.

Growth and decline of route mileage

Year	Mileage	Year	Mileage
1830	23	1916	254,000
1840	2,818	1920	252,865
1850	9,021	1930	249,619
1860	30,626	1940	234,182
1870	52,922	1950	224,331
1880	93,267	1960	217,551
1890	163,605	1970	209,001
1900	193,366	1980	183,077
1910	240,313	1990	162,254

Post-war decline of railroad inter-city passenger traffic, 1945–93 (in millions of passenger miles)

Year	Passenger miles	Year	Passenger miles
1945	93,535	1970	10,903
1950	32,481	1975	10,075
1955	28,695	1980	11,500
1960	21,574	1993	13,138
1965	17,557		

Source: Association of American Railroads

The automobile age

Chronology of major developments

1895   The first automobile journal, *Horseless Age*, heralds increasing interest in automobiles. Charles and Frank Duryea of Springfield, Massachusetts, win Chicago *Times Herald* sponsored race.

1899   First annual figures for automobile production show 2,000 cars built.

1903   Association of Licensed Automobile Manufacturers (ALAM) formed, aims to limit competition in and entry into motor industry.

1908   Henry Ford introduces Model 'T' which wins massive popularity. General Motors formed by William C. Durant.

1910   Motor vehicle registrations reach 458,500.

1913–14 Perfection of mass production techniques at the Ford Highland Park plant in Michigan.

1916   Passage of Federal Aid Road Act, the first national legislation to assist road-building. Money appropriated for five-year period to improve rural post roads.

1919   First four states introduce automobile licence fees.

1921   Congress provides for aid to states (via US Bureau of Public Roads) for construction of inter-city highways (Federal Highway Act).

1929   Motor vehicle registration reaches 26.7 million. Production peaks at 5.3 million (not reached again until 1949). Ford, General Motor and Chrysler account for 80% of production – the 'Detroit Big Three'.

1932   National Automobile Chamber of Commerce becomes Automobile Manufacturers Association.

1937   Unions take hold as General Motors and Chrysler defeated by United Automobile Workers. Reinforced when Ford forced to submit in 1941.

1939   Automatic transmission introduced in the Oldsmobile.

1954   American Motors formed from merger of Nash-Kelvinator and Hudson.

1956   Interstate Highway Act. Congress authorizes construction of national network of limited access highways. By 1975, 36,000 miles completed.

1965   Motor Vehicle Air Pollution Act.

1966   Traffic and Motor Vehicle Safety Act.

1973   Urban public transport is made eligible for funding from the federal government's highway trust fund.

1973–74 World energy crisis shakes the 'automobile culture'. Rise in sales of small cars at expense of 'gas-guzzlers'.

1974   National speed limit of 55 m.p.h. established by the Emergency Highway Energy Conservation Act in order to save petrol (2 Jan.).

1984   New York requires drivers to wear seat belts, the first state to do so (12 July).

Total highway expenditure (all branches of government) ($ billion)

1921	1 (just under)
1939	2.4
1949	4.2
1959	10.9
1971	23.4
1990	36.5
1994	37.1

Motor vehicles produced, 1921–94 (000s)

1921	1,900
1929	4,900
1935	3,947
1965	9,306[1]
1975	6,713[1]
1985	6,739[1]
1990	6,078
1994	6,614

[1] Passenger cars only.

Air transportation

Chronology of major developments

1903   Slow development of air transportation after first controlled flight by Orville and Wilbur Wright on 17 December.

1914   First commercial passenger flight (on seasonal basis) in Florida between Saint Petersburg and Tampa (1 Jan.).

1918   Federal government begins to provide airmail service (15 May).

1924   First night mail began (1 July).

1927   Solo flight of Charles A. Lindbergh from New York to Paris begins wave of enthusiasm for air travel. Formation of the 'big four' domestic airlines (United Airlines, Eastern Airlines, Transcontinental Air Transport and American Airlines).

1930   Air Mail Act passed. Subsequently widely attacked.

1938   Civil Aeronautics Act places all sixteen domestic airlines, to-
gether with Pan American, under economic regulation of Civil
Aeronautics Authority (later renamed Civil Aeronautics Board
(CAB)).

1958   Federal Aviation Agency takes over all aspects of the federal
regulation of aviation (examination of causes of accidents remains with Civil Aeronautics Board).

1966   Federal Aviation Agency becomes Federal Aviation Administration.

1967   United Airlines becomes first airline to exceed $1 billion rev-
enue in a single year.

1971   US Senate votes not to provide funding for the development of
an American supersonic passenger aeroplane (24 Mar.).

1976   First regularly-scheduled commercial supersonic flights begin.
British Airways and Air France begin service to Washington
(24 May).

1978   De-regulation of US domestic air transportation by the Airline
Deregulation Act, abolishing the federal government's control
of airline ticket prices and routes. The Act leads firstly to the
emergence of numerous smaller carriers and then to consolidation in the industry.

1981   Nationwide strike by the Professional Air Traffic Controllers
Organization (PATCO) (3 Aug.). President Reagan orders an
immediate return to work and then dismisses those who refuse,
relying upon military personnel to operate the system.

1994   Chicago O'Hare, world's busiest airport, handles over 66 million passengers and 883,000 aircraft movements.

Growth of air passenger travel since 1945 (millions of passenger miles)

1945	3,362
1950	10,072
1955	22,741
1960	31,730
1965	53,719
1970	109,499
1975	136,432
1980	204,368
1990	457,900
1994	519,200

Source: Civil Aeronautics Board

SECTION FOUR

Foreign affairs and defence

Foreign affairs, treaties and alliances

Secretaries of State (since 1789)

An Act of Congress created the Department of Foreign Affairs on 27 July 1789. On 15 September its name was changed to the Department of State. The head of the Department of State (the first of the executive Departments of the US government) and the most senior member of the President's Cabinet is the Secretary of State. He or she is responsible, under the President, for the formulation and execution of the foreign policy of the United States; for the activities of other government departments and agencies overseas; and for the operations of the Foreign Service, the diplomatic service of the United States. As the ranking Cabinet member, he or she is first in line of succession to the Presidency after the Vice-President, the Speaker of the House of Representatives and the President *pro tempore* of the Senate.

1789	John Jay	1853	William L. Marcy
1789	Thomas Jefferson	1857	Lewis Cass
1794	Edmund Randolph	1860	Jeremiah S. Black
1795	Timothy Pickering	1861	William H. Seward
1800	John Marshall	1869	Elihu B. Washburne
1801	James Madison	1869	Hamilton Fish
1809	Robert Smith	1877	William M. Evarts
1811	James Monroe	1881	James G. Blaine
1817	John Quincy Adams	1881	F.T. Frelinghuysen
1825	Henry Clay	1885	Thomas F. Bayard
1829	Martin Van Buren	1889	James G. Blaine
1831	Edward Livingston	1892	John W. Foster
1833	Louis McLane	1893	Walter Q. Gresham
1834	John Forsyth	1895	Richard Olney
1841	Daniel Webster	1897	John Sherman
1843	Abel P. Upshur	1898	William R. Day
1844	John C. Calhoun	1898	John Hay
1845	James Buchanan	1905	Elihu Root
1849	John M. Clayton	1909	Robert Bacon
1850	Daniel Webster	1909	Philander C. Knox
1852	Edward Everett	1913	William J. Bryan

1915	Robert Lansing	1961	Dean Rusk
1920	Bainbridge Colby	1969	William P. Rogers
1921	Charles E. Hughes	1973	Henry A. Kissinger
1925	Frank B. Kellogg	1977	Cyrus R. Vance
1929	Henry L. Stimson	1980	Edmund J. Muskie
1933	Cordell Hull	1981	Alexander M. Haig, Jr
1944	E.R. Stettinius, Jr	1982	George P. Shultz
1945	James F. Byrnes	1989	James A. Baker
1947	George C. Marshall	1992	Lawrence S. Eagleburger
1949	Dean G. Acheson	1993	Warren M. Christopher
1953	John Foster Dulles	1997	Madeleine Albright
1959	Christian A. Herter		

The rise of American diplomacy, 1778–1914

The newly independent United States rapidly began to establish diplomatic relations, at first with the major powers of *ancien regime* Europe. France led the way in 1778. During the nineteenth century, American attention centred first on Latin America, but also further afield – with China (1843) and Egypt (1848). By 1914 America's diplomatic influence was world-wide.

1778	14 Sept.	France
1779	28 Sept.	Spain
1780	19 Dec.	Russia
1781	16 Aug.	Holland
1782	28 Sept.	Sweden
1785	24 Feb.	United Kingdom
1791	21 Feb.	Portugal
1797	1 June	Prussia
1823	27 Jan.	Chile
1823	27 Jan.	Colombia
1823	27 Jan.	Mexico
1825	7 Mar.	Guatemala
1825	9 Mar.	Brazil
1826	2 May	Peru
1827	3 Mar.	Denmark
1831	15 Apr.	Ottoman Empire
1832	27 Jan.	Argentina
1832	14 Apr.	Belgium
1835	3 Mar.	Venezuela
1838	8 Feb.	Austria
1840	5 June	Sardinia
1843	3 Mar.	China

1848	10 Apr.	Ecuador
1848	14 Aug.	Egypt
1851	12 Mar.	Nicaragua
1853	16 Mar.	Switzerland
1853	29 Mar.	El Salvador
1853	29 Mar.	Costa Rica
1853	29 Mar.	Honduras
1859	19 Jan.	Japan
1861	8 June	Paraguay
1862	12 July	Haiti
1863	11 Mar.	Liberia
1867	5 Apr.	Uruguay
1868	11 Mar.	Greece
1880	11 June	Romania
1882	7 July	Serbia
1882	13 July	Thailand
1883	29 Jan.	Persia
1883	27 Feb.	Korea
1883	12 Nov.	Dominican Republic
1901	24 Apr.	Bulgaria
1902	20 May	Cuba
1903	5 June	Luxembourg
1905	8 Mar.	Morocco
1905	8 Mar.	Norway
1908	20 July	Ethiopia

Chronology of major foreign treaties and agreements (since 1778)

1778   Treaty of Alliance with France.

1782   Commercial Treaty with the Netherlands.

1783   Treaty of Paris ending Revolutionary War. Commercial Treaty with Sweden.

1785   Commercial Treaty with Prussia.

1786   Treaty of Peace and Friendship with Morocco.

1788   Consular convention with France.

1794   Jay's Treaty with Britain (resolves continuing problems of 1783 Treaty of Paris).

1795   First of series of treaties with Barbary States (Algiers, 1795; Tripoli, 1796; Tunis, 1797) secures safe transit for merchant ships by payment of subsidies. Treaty of San Lorenzo (Pinckney's Treaty) with Spain. United States secures right to deposit river cargoes in New Orleans for subsequent trans-shipment.

1800   Commercial convention with France (30 Sept.).

1803   Treaty with France. Louisiana ceded to US (30 Apr.).

1809   Start of diplomatic relations with Russia.

1814   Treaty of Ghent concludes peace with Britain (24 Dec.) (followed by 1816 commercial treaty, agreement on demilitarization of Great Lakes, 1817 and convention of 1818 on northern boundary and coastal fishing).

1817   Rush–Bagot Agreement with Britain on demilitarization of the Great Lakes (Apr.).

1818   Convention with Britain settles variety of boundary questions (Oct.).

1819   Treaty with Spain (Adams–Onís Treaty, 22 Feb.). US acquires East Florida and Oregon Territory north of the 42nd parallel. Spain relinquishes claims to West Florida.

1822   Pressure grows to recognize independent states of South America (see p. 230 for individual countries).

1823   Promulgation of Monroe Doctrine (see p. 340).

1842   Webster–Ashburton Treaty adjusts north-east boundary with Canada (9 Aug.).

1844   Treaty of Wang-hsia with China (3 July).

1846   Treaty with Britain settling the Oregon boundary with Canada along 49th parallel (15 June).

1848   Treaty of Guadalupe Hidalgo concludes Mexican War and settles boundary (2 Feb.) (but see 1854).

1850   Clayton–Bulwer Treaty (compromise over Panama) (19 Apr.).

1854   Gadsden Purchase Treaty modifies Mexican boundary (30 Dec.). Treaty of Kanagawa signed with Japan (31 Mar.). Marcy–Elgin Treaty with Canada (regarding fishing and trade).

1867   Treaty with Russia to acquire Alaska (30 Mar.).

1868   Burlingame Treaty with China.

1871   Treaty of Washington signed (for adjustment of Alabama claims).

1876   Samoan Treaty ratified by Senate.

1882   Treaty with Korea recognizing its independence (22 May).

1889   Berlin Treaty signed (for tripartite control over Samoa).

1892   Treaty for Arbitration of sealing disputes in Bering Sea.

1898   Treaty of Paris ends Spanish–American War (see p. 242 for territories acquired by US).

1899   'Open Door Policy' propounded by John Hay.

1901   Hay–Pauncefote Treaty paves way for US construction of Panama Canal as an international waterway.

1903   Treaty on Relations with Cuba (incorporates Platt Amendment on Cuban independence). Guantánamo Bay leased to US as naval base.

1916   Agreement with Denmark to purchase Virgin Islands.

1921   Peace treaties signed with Austria, Germany and Hungary (25–29 May).

1922   Washington Naval Agreement (with Britain, France, Italy, Japan and others) restricts size of navies (6 Feb.).

1923   War Debt Convention with Britain (19 June).

1926   Treaty of Alliance with Panama (28 July).

1928   Briand–Kellogg Pact. US and major powers renounce war as a means to settle disputes (27 Aug.).

1930   London Naval Agreement expands 1922 Washington Naval Agreement.

1931   Protocol on Hoover Plan to suspend German reparations for one year.

1933   US signs multilateral Montevideo Convention on Extradition.

1934   US agrees independence of Philippines from 1945.

1936   Treaty with Panama (2 Mar.).

1941   US enacts Lend-Lease Bill for aid to Britain. Atlantic Charter agreed by Roosevelt and Churchill.

1942   Washington Pact of 26 United Nations (1 Jan.).

1943   Casablanca Conference of wartime Allies agrees on demand for unconditional surrender of Nazi Germany (26 Jan.). Followed by Cairo Meeting (22–26 Nov.) and Tehran Meeting (26 Nov.–2 Dec.).

1944   Bretton Woods Agreement to set up World Bank and International Monetary Fund.

1945   Yalta Agreement (11 Feb.) with Britain and Russia on the future of Germany, Europe and world security. US signs charter of United Nations (26 June).

1947   US Marshall Plan provides aid for reconstruction in war-devastated Europe.

1948   US adheres to GATT (General Agreement on Tariffs and Trade). Treaty forming Organization of American States (OAS) for joint resistance to attack signed by USA and 20 other Latin American countries (in force from 1951).

1949   US is a founder member of NATO (North Atlantic Treaty Organization) with ten other nations.

1950   Defence agreement with South Korea (26 Jan.). For Korea, see also p. 245.

1951   Pacific Security Treaty between United States, Australia and New Zealand (ANZUS Pact, 1 Sept.). Japan signed Mutual Security Pact with the United States, permitting the US to remain indefinitely in Japan.

1952   US–Japanese Agreement (28 Feb.) on bases in Japan.
         US–Israeli defence agreement (23 July).

1953   Armistice signed in Korean War (27 July) at Panmunjon. Mutual defense agreement between United States and Spain (26 Sept.) allowing US bases. Mutual Defense Treaty of United States with South Korea (1 Oct.).

1954   South-East Asia Collective Defense Treaty (8 Sept.) signed by US and seven other nations pledging joint action to protect South Vietnam and other nations in the area. Mutual Defense Treaty with Nationalist China signed by US (2 Dec.).

1955   US–Canadian agreement on operation of Early Warning System (5 May) (extended in 1958 to set up NORAD, North American Air Defense Command). Austrian State Treaty (15 May) between the US, Britain, Russia and France established Austria as neutral, sovereign state.

1959   Ten-Power Committee on Disarmament set up (7 Sept.) representing US, Britain, Canada, France, Italy, Bulgaria, Czechoslovakia, Poland, Romania and the Soviet Union.

1960   Japanese–US Treaty of mutual security (19 Jan.).

1961   Organization for Economic Co-operation and Development (OECD, 30 Sept.) replaces the OEEC and includes United States and Canada.

1963   'Hot-line' agreement reached between the United States and Soviet Union (5 Apr.). Partial Test-Ban Treaty signed on nuclear testing with Britain and Russia (5 Aug.).

1967   Treaty banning nuclear weapons in space opened for signature in London, Moscow and Washington (27 Jan.).

1968   Nuclear Non-Proliferation Treaty agreed and opened for signature (1 July).

1971   Sea-bed Treaty prohibiting the use of the sea-bed for nuclear weapons opened for signature (11 Feb.). Agreement with Japan on transfer of sovereignty over the Ryukyu Islands (17 June).

1972   SALT I Anti-Ballistic Missile (ABM) agreement and five-year interim agreement on limitation of strategic arms signed by US and Soviet Union (26 May).

1973   Agreement to end the war and restore peace in Vietnam with North and South Vietnam and the South Vietnamese Provisional Revolutionary Government (27 Jan.).

1974   Protocol to the US–Soviet SALT ABM agreement limited deployment to a single area (3 July); US–Soviet Threshold Test Ban Treaty signed, limiting underground nuclear tests (3 July); Vladivostok Accord between United States and Soviet Union (24 Nov.) established framework for future negotiations controlling strategic arms race.

1975   Act of the Helsinki Conference, 'Helsinki Agreement', (1 Aug.) between 35 nations regarding European security, including a reaffirmation of human rights and proposals for economic collaboration between eastern and western 'blocs'. Israeli–US agreement on establishment of early warning system in Sinai (1 Sept.).

1976   US–Soviet Treaty restricting nuclear explosions for peaceful purposes (28 May).

1977   Basic treaty and neutrality with Panama, settling future of Panama Canal (7 Sept.).

1978   Camp David agreements between Israel and Egypt for conclusion of peace treaty and overall Middle East settlement (17 Sept.).

1979   Agreement with Philippines on use of bases (6 Jan.). SALT II Agreement signed by United States and Soviet Union, restricting numbers of strategic offensive weapons (18 June).

1980   Agreement for normalization of relations with China (17 Sept.).

1981   US, Israel and Egypt sign agreement for peace-keeping force in Sinai (10 July). Inhumane Weapons Convention signed in Geneva (18 May).

1983   Agreement with Philippines for continued use of bases (1 June).

1984   Agreement with Soviet Union to expand and improve the 'Hot Line' (17 July).

1985   Agreement with Canada for new chain of ground radar stations across Canadian Arctic and northern Alaska to be known as North Warning System (18 Mar.).

1990   Treaty on the Final Settlement with Respect to Germany signed with East Germany, West Germany, France, Great Britain and Soviet Union (12 Sept.).

1991   Agreement with Philippines over US bases (27 Aug.). Defense pact signed with Kuwait (Sept.). START I agreement signed (31 July).

1992   North American Free Trade Association (NAFTA) agreement with Canada and Mexico (13 Aug.).

1993   START II agreement signed with President Yeltsin of Russia (3 Jan.).

1994   Agreement to open diplomatic liaison offices with Vietnam (May) following 1992 easing of economic embargo.

1995   Dayton Agreements hosted by US on future of Bosnia-Hercegovina.

Chronology of American overseas expansion (since 1853)

From the mid-nineteenth century America gradually became involved in overseas expansion and annexation, particularly in the Pacific. Key events have been:

1853   Commodore Matthew Perry sails US fleet into Tokyo Bay. Beginning of trading relations with Japan and increased US interest in Asia-Pacific region.

1867   Annexation of Midway Islands. Subsequently, the two islands (Sand Island and Eastern Island) under control of US Navy. Purchase of Alaska arranged for $7,200,000. Transferred to US (18 Oct.).

1872   Naval base established at Pago Pago on Samoa.

1893   Queen Liliuokalani deposed in Hawaii. Republic proclaimed (1894) with Sanford B. Dole as President. US marines aided overthrow of government in 1893 and Hawaii became an American protectorate (until annexed in 1898).

1898   Puerto Rico ceded by Spain (10 Dec.); Guam ceded (administered by US Navy, 1899–1950). US buys Philippines for $20 million. Annexation of Hawaii.

1899   Secretary of State John Hay proposed 'Open Door Policy' with regard to China. Agreement with Germany to divide Samoan Islands between them (2 Dec.). Britain withdraws its claims. US claims Wake Island (as trans-Pacific telephone cable station).

1900   Chiefs of Samoan Islands cede them to US; US Navy administers islands (until 1951). Congress formally accepts cession in 1929. Hawaii becomes a US Territory.

1903   The Canal Zone (surrounding strategic Panama Canal) is acquired.

1916   Treaty with Denmark (signed 4 Aug.) for purchase of Virgin Islands.

1917   Jones Act creates Territory of Puerto Rico (2 Mar.). US citizenship granted to Puerto Ricans. Virgin Islands purchased from Denmark for $25 million (31 Mar.).

1927   US citizenship granted to Virgin Islanders.

1941   Japan bombs Pearl Harbor. Rapid Japanese conquests in Pacific; Guam falls (7–13 Dec.).

1944   Guam recaptured (21 July–10 Aug.).

1947   US receives UN Trusteeship over Pacific Islands (18 July). These include Northern Marianas, Micronesia, Belau and the Marshall Islands.

1950   US Territory of Guam created (1 Aug.) under Department of Interior. Islanders become US citizens.

1951   Department of Interior takes over administration of Samoan Islands.

1952   Puerto Rico becomes Commonwealth (25 July) with own constitution (adopted 3 Mar.).

1959   Alaska becomes 49th state (3 Jan.). Hawaii becomes 50th state (21 Aug.).

1962   US Trust Territory of the Pacific placed under Department of Interior (7 May).

1976   Voters in Guam approve continued status as US Territory.

1977   US–Panamanian agreement to return Canal Zone to Republic of Panama by the year 2000.

1978   Northern Marianas become US Commonwealth.

1979   Virgin Islands reject home rule (6 Mar.). Federated States of Micronesia established as self-governing state.

1980   Grant of limited independence to Marshall Islands.

1981   Virgin Islanders reject home rule constitution in referendum (7,157 for; 4,821 against). Belau becomes self-governing.

1982   Voters in Guam favour Commonwealth status as opposed to statehood.

America and the League of Nations: A chronology

1916   President Wilson first suggests the need for a 'Peace League'.

1918   Wilson's 'Fourteen Points' includes the idea of an association of nations (Jan.)

1919   At Paris Peace Conference, 27 nations agree to Wilson's proposal for a League of Nations (Feb.). The Agreement or Covenant setting up the League is written into the Treaties of Versailles (28 June) and Saint-Germain (10 Sept.). Headquarters of League set up in Geneva. Albert Thomas, French Socialist, first director of the International Labour Organization, one of the League's committees; other committees established to deal with world health, communications, and education, not restricted to signatories of the Covenant. League begins allocation of mandates of former colonies to victorious powers and their allies. First signs of hostility to the Covenant in the United States – Wilson goes on pro-League tour of the United States (Sept.). United States Senate votes against amended League of Nations in two votes (Nov.).

1920   United States boycotts first meeting of the League (Jan.); membership of League finally rejected by Senate (Mar.).

1921   New US President Harding rejects the League of Nations (Apr.).

America and the birth of the United Nations: A chronology

1941   Atlantic Charter issued by US President Franklin D. Roosevelt and British Prime Minister Winston Churchill detailing eight points to 'base their hopes for a better future for the world' (14 Aug.).

1942   Declaration by United Nations signed by 26 nations in Washington, approving basic points of Atlantic Charter; first official use of name 'United Nations' (1 Jan.).

1943   Moscow Declaration on General Security signed by Britain, China, Soviet Union and United States, recognizing 'the necessity of establishing at the earliest practicable date a general international organization, based on the principle of sovereign equality' (30 Oct.).

1944   Dumbarton Oaks Conference in Washington, DC at which representatives of 39 nations discuss over three months proposals for establishing United Nations organization, agreeing on Security Council as executive branch of UN (21 Aug.).

1945   UN Charter approved by delegates of 50 nations at international conference in San Francisco (26 June). UN Charter goes into effect upon ratification by majority of nations, including Britain, China, France, Soviet Union, and United States (24 Oct.).

1946   Gift of $8,500,000 from US millionaire John D. Rockefeller Jr accepted by UN to buy 18 acres in New York City as site of permanent headquarters (14 Dec.).

Warfare and the Armed Services

Major wars since 1775

Note: Additional chronological material can be found in Section I, Political Chronology, pp. 1–53.

War of Independence, 1775–83

Otherwise known as the Revolutionary War, the great conflict in which the English colonies in North America became free of Great Britain and established themselves as the United States. The first shots of the war were fired on 19 April 1775 when British troops sent from Boston to destroy stores of the Massachusetts militia at Concord were opposed at Lexington. George Washington was appointed Commander-in-Chief of the rebels' Continental Army on 15 June 1775. An American attack on Canada failed, but in March 1776 the British were forced to evacuate Boston. The Americans issued their Declaration of Independence on 4 July 1776. In September 1776 the British occupied New York, and Washington retreated across the Delaware River into Pennsylvania. However, on 26 December 1776 he recrossed the river and defeated an army of Hessian auxiliaries at Trenton. In 1777 a British plan to divide the rebels by a threefold attack, with Burgoyne advancing from Canada, in cooperation with St Leger from Lake Ontario and Howe from New York, was a complete failure and resulted in Burgoyne's surrender at Saratoga on 17 October 1777. In 1778 the scope of the conflict widened as France declared war on Britain on 17 June. Spain declared war on 21 June 1779, and Britain declared war on Holland on 20 December 1780. British command of the seas was further challenged by the Armed Neutrality of the North formed by Russia, Sweden and Denmark in 1780. In 1781 General Cornwallis was besieged at Yorktown by Washington and Rochambeau on land and by the French fleet under de Grasse, and forced to surrender on 19 October. This ended any chance of a British suppression of the rebellion, but command of the seas was restored by Admiral Rodney's victory over de Grasse at the Battle of the Saints in the West Indies on 12 April 1782. Peace was concluded and the independence of the United States recognized by the treaty of Versailles signed on 3 September 1783.

War of 1812

War fought between Great Britain and the United States between 1812 and 1815 and often referred to in America as the Second War of Independence. Great Britain, in the course of her long war against Napoleonic France, had frequently disregarded American rights of neutrality and seized American ships trading with France. The destruction of American commerce – and the possibilities offered to the United States by the annexation of Canada and Florida (which belonged to Britain's ally Spain) – eventually forced an American declaration of war in June 1812. An American plan for a threefold attack on Canada failed, and a British force under General Brock forced the surrender of Detroit on 16 August 1812. In April 1813 the Americans captured and burnt Toronto, and in September defeated the British in the Battle of Lake Erie and recaptured Detroit. In August 1814 a force of 4,000 British veterans landed in Chesapeake Bay, defeated the Americans at Bladensburg and burnt parts of Washington. A peace treaty was signed at Ghent in Belgium on 24 December 1812, largely restoring the pre-war situation. Before news of the peace reached America, General Pakenham was killed on 8 January 1815 leading an unsuccessful British attack on New Orleans. The end of the Napoleonic Wars had effectively resolved the question of interference with trade and both sides had willingly concluded peace. Nonetheless the war was important for stimulating a greater degree of unity and self-identification within the United States and for ending her diplomatic dependence upon Europe.

Mexican–American War, 1846

War between the United States and Mexico, which broke out in 1846 after the American annexation of Texas (see Alamo). It was deeply unpopular in the Northern states because of the possibility it might lead to an increase in the territory of the slave-holding South and the whole conflict was known as 'Mr. Polk's War' after the then President. In September 1847 an American army, composed largely of untrained volunteers under General Winfield Scott, captured Mexico City and the Mexicans sued for peace. They recognized the United States' acquisition of present-day California, Arizona and New Mexico and the establishment of the Rio Grande River as the border of Texas. See Gadsden Purchase.

The American Civil War, 1861–65

The greatest conflict in American history, the Civil War began in April 1861 after the military forces of the secessionist Confederate States of America (q.v.) attacked one of the remaining federal military installations in the South – Fort Sumter in Charleston, South Carolina. The under-lying causes of the war were the dispute over slavery (which Northern political opinion wished to exclude from the Western Territories of the US and, latterly, abolish outright), and the tension over the relative importance of the two regions within the American Union. Beginning with South Carolina in December 1860, eleven states withdrew in response to the election of the first Republican President, Abraham Lincoln (q.v.), whom they feared was pro-abolition; a new confederation of Southern states was established in February 1861.

Despite the North's significant advantage in population and industrial resources, the Confederate military managed for four years to prevent the reconquest of the Southern states by the federal government. At the outset the US Army was relatively small – the President and Congress were forced to call for a million volunteers after the Confederates won the first engagement at Bull Run (Manassas) in northern Virginia in July 1861; whereas the Southern state militias had been organizing themselves since John Brown's raid upon Harper's Ferry in 1859. The Union's strategy throughout the war was to advance upon the South along its major waterways, principally those of the Yorktown peninsula in Virginia, to threaten the Confederate capital of Richmond, and the Tennessee and Mississippi, to isolate the West and Texas. Throughout the war Southern ports were closely blockaded by the US Navy.

Northern Virginia was ably defended by General Robert E. Lee (q.v.) who throughout 1862 out-fought his less dynamic Union opponent General George B. McClellan, even going so far as to invade Maryland, though he was stopped on 17 September at the Battle of Antietam in some of the bloodiest fighting of the war. President Lincoln dismissed McClellan for his failure to crush Lee; Union command eventually passed to General 'Fighting Joe' Hooker, who was no more successful, and operations in the Eastern theatre descended into a war of attrition. Lee gambled once more upon an invasion of the North to force Lincoln to seek peace; he invaded Pennsylvania but was defeated by Union forces under Major-General George G. Meade at Gettysburg (1–4 July 1863): thereafter the South never again threatened the North.

In the West the Union forces were more successful under the deter-mined General Ulysses S. Grant (q.v.). They captured western Tennes-see and most of the Mississippi valley; New Orleans had fallen in May 1862 and eventually the Confederate stronghold of Vicksburg was taken, also on 4 July 1863. President Lincoln then gave Grant command of all Union forces; during 1864 the latter engaged Lee in Virginia in some of the bloodiest fighting of the war, while his deputy General William T. Sherman secured Tennessee and then invaded Georgia. Sherman cap-tured and burnt Atlanta in November 1864 and pushed northwards into South Carolina, the heart of the Confederacy, devastating the land as he went. Meanwhile Grant's dogged pursuit of Lee eventually exhausted the Confederates and Lee surrendered at Appomattox Court House in western Virginia on 9 April 1865, effectively ending the war.

The conflict was significant for being the first recognizably 'modern' war, fought by mass conscripted armies (over a million men served in the Union forces), and for determining the question of the relationship between the individual states and the federal union. Henceforth it was an established fact that the several states had surrendered a measure of sovereignty when creating the United States of America in 1787–90 and that therefore they were not at liberty to secede. The abolition of slavery was also achieved; President Lincoln issued an Emancipation Proclamation on 1 January 1865 and the Thirteenth Amendment to the Constitution abolishing involuntary servitude was ratified in December 1865.

Spanish–American War, 1898–99

On 15 February 1898 the US battleship *Maine* was mined in Havana Harbor (with 260 killed). Responsibility was never firmly fixed, but Congress recognized the independence of Cuba (where Cuban rebels were fighting the Spanish colonial power). Spain declared war on the United States on 24 April. The US won the Battle of Manila Bay (1 May) and destroyed the Spanish fleet off Santiago, Cuba, on 3 July. By the Treaty of Paris, Spain ceded Guam and Puerto Rico, Cuba became independent (but under US military control until 1902) and America bought the Philippines for $20 million.

World War I, 1914–18

On 28 July 1914 Austria-Hungary declared war on Serbia, whom she blamed for the assassination of the Austrian heir to the throne a month earlier. Austria was supported by her ally Germany, but they were faced by the 'Entente' powers of Russia, France and Britain. The United States declared her neutrality on 5 August, but offered to mediate in the conflict. In late 1914 the Germans failed to capture the French capital, Paris, and on the Western Front the war settled into the deadlock of trench warfare, while in the East the Germans defeated the Russian invasion of Prussia. In 1915 the Entente powers unsuccessfully attempted to break the deadlock on the Western Front by expeditions to the Dardanelles and Salonika, while American political opinion began to move decisively against Germany because of her submarine attacks on Allied and neutral shipping on the high seas. On 7 May the British passenger ship *Lusitania* was sunk without warning; 114 American passengers were among the dead. US President Wilson demanded an apology and reparations, and Germany eventually agreed to abide by international law on maritime warfare. In 1916 both sets of combatants launched grand offensives on the Western Front, the Germans against Verdun and the Allies on the Somme, but failed to break the deadlock. At sea the Germans and British fought the inconclusive Battle of Jutland. The following year marked the turning point in the war. The Russian Revolutions of February and October 1917 eventually led to Russia's withdrawal (and capitulation to the Germans at the Treaty of Brest-Litovsk). On 3 February the United States broke off diplomatic relations with Germany, in response to Germany's adoption of unrestricted submarine warfare four days earlier. On 24 February the British Secret Service released the 'Zimmerman telegram', instructions from the German Foreign Minister to his Ambassador in Mexico to seek that country's entry into the war on the side of the Central Powers in return for those parts of the United States taken from Mexico after the 1846–48 war. The telegram pushed the US into a declaration of war against Germany on 2 April. An American Expeditionary Force under General Pershing arrived in France in June but was not yet ready to operate independently. On 8 January 1918 President Wilson proposed his 'Fourteen Points' for post-war reconstruction, including a League of Nations to guarantee peace. The Germans launched their last great offensive in the spring but this was halted, and in September the Allies, including over a million American troops, began their final offensive on the Somme which forced Germany to conclude an armistice on 11 November. Her allies, Austria and Turkey, had already given up the fight, the Austrians defeated in northern Italy and the Turks by the British in the Middle East. The American contribution, particularly her industrial might, had been decisive; and President Wilson's Fourteen Points dominated the Paris Peace Conference which led to the Treaty of Versailles on 28 June 1919 – the treaty which also established the League of Nations.

World War II, 1939–45

German forces invaded Poland on 1 September 1939, which led to declarations of war by Britain and France on 3 September. The United States formally declared its neutrality two days later, but as in World War I the balance of American opinion was firmly with the Allies; in November President Roosevelt signed a Neutrality Act which effectively allowed Britain and France to buy American weapons. The German invasion of Norway and Denmark in April 1940 and of the Low Countries in May, and the collapse of France in June, isolated Great Britain, but in the Battle of Britain the Luftwaffe failed to destroy the RAF and Hitler's plan to invade England was abandoned. The German airforce then resorted to bombing attacks on British cities (the 'Blitz'). In September the United States agreed to give 50 obsolete naval destroyers to Britain in return for leases on naval bases, effectively beginning the Lend-Lease military aid programme. For the next year Britain stood alone against Germany and her ally Italy, which had declared war on 10 June 1940, thus widening the war to include British and Italian forces in North Africa. In 1941 the war was vastly extended by the German attack on the Soviet Union on 22 June and the United States offered aid to the Russians as well. On 14 August President Roosevelt and Prime Minister Churchill issued the Atlantic Charter which set out the principles of freedom on which the Allied nations would fight the war. During October and November US naval forces skirmished with Germany's in the Atlantic, while the United States negotiated with Japan to resolve deep divisions over trade and Japan's invasion of China. On 7 December 1941, without warning, Japanese naval forces attacked the American base at Pearl Harbor, Hawaii, resulting in a US declaration of war the following day; to aid her Japanese ally, Germany (and Italy) declared war on America on 11 December. The following year was initially one of Allied reversals in the Pacific, as Japanese forces defeated the Americans, British and Dutch in the Philippines, Malaya and Indonesia (which in February provoked the internment of Japanese-Americans in the United States) but the tide was turned at the Battle of Midway in June. By early 1943 the German invaders of Russia had been defeated at Stalingrad (2 February) and by May Anglo-American armies had overcome the Italians and Germans in North Africa, leading to the invasion of Italy in July. The three Allied leaders, Roosevelt, Stalin and Churchill, met at Tehran in Iran in November 1943 to plan the invasion of Western Europe. On 6 June 1944 Anglo-American forces launched the largest seaborne invasion in history, landing in Normandy and opening the 'Second Front' in France. Through 1944 the Anglo-American airforces continuously attacked German cities and the Russians pushed the Germans out of Eastern Europe, reaching the Hungarian plain by the autumn. In the Pacific theatre American forces accelerated their 'island-hopping' advance towards Japan, which culminated in October in the largest naval engagement in history, the Battle of Leyte Gulf, which destroyed most of the Japanese navy and led to the recapture of the Philippines by July 1945. In the European theatre Germany itself was invaded from East and West, and American and Russian forces met at the River Elbe on 28 April 1945. The Germans surrendered unconditionally on 7 May, but the war against Japan continued as British forces advanced through Indo-China and the United States launched an unrestricted aerial and submarine offensive against the Japanese home islands, culminating in the first use of atomic bombs, dropped on Hiroshima (6 Aug.) and Nagasaki (9 Aug.). Japan surrendered on 14 August 1945. By her participation in the war, the United States emerged as the world's decisive economic, military and political power and the only major combatant whose homeland had not been severely damaged.

Korean War, 1950–53

North Korean troops invaded the South on 25 June 1950. The United Nations decided to intervene following an emergency session of the Security Council, which was being boycotted by the Soviet Union. The first US troops landed at Pusan airport on 1 July 1950. General MacArthur mounted an amphibious landing at Inchon on 15 September 1950, and Seoul was recaptured on 26 September. The advance of the UN forces into North Korea on 1 October 1950 led to the entry of China into the war on 25 November 1950. Seoul fell to the Chinese on 4 January 1951, but was retaken by UN forces on 14 March 1951. General MacArthur was relieved of his command on 11 April 1951 after expressing his desire to expand the war into China. Truce talks began on 10 July 1951, and an armistice was finally signed at Panmunjon on 27 July 1953. United States casualties included 33,699 dead, 103,284 wounded in action and 13,000 missing or taken prisoner (of whom 5,000 returned).

Vietnam War, 1959–75

Military conflict in South-East Asia, which in its widest sense extended from the surrender of the Japanese forces in Indo-China and the re-establishment of the French colonial regime in 1945 to the defeat of the Republic of South Vietnam by the communists in 1975. The French were expelled from Vietnam by the nationalist forces in 1954, following their military defeat at Dien Bien Phu, despite having received substantial American economic and military aid (granted to counter the support being given to the communist nationalists by the Chinese). At the Geneva Peace Conference the country was divided between the communist People's Republic of Vietnam north of the 17th parallel and the Republic of South Vietnam to the south. The division was temporary pending elections. The communists in South Vietnam (the Viet Cong) built up their strength and launched their first attack on the South Vietnamese armed forces on 8 July 1959 near Bien Hoa, killing two American advisers. A state of emergency was proclaimed in the south on 19 October 1961. After attacks on the USS *Maddox* and *Turner Joy*, the US Congress passed the Gulf of Tonkin resolution on 7 August 1964, giving President Johnson wide military powers in South Vietnam. The sustained bombing of North Vietnam by US aircraft (Operation 'Rolling Thunder') began on 7 February 1965. The first American combat troops landed at Da Nang on 8 March 1965 and engaged the Viet Cong on 15 June. On 30 January 1968, communist forces launched their Tet Offensive with heavy attacks on Saigon, Hue and 30 provincial capitals. On 31 March 1968 President Johnson announced the end of the bombing of the North, and on 13 May 1968 peace discussions began in Paris. On 25

January 1969 these discussions were transformed into a formal conference. American and South Vietnamese troops invaded Cambodia in 1970, and the South Vietnamese made an incursion into Laos in 1971. A new communist offensive against the South began on 30 March 1972, and this led to a resumption of American bombing of the North on 6 April. The last American ground combat units were withdrawn on 11 August 1972. American bombing was halted on 15 January 1973, and a peace agreement was signed in Paris on 27 January. Two years later, a North Vietnamese offensive, which began on 6 January, overran the South, and Saigon was occupied on 30 April 1975. The war, the longest in US history, cost 211,000 American lives. It was deeply unpopular, particularly among the young, economically ruinous to the United States, and caused a tremendous crisis of confidence in the political system.

The Gulf War, 1990–91

On 2 August 1990, Iraqi troops launched a surprise attack on Kuwait and invaded the country, which President Saddam Hussein then annexed on 7 August, and on 28 August declared it to be the 19th province of Iraq. The UN Security Council condemned the invasion and demanded the immediate withdrawal of the Iraqi troops. On 10 August, a similar declaration was made by the Arab League (only Libya and the Palestine Liberation Organization voted against the declaration). Due to the failure of diplomatic means, the UN voted for economic sanctions against Iraq (6 August) and the United States – in alliance with other countries – started to build up large military forces in the area. On 28 November, the UN Security Council authorized its member states to use force against the aggressors if Iraq did not withdraw its troops from Kuwait by 15 January 1991. After acquiring an absolute supremacy in the air within a matter of days, the US Air Force, together with its allies, bombed Iraqi positions and major cities for more than a month – carrying out saturation bombing missions. In response, Saddam Hussein launched 'Scud' air missiles on Israel and Saudi Arabia, had hundreds of thousands of tons of oil poured into the Persian Gulf, and set 500 Kuwaiti oil wells on fire. On 23 February, a land offensive was also launched and by 26 February Kuwait was fully liberated. On 28 February – after Iraq's total defeat – US President Bush ordered a cease-fire.

Summary of deaths in major conflicts, 1775–1973[1]

War of Independence	10,600
War of 1812	6,800
Mexican War	17,400
Civil War	806,000[2]

Spanish–American War	4,100
World War I	320,500
World War II	1,076,000
Korean War	157,500
Vietnam War	211,000

[1] Figures rounded to nearest hundred.
[2] Estimate includes deaths of Confederates in Union prisons.

Minor wars and military campaigns since 1890

In addition to the major conflicts listed in the previous section, the rise of American power in the late nineteenth century led to increasing intervention in more localized conflicts, especially in Latin America and the Caribbean where America acted as the 'regional gendarme'. Some of the more noteworthy have included the following:

1893   Marines land in Hawaii to help overthrow government. Hawaii then proclaimed a US protectorate.

1900   Marines and army help international forces relieve Peking during the Boxer Rebellion in China.

1903   US forces from *USS Nashville* halt the advancing Colombian army at Panama. US recognizes independence of Republic of Panama on 6 November 1903.

1904   Minor intervention in Dominican Republic to enforce debt repayments and administer customs from 1905 to 1907.

1906   Intervention in Cuba (lasted until 1909).

1912   Renewed intervention in Cuba (lasted until 1917). Marines land in Nicaragua to protect US interests (14 Aug.). A small contingent remained until 1925.

1914   Tampico incident in Mexico leads to landing of US forces. Veracruz bombarded. War averted by mediation of Argentina, Brazil and Chile and abdication of Mexican dictator, Victoriano Huerta.

1915   Military occupation of Haiti begins. Treaty makes Haiti effectively a US protectorate. Occupation lasts until troops withdrawn in 1934.

1916   Punitive expedition by General Pershing in Mexico against raids by Pancho Villa. US troops withdrawn when war with Germany became imminent.

1917   Marines occupy Cuba (lasted until 1923).

1919   Honduran ports occupied by US marines.

1924   US marines land in Honduras.

1926   US marines occupy Nicaragua until 1933 and organize the National Guard. Control of the National Guard becomes the cornerstone of political power in Nicaragua and the guarantor of the Somoza 'dynasty' for 45 years.

1932   US Navy on standby during the *matanza* in El Salvador.

1956   Suez crisis in Egypt leads to US Fleet evacuating Americans.

1957   US Fleet despatched to Eastern Mediterranean during Jordan crisis.

1958   US forces sent to aid of Lebanon. Troops land in Beirut in July to aid government of President Chamoun. All withdrawn by year end.

1962   US naval forces on alert in Cuban Missile Crisis (q.v.), acting to 'quarantine' island.

1965   Dominican civil war. On 28 April 1965, 400 US marines were sent in to prevent a left-wing takeover, and during the next month a further 24,000 American troops were landed. A cease-fire was signed on 6 May and at the end of May an Inter-American Peacekeeping Force was formed to keep the warring factions apart.

1983   Lebanon civil war. Marines join international peacekeeping force in September 1983. Marine compound in Beirut bombed on 23 October 1983 with loss of 241 marines. Contingent ordered to be withdrawn, 7 February 1984.

1983   Invasion of Grenada. On 19 October 1983 the army took control in Grenada after a power struggle led to the murder of Prime Minister Maurice Bishop. On 21 October the Organization of Eastern Caribbean States appealed to the United States to intervene and on 25 October US marines and airborne troops invaded Grenada, together with token contingents from six Caribbean countries. Resistance from the Grenadian army and 700 Cuban construction workers was overcome and order restored by 27 October 1983.

1989   Panama invasion. On 15 December 1989 the corrupt President Noriega of Panama declared that a state of war existed between his country and the United States. An off-duty US marine, Lieutenant Robert Paz, was killed at a road-block on 16 December. American forces began the invasion of Panama, codenamed Operation Just Cause, on 20 December. Fighting ended on 31 December. President Noriega took refuge in the Vatican embassy in Panama City, but gave himself up to US forces on 3 January 1990.

1991   Somalia civil war. Following protracted civil war, which had originally begun in 1981, law and order broke down completely. Following widespread famine, a US-led UN force landed in Somalia in December 1991. The last US peacekeepers left in March 1994.

1995   Dayton Peace Accord commits US troops to Bosnia.

The Armed Forces: Chronology of internal events to the end of the Vietnam War

(For wars, see separate list, pp. 239–46.)

1775	Birth of the US Army (14 June) when 2nd Continental Congress appoints committee to draw up rules for the New England Army. George Washington appointed Commander-in-Chief by Congress (15 June). Congress calls for purchase of naval vessels (13 Oct.). Marine Corps founded (10 Nov.).
1776	Congress votes to expand army to 88 infantry battalions (Oct.). A further 22 battalions authorized (Dec.).
1789	US Army officially established by Congress.
1790	First authorizations by Congress for US Coast Guard.
1794	Congress authorizes construction of frigates to deal with Barbary Pirates. War Department established (one of first four Cabinet departments established under Washington).
1798	Creation of Navy Department (Apr.) under a Secretary of the Navy with Cabinet rank.
1802	US Military Academy of West Point founded.
1813	Congress creates embryonic General Staff.
1817–25	Lasting administrative structure established by Secretary of War John C. Calhoun.
1845	Naval School established at Fort Severn, Annapolis, Maryland (renamed US Naval Academy, 1850).
1865	Peak strength of one million men at climax of Civil War. In all, 2,500,000 men served at some time in Civil War. Demobilization reduces regular strength to 45,000 (1869).
1898	Spanish–American War creates need for army capable of fighting overseas.
1899	Series of modernizing reforms begun under Secretary of War Elihu Root. Chief of Staff (heading a general staff) replaces commanding general and made responsible to Secretary of War. General Staff Corps established. Establishment of Army War College (1901). Total modernization of school system.
1903	Dick Act reorganized the National Guard as the Organized Militia.
1916	National Defense Act. Army and National Guard enlarged. Reserve Corps added to Army. Reserve Officers Training Corps set up.
1918	Army Air Service established (under aegis of US Army).
1920	Demobilized Army reduced to 202,000 men (from peak 3,685,000 in World War I). National Defense Act confirms the three components of the Army: the Regular Army, the National Guard and the Organized Reserve.

1926	Army Air Corps formed (until 1941 when becomes Army Air Forces).
1946	Wartime army structure dismantled. Army Service Forces abolished. Power of General Staff restored.
1947	Department of Defense established (26 July) as National Defense Establishment. Name changed to Department of Defense (10 Aug. 1949). Secretaries of Army, Navy and Air Force are subordinate to Secretary of Defense. US Air Force established as an independent military service (18 Sept. 1947).
1954	Eisenhower signs Bill creating US Air Force academy (1 Apr.). First cadets enter Lowry Air Force Base, Denver (11 July 1955). Permanent home created north of Colorado Springs.
1956	Establishment of CONARC (Continental Army Command).
1962	Two new commands created; Army Material Command and Combat Developments Command.
1973	Further reorganization creates Training and Doctrine Command, and Force Command. New era begins with withdrawal from Vietnam (March) and ending of the draft (1 July).

The Cold War, nuclear rivalry and detente, 1942–91

The Cold War: a background note

The term was first used in Congress on 12 March 1947 during a debate on the Truman Doctrine (q.v.). Europe was at this time effectively divided into Allied and Soviet spheres of interest following the rejection by the Eastern European states of American financial aid offered under the Marshall Plan (q.v.) and the spread of communist regimes in these countries. The establishment of NATO (1949) and the signing of the Warsaw Pact treaty (1955) completed the division of the continent into two hostile military alliances. The Cold War was marked by a series of political crises around the globe involving the allies of the USSR and US, notably the Berlin Air Lift of 1948, the communist takeover of China in 1949, the Korean War of 1950–53, the Russian invasion of Hungary in 1956 and of Czechoslovakia in 1968, and the Cuban Missile Crisis (q.v.) of 1962. Western outrage at these examples of Soviet expansionism were tempered by the British and French involvement in the Suez Crisis of 1956 and the American participation in the Vietnam War (q.v.) in the 1960s and 1970s. However, from the early 1970s onwards both superpowers attempted to reach an accommodation over the limitation of strategic nuclear weapons, which produced the two SALT treaties of 1972 and 1979 and the INF treaty of 1987 (see SALT and START).

Despite the Reagan Administration's initial hostility towards Russia, which produced a massive American rearmament, by the late 1980s the Cold War had been effectively ended by a new political understanding reached with Soviet President Gorbachev.

America and the nuclear age: Chronology

1942   Manhattan Project begins work on the production of an atomic bomb (June).

1945   The first successful explosion of an experimental atomic device takes place at Alamogordo, New Mexico (16 July).
US Air Force B–29 bomber, Enola Gay, drops the first atomic bomb, nicknamed 'Little Boy', on the Japanese city of Hiroshima (6 Aug.). A second atomic bomb, nicknamed 'Fat Man', is dropped on Nagasaki (9 Aug.).

1946   The United States carries out the first nuclear test in peacetime at Bikini Atoll in the Marshall Islands (1 July). President Truman signs the Atomic Energy Act, restricting exchange of information with other nations on atomic energy (1 Aug.).

1949   The Soviet Union explodes an atomic bomb, ending the American monopoly of nuclear weapons (29 Aug.).

1952   Great Britain tests its first atomic bomb (3 Oct.). The United States explodes the first hydrogen device at Eniwetok lagoon in the Marshall Islands (1 Nov.).

1953   The Soviet Union tests its first hydrogen bomb in Siberia (12 Aug.).
Atoms for Peace: President Eisenhower announces a plan at the UN General Assembly for a pool of fissile material to be available for peaceful purposes (8 Dec.).

1954   Massive Retaliation: doctrine propounded by Secretary of State John Foster Dulles (12 Jan.). The USS Nautilus, the first American atomic-powered submarine, is commissioned (30 Sept.).

1955   At the Geneva summit, President Eisenhower puts forward his 'open skies' proposal (21 July).

1957   The UN International Atomic Energy Agency is established (29 July). The first British hydrogen bomb is exploded near Christmas Island (15 Aug.). The Soviet Union announces the successful launch of an intercontinental ballistic missile (26 Aug.).

1960   France explodes its first atomic device in the Sahara (13 Feb.). A Polaris missile from the USS George Washington is successfully fired underwater for the first time (20 July). The first Polaris nuclear submarine, USS George Washington, becomes operational (15 Nov.). US Secretary of Defense Robert McNamara announces new strategy of 'flexible response' (16 June). Cuban Missile Crisis (22–28 Oct.) (*see* p. 314). President Kennedy meets British Prime Minister Harold Macmillan at Nassau in the Bahamas and agrees to make US Polaris missiles available to Great Britain for use with British warheads (18–20 Dec.).

1964   The first Chinese atomic explosion takes place at Lop Nor in Sinkiang Province (16 Oct.).

1965   US Secretary of Defense Robert McNamara announces that the United States would rely on threat of 'assured destruction' to deter a Soviet attack (18 Feb.).

1966   NATO establishes the Nuclear Defense Affairs Committee (all members except France, Iceland and Luxembourg) and the Nuclear Planning Group (all members except France and Iceland).

1967   The first Chinese hydrogen bomb test is carried out (17 June). NATO adopts a strategy of 'flexible response', based on maintaining the capability of threatening a balanced and flexible range of responses, conventional and nuclear, to all levels of aggression (14 Dec.).

1968   France explodes its first hydrogen bomb (25 Aug.).

1969   President Nixon announces the decision to deploy a ballistic missile defence system, 'Safeguard' (14 Mar.).

1970   The first successful underwater launch of a Poseidon missile is accomplished from the *USS James Madison* (3 Aug.).

1974   US Secretary of Defense James Schlesinger announces a new doctrine of 'limited strategic strike options' in the event of a nuclear war (10 Jan.). India explodes its first atomic device at Pokharan in the Rajasthan desert (18 May).

1977   The United States announces that it has tested an Enhanced Radiation Weapon or 'neutron bomb' (7 July).

1978   President Carter announces the postponement of a decision on the production and deployment of the neutron bomb (7 Apr.).

1979   A major nuclear accident in the United States at Three Mile Island, near Harrisburg, Pennsylvania (28 Mar.). NATO announces its intention to modernize its long-range theatre nuclear systems by the deployment of 464 ground-launched cruise missiles and 108 Pershing II medium-range ballistic missiles in Europe (12 Dec.).

1980   President Carter signs Presidential Directive 59, emphasizing the possibility of flexible, controlled retaliation against a range of military and political targets in a prolonged nuclear war (25 July). The US Department of Defense announces its intention to build an Advanced Technology, or 'stealth', bomber with a greatly reduced radar detectability (22 Aug.).

The US nuclear arsenal (from the Cuban Missile Crisis to the fall of the Soviet Union)

	1963	1968	1976	1980	1985
Intercontinental Ballistic Missiles (ICBM)	424	1,054	1,054	1,054	1,026
Strategic Long-Range Ballistic Missiles (SLBM)	224	656	656	656	640
Long-Range Bombers (LRB)	630	600	373	338	241

America, disarmament and detente: Chronology

1957   Adam Rapacki, foreign minister of Poland, proposes creation of a nuclear-free zone in central Europe. The plan is rejected by NATO (2 Oct.).

1959   The Ten-Power Committee on Disarmament established (7 Sept.).

1962   The first meeting in Geneva of the Eighteen Nation Disarmament Committee (14 Mar.).

1963   A 'Hot Line' agreement is reached between the United States and the Soviet Union (5 Apr.). The Partial Test-Ban Treaty, outlawing nuclear tests in the atmosphere and outer space and under water is concluded (5 Aug.).

1964   Statements by the United States and the USSR agreeing to the reduction of fissionable materials production (20 Apr.).

1967   A treaty banning nuclear weapons in outer space is opened for signature in London, Moscow and Washington (27 Jan.). The Treaty of Tlatelolco, prohibiting nuclear weapons in Latin America, is opened for signature in Mexico City (14 Feb.).

1968   The Non-Proliferation Treaty is opened for signature in London, Moscow and Washington (1 July). Treaty prohibits nuclear-weapon states from transferring or assisting in the manufacture of nuclear weapons and prohibits non-nuclear-weapon states from acquiring or manufacturing them. Non-nuclear-weapon states undertake to conclude safeguards agreements with the International Atomic Energy Agency to prevent diversion of nuclear energy from peaceful uses to nuclear weapons.

1969   Eight new members join the 18-nation Disarmament Committee, which is renamed the Conference of the Committee on Disarmament (26 Aug.). Five additional members join on 1 January 1975. Preparatory negotiations on Strategic Arms

Limitation Talks (SALT) between the United States and the Soviet Union begin in Helsinki (17 Nov.).

1970   Strategic Arms Limitation Talks are opened in Vienna (16 Apr.).

1971   The Sea-Bed Treaty prohibiting the emplacement of nuclear weapons on the sea-bed is opened for signature in London, Moscow and Washington (11 Feb.). US–Soviet Hot Line modernization agreement (30 Sept.). US–Soviet nuclear accidents agreement, including notification of unauthorized detonation of nuclear weapons and advance warning of planned missile launches extending beyond the national territory (30 Sept.).

1972   US–Soviet agreement on the prevention of incidents involving naval vessels on the high seas and the flight of military aircraft over the high seas (25 May). US–Soviet SALT antiballistic missile agreement, limiting deployment of ABM systems to two areas in each country, with no more than 100 launchers and 100 interceptor missiles in each deployment area (26 May). US–Soviet SALT interim agreement on limitation of strategic arms (26 May). In September 1977 the United States and the USSR state that although the interim agreement is due to expire on 3 October 1977, they intend to refrain from any actions incompatible with its provisions. US–Soviet agreement on the basic principles of relations between the two countries, including doing their utmost to avoid military confrontations and to prevent the outbreak of nuclear war (29 May). US–Soviet memorandum of understanding regarding the establishment of a Standing Consultative Commission to promote objectives and implementation of nuclear accidents agreement of 1971 and SALT agreements of 1972.

1973   US–Soviet agreement on the basic principles of negotiations on the further limitation of strategic offensive arms (21 June). US–Soviet agreement on the prevention of nuclear war (22 June).

1974   A Protocol to the US–Soviet SALT ABM agreement, limiting ABM deployment to a single area, is agreed to (3 July). A US–Soviet Threshold Test-Ban Treaty is signed, limiting underground nuclear tests (3 July). The Vladivostok Accord between the United States and the Soviet Union, setting out the framework for future negotiations on controlling the strategic arms race, is reached (24 Nov.).

1976   A US–Soviet Treaty restricting nuclear explosions for peaceful purposes is ratified (28 May).

1979   A SALT II agreement is signed by the United States and Soviet Union, restricting numbers of strategic offensive weapons (18 June). The treaty establishes a ceiling of 2,400 on all types of strategic delivery vehicles, to be reduced to 2,250 by the end of

1981 (18 June). The US Congress refuses to ratify the agreement following the Soviet invasion of Afghanistan in December 1979.

1984   US–Soviet agreement to expand and improve the operation of the Hot Line (17 July).

1987   US–Soviet treaty on the elimination of intermediate nuclear forces (INF) signed in Washington (8 Dec.).

1991   US–Soviet START agreement (30 July). Not ratified by US Senate.

1993   START II agreement between President Bush and President Yeltsin (1 Jan.).

The Central Intelligence Agency

An agency of the US government, headed by a director appointed by the President with Senate approval, that works under the National Security Council to co-ordinate intelligence activities in the interest of national security. The CIA evaluates intelligence information provided by the Army, Navy, Air Force, State Department and other intelligence-gathering civilian and military agencies. This information is disseminated among various units of the national government to aid the formulation of foreign and defence policy. The CIA also engages in world-wide intelligence-gathering activities. The Congressional Charter establishing the CIA specifically prohibits the use of its resources for internal surveillance. As a result of alleged breaches of the charter, Congress has created a select committee to oversee CIA operations.

CIA Directors

Director	Served
Adm. Sidney W. Souers	1946
Gen. Hoyt S. Vandenberg	1946–47
Adm. Roscoe H. Hillenkoetter	1947–50
Gen. Walter Bedell Smith	1950–53
Allan W. Dulles	1953–61
John A. McCone	1961–65
Adm. William F. Raborn Jr	1965–66
Richard Helms	1966–73
James R. Schlesinger	1973
William E. Colby	1973–76
George Bush	1976–77
Adm. Stansfield Turner	1977–81
William J. Casey	1981–87
William H. Webster	1987–91
Robert M. Gates	1991–93
R. James Woolsey	1993–95
John M. Deutch	1995–96

SECTION FIVE

Biographies

Abzug, Bella (1920–):   Politician; born Bella Savitsky. Practised law privately before being elected in 1970 to the US House of Representatives from New York City on an openly antiwar platform. Served two terms; chaired the subcommittee on government information and was assistant Democratic whip under Speaker Tip O'Neill. A strong advocate of women's rights and freedom of information, she launched official investigations into illegal government surveillance of minority groups. Co-founder in 1971 of the National Women's Political Caucus. Retired from the House to campaign unsuccessfully for the Democratic Party nomination for the US Senate from New York in 1976 and the following year ran for mayor of New York City. Appointed co-chair of the National Advisory Committee for Women, but dismissed by President Carter in 1979 for criticising a reduction in federal funding for women's programmes.

Acheson, Dean (1893–1971):   Statesman. As Secretary of State from 1949 to 1953 he played a key role in establishing NATO and in formulating American policy during the Korean War (q.v.). Attacked by Senator McCarthy and his supporters for being weak on communism.

Adams, John (1735–1826):   2nd President of the United States, 1797–1801. Delegate to the Continental Congress, 1774–77. Served as Commissioner to France, 1778–79. Drafted Massachusetts Constitution, 1779. Served again as diplomat in Europe, 1780–88. First envoy to Britain, 1785. A Federalist, he served as Vice-President under Washington for two terms. His term of office was overshadowed by factional intrigues. His son was John Quincy Adams (q.v.).

Adams, John Quincy (1767–1848):   6th President of the United States, 1825–29. Son of the 2nd President, John Adams, John Quincy Adams provides the only example of an American President whose father also held that office. He had previously negotiated the peace treaty between the United States and Great Britain after the War of 1812. He entered the White House with no political party and little real popular support.

Adams, Samuel (1722–1803):   Leader of the revolution. Helped organize Sons of Liberty, 1765 (to oppose Stamp Act) and the Boston Tea Party, 1773. Delegate to Continental Congress, 1774–82. Signed Declaration of Independence, 1776. Subsequently Lieutenant-Governor (1789–93) then Governor (1793–97) of Massachusetts.

Addams, Jane (1860–1935):   Pacifist and social reformer. Founder of Hull House, Chicago (the first settlement house). First woman President of National Conference of Charities and Corrections (1909). Shared 1931 Nobel Peace Prize.

Agnew, Spiro (1918–96):   Vice-President of the United States, 1969–73. Republican politician, distinguished only as Nixon's (q.v.) surprise running-mate (chosen to secure the Southern vote) and also for his forced resignation in 1973 over his financial affairs.

Albright, Madeleine (1937–):   Nominated in December 1996 as the first woman Secretary of State by President Clinton. A Czech-born refugee from communism who served as Ambassador to the United Nations, 1992–96. Hard-working and outspoken, but something of an unknown quantity as a strategic thinker. At the United Nations she had urged UN involvement in Somalia, air attacks on Bosnian-Serb installations and vetoed the reappointment of Boutros Ghali as UN Secretary General.

Allen, Richard (1760–1831):   Born a slave in Philadelphia, Allen founded the Bethel African Methodist Episcopal Church, 1794, the first black religious denomination in the United States.

Anthony, Susan Brownell (1820–1906):   Campaigner for women's rights. Co-founder, with Elizabeth Cady Stanton (q.v.), of the National Woman Suffrage Association, 1869 (subsequently President, 1892–1900). Her trial (after she was arrested for voting in 1872) gave much publicity to the NWSA. Also advocated temperance and abolition.

Arthur, Chester (1829–86):   21st President of the United States, 1881–85. Formerly Vice-President to his Republican predecessor James Garfield, his Administration was dominated by the question of civil service reform. He was primarily a machine politician from New York who was nicknamed 'the Gentleman Boss'. His refusal of the nomination in 1884 was due to illness (unknown to his supporters he had Bright's disease).

Austin, Stephen Fuller (1793–1836):   Pioneer of Texas settlement (establishing first settlement on Brazos River in 1821). Led demands for independence from Mexico. First Secretary of State, 1836, in independent Texas Republic. The state capital is named after him.

Baker, James Addison (1930–):   US Secretary of the Treasury, 1985–88, under Reagan. Co-chairman of the campaign to elect George Bush president. Secretary of State, 1989–August 1992. Faced a major test with the Gulf War of 1991 (see p. 246).

Baruch, Bernard (1870–1965):   Long-serving adviser to US Presidents (from Woodrow Wilson to Kennedy). A key figure in planning the development and control of atomic energy.

Beecher, Henry Ward (1813–87): Reforming pastor at Plymouth Congregational Church, Brooklyn, New York for 40 years after 1847. Popular advocate of abolition and the cause of women's rights. Highly publicized trial for adultery (1874–75) but no verdict reached. Brother of Harriet Beecher Stowe, author of *Uncle Tom's Cabin.*

Blaine, James Gillespie (1830–93): Republican politician. US Secretary of State, 1881, 1889–92. Speaker of the House, 1869–75. Republican presidential candidate, 1884, but defeated partly because of backlash in New York where Democrats had been accused (by one of his supporters) of 'rum, Romanism and rebellion'.

Bond, (Horace) Julian (1940–): Black activist, politician and lawyer. Co-founder of the Student Nonviolent Coordinating Committee (SNCC) in 1960 and subsequently its communications director. Elected to the Georgia State Assembly in 1965, but refused his seat by the legislature because of SNCC's declaration that US involvement in the Vietnam War violated international law. Twice re-elected and refused admission until the US Supreme Court ruled in his favour in 1966; served in the Georgia legislature until 1987. Was nominated for vice-president on the (unsuccessful) ticket of Eugene McCarthy (q.v.) at the Democratic National Convention in 1968 but withdrew his name because he was under the constitutionally specified minimum age. Ran unsuccessfully for the US House of Representatives in 1986.

Boone, Daniel (1734–1820): Famous early Kentucky explorer and Indian fighter. Pioneered the 'Wilderness Road' through the Cumberland Gap. Boonesborough (Kentucky) was built by him, 1775.

Booth, John Wilkes (1838–65): Shakespearean actor who assassinated President Lincoln, 1865. Wilkes was himself killed twelve days later near Port Royal, Virginia.

Bradley, Omar Nelson (1893–1981): World War II military commander. Led US ground forces in D-Day Normandy landing, June 1944, then led 12th Army Group in conquest of German-occupied western Europe. US Army Chief of Staff, 1948–49, subsequently first chairman of Joint Chiefs of Staff, 1949–53.

Brandeis, Louis Dembitz (1856–1941): A liberal-inclined Associate Justice of the Supreme Court, 1916–39. Famous for his liberal dissent to the conservative judgments of the Court. A key figure of the New Deal era.

Breckinridge, John Cabell (1821–75):   Kentucky Democrat politician. Became youngest Vice-President, 1857–61. Representative (1851–55), subsequently Senator (1861) for Kentucky. Opposed Lincoln's war policy, becoming a Confederate general (1862–64) and Confederate Secretary of War, 1865.

Brown, John (1800–59):   Abolitionist who led the raid on Pottawatomie Creek, Kansas, in 1856 (killing five pro-slavery settlers). Subsequently helped capture Harpers Ferry, Virginia, on 16 October 1859 in the hope of starting a slave revolt. After capture and trial he was hanged on 2 December 1859.

Bruce, Blanche Kelso (1841–98):   First black to complete full term as Senator (as a Republican) for Mississippi, 1875–81. Born a slave near Farmville, Virginia. Register of US Treasury, 1881–85, 1897–98.

Bryan, William Jennings (1860–1925):   Democrat politician. Advocated free coinage of silver (famous for his 'Cross of Gold' speech at 1896 Democratic convention). Unsuccessful Democrat candidate in 1896, 1900 and 1908 presidential elections. As Secretary of State under Woodrow Wilson, he opposed US involvement in World War I (resigning in protest at Wilson's warnings to Germany over submarine attacks).

Buchanan, James (1791–1868):   15th President of the United States, 1857–61. During his Administration seven Southern states seceded from the United States over the issue of the abolition of slavery, to form the Confederate States of America. Ironically, he had been elected as a president who could hold the nation together over the slavery question. He had earlier sought the presidential nomination in 1844, 1848 and 1852. Elected with less than a majority of the popular vote, he defeated John C. Frémont (first candidate of the new Republican Party), the Whig Millard Fillmore and a 'know-nothing' candidate. His moderate views alienated extremists in both North and South.

Buchanan, Pat (Patrick Joseph) (1938–):   Politician. After a career in political journalism, served as speechwriter to Presidents Nixon and Ford and as director of White House communications in the Reagan Administration, 1985–87. Campaigned unsuccessfully for the Republican Party nomination for President, 1992 and 1996, as the candidate of the conservative Right.

Bunche, Ralph Johnson (1904–71):   Diplomat who mediated in 1948–49 Arab–Israeli conflict. United Nations Under-Secretary of State, 1955–71. First black American to be awarded Nobel Peace Prize, 1950.

Burr, Aaron (1756–1836): Democratic-Republican politician. The 3rd Vice-President, 1801–05 (the US House of Representatives having decided on Jefferson after a tie vote). Earlier Attorney General for New York, 1789–90 and US Senator, 1791–97. Killed Alexander Hamilton in a duel, 1804. Organized expedition against Spanish colonies and Mexico. Indicted for treason (for plotting to create a separate western Empire) but acquitted, 1807.

Bush, George Herbert Walker (1924–): 41st President of the United States, 1989–93. Republican politician. Gained lengthy experience as Vice-President, 1981–89, serving under Reagan (q.v.). The first Vice-President to be elected President since Martin Van Buren in 1836. Inherited Reagan's legacy of massive budget deficit, a drugs crisis and external problems in Panama. Bush ordered the December 1989 invasion of Panama to overthrow the Noriega regime and seize the dictator. Defeated by Democrat Bill Clinton in November 1992 presidential election.

Calhoun, John Caldwell (1782–1850): 7th Vice-President of the United States (and the first to resign office). Democratic Representative, South Carolina, 1811–17 (later Senator, 1832–43). Secretary of War, 1817–25. Vice-President, 1825–32. Secretary of State, 1844–45. Resigned as Vice-President, 1832, to lead nullification (q.v.) fight against President Jackson. Opposed the Mexican War and the Compromise of 1850.

Carmichael, Stokely (1941–): West-Indian born radical student activist. Emigrated to the United States from Trinidad in 1951. Joined the Student Nonviolent Coordinating Committee (SNCC) at university. Participated in the civil rights movement as a 'Freedom Rider' in 1961, exposing segregation on interstate transportation in the South, and in 1964 co-founded the Lowndes County Freedom Organization (see p. 104) during SNCC's voter registration campaign in Alabama. Became chairman of SNCC in 1966 but, increasingly frustrated with the integrationist strategy of Martin Luther King (q.v.), espoused the separatist doctrine of 'Black Power'. Abandoned SNCC in 1968 and travelled abroad, widely condemning US intervention in Vietnam, before emigrating to Guinea in West Africa. Co-founded the All-African People's Revolutionary Party and adopted the name Kwame Toure.

Carnegie, Andrew (1835–1919): One of the great philanthropists of modern America. A Scottish-born industrialist who developed Carnegie Steel Company. His fortune helped provide for 2,500 public libraries in English-speaking countries.

Carraway, Hattie Wyatt (1878–1950): Democratic politician. Achieved fame on appointment in November 1931 to US Senate (Democrat,

Arkansas) on the death of her husband. Elected as first woman to Senate, January 1932. Re-elected (for full terms) 1932 and 1938.

Carter, James Earl (Jimmy) (1924–):   39th President of the United States, 1977–81. Democrat Senator for Georgia, 1962–66. Elected Governor of Georgia 1971. Defeated Ford (q.v.) in presidential election, 1976. Negotiated Panama Canal Treaty, treaty between Egypt and Israel at Camp David and the unratified SALT II. Weakened by bad relations with Congress, failure to surmount world oil crisis and economic recession. Bungled rescue attempt of American Embassy hostages in Iran contributed to defeat by Reagan (q.v.) in presidential election, 1980.

Chase, Salmon Portland (1808–73):   Republican politician from Ohio. As 6th Chief Justice of the United States (1864–73) presided over 1868 impeachment trial of Andrew Johnson. Played key role financing Union expenses as Lincoln's Secretary of the Treasury, 1861–64. Earlier he had opposed Compromise of 1850 and Kansas-Nebraska Act.

Chavez, Cesar Estrada (1927–93):   Leading trade union organizer for Mexican-American migrant farm workers. Born in Arizona, he forced producers to agree to union contracts after nation-wide grape and lettuce boycotts in the 1960s and 1970s.

Christopher, Warren (1926–):   Appointed US Secretary of State in 1993. A lawyer and diplomat, he served as Deputy Secretary of State under President Carter. He was an adviser to Bill Clinton during his 1992 presidential campaign and acted as co-director of President Clinton's transition team. Played key role in Middle East peace process and in negotiations to end war in Bosnia. Retired from office, 1996.

Clark, William (1770–1838):   Joint explorer (with Meriwether Lewis) of the newly acquired Louisiana Territory (1804–06). Later Governor of Missouri Territory (1813–20). Younger brother of George Rogers Clark (1752–1818), frontiersman and revolutionary hero.

Clay, Henry (1777–1852):   Unsuccessful Whig presidential candidate, 1824, 1832 and 1844. Long-serving Representative and Senator from Kentucky. Led 'war hawks' in 1812. Secretary of State, 1825–29. Key role mediating 1820 Missouri Compromise and also sponsored Compromise of 1850.

Cleaver, (Leroy) Eldridge (1935–):   Radical black activist and author. After an early life spent in prison for violent crimes, became a follower of Malcolm X (q.v.) and subsequently 'minister of information' for the

Black Panther Party (see p. 104). Arrested following Martin Luther King's (q.v.) assassination in 1968, he absconded and fled abroad to Algiers where he established an international section of the Party. Returned to the United States of his own volition in 1975 and entered a plea-bargain with the authorities to avoid a charge of attempted murder, reportedly becoming a born-again Christian. Published his autobiography *Soul on Ice* (1968) describing the powerlessness of contemporary black life.

Cleveland, Grover (1837–1908):   22nd President (1885–89) and 24th President of the United States (1893–97). A Democrat, his two Administrations were separated by that of his Republican opponent Benjamin Harrison. Cleveland was the only President in American history to serve two non-consecutive terms in office. He was the first Democrat to be elected after the Civil War. His career included being Governor of New York (1883–84) where he attacked Tammany Hall corruption. Elected as a champion of honesty and reform (aided by the Mugwumps (q.v.), reform-minded Republicans). Frustrated in office by Republican-dominated Senate. His second Administration inherited the 1893 financial panic (Cleveland forced the repeal of the Sherman Silver Purchase Act) and the problem of the 1890 Chicago Pullman strike (his despatch of federal troops alienated the labour vote). With continuing economic recession, the 1896 Democratic convention refused him a third term.

Clinton, De Witt (1769–1828):   New York politician. Nephew of George Clinton (q.v.). Unsuccessfully contested presidency, 1812, as Federalist and Peace Party candidate. Three times Mayor of New York City (1803–07, 1810–11, 1813–14). Leading advocate of Erie Canal (opened by him in 1825), linking Hudson River with the Great Lakes.

Clinton, George (1739–1812):   Democratic-Republican politician. Delegate to Continental Congress, 1775–76. Brigadier General of Militia in War of Independence, 1776–77. First (and long-serving) State Governor of New York, 1777–95 and again 1801–04. Served as 4th Vice-President of the United States, under Jefferson and Madison, 1805–12.

Clinton, William Jefferson (Bill) (1946–):   42nd President of the United States, having defeated George Bush in the November 1992 presidential elections. Inaugurated January 1993. Governor of Arkansas 1979–80 and 1983–92. His immediate policy concerns as his Administration began were the economy, the health-care system and foreign trade. His first Administration suffered several setbacks – the failure of health-care reform, the advent of the right-wing republican 'Contract with America', the widespread mid-term Democratic losses of 1994 and the continuing allegations arising from the Whitewater affair. His wife, Hillary, played an important political role. Re-elected in November 1996 (defeating Republican Bob Dole).

Coolidge, (John) Calvin (1872–1933):   30th President of the United States, 1923–29. Massachusetts Republican state legislative member, 1912–15, Lieutenant Governor, 1916–18, Governor, 1918. Elected as Harding's Vice-President in 1920. Succeeded to the Presidency on Harding's death, August 1923, going on to win the 1924 presidential election. Conducted *laissez-faire* policy domestically and non-intervention abroad. Declined nomination for further term, 1928. Apparent prosperity of Coolidge era exposed as illusory by the Wall Street Crash seven months after he left office.

Crazy Horse (*c.* 1844–77):   Sioux Indian chief. Leader of the Sioux War of 1876–77. Led massacre of George Custer (q.v.) and his troops in Battle of the Little Big Horn.

Custer, George Armstrong (1839–76):   Civil War soldier who rose to Brigadier General at the age of 23. His disastrous cavalry attack on the Sioux Indians, led by Crazy Horse and Sitting Bull, at the Battle of the Little Big Horn on 25 June 1876 (Custer's Last Stand) killed both Custer himself and all his 225-strong column.

Dallas, George Mifflin (1792–1864):   Democratic politician who served as 11th Vice-President of the United States (1845–49) under James Knox Polk. Mayor of Philadelphia, 1829. Subsequently Democrat Senator for Pennsylvania, 1831–33, Minister to Russia, 1837–39 and Minister to Britain, 1856–61.

Davis, Jefferson (1808–89):   President of the Confederate States of America, 1861–65. Born in Kentucky, his early career included service in the Mexican War (at battles of Monterrey and Buena Vista, 1846–47). As Democratic Senator for Mississippi (1847–51) opposed Compromise of 1850. Served under Pierce as Secretary of War, 1853–57. The leading figure of the Confederate States during the Civil War, he was imprisoned on treason charges from 1865–67.

Dawes, Charles Gates (1865–1951):   Politician and diplomat. 30th Vice-President of the United States, serving under Calvin Coolidge, 1925–29. Architect of Dawes Plan for re-scheduling post-World War I reparation payments owed by Germany (for which he was jointly awarded 1925 Nobel Peace Prize). Ambassador to Britain, 1929–32. Chairman of Reconstruction Finance Corporation, 1932.

Debs, Eugene Victor (1855–1926):   Socialist trade union leader, founder of the American Railway Union (ARU) in 1893. Jailed a year later for disobeying federal injunction to support striking Chicago Pullman workers (despite celebrated defence by Clarence Seward Darrow). Stood five times as presidential candidate, 1900–20. His best performance was in 1920, when he obtained 920,000 votes fighting the campaign from jail. *See also* Socialist Party, p. 114.

Dewey, Thomas Edmund (1902–71):   Republican politician. Twice unsuccessfully contested presidency (1944 and 1948). Long-serving Governor of New York, 1943–54. Prominent in the 1930s as special prosecutor of gangsters such as Lucky Luciano.

Dickinson, John (1732–1808):   Writer and politician who drafted documents of seminal importance in the revolution. They included the *Declaration of Rights and Grievances of the Colonists of America* (1765), although he supported the colonies remaining in the British Empire. President of Delaware (1781–82), then Pennsylvania, 1782–85, and presided at Annapolis Convention, 1786.

Douglas, Stephen Arnold (1813–61):   Democrat Senator for Illinois, 1847–61. His support helped secure Compromise of 1850 and he sponsored 1854 Kansas-Nebraska Act. Unsuccessful Democrat presidential candidate against Abraham Lincoln in 1860 (though he had defeated Lincoln in the celebrated Illinois Senate contest in 1858).

Douglass, Frederick (1817–95):   Black abolitionist and publicist. Born a mulatto slave in Maryland, escaping in 1838 to settle temporarily in Massachusetts. Founded *North Star* newspaper, 1847. Recruited two black regiments in Civil War to fight for Union Army. Consul-General to Haiti, 1889–91.

Du Bois, William Edward Burghardt ('W.E.B.') (1868–1963):   Black historian, sociologist and civil rights leader. A founder of the National Association for the Advancement of Colored People (NAACP, see p. 341). Edited its magazine, *Crisis,* 1910–34. Broke with NAACP in 1948 over its lack of radicalism. Joined Communist Party, 1961, eventually emigrating (1962) to Ghana where he took up citizenship.

Dulles, John Foster (1888–1959):   American Secretary of State, 1953–59. An advocate of a hard-line against communism, his foreign policy was obdurately opposed to negotiation with Russia and to American recognition of Communist China. Strongly opposed the Anglo-French invasion of Egypt in 1956 – the 'Suez Crisis'. *See also* Massive Retaliation, p. 339.

Eddy, Mary Baker (1821–1910):   The founder of Christian Science (Church of Christ, Scientist, chartered in 1879). Author of *Science and Prayer*. Set up *Christian Science Monitor*, 1908.

Eisenhower, Dwight David (1890–1969):   Statesman and military commander. After the Japanese attack on Pearl Harbor on 7 December 1941, he became assistant Chief of Staff in charge of the Operations Division in Washington. He was in command of the European theatre of operations in 1942, and successively Commander of the Allied forces in North Africa, 1942–44, Supreme Commander of the Allied Expeditionary Force in the Western Zone of Europe, 1944–45, Commander of the US Occupation Zone in Germany in 1945, Chief of Staff of the United States Army, 1945–48, and Supreme Commander of the North Atlantic Treaty Forces in Europe, 1950–52. In 1952, Eisenhower won the Republican nomination for the presidency, and then the presidency itself. In September 1955 he suffered a severe heart attack, and in June 1956 underwent a serious operation for intestinal disorder. He nevertheless secured re-election in November 1956. He was succceeded in office by President John F. Kennedy (q.v.) in February 1961.

Ellsworth, Oliver (1745–1807):   Third Chief Justice of the United States, 1796–1800. Diplomat and Senator. Connecticut delegate to Continental Congress, 1777–84. Special envoy to Paris, negotiating 1800 treaty ending undeclared Franco–US naval war. Federalist Senator for Connecticut, 1789–96. Architect of 1789 Federal Judiciary Act.

Evers, Medgar (1925–63):   Black civil rights activist. A native of Mississippi, he worked in that state to organise local sections of the National Association for the Advancement of Colored People (NAACP). Became its first field secretary in Mississippi in 1954, promoting black voter registration. His murder in June 1963 immediately following President Kennedy's declaration of federal support for civil rights made him a nationally-known martyr. In 1994 Byron de la Beckwith was finally convicted of his slaying.

Farmer, James Leonard (1920–):   Black civil rights leader. A founder of the Congress of Racial Equality (CORE) (q.v.) in 1942 and subsequently its national director. Assistant Secretary of Health, Education and Welfare, 1969–70.

Farrakhan, Louis (1933–):   Black political leader of the Nation of Islam; born Louis Eugene Walcott. Joined the Nation of Islam (Black Muslims) under its leader Elijah Muhammad (q.v.) in 1955 and served under Muhammad's own disciple Malcolm X (q.v.). Denounced Malcolm

X's desertion of the movement in 1964 and, following Muhammad's death in 1975, formed his own sect within the Nation which adopted that name and followed a more radical path of separatism. His public oratory has been widely denounced as anti-semitic in the extreme. In 1995 led the 'Million Man March' in Washington, DC to promote self-help within the black community.

Fillmore, Millard (1800–74): 13th President of the United States, 1850–53. Formerly Vice-President to his Whig predecessor, Zachary Taylor, he secured the so-called Compromise of 1850 which admitted California to the Union as a state free of slavery but also allowed the inhabitants of other Western Territories themselves to decide whether to permit slave-holding. However, his attempts at conciliation alienated both sides. The anti-slavery wing of the Whig Party denounced his strict enforcement of the 1850 Fugitive Slave Law. He lost Whig support in 1852, the nomination going to the more radical anti-slavery General Winfield Scott.

Ford, Gerald Rudolph (1913–): 38th President of the United States, 1974–77. Michigan Republican Congressman, 1948–73. Nixon's Vice-President on resignation of Agnew (q.v.), 1973. Succeeded as President following Nixon's resignation over the Watergate scandal, 1974. Unique in holding both offices without election. Pardoned Nixon and amnestied Vietnam War draft evaders, 1974. Defeated by Carter (q.v.) in presidential election, 1976.

Forrest, Nathan Bedford (1821–77): One of the most successful (and legendary) Confederate generals in the Civil War, rising rapidly from the ranks. Led brilliant cavalry attacks at Shiloh, Murfreesboro and Chickamauga. In 1867 became Grand Wizard of the Ku Klux Klan.

Franklin, Benjamin (1706–90): One of the founding fathers of the independent United States. His early career included the editorship of the *Pennsylvania Gazette* (which he had founded), 1729–66, and *Poor Richard's Almanack*. Wrote Albany Plan for uniting American colonies, 1754. Helped formulate and draft 1776 Declaration of Independence, the French alliance in 1778 and the 1787 Constitution. First Postmaster-General of the United States, 1775–76. Subsequently served as Ambassador to France, 1776–85, and President of Pennsylvania.

Frémont, John Charles (1813–90): Explorer, soldier and political leader. Helped secure California in Mexican War (briefly its first Governor). Made a fortune from gold after court martial from army. Free-Soil Democrat Senator for California, 1850–51. First Republican presidential candidate, 1856. Governor of Arizona Territory, 1878–81.

Friedan, Betty (1921–):   Women's rights activist and author, born Bettye Naomi Goldstein. After an early career as a radical trades union journalist, in 1963 published *The Feminist Mystique* which described the contemporary alienation of the middle-class American woman. Co-founded, with others attending the Third National Conference of the Commission on the Status of Women (established 1961), the National Organization for Women (NOW) on 30 June 1966 and served as its first president.

Gallatin, Albert (1761–1849):   Swiss-born politician and diplomat. Served under Jefferson and Madison as US Secretary of the Treasury, 1802–14. Negotiated Treaty of Ghent, 1814 (ending war with Britain). Subsequently minister to France (1815–23) and Britain (1826–27).

Garfield, James (1831–81):   20th President of the United States, 1881. He was assassinated after six months in office by a disgruntled office-seeker (the second US president to be assassinated). Elected to Congress in 1863 as a staunch Republican advocate of radical reconstruction. Republican minority leader of the House during Rutherford Hayes's term of office. A dark-horse candidate in 1880 (behind Ulysses Grant and James G. Blaine), Garfield was nominated on the 36th ballot. His short Administration was marked by antagonism with his erstwhile sponsor, Senator Roscoe Conkling of New York.

Garrison, William Lloyd (1805–79):   Vehement Massachusetts publicist for abolition. One of the chief organizers of the American Anti-Slavery Society, 1833. Published abolitionist newspaper *The Liberator*, 1831–65. Many early historians saw him as the most important leader of the abolitionist cause.

Gates, Horatio (*c.* 1728–1806):   Military commander in War of Independence, whose fortunes fluctuated greatly. He commanded the victorious army at Saratoga in 1777, forcing a major British surrender. In turn his own army was destroyed at Camden, South Carolina, in 1780 by Cornwallis.

George, Henry (1839–97):   The chief advocate of the 'single tax' on land use. His ideas widely disseminated with the publication of *Progress and Poverty* (1879). Unsuccessful in two bids (1886, 1897) to become Mayor of New York.

Geronimo (1829–1909):   Apache Indian. His Apache warriors attacked settlers in Arizona and New Mexico. He surrendered in 1886.

Gerry, Elbridge (1744–1814):   Democratic-Republican politician. Massachusetts delegate to Continental Congress, 1776–85. Delegate to

Constitutional Convention, 1787 (but refused to sign US constitution). US Representative (Republican, Massachusetts), 1789–93. Governor of Massachusetts, 1810–12. 5th Vice-President of the United States (dying in office).

Gingrich, Newton Leroy (Newt) (1943–):   Republican politician. Foremost advocate of the populist 'New Right' and the 'Contract with America'. Georgia Congressman since 1979. House Republican Whip, 1989–94. After Republican mid-term landslide in November 1994, the Speaker of the House. Narrowly re-elected Speaker, January 1997.

Goldwater, Barry Morris (1909–):   Republican politician, the archetypal conservative. Republican Senator for Arizona, 1953–65, 1969–86. Unsuccessfully contested 1964 presidential election on right-wing platform.

Gompers, Samuel (1850–1924):   One of the towering figures of the labour movement. Played key role in founding American Federation of Labor (AFL). Its long-serving president, 1886–94, 1896–1924, he strongly believed that labour should not form a separate independent political party.

Gore, Albert Jr (Al) (1948–):   Vice-President of the United States since January 1993. Running-mate of Bill Clinton. Former Senator for Tennessee, as was his father, Albert Gore Snr.

Grant, Ulysses Simpson (1822–85):   18th President of the United States, 1869–77. Elected in 1868 as a national hero after his victories for the Union army in the Civil War, his Administration became engulfed in blatant corruption and acrimonious politics. Early Civil War successes against two Confederate strongholds (Fort Henry and Fort Donelson) were followed by the brilliant capture of Vicksburg (1863). Given supreme command of Union armies (1864) and accepted surrender of Confederate Robert E. Lee at Appomattox Court House (9 April 1865). Re-elected President in 1872, the scandals of his second term even exceeded those of his first four years in office. Despite support of the Stalwarts (q.v.), failed to be nominated for a third term in 1880.

Greeley, Horace (1811–72):   Politician and editor. Founder and long-time editor of New York *Tribune*, 1841–72. His support assisted Lincoln in securing 1860 Republican presidential nomination. Campaigner for abolition and protective tariffs. Unsuccessfully contested 1872 presidential election as Democratic and Liberal Republican candidate against Ulysses S. Grant.

Greene, Nathanael (1742–86): Soldier. Major-General in War of Independence, distinguishing himself at Trenton, Brandywine, etc. Quartermaster-General of Continental Army, 1778–80. Under his leadership, his troops inflicted a major series of defeats on the British in the Southern states.

Haig, Alexander Meigs (1924–): Soldier and politician. Brigade commander in Vietnam, 1966–67. President Nixon's military adviser, 1969–73, and White House Chief of Staff, 1973–74. Supreme Allied Commander NATO forces Europe, 1974–78, where he survived an assassination attempt. Appointed Reagan's Secretary of State, 1981, he resigned in 1982 after increasing conflict with the Administration over foreign policy.

Hamilton, Alexander (c. 1757–1804): With Washington and Jefferson, one of the key figures in the early years of independence. The leader of the conservative Federalists opposed to Jefferson's more liberal Democratic-Republicans. Washington's *aide-de-camp* in War of Independence, commanding regiment at Yorktown in 1781. Delegate representing New York in Continental Congress, 1781–83. A signatory to the US Constitution, 1787. Played key role as first US Secretary of the Treasury, 1789–95, in building sound structure for the national finances. Killed in 1804 in a duel with Vice-President Aaron Burr. Athough opinionated and lacking trust in the democratic process, he was a towering figure of high intellectual and administrative ability.

Hancock, John (1737–93): Leader of independence movement in Massachusetts. Joined with Samuel Adams in 1768 in colonial resistance to British. The first signatory of the Declaration of Independence, 1776. President of the Continental Congress, 1775–77, 1785–86. First State Governor of Massachusetts, 1780–85, 1787–93.

Harding, Warren Gamaliel (1865–1923): 29th President of the United States, 1921–23. Ohio Republican State Senator, 1890–1902. Lieutenant Governor, 1904–06. Elected to Senate, 1914. Won landslide presidential election victory on 'back to normalcy' platform, 1920. Facing depression, Harding reduced taxes, increased tariffs and introduced immigration controls. Called 1921–22 Washington Disarmament Conference to limit size of navies. Death in office, 1923, followed by revelations of administrative corruption (notably the Teapot Dome scandal), though the extent of Harding's awareness of these events was unclear.

Harrison, Benjamin (1833–1901): 23rd President of the United States, 1889–93. Like the rule of his Democratic opponent Cleveland, Harrison's Administration was dominated by questions of the currency and monetary policy. A grandson of William Henry Harrison (q.v.), Harrison received fewer popular votes than Cleveland in 1888. Although lacking charisma, his main-line Republican Administration saw support for the McKinley tariff, the liberal Disability Pension Act and the beginnings of the later Pan-American Union. Defeated by Cleveland in 1892, partly because the Republicans were identified as the party of big business.

Harrison, William Henry (1773–1841): 9th President of the United States, 1841. A national hero for his distinguished military service, Harrison was elected on the Whig ticket aged 68. At his inauguration ceremony in March 1841 he developed pleurisy and died after only a month in office (the first President to die in the White House). His early career included the Governorship of Indiana Territory (1800–12). In 1811 defeated the Shawnee Indians at Tippecanoe and in 1813 defeated the British (and their Indian allies) at the Battle of the Thames River. Unsuccessfully nominated by dissident Whigs for President in 1836. Won in 1840 on a demagogic platform with John Tyler as his running-mate.

Hayden, Thomas Emmett (Tom) (1939–): Radical student leader, one of the leading lights of the New Left movement in the 1960s and a co-founder of Students for a Democratic Society (SDS). Provided the original draft of the Port Huron Statement. Was involved in demonstrations at the Democratic National Convention in Chicago in 1968 and was one of the 'Chicago Eight' who in 1969 were tried on charges of conspiracy to incite riot. Elected to the California State Assembly in 1982 and to the State Senate in 1992.

Hayes, Rutherford (1822–93): 19th President of the United States, 1877–81. A Republican, his election was disputed but eventually agreed to by the Democratic Party in return for the cessation of federal military rule over the former Confederate states in the South, an act which antagonized the extremists in his own party. His attempts at civil service reform also angered Republican leaders. During his Administration, economic depression brought about the first nation-wide strike by railroad workers in 1877. Hayes declined to seek renomination.

Henry, Patrick (1736–99): Revolutionary patriot leader from Virginia. Commanded Virginia Militia, 1775–76. Delegate to the Continental Congress, 1774–76. First State Governor of Virginia, 1776–79. The lack of a Bill of Rights caused him to oppose the adoption of the US Constitution.

Hoffman, Abbie (1936–89): Radical activist. Participated in the civil rights movement's Freedom Summer in Mississippi in 1963 and later founded, with Jerry Rubin (q.v.), the Youth International Party or Yippies. Was active in protests against the Vietnam War, participating in the famous march of 21 October 1967 that attempted to besiege the Pentagon building (which Hoffman attempted to levitate). Organised the Yippie's Festival of Life at the 1968 Democratic National Convention in Chicago and the following year was prosecuted as one of the 'Chicago Eight' on charges of conspiracy to incite riot. His career as an activist was interrupted in 1973 by his arrest for drug peddling, after which he withdrew from public life until the 1980s when he re-emerged to promote environmental causes. Committed suicide in 1989.

Holmes, Wendell Court (1841–1935): Associate Justice of the US Supreme Court, 1902–32. His constant opposition to the conservatism of his colleagues with regard to social legislation led to his nickname 'The Great Dissenter'.

Hoover, Herbert Clark (1874–1964):   31st President of the United States, 1929–33. Businessman and organizer of relief operations following World War I. Appointed Secretary of Commerce by President Harding, 1921. Elected Republican President in 1928, his attempts to combat the Depression through a Reconstruction Finance Corporation and the relief of state debts failed. Defeated by Roosevelt in 1932 presidential election. Appointed co-ordinator of food supplies to war-ravaged countries, 1946. Headed Hoover Commission to reorganize federal government structure, 1947–49, 1953–55.

Hoover, (John) Edgar (1895–1972):   Head of US Federal Bureau of Investigation. Lawyer in Department of Justice, 1917. Special assistant to Attorney General, 1919. FBI Assistant Director, 1921; Director, 1924–72, serving under eight Presidents. Reorganized Bureau, concentrating on gangsters in the 1930s, enemy spies in the 1940s and communist subversion after 1945. His role became increasingly controversial in the 1960s, when the FBI was accused of harassing anti-Vietnam War and black civil rights activists.

Houston, Samuel (1793–1863):   A maker of modern Texas. Commanded army of American settlers in Texas War of Independence, 1836, defeating Mexicans at Battle of San Jacinto (21 April 1836). President of Texas Republic, 1836–38, 1841–44. Governor of Texas, 1859–61, but deposed for his opposition to secession. The state capital is named after him.

Hughes, Charles Evans (1862–1948):   12th Chief Justice of the United States, 1930–41. Bitter opponent of F.D. Roosevelt's 'court packing'. Unsuccessful Republican presidential candidate, 1916. Secretary of State under both Harding and Coolidge.

Hull, Cordell (1871–1955):   Democratic politician. Long-serving Representative (then Senator) for Tennessee. Played key role as Roosevelt's Secretary of State, 1933–44, implementing start of 'good neighbour' policy (q.v.) with Latin America. Helped develop structure of United Nations, 1944. Awarded Nobel Peace Prize, 1945.

Humphrey, Hubert Horatio (1911–78):   Democratic politician. Served as Lyndon Johnson's Vice-President, 1965–69. Senator for Minnesota, 1949–65, 1971–78. His liberal views did not help his unsuccessful Democratic bid for the Presidency in 1968.

Jackson, Andrew (1767–1845):   7th President of the United States, 1829–37. The first 'log cabin' President, who was seen as an upstart by his opponents and symbol of the democratic sentiments of the age by his supporters. His Administration is viewed as one of the most important in US history. Became Major General in War of 1812, acquiring nickname 'Old Hickory' for his personal toughness. In 1824, won plurality of the electoral votes, not the majority required and John Quincy Adams became President. In 1828 Jackson comfortably defeated re-election attempt by Adams. Adopted strong pro-Union stance in Nullification Crisis (see p. 345). Re-elected in 1832, in 1836 he gave his support to Vice-President Martin Van Buren.

Jackson, Reverend Jesse Louis (1941–):   Clergyman and civil rights leader. Radical black politician who unsuccessfully sought the Democratic presidential nomination in 1984 and 1988.

Jackson, Thomas Jonathan (1824–63):   'Stonewall' Jackson, one of the best Confederate generals, who defeated the Union Army at Bull Run in 1861 and again in 1862. He led the Shenandoah Valley campaign, 1862, and inflicted the reverse on his Union opponents at Chancellorsville, 1863. He was accidentally killed by his own troops.

Jay, John (1745–1829):   One of the key figures of the early years of US independence. New York delegate to Continental Congress, 1774–79, and its President, 1778–79. Helped negotiate 1783 Peace Treaty with Britain. Secretary of Foreign Affairs, 1784–89. Played prominent role in urging ratification of US Constitution. Negotiated settlement of outstanding disputes with Britain in Jay's Treaty of 1794. The first Chief Justice of the United States, 1790–95. Governor of New York, 1795–1801.

Jefferson, Thomas (1743–1826):   3rd President of the United States, 1801–09. One of the commanding figures of the early years of the new nation. Delegate to Continental Congress, 1775–76. Chosen to write the Declaration of Independence, 1776. Governor of Virginia, 1779–81. Delegate to Congress, 1783–84. Secretary of State, 1789–93. Vice-President under John Adams, 1797–1801. A major achievement of his Presidency was the Louisiana Purchase of 1803. He also sought as President to curb the growing power of the Supreme Court. His opposition to Hamilton and the Federalist Party helped create the Republican group (the antecedents of the present Democratic Party). His range of interests and intellectual qualities was equalled only by Benjamin Franklin.

Johnson, Andrew (1808–75):   17th President of the United States, 1865–69. A Southerner and Democrat, he was Vice-President to his Republican predecessor, Abraham Lincoln, and succeeded to the Presidency upon the latter's assassination. He was impeached before the Senate (the only President to be so charged) for obstructing the policy of Congress towards the former Confederate states but was acquitted. As President his major issue with the Radical Republicans was the rigour of their Reconstruction policy.

Johnson, Lyndon Baines (1908–73):   36th President of the United States, 1963–69. Elected to the House of Representatives in 1938 and to the Senate in 1948. Became Democratic leader in the Senate in 1953. Despite suffering a severe heart attack in 1955, he held the post until he became Vice-President of the United States in January 1961. After completing the presidential term to which the assassinated President Kennedy had been elected, he was nominated to run as Democratic candidate for the Presidency in 1964, an election which he won by a large majority. Because of disenchantment within the Democratic Party over his Administration policies towards Vietnam, he did not run for re-election in 1968. He was succeeded by Richard M. Nixon (q.v.).

Johnson, Richard M. (1780–1850):   Democratic Kentucky politician. Vice-President, 1837–41, under Van Buren, the only Vice-President ever elected by the US Senate.

Jordan, Barbara (1936–96):   Black politician, lawyer and community leader. A native of Texas, she practised law before being elected to the State Senate in 1966. In 1972 was elected to the US House of Representatives as the first black congresswoman from the Deep South. Achieved national prominence as a member of House judiciary committee during the hearings on the impeachment of President Richard Nixon (q.v.). Delivered the keynote address at the Democratic National Convention in 1976. Retired to academic life in 1977.

Kennedy, Edward (Ted) Moore (1932–):   Youngest of the three Kennedy brothers (see below). Democratic politician. Senator for Massachusetts since 1962. His career towards higher office was derailed by the fatal Chappaquiddick incident (see p. 310).

Kennedy, John Fitzgerald (1917–63):   The 35th President of the United States, 1960–63. Born in Boston, Massachusetts. The son of Joseph Kennedy, a successful businessman and Ambassador to the United Kingdom, and a Roman Catholic. He graduated from Harvard University in 1940 and served in the US Navy. Elected to the House of Representatives in 1946. He defeated Henry Cabot Lodge for one of the Massachusetts Senate seats in 1952, and in November 1960 defeated Richard Nixon (q.v.) in the presidential election by a narrow margin. On 22 November 1963 he was assassinated in Dallas, Texas. A commission under the Chief Justice of the US Supreme Court, Earl Warren, concluded that he had been killed by one Lee Harvey Oswald, acting alone. He was succeeded by the Vice-President, Lyndon Baines Johnson (q.v.), on the afternoon of his death. His short period as President witnessed the Cuban Missile Crisis. His style and charisma made him one of the most admired and popular Presidents of modern times (the youngest ever elected).

Kennedy, Robert Francis (1925–68):   Democratic politician. Presidential campaign manager for his brother, John F. Kennedy, 1960. US Attorney General, emphasizing civil rights and investigating institutionalized crime, 1961–64. Democratic Senator for New York, 1965–68. Assassinated in Los Angeles, 5 June 1968, while campaigning for Democratic presidential nomination on black rights and anti-Vietnam War platform.

King, Martin Luther (1929–68):   American black civil rights leader. Ordained as Baptist minister, 1947. Began non-violent civil rights campaign in Montgomery, Alabama, leading boycott of racially segregated buses, 1955–56. Founded Southern Christian Leadership Conference, 1957. An effective orator, notably in his Washington 'I have a dream' speech, 1963. Awarded Nobel Peace Prize, 1964. His assassination in Memphis, Tennessee, 4 April 1968, provoked widespread black riots throughout America. In the generation since his death, he has remained the major inspiration in the struggle for racial equality in the United States.

King, Rufus (1755–1827):   Federalist politician. Senator, 1789–96, 1813–25. Unsuccessful candidate for Presidency, 1816. Delegate to Congress from Massachusetts, 1784–87. Signed US Constitution, 1787. Minister to Britain, 1796–1803, 1825–26.

Kissinger, Henry (1923–): American academic and politician. German-born, US citizen, 1943. Professor of Government, Harvard, 1958–71. Adviser in Nixon's (q.v.) presidential campaign 1968. White House National Security Adviser, 1969–73, playing a greater foreign policy role than the Secretary of State. Conducted diplomatic missions in Middle East, Southern Africa and Vietnam. Joint Nobel Peace Prize winner with Vietnamese negotiator Le Duc Tho for extricating US from Vietnam. Secretary of State under Nixon and Ford, 1973–77. Kissinger practised a *realpolitik* of great-power diplomacy.

La Follette, Robert Marion (1855–1925): Progressive leader who unsuccessfully contested Presidency, November 1924. Representative (Republican) from Wisconsin, 1885–91. Governor of Wisconsin, 1901–05. Progressive Senator for Wisconsin, 1906–25. Opposed both US entry into World War I and also participation in League of Nations.

LaGuardia, Fiorello Henry (1882–1947): New York politician. A maverick Republican, who led the anti-Tammany Hall 'Fusion' slate in 1933. Mayor of New York (the first reform Mayor in New York's history to succeed himself) who successfully attracted New Deal funding to tackle problems of New York poverty and housing.

Lee, Richard Henry (1732–94): Virginia delegate to Continental Congress, 1774–79. Played key role in early constitutional developments, introducing resolution for Declaration of Independence (7 June 1776). Later keen proponent of Bill of Rights. Senator for Virginia, 1789–92.

Lee, Robert E. (1807–70): One of the most famous Confederate generals of the Civil War, commanding Confederate Army of Northern Virginia, 1862–65. His skills and strategy gave victory to his numerically inferior forces (e.g., at the Second Battle of Bull Run and Fredericksburg), but he was defeated at Gettysburg in 1863. Appointed General-in-Chief of the Confederate Armies, 1865. It was Lee who surrendered at Appomattox Court House in 1865.

Lewis, John Llewellyn (1880–1969): Veteran labour leader. For 40 years (1920–60) President of United Mine Workers (UMW). In 1935 organized the CIO (Committee for Industrial Organization). President of the CIO after its expulsion from the American Federation of Labor (AFL) in 1938 until 1942. A policy dispute caused him to pull the UMW out of the CIO in 1942.

Lewis, Meriwether (1774–1809): Joint leader (with William Clark) of the expedition to explore the Louisiana Purchase, 1804–06. Subsequently Governor of Louisiana Territory, 1807–09.

Lincoln, Abraham (1809–65): 16th President of the United States, 1861–65, whose presidency spanned the bitter divisions of the Civil War. Born in a log cabin in Hardin County, Kentucky. Built up a prosperous legal business in Springfield, Illinois. Married Mary Todd of Kentucky, daughter of a slaveowner, 1842. Elected to the Illinois legislature as a Whig, 1834, serving three terms, and to the US Congress, 1846, where he served only one because of his opposition to the Mexican War. Brought back to politics by his opposition to the Kansas-Nebraska Act, eventually joining the newly formed Republican Party in 1856. Stood as Republican candidate for the US Senate from Illinois, 1858, engaging in a famous series of debates with his Democrat rival, Stephen Douglas (q.v.); Douglas won, but Lincoln's reputation was assured. Won the presidential nomination of his party on the third ballot, 1860, though William Seward (q.v.) was the early favourite. In the election faced the opposition of two Democratic candidates – his old rival Douglas and John Breckinridge (Southern Democrat) who represented the slaveholding South – and John Bell of the Constitutional Union Party, but won with 40% of the popular vote and 180 electoral votes. Inaugurated President on 4 March 1861, eleven Southern states having withdrawn in the meantime to establish the Confederate States of America; Lincoln declared that he had no intention of seeking to abolish slavery in the South. A Confederate attack on Fort Sumter in Charleston harbour, South Carolina on 12 April prompted him to declare a state of rebellion and to raise 75,000 volunteers for the defence of the Union. Issued his first Emancipation Proclamation, September 1862, declaring free, with effect from 1 January 1863, those slaves in states still in rebellion. Promoted General Ulysses Grant to be general of the Union forces, 1864. Nominated as presidential candidate of the National Union Party (Republican-War Democrat coalition) and re-elected, with 55% of the vote, over Democrat George McClellan, November 1864. Shot on 14 April 1865 at Ford's Theater in Washington, DC by Confederate sympathizer, John Wilkes Booth (q.v.), and died the following morning.

Livingstone, Robert (1746–1813): Diplomat and statesman. In early career a New York delegate to Continental Congress, 1775–77. First Secretary of Foreign Affairs, 1781–83. While Minister to France, 1801–04, negotiated the crucial Louisiana Purchase (see p. 338). Long-serving Chief Judge of New York, 1777–1801.

Lodge, Henry Cabot (1850–1924): Republican politician. Massachusetts Senator, 1893–1924. Played leading role in calling for US involvement in World War I, but led opposition to Treaty of Versailles and to United States joining League of Nations.

Lodge, Henry Cabot (1902–85):   Ambassador and politician. Republican Vice-Presidential candidate (unsuccessful) in 1960 election. Ambassador to United Nations, 1953–60. Subsequently Ambassador to West Germany, South Vietnam, etc. Republican Senator for Massachusetts, 1937–44, 1947–53.

Lovejoy, Elijah Parish (1802–37):   Newspaper editor. Attacked and killed by a pro-slavery mob in Alton, Illinois, while editor of the anti-slavery *Observer*. His death provided a martyr for the abolitionist cause.

MacArthur, Douglas (1880–1964):   US General. Army Chief of Staff, 1930–35. Supreme Allied Commander, South West Pacific, World War II. Received Japanese surrender, 1945. Led occupation forces in Japan, 1945–51, playing a decisive role in preserving Japanese stability. Commander-in-Chief, UN forces in Korean War, 1950–51. Dismissed by Truman (q.v.) for urging spread of war into China, contrary to official policy. Failed to win nomination as candidate in 1952 presidential election.

McCarthy, Joseph (1909–57):   Republican politician. Senator for Wisconsin 1946–57. McCarthy alleged in 1950 that over 200 Government employees were either Communist Party members or sympathizers, though he provided no evidence. Chairman of the Senate Sub-committee on Investigations, 1953, where he accused numerous Democrats and liberals of communist sympathies. His attacks on the Army aroused President Eisenhower's antagonism, leading to a Senate motion of censure against McCarthy in 1954 which ended his career.

McClellan, George Brinton (1826–85):   Civil War general. Commanded Union Army of Potomac, responsible for its reorganization after initial defeat at Bull Run. Relieved of command by President Lincoln when, after forcing Robert E. Lee to retreat after Antietam, failed to take Richmond. Fought unsuccessful campaign as Democratic candidate for Presidency, 1864.

McGovern, George Stanley (1922–):   Democratic politician. Democratic Representative (1957–61) then Senator (1963–81) for South Dakota. Unsuccessfully fought a liberal campaign against the incumbent Richard Nixon for Presidency in 1972, warning of the depths of Nixon's deceit. These warnings were justified when the Watergate scandal erupted (see p. 364).

McKinley, William (1843–1901):   25th President of the United States, 1897–1901. A Republican, he presided over the Spanish–American War of 1898. His Presidency marked a transition in American politics, with the final taming of the frontier and the advent of an industrial society. McKinley was also the last President to have served in the Civil War. His Presidency saw the acquisition of Puerto Rico, Guam and the Philippines. He was re-elected in 1900, but was assassinated in Buffalo on 6 September 1901 by Leon Czolgosz, a Polish anarchist.

Madison, James (1751–1836):   4th President of the United States, 1809–17. A key figure in the founding years of modern America, as the architect of the Constitution and a founder of the Democratic-Republican Party, as well as author of the Virginia Resolution (see p. 363) and of much of the Federalist Papers (q.v.). His early career included membership of the executive council of Virginia during the War of Independence and as delegate to the Continental Congress. The leading advocate for strong federal government in the 1787 Constitutional Convention. Served four terms as Representative in new Congress, playing leading role in securing Bill of Rights. Friend of Thomas Jefferson and avowed enemy of Hamilton. Secretary of State under Jefferson, 1801–08. Helped secure Louisiana Purchase as well as avoiding US involvement in Napoleonic Wars. Successful candidate for President, 1808. During his Administration the United States was, for a second time, at war with Great Britain, 1812–14, chiefly over the issue of British abuse of American rights of neutrality upon the high seas (where Madison succumbed to the war party of Henry Clay and John C. Calhoun). Re-elected 1812, despite reverses in the war. Later military reverses in his Presidency included defeat at Bladensburg and the burning of the White House (see. p. 240).

Malcolm X (1925–65):   Radical black religious and political leader. National organizer for Nation of Islam. Withdrew from the Nation of Islam in March 1964 to create his own organization closer to orthodox Islam and subsequently moderated his attacks upon whites. Assassinated in Harlem by supporters of the Nation of Islam, with whom he had had violent public disagreements.

Marshall, George Catlett (1880–1959):   Army officer and cabinet member. Army Chief of Staff from 1939 to 1945. Special ambassador to China, November 1945–January 1947. As Secretary of State (1947–49), he developed the European Recovery Program (also referred to as the Marshall Plan) to foster post-war economic recovery in Europe. He resigned as Secretary of State in January 1949, but came out of retirement to become Secretary of Defense in September 1950.

Marshall, John (1755–1835):   Long-serving 4th Chief Justice of the United States (1801–35) who played major role in establishing the powers of the Supreme Court and in broadening the frontiers of federal government. Briefly Representative (Federalist) from Virginia, 1799–1800 and Secretary of State, 1800–1. Among his key decisions as Chief Justice was the 1803 *Marbury v Madison* ruling which established the Supreme Court's power to declare individual laws unconstitutional.

Marshall, Thurgood (1908–93):   Leading black lawyer who in 1967 became first black to be appointed as Associate Justice of US Supreme Court. Played prominent role as head of legal services at the National Association for the Advancement of Colored People (NAACP) in winning desegregation issues over housing, schools, etc. US Solicitor-General, 1965–67. Retired from Court in June 1991.

Meade, George Gordon (1815–72):   Civil War general who turned the course of the war by his victorious command of the Union Army of the Potomac, defeating Robert E. Lee at Gettysburg (1863).

Mondale, Walter Frederick (1928–):   Democratic politician. Served as 42nd Vice-President of the United States, 1977–81. Democratic Senator from Minnesota, 1964–77. Unsuccessfully contested 1984 presidential election against Ronald Reagan.

Monroe, James (1758–1831):   5th President of the United States, 1817–25. Democratic-Republican politician of high administrative ability. A leading Jefferson supporter in the Senate. Minister to France, 1794–96 (and enthusiastic supporter of the revolution). Elected Governor of Virginia, 1799. Secretary of State under Madison (1811–17). Easy victor in 1816 presidential election, his Presidency began as the 'Era of Good Feelings'. Re-elected in 1820 without opposition, but his second term plagued by rising dissent over extension of slavery to the new territories (temporarily calmed by 1820 Missouri Compromise). During his terms in office, Florida was acquired in 1819 and the newly independent Latin American countries received diplomatic recognition in 1823 (see p. 230). Monroe's most lasting legacy was perhaps his promulgation of the Monroe Doctrine of 1823, by which the United States declared its intention to prevent any further European colonization in the Americas.

Morris, Robert (1734–1806):   Financier who played key role in the War of Independence by pledging his own personal credit to help supply Washington's army at Battles of Trenton and Princeton (1776). US Superintendent of Finance, 1781–84. Earlier he had been Pennsylvania's delegate to Continental Congress. In later life, eventually jailed for debt. Known as 'Financier of the American Revolution'.

Moseley-Braun, Carol (1947–):   Black politician. A native of Chicago, served as assistant US attorney for Illinois before being elected to the State House of Representatives in 1978. Served as recorder of deeds for Cook County, 1988–92. In 1992, being opposed to incumbent US Senator Alan Dixon's support for Supreme Court nominee Clarence Thomas (q.v.), she campaigned for the Democratic Party nomination for Dixon's seat and won an upset victory, subsequently becoming the first black woman to be elected to the US Senate.

Mott, Lucretia Coffin (1793–1880):   One of the most important social reformers. Abolitionist who aided escape of slaves through 'underground railroad'. Campaigner for women's rights. With Elizabeth Cady Stanton (q.v.) organized first women's rights convention at Seneca Falls, New York, 1848.

Muhammad, Elijah (1897–1975):   Black religious leader; born Elijah Poole. An early disciple of Wallace Fard, founder of the Nation of Islam (Black Muslim) movement, he succeeded Fard when the latter disappeared in 1934 and moved his base of operations from Detroit to Chicago. Was violently critical of American racism and advocated black separatism; his own disciple Malcolm X (q.v.) broke with the movement in 1964 but there is no definitive evidence that Muhammad was behind Malcolm's assassination a year later. Following his death in 1975, Muhammad's own son led the Nation of Islam to join the established US Muslim community, so provoking a separatist sect under Louis Farrakhan (q.v.).

Newton, Huey P. (1942–89):   Black radical activist. Co-founder in 1966 with Bobby Seale (q.v.) of the Black Panther Party (see p. 104) in Oakland, California, to protect blacks against police brutality and racial discrimination. Convicted of the manslaughter of a policeman in 1967 (though this decision was later reversed). Announced in 1971 that the Party would adopt a manifesto of non-violence and organize for community service rather than political action. Fled to Cuba in 1974 following a further murder charge but returned to the United States three years later. Following the demise of the Party in 1982, devoted himself to community service activities but was found murdered by unknown assailants in Oakland in 1989.

Nimitz, Chester William (1885–1966):   World War II naval commander. Commanded US Pacific Fleet, 1941–45. Led Pacific island-hopping campaign that eventually led to Japanese defeat. The Japanese surrender was signed aboard his flagship, the *USS Missouri* on 2 September 1945.

Nixon, Richard Milhous (1913–94):   37th President of the United States, 1968–74. Elected as Republican to House of Representatives, 1946, and the Senate, 1950. Vice-President under Eisenhower (q.v.), 1953–61. Narrowly defeated by Kennedy (q.v.) in presidential election, 1960. Won presidential election, 1968. Ended American involvement in Vietnam, eased US–Soviet relations and opened diplomatic links with Communist China. Re-elected President, 1972. Controversial second term saw resignation of Vice-President Agnew (q.v.), 1973, and Nixon's own resignation, 1974, under threat of impeachment for involvement in Watergate conspiracy (see p. 364).

O'Connor, Sandra Day (1930–):   Politician and judge. Republican Senator for Arizona, 1969–75. Appointed by Reagan as first woman Associate Justice of US Supreme Court.

Patton, George Smith (1885–1945):   World War II commander. Led the US Third Army in Europe, with his army leading the liberation of France, Germany, etc. Known as 'Old Blood and Guts'.

Perkins, Frances (1882–1965):   Secretary of Labor under Roosevelt and Truman, 1933–45. The first woman to become member of presidential cabinet. Subsequently Civil Service Commissioner, 1946–53.

Perot, (Henry) Ross (1930–):   Maverick right-wing populist, founder of Perot Systems Corporation. A billionaire industrialist who contested 1992 presidential election on anti-government, independent platform, taking 19% of the vote. Founded Reform Party (q.v.) in 1995. Unsuccessfully contested 1996 presidential election, taking only 9% of the vote.

Perry, Matthew Calbraith (1794–1858):   Naval officer who in 1854 forced the opening of two Japanese ports to US trade. The younger brother of Oliver Hazard Perry (1785–1819) who defeated British in Battle of Lake Erie, 1813.

Pershing, John Joseph (1860–1948):   Leading US commander in World War I. Commanding General of US troops in Europe, 1917–19. US Army Chief of Staff, 1921–24. Known as 'Black Jack'.

Pierce, Franklin (1804–69):   14th President of the United States, 1853–57. A Jacksonian Democrat who was elected to the Senate in 1836 when aged only 32. A dark-horse presidential candidate who secured the 1852 nomination on the 49th ballot. A Northern democrat whose pro-South sympathies caused him to misjudge the growing national animosity to slavery. His attempt to sponsor a compromise in the worsening dispute between North and South over the extension of slavery into the Western Territories of the US led to the 1854 Kansas-Nebraska Act (overturning the 1820 Missouri Compromise). He successfully completed the purchase of the southern parts of Arizona and New Mexico (the Gadsden Purchase) but failed to acquire Alaska or annex Hawaii. Rejected for renomination in 1856 because of the Kansas-Nebraska Act.

Pinchback, Pinckney Benton Stewart (1837–1921):   Black politician. Born the son of a slaveholder and free black mother, fled the South with his family in 1848 upon his father's death; during the Civil War served in the Union army. Active in Republican politics in Reconstruction Louisiana, serving in the State Senate in 1868, as lieutenant-governor of the state in 1871 and as acting governor during impeachment proceedings against the incumbent in 1872–3. Elected to the US Congress in 1872, he was refused his seat when his Democratic opponent successfully challenged the result. Elected to the US Senate in the subsequent year but again denied his seat owing to alleged irregularities, which led to his retirement from politics.

Pinckney, Charles Cotesworth (1746–1825):   Soldier and politician. Major General in US Army after 1798 (ranking third in command after Washington and Hamilton). South Carolina delegate to Constitutional Convention, 1787. Unsuccessful as vice-presidential candidate (to President John Adams) in 1800. Unsuccessful as Federalist presidential candidate, 1804 and again in 1808.

Polk, James Knox (1795–1849):   11th President of the United States, 1845–49. A Democrat, he won the 1844 Convention as the dark-horse, unity candidate supported by Andrew Jackson. Known as 'Young Hickory' to his supporters. An avowed expansionist who won a narrow victory over the Whig Henry Clay. Served in Congress (for Tennessee), 1825–39, becoming Speaker of the House. He concluded with Great Britain the Oregon Treaty of 1846 fixing the western boundary with Canada, and fought the Mexican War of 1846–48, by which the US acquired all Mexican territory north of the Rio Grande River (see p. 240). His attempt to purchase Cuba from Spain was rebuffed.

Powell, Colin Luther (1937–):   Army officer. National Security Adviser, 1987–88. Commander-in-Chief, US Forces, April–September 1989, Fort McPherson, Georgia. Chairman, Joint Chiefs of Staff, 1989–93. Secured overwhelming defeat of Saddam Hussein's forces in the Gulf War (see p. 246). The highest-ranking black American general. Refused to be drafted as Republican candidate in 1996 presidential elections despite his widespread popularity.

Randolph, A. Philip (1889–1979):   Black trades unionist and civil rights activist. Following a career as an academic in New York City and as a Socialist Party candidate, became founding president of the Brotherhood of Sleeping Car Porters in 1925, the first major black trade union. Amalgamated the union with the emergent Congress of Industrial Organizations (CIO) in 1938 in protest against the segregation policy of the American Federation of Labor (AFL). In 1941 won from President Roosevelt an executive order forbidding racial discrimination in the federal government by threatening to lead a massive protest march to Washington, DC, and (by establishing the League for Nonviolent Civil Disobedience Against Military Segregation) in 1948 induced President Truman to end segregation in the armed forces. Became vice-president of the merged AFL-CIO in 1955.

Randolph, Edmund (1753–1813):   Governor of Virginia, 1786–88. Served as first US Attorney General, 1789–94. Secretary of State, 1794–95 (resigned after false allegation of bribery against him). Counsel for Aaron Burr in 1807 (securing his acquittal in famous treason trial).

Rayburn, Sam (1882–1961):   Veteran Texas Democrat politician. Elected to Congress, 1913–61 (25 consecutive times). Speaker of the House of Representatives, 1940–47, 1949–53 and 1955–61. Played key role in helping to secure votes to carry out Roosevelt's New Deal and subsequent reforms of Harry Truman.

Reagan, Ronald (1911–):   40th President of the United States, 1981–89. Film actor. Republican Governor of California, 1967–74. Defeated Carter (q.v.) in 1980 presidential election; re-elected, 1984. First term marked by 'Reaganomics': tax cutting, reductions in public spending (which hurt the poor) and maintenance of high military expenditure. Expressed intense anti-Soviet rhetoric. Formed close friendship and alliance with Margaret Thatcher (e.g., during Falklands War). Military intervention in Grenada, 1983. In second term developed warmer relations with Soviet Union under Gorbachev with summit meetings at Geneva and Reykjavik. Reagan's hitherto impregnable personal popularity was undermined from 1986 by controversy over covert arms sales to Iran and support for Contra forces in Nicaragua. But his support for his Vice-President ensured victory for George Bush in 1988. Reagan's enduring popularity (considering his lack of real achievement, especially in the domestic arena) remains a paradox.

Revels, Hiram (1822–1901):   Black politician. Born a free black in North Carolina, he became a minister in the African Methodist Episcopal Church and during the Civil War an army chaplain. Settling in Mississippi after the War, was elected firstly to the State Senate in 1869 and the following year to the US Senate, the first black to be so chosen. Served out the unexpired term (1870–71) of Jefferson Davis (q.v.), the ex-President of the Confederate States. Retired to academic life, later criticising the Reconstruction government of Mississippi as corrupt and supporting the restoration of the Democratic Party.

Revere, Paul (1735–1818): Revolutionary hero, whose patriotic ride from Boston to Lexington, Massachusetts, warning that the British were moving to arrest Samuel Adams and John Hancock, remains one of the most famous episodes of the War of Independence. Founded Revere Copper Company.

Rockefeller, John Davison (1839–1937): The founder of Standard Oil (in 1870) and the epitome of American big business. A billionaire whose oil monopoly was broken by the Supreme Court in 1911. His many benefactions included the Rockefeller Institute of Medical Research (1901) and the Rockefeller Foundation.

Rockefeller, Nelson Aldrich (1908–71): Republican politician, grandson of John D. Rockefeller (q.v.). 41st Vice-President of the United States, 1974–77. Unsuccessfully sought Republican presidential nomination, 1964 and 1968. Governor of New York four times, 1959–73.

Roosevelt, Franklin Delano (1882–1945): 32nd President of the United States, 1933–45. Democrat State Senator, New York, 1911–12. Assistant Secretary to the Navy, 1913–20. Crippled by polio, 1921. Governor of New York, 1928. Defeated Hoover in presidential election, 1932. Instituted 'New Deal' to counter Depression, with 'Hundred Days' of legislation, 1933. Devalued dollar and extended federal government role through public works, agricultural support, labour legislation and business protection. Re-elected 1936, 1940, 1944. Attacked for radicalism, some legislation was declared unconstitutional by the Supreme Court, 1935. Maintained wartime neutrality, 1939–41, but supported Britain materially through Lend-Lease. Declared war on Japan and Germany after Pearl Harbor, December 1941. Attended wartime conferences with Stalin and Churchill, notably Yalta, which delineated East–West post-war spheres of European influence. Died in office at moment of victory over Germany. The outpouring of grief at his death testified to his place as one of the greatest figures of the century. His wife, Eleanor ('the conscience of the White House'), was a powerful campaigner for social reform.

Roosevelt, Theodore (1858–1919): 25th President of the United States, 1901–09, at 42 the youngest ever to achieve the office. A Republican who stood unsuccessfully for Mayor of New York (at age of 28). Governor of New York State from 1898. Elected Vice-President to McKinley in 1900 presidential election. Became President 14 September 1901, following assassination of McKinley in Buffalo, Re-elected 1904. His mediation in the Russo–Japanese War led to his award of Nobel Peace Prize. Secured election of William H. Taft as his successor, 1908. However Taft's essential conservatism caused Roosevelt to found the Progressive Party (see p. 111). As its presidential candidate in 1912 he split the Republican vote, thus ensuring the election of the Democrat, Woodrow Wilson. A popular President (the only New Yorker ever to hold the post) with strong intellectual interests, but glorying in use of military power.

Rubin, Jerry (1938–94):   Radical activist, participant in the Free Speech Movement at Berkeley and co-founder, with Abbie Hoffman (q.v.), of the Youth International Party or Yippies. As a leader of the radical wing of the movement against the Vietnam War took part in the 'March on the Pentagon' of 21 October 1967 and in the Yippie's Festival of Life at the 1968 Democratic National Convention in Chicago, which led to his prosecution the following year as one of the 'Chicago Eight' on charges of conspiracy to incite riot. Latterly became a Wall Street venture capitalist and promoter of alternative health therapies, until his death in a road accident in Los Angeles.

Schurz, Carl (1829–1906):   Republican politician, general, diplomat and newspaper editor. His many talents embraced a career as Minister to Spain, 1861–62, and general in the Union Army, 1862–63. He had earlier supported Lincoln's nomination in 1860. Republican Senator, 1869–75. Served as Secretary of the Interior, 1877–81, initiating civil service merit system in his department and also reform of treatment of Indians. His newspaper career embraced editorships of Detroit *Post*, 1866–67, and the New York *Evening Post*, 1881–83.

Scott, Winfield (1786–1866):   Military commander and Whig presidential candidate. Military reputation established in War of 1812 at battles of Chippewa and Lundy's Lane (1814). Nicknamed 'Old Fuss and Feathers'. Commanding General, US Army, 1841–61. Captured Mexico City in Mexican War, 1847. Although he commanded Union Army at outset of Civil War, retired in November 1861.

Seale, Bobby (1936–):   Black radical activist. Co-founder in 1966 with Huey P. Newton (q.v.) of the Black Panther Party (see p. 104) in Oakland, California, to protect blacks against police brutality and racial discrimination. After service in the US Air Force he was drawn into politics by the example of Malcolm X (q.v.). Led demonstrations against the

Vietnam War at the 1968 Democratic National Convention in Chicago, which led to his prosecution the following year as one of the 'Chicago Eight' on charges of conspiracy to incite riot. During the trial he repeatedly argued with the judge that his constitutional rights were being denied, which resulted in his being cited for contempt of court and jailed for four years. In 1971 was tried for the alleged 1969 murder of a police informer but the jury was unable to reach a decision. Thereafter renounced violence for political purposes and became a community activist. Ran unsuccessfully for mayor of Oakland in 1973.

Seward, William Henry (1801–72): Whig, later Republican, politician. First Whig Governor of New York, 1839–42. New York Senator, 1849–55 (Whig), 1855–61 (Republican). Strong opponent of slavery. Secretary of State under Lincoln and Johnson, 1861–69. Purchased Alaska from Russia ('Seward's Folly'). Wounded by accomplice of Booth the same night Lincoln was assassinated.

Sheridan, Philip Henry (1831–88): Leading Civil War general. Led charge on Missionary Ridge in 1863 Battle of Chattanooga. Cavalry Commander of Army of Potomac under Ulysses S. Grant (q.v.), finally driving Confederate troops out of Shenandoah Valley. Rose to become Commanding General of US Army, 1884–88.

Sherman, William Tecumseh (1820–91): Leading Civil War general. Commander of the Union armies of the West. Led famous 'March to the Sea' across Georgia. Secured capture of Atlanta (1 September 1864) and Savannah (22 December) before marching north to accept surrender of the Confederate General Johnston at Durham, North Carolina (26 April 1865). Refused to be nominated for Presidency. Commanding General of the US Army, 1869–84.

Shultz, George (1920–): US Secretary of State, 1982–88. An economist, he was, under Nixon, Secretary of Labor, 1969–70; Director, Office of Management and Budget, 1970–72; and Secretary of the Treasury, 1972–74. He was appointed Secretary of State by President Reagan in 1982.

Sitting Bull (1834–90): Sioux Indian chief (see Little Big Horn, p. 337).

Smith, Alfred Emanuel (1873–1944): Democratic politician. Long-serving Governor of New York, 1919–20, 1923–28. The first Roman Catholic to run for President (being defeated by Hoover in 1928). In favour of repeal of prohibition. Despite the controversy he provoked, a Democrat defeat in 1928 was probably inevitable given the seeming Republican prosperity of the 1920s.

Stanton, Edwin McMasters (1814–69):   Lincoln's Secretary of War, 1862–68, during the Civil War. His removal by President Andrew Johnson (for Stanton's stern regime in the occupied Southern states) brought about Johnson's own impeachment by the Radical Republicans.

Stanton, Elizabeth Cady (1815–1902):   One of the leading figures in the rise of the women's movement and passionate advocate of numerous reform causes. With Lucretia C. Mott (q.v.) organized first women's rights convention, 1848, at Seneca Falls, New York. Organized National Woman Suffrage Association (with Susan B. Anthony). Prominent in abolition and temperance movements.

Steinem, Gloria (1934–):   Author and feminist activist. Founded *Ms.* magazine in 1970.

Stephens, Alexander Hamilton (1812–83):   Leading Confederate politician. Whig (then Democrat) Representative from Georgia, 1843–59, 1873–82. Vice-President of the Confederate States. Represented Confederacy at Hampton Roads, Virginia, Peace Conference with Lincoln (February 1865). Imprisoned after the war, eventually returning as Governor of Georgia, 1882–83.

Stevens, Thaddeus (1792–1868):   Whig, then Republican, politician. Representative from Pennsylvania, 1849–53, 1859–68. Leader of the Radical Republicans after the Civil War, demanding severe measures against the South. Managed impeachment of Andrew Johnson in 1868. A symbol of Northern revenge.

Stevenson, Adlai Ewing (1835–1914):   Democrat politician. Representative for Illinois, 1875–77, 1879–81. Served under Grover Cleveland as 23rd Vice-President, 1893–97. Unsuccessfully fought Vice-Presidency, 1900.

Stevenson, Adlai Ewing (1900–65):   Democrat politician. Governor of Illinois, 1949–53. Unsuccessful Democrat candidate against Eisenhower in presidential elections, 1952 and 1956. US Ambassador to the United Nations 1961–65. The grandson of Adlai Stevenson (1835–1914) (q.v.).

Stowe, Harriet Beecher (1811–96):   Abolitionist author. Daughter of noted Congregationalist preacher Lyman Beecher of Litchfield, Connecticut. Served as a schoolteacher in Cincinnati, Ohio, whence her family moved in 1832, and married Calvin Stowe, professor of theology at the seminary of which her father was president. Wrote the great antislavery novel *Uncle Tom's Cabin* (1852).

Stuart, James Ewell Brown ('Jeb') (1833–64):   Confederate soldier. Cavalry General (the 'eyes of the army') in Civil War. Killed at Yellow Tavern in Battle for Richmond.

Taft, William Howard (1857–1930):   27th President of the United States, 1909–13. A Republican, he supported the policies of his friend and predecessor, Theodore Roosevelt. A lawyer who became Governor of the Philippines, 1901–04. A close ally of Theodore Roosevelt, who appointed him Secretary of War, 1904–08. Chosen by Roosevelt as his successor, he defeated the Democrat William Jennings Bryan in 1908. The Presidency was Taft's first elective office, and this was reflected in his difficulties managing both the party and politicians. His growing conservatism caused the Progressives (see p. 111) to break away. Taft came third in the 1912 election. He later served on the US Supreme Court as Chief Justice, 1921–30, the only man ever to hold both offices.

Taney, Roger Brooke (1777–1864):   Public servant. The 5th Chief Justice of the United States, 1836–64. He had earlier been Attorney General under Jackson, 1831–33. The Senate refused to confirm him as Secretary of the Treasury in 1834 because of his opposition to the Second Bank of the United States. His crucial ruling was in the Dred Scott case (see p. 318) in 1857, a ruling that helped bring the Civil War closer.

Taylor, Zachary (1784–1850):   12th President of the United States, 1849–50. As commander of the American forces during the Mexican War of 1846–48, he greatly enhanced his reputation, especially at the Battle of Buena Vista, paving the way for nomination as Whig presidential candidate in 1848. A slaveowner and essentially a conservative, he had never held elective office when he won the Presidency (largely on his war record). Much influenced by the anti-slavery Whig William H. Seward (q.v.), Taylor opposed the extension of slavery into the Western Territories. The Compromise of 1850 (see p. 18) was drawn up, but Taylor died before he could veto it.

Thomas, Clarence (1948–):   Associate Justice of the US Supreme Court from 1991. After a legal career in Missouri, became assistant secretary of education in 1981–82 under President Reagan. Served as chairman of the Equal Employment Opportunities Commission (1982–90) and on the US Court of Appeals for the District of Columbia (1990–1). Nominated by President Bush to succeed Thurgood Marshall (q.v.) on the Supreme Court. His confirmation by the Senate seemed unremarkable until he was accused of sexual harassment by a former subordinate, Anita Hill, which ignited a controversy about how seriously the all-male Judiciary Committee took women's rights.

Tilden, Samuel Jones (1814–86):   Democratic politician. Played key role in New York as leader of reform group against corruption of the Tweed Ring (see p. 361). Served as Governor of New York, 1875–76. Fought 1876 presidential election, winning majority of popular vote, but Presidency denied him. Presidency awarded to Rutherford Hayes by election commission controlled by the Republicans.

Tompkins, Daniel D. (1774–1825):   Vice-President of the United States, 1817–25, under President James Monroe. A Democratic-Republican. As Governor of New York, 1807–17, put through state law ending slavery in New York.

Truman, Harry S. (1884–1972):   33rd President of the United States, 1945–53. Served in US Army in France, 1918. Democratic Senator, Missouri, 1935–44. Elected as Roosevelt's Vice-President 1944, succeeding him on death in April 1945. Authorized dropping of atomic bombs on Japan, August 1945. Surprise victor in 1948 presidential election on 'Fair Deal' civil rights and social reform platform, but unable to push legislation through conservative Congress. Vigorous anti-communist foreign policy: Truman Doctrine (see p. 360), Marshall Plan for 'European recovery (see p. 339), Berlin airlift, creation of NATO, and US participation in Korea.

Truth, Sojourner (1797–1883):   The assumed name of Isabella van Wagener, black religious leader and abolitionist. Born into slavery in New York, she was freed in 1827 upon its abolition in that state. Became attached to the household of Elijah Pierson, leader of the religious sect the Retrenchment Society. Assumed the name Sojourner Truth in 1843 and thereafter became an itinerant religious preacher and antislavery activist. Settled in Michigan in the early 1850s and supported the raising of black troops for the Union Army during the Civil War. Received in the White House by President Lincoln in 1864. Latterly worked for the National Freedmen's Relief Association.

Tubman, Harriet (c. 1820–1913):   One of the best-known black abolitionists. Escaped from slavery in Maryland, 1849. Aided many hundreds of slaves to escape via the 'underground railroad' (see p. 361).

Turner, Nat (1800–31):   The leader of the major slave uprising of 1831 in Virginia (see p. 139).

Tyler, John (1790–1862):   10th President of the United States, 1841–45. Formerly Vice-President to his Whig predecessor, William Henry Harrison, who died in office (the first President to succeed because of the death of an incumbent). His Administration was a bitter disillusion to his Whig supporters, as in his veto of the bill re-establishing the national bank. Most of his Administration resigned. However, his Administration concluded with Great Britain the Webster–Ashburton Treaty of 1842, fixing the eastern border between the US and Canada. He also secured the annexation of Texas. In 1844 the Whigs rejected Tyler in favour of Clay.

Van Buren, Martin (1782–1862): 8th President of the United States, 1837–41. Formerly Vice-President to his Democratic predecessor, Andrew Jackson, and one of Jackson's key advisers. A skilful political operator (nicknamed the 'Red Fox'), he lost popularity in the financial panic of 1837. He opposed the annexation of Texas to the US for fear of increasing the power of the slave-holding South, a stance which probably later cost him the 1844 nomination. In 1840 he had been defeated in his attempts at re-election. A friend of labour who helped secure the 10-hour day for federal employees.

Vance, Cyrus (1917–): Diplomat and lawyer. He became Secretary of the Army in 1962, and Deputy Secretary of Defense in 1964, in which post he strongly defended the Vietnam War. He was a member of the Vietnam peace talks negotiating team in Paris, 1968–69, and Secretary of State, 1977–80, under President Carter. Vance supported diplomatic recognition of the united Vietnam. He resigned in 1980 following a failed attempt to rescue American hostages in Iran. He attempted unsuccessfully with Lord Owen to negotiate a peaceful solution to the Bosnian problem in 1993.

Wald, Lillian D. (1867–1940): Leading social reformer, involved in campaigns against child labour and sweatshops. Social worker in New York. Founder of Henry Street Settlement.

Wallace, George (Corley) (1919–): Right-wing Democratic and populist politician. Served as Governor of Alabama, 1962–66, 1970–74. Founder of anti-liberal American Independent Party and fought 1968 presidential election. Seriously injured in assassination attempt (May 1972) which left him paralysed. Led the fight of the South against racially integrated education. A symbol of white intransigence who later recanted his segregationalist views.

Warren, Earl (1891–1974): Liberal 14th Chief Justice of the United States, 1953–69. A long string of rulings on such varied issues as racial segregation in schools, freedom of the press, religious services in schools and obscenity definitions marked the liberal tenure of his office. Earlier he had unsuccessfully contested the Vice-Presidency in

1948 as a Republican (and also lost out to Eisenhower for the Republican presidential nomination in 1952). Headed the Warren Commission to investigate the John F. Kennedy assassination.

Washington, George (1732–99):   The founding father of the independent United States and its first President. Born on his family's estate on the Potomac River in Westmoreland County, Virginia, the son of a prosperous planter family which had emigrated from England in 1656. Served as a major and later colonel in the Virginia militia in the French–Indian (Seven Years) War, 1752–58, distinguishing himself in 1755 by rescuing the disastrous expedition of General Braddock. Served in the Virginia House of Burgesses, 1759–74, where he protested against British colonial policy but did not yet favour separation. Married widow Martha Custis, 1759; the couple had no children of their own. Served as a member of the Virginian delegation to the First and Second Continental Congresses, 1774–75, and in the latter year was appointed Commander-in-Chief of the Continental Army. Despite victories at Trenton (December 1776) and Princeton (January 1777), Washington's army suffered reverses in 1777 and the Continental Congress debated removing him as supreme commander. Rebuilt his army in its winter quarters in Valley Forge, Pennsylvania, December 1777–June 1778, turning it into a disciplined force which won a decisive victory at Yorktown in October 1781 and forced the eventual British capitulation. Resigned his commission and retired to private life, 1783. Elected president of the Constitutional Convention in Philadelphia, 1787. Overwhelmingly elected first President of the United States, 1789, and likewise re-elected, 1792. Established the federal government on a permanent basis and created the custom that heads of departments of state should act together as a cabinet under presidential leadership, rather than under congressional direction. Voluntarily refused to seek a further term and announced his retirement with a published Farewell Address, 1796, leaving office in March 1797. Retired to private life, but accepted command of the American forces during a brief war scare with France in 1798. Died at his home, December 1799.

Weaver, Robert Clifton (1907–):   Noted economist. First black member of the Cabinet. Secretary, Department of Housing and Urban Development, 1966–69. Author of *Negro Labor: A National Problem* (1946) and *The Negro Ghetto* (1948).

Webster, Daniel (1782–1852):   Federalist (later Whig) politician who negotiated settlement of the Maine boundary dispute with Britain (the Webster–Ashburton Treaty of 1842). Representative (later Senator), first for New Hampshire then for Massachusetts. Unsuccessful Whig candidate for President, 1836. Had earlier opposed War of 1812 and supported protective tariffs. Served as Secretary of State, 1841–43 and 1850–52. An opponent of the Mexican War and supporter of the Compromise of 1850. Regarded as the greatest American orator of the nineteenth century.

Willard, Frances Elizabeth Caroline (1839–98):   Teacher and social reformer who joined temperance movement in 1874. President, Woman's Christian Temperance Union from 1879 to 1898. Also President of International World Women's Christian Temperance Union.

Willkie, Wendell Lewis (1892–1944):   Republican politician and lawyer. President in 1930s of electric utility company, Commonwealth and Southern Corporation. Unsuccessfully campaigned for Presidency against Franklin D. Roosevelt in 1940. His adoption as candidate in 1940 (he had previously been a liberal Democrat in his early life, and only changed affiliation in 1939) was an extraordinary event. His support for Roosevelt's pro-British stance alienated some Republicans.

Wilson, Thomas Woodrow (1856–1924):   28th President of the United States, 1913–19. Lawyer and academic. Democratic Governor, New Jersey, 1910. Inaugurated President, 1913. Liberal domestic policy. 'Big Stick' policy in Latin America. Determined on neutrality in World War I. Re-elected to Presidency, 1916; declared war on Germany, 1917. Announced Fourteen Points (see p. 323) for reshaping post-war world on basis of national self-determination and the creation of an international forum, January 1918. Congress refused to ratify Wilson's signing of Versailles Treaty, particularly objecting to participation in League of Nations. Awarded Nobel Peace Prize, 1919. Suffered incapacitating stroke, 1919.

SECTION SIX

Glossary of terms

Abolitionists Political activists who campaigned for the abolition of slavery in the US. The movement was concentrated in the northern and more heavily industrialized states which had abandoned the system towards the end of the eighteenth century. Abolitionism was remarkable for being an international movement (American anti-slavery groups had their counterparts in Great Britain), heavily influenced by religious fundamentalism and composed of both white and black activists working together. From 1839 the movement was divided between the radical American Anti-Slavery Society led by William Lloyd Garrison of Boston, which regarded the US Constitution as being pro-slavery, and the more conservative American and Foreign Anti-Slavery Society which favoured gradual emancipation by legal means. Constitutional abolitionism was endorsed by the Republican Party (q.v.) and by the Freesoilers (q.v.) and, following the defeat of the Confederate States (q.v.) in the American Civil War (1861–65), slavery was abolished by the Thirteenth Amendment to the Constitution. After the war abolitionists engaged in humanitarian and civil rights work among the former slaves (*see* Freedmen's Bureau), but the American Anti-Slavery Society itself was wound up in 1870.

Acceptance speech Speech by which a candidate for the US Presidency accepts nomination at the party convention, usually outlining his programme for office.

ACLU American Civil Liberties Union, founded in 1920. The ACLU is a liberal activist organization which campaigns to protect the constitutional rights of all Americans, including political extremists.

ACU American Conservative Union, founded in 1964. It publishes an index of the conservatism of members of Congress which is based on their voting records on measures in Congress.

ADA Americans for Democratic Action, a liberal group established in 1947 which, like the ACU, produces an index of the ideological positions of members of Congress.

Affirmative action A policy of remedying the effects of past racial or other discrimination, as distinct from equal opportunities legislation which simply forbids unequal treatment. In general, programmes for affirmative action concern the proportion of minorities employed in hitherto inaccessible occupations. Affirmative action is required by law or regulation for all governmental agencies and for recipients of public funds (such as contractors or universities). In effect, legislative action is designed to consolidate the progress made in legal, social and political redress of minority grievances with tangible advantages in job and educational opportunity, but critics of the system regard it as a form of 'reverse discrimination'.

AFL–CIO The American Federation of Labor–Congress of Industrial Organizations, a confederation of North American trades unions equivalent to the TUC in Great Britain. The AFL arose out of the nineteenth-century craft union tradition of the Knights of Labor, under the directorship of Samuel Gompers (1886–1924). The CIO was founded in 1937 as a breakaway movement of general unions in mass production industries whose unskilled workers had not been incorporated in the AFL. The two rival confederations amalgamated in 1955 creating a combined organization of labour unions with a membership of 17 million. Its political influence stems in part from its organizational and financial assistance to the Democratic Party.

***Alabama* claims** Legal claims for damages made by the US against Great Britain after the American Civil War (q.v.) for losses to her shipping caused by Confederate raiders built in British yards, the most famous of which was the *Alabama*.

Alamo A mission in San Antonio, Texas and the site in 1836 of a noted defence against the Mexican army by a garrison of the American settlers who had rebelled against Mexican rule. Those who fell included the noted frontiersman Davy Crockett. The example of the defence of the Alamo inspired the settlers' army which under General Sam Houston defeated the Mexican forces at the battle of San Jacinto. Texas became an independent republic until it joined the United States in 1845.

Albany Plan Plan of union proposed by Benjamin Franklin and adopted at the Albany Congress of June 1754. Franklin's plan was for a permanent confederation among the British colonies in America with an elected parliament to organize their defence and the authority to raise taxes. The plan was rejected by the individual colonial assemblies.

Alliance for Progress An initiative of the Kennedy Administration (1961–63) to promote economic development in Latin America through extensive US assistance and so forestall the spread of communism in the western hemisphere. The Alliance was founded in August 1961 when 20 American states subscribed to its charter at Punta del Este in Uruguay. Its declared aim was to raise living standards by 2.5% per annum, but the American aid was insufficient for the purpose and the Alliance was a failure.

Alphabet agencies   Popular name for the administrative agencies created by the New Deal (q.v.). The most important of these were the Agricultural Adjustment Administration (AAA) to stabilize the market for farm produce; the Works Progress Administration (WPA) to provide public-sector jobs; the Federal Emergency Relief Administration (FERA) to provide welfare payments to the states; and the National Recovery Administration (NRA) to stabilize industrial trading conditions. *See* TVA.

Amendment   The action of a legislative body in altering any measure before it, or any previously enacted law, or, more usually, any change to be made to the constitution of a state or to the US Constitution. The means of amending the latter are stipulated in Article V: proposed amendments, which the President cannot veto, must be ratified by three-quarters of the legislatures of the states or by conventions called for the purpose.

America First Committee   Pacifist organization established in 1940 which opposed US participation in World War II and military aid to the Allies. It was dominated by conservative isolationists (q.v.).

American System   An economic programme proposed by Henry Clay after the War of 1812 (q.v.) to lessen American dependence upon foreign powers. It included a national bank, federal assistance for the development of transportation, and tariffs to protect American industry. The system was favoured by the Whig Party (q.v.).

Anti-Trust laws   Laws to regulate or prohibit 'unfair' competition or combinations among producers that tend to hinder fully competitive trade. The enforcement of such laws is carried out by the Antitrust division of the Department of Justice and the Federal Trade Commission. Combinations in restraint of trade were first prohibited by the Sherman Anti-Trust Act of 1890.

Apportionment   The allocation of legislative seats. By the Apportionment Act of 1929, Congress fixed the number of House seats at 435 and provided that the Bureau of the Census should redistribute the seats among the 50 states after each decennial census. Each state is assigned at least one seat and the remainder are divided among the states according to population. This process helps avoid the possibility of large over- or under-representation in a society with a highly mobile population and a Constitution which requires each person's vote to have as nearly equal a weight as possible.

Appropriation   A bill in Congress which raises money for those specific purposes which have previously been established by 'authorization' bills.

Arms race   Any process of competition between two or more powers to develop a greater number of and more technically sophisticated weapons; but usually understood to refer to the post-war rivalry between the USA and the former USSR over deployment of nuclear weapons.

Articles of Confederation   *See* p. 55.

Atlantic Charter   Agreement reached in August 1941 between US President Franklin Roosevelt and British Prime Minister Winston Churchill which set out the basis upon which the two powers would co-operate internationally after the conclusion of World War II. The terms included recognizing the right of all peoples to consent to their own government and the establishment of a system of collective security. The Charter formed the basis of the subsequent alliance of the United Nations against Germany and Japan, and was endorsed by the other Allied combatants.

Atom spies   Alleged members of a Soviet spy ring which had penetrated the Manhattan Project (q.v.). Following the confession in Great Britain in 1950 of the Anglo-German scientist Klaus Fuchs, the FBI arrested eight persons named in the press as having supplied nuclear secrets to the USSR. Two of that number, Julius Rosenberg and his wife Ethel, were tried for conspiracy and sentenced to death. The Supreme Court considered their case five times but they were finally executed in 1953, the only persons ever sentenced to death for espionage in peacetime. *See* House Un-American Activities Committee *and* McCarthyism.

Attorney General   The head of the US Department of Justice and a senior member of the Presidential Cabinet. The Attorney General serves both as legal adviser to the President and to the executive branch of the federal government as a whole. He is also chief law-enforcement officer of the United States. In this latter capacity the Attorney General directs the work of federal district attorneys, US Marshals and the federal penal institutions. Criminal investigation and the conduct of litigation involving the United States are his responsibility. Each of the states has an Attorney General who is often an elected official.

Balanced budget   A budget of any governmental authority in which the receipts and expenditures are equal to one another. Certain state constitutions require that the budget of that state government shall be in balance in any financial year (i.e., it is not permitted to run a deficit) and periodically bills are introduced into Congress or constitutional amendments proposed to require the same of the federal government.

Balanced ticket A party's list of candidates at an election designed to represent, and so to appeal to, the regional, ethnic, religious and gender composition of the electoral district.

Bamboo Curtain Term used to describe the diplomatic isolation of the People's Republic of China from the communist revolution of 1949 until 1972, when President Nixon visited Peking to restore US diplomatic relations and China joined the United Nations. *See* Iron Curtain.

Barnburners Anti-slavery faction within the Democratic Party (q.v.) who favoured the Wilmot Proviso (q.v.) of 1846. Supporters of Martin Van Buren of New York state, the Barnburners split the party to form the Freesoilers (q.v.) and thus allowed the election of the Whig President Zachary Taylor in 1848.

Baruch Plan Proposal made in June 1946 by Bernard Baruch, US representative to the UN Atomic Energy Commission, to place all sources of nuclear power under international control. It was rejected by the Soviet Union.

Bay of Pigs Coastal area in southern Cuba and site in April 1961 of an abortive armed landing by Cuban exiles opposed to the communist regime of Fidel Castro, which the United States sought to destabilize. The anti-Castro forces had been secretly trained in the US by the CIA; the operation was planned during the later stages of the Eisenhower Administration and continued by President Kennedy, but Kennedy's refusal to allow American military air-cover during the landing resulted in the rebels' rapid defeat and capture. It marked the first serious foreign policy reversal of the Kennedy Administration and resulted in Cuba's closer alignment with the USSR. *See* Cuban Missile Crisis.

Beauty contest A primary election in which American voters may demonstrate their support for a candidate, but the result of which is not binding on the delegates.

Bering Sea Controversy Dispute between the United States and Great Britain over the extension of American territorial waters in the Bering Sea. The United States had purchased Alaska from Russia in 1867 and claimed that the territorial rights transferred to her included control over the eastern part of the Bering Sea, from which she sought to exclude British seal fishing ships. The dispute went before an international arbitration tribunal in 1893 which awarded damages to the British sealers.

Bible Belt   Term describing the morally conservative and religiously fundamentalist Southern states of the United States.

Big Five   Permanent members of the Security Council of the United Nations (q.v.), namely the United States, Russia, France, United Kingdom and the People's Republic of China.

Big Four   Representatives of the principal Allied powers at the Paris Peace Conference of 1919, which produced the Treaty of Versailles. They were President Woodrow Wilson of the United States and Prime Ministers Lloyd George of Great Britain, George Clemenceau of France, and Vittorio Orlando of Italy.

Big Three   Leaders of the three major Allied powers of World War II – President Franklin Roosevelt of the United States, Marshal Stalin of the Soviet Union and Prime Minister Winston Churchill of Great Britain.

Bill of Rights   *See* p. 58.

Bimetallism   Use of both gold and silver as monetary standards in any system of currency. The United States effectively adopted the gold standard in 1834 when Congress fixed the legal ratio between silver and gold for monetary purposes at 16 to 1. The Coinage Act of 1873 demonetized silver altogether. This, however, was antithetical to the interests of those exploiting the new silver mines of Nevada, who otherwise would have been able to sell silver to the US Treasury at a fixed ratio. The silver interests were supported by farmers' groups in the Mid-West who sought an inflationary expansion of the money supply through silver currency in order to reduce the real value of their debts. The demands subsided with economic expansion during the 1880s but the onset of a severe depression at the end of the decade led to renewed calls for bimetallism on the part of radical agrarian parties, the Populists (q.v.), and later the Democratic Party itself in the 1896 presidential campaign. *See* Cross of Gold Speech, Goldbugs *and* Greenback.

Bipartisanship   Any process of co-operation between the two main political parties in support of a particular policy or piece of legislation.

Birchers   Members of the John Birch Society, an extreme right-wing political grouping founded in 1958 and which believes that international communism poses a direct threat to American Christian democracy. It is named for US Captain John Birch, executed as a spy by the Chinese communists in 1945, who is regarded by the Right as the first victim of the Cold War.

Black Codes Laws enacted by Southern states in 1865 and 1866 after the American Civil War (q.v.) to maintain the legal subordination of the newly emancipated slaves. In most states blacks were forbidden to vote, to bear arms, to testify against white persons or to marry them. In many cases the laws largely remained in force until the Civil Rights Movement (q.v.) of the 1950s and 1960s.

Black Monday Term for the collapse of the New York Stock Exchange on 19 October 1987, when the Dow Jones (q.v.) Industrial Average fell 508 points (23%), causing major falls in other world stock markets. It was the worst one-day decline since the Wall Street Crash (q.v.).

Black Muslims Puritanical movement of black Americans, also known as the Nation of Islam, whose twin pillars of belief are Negro superiority and racial separation. It was founded in 1930 and led by Elijah Muhammad; the most influential member was Malcolm X, who was assassinated in February 1965 after he had broken with the group to found his own internationalist Organization for Afro-American Unity. The Nation of Islam was influential again during the 1980s under Louis Farrakhan. *See* Black Power.

Black Panther Party A paramilitary Black Power (q.v.) organization established in Oakland, California in 1966 by Huey Newton and Bobby Seale which was active in resisting the police (see p. 104).

Black Power Radical black movement which emerged in the United States in the 1960s partly as a result of dissatisfaction with the lack of progress with the Civil Rights Movement (q.v.). Black Power activism had many strands, but all its practitioners rejected the belief that blacks should integrate with white society and proclaimed blacks' cultural equality. The movement's readiness to contemplate violence led to fears of inter-racial civil war in the era of urban riots beginning with Watts (q.v.). Its influence diminished substantially in the 1970s.

Black Thursday 24 October 1929, the day the Wall Street Crash (q.v.) began.

Bleeding Kansas Period of militant rivalry in 1856 during the settlement of the Kansas Territory when pro- and anti-slavery settlers resorted to violence to press the claims of each party as the legitimate government of the territory. Before the federal government restored order, 200 settlers had been killed, including five murdered at the 'Pottawatmoie Creek Massacre' by the fanatical abolitionist John Brown (who was later to be executed for leading a raid on the federal arsenal at

Harpers Ferry, Virginia in 1859). *See* Missouri Compromise *and* Popular Sovereignty.

Bloc   A cross-party coalition of American legislators who unite to vote on a single issue of common interest.

Block Grant   Transfer of revenue from the federal government to state and local governments, first adopted in 1966. Payments made in block grants may be used only for broadly defined areas of governmental activity, but the local authority is free to develop specific programmes or policies at its own discretion.

Blue Eagle   Symbol of the National Recovery Administration, an early agency of the New Deal (q.v.) whose object was to stabilize industrial production through regulation. The display of the Blue Eagle in a workplace or shop indicated that that employer accepted the NRA's conditions on working hours and wages.

Blue laws   Moral laws among Puritan communities of the colonial period to enforce the Sabbath and prohibit certain kinds of behaviour; and a term now applied to state or local laws banning commercial activity on Sundays, etc.

Boll Weevils   Nickname for those congressional Democrats from Southern states who, being more conservative, often vote with Republican members. In the early 1980s they were a significant component of President Reagan's bipartisan coalition in Congress. The name is derived from the beetle which is a pest to cotton.

Bonus Marchers   Some 22,000 unemployed US veterans of World War I who travelled to Washington DC in June 1932 during the Great Depression to try to persuade the government to pay immediately a bonus due to them in 1945. President Hoover did not wish to unbalance the federal budget by complying and after one month ordered the army, under General MacArthur, to evict them from the capital, which was done with excessive force.

Boondoggle   Any unnecessary project for which public expenditure is authorized. *See* Pork Barrel.

Boss   Term traditionally applied to the leader of a (often municipal) political 'machine' or group of supporters, who are capable of mobilizing large numbers of voters at elections. The boss would frequently be a leading publicly elected official who would nominate his supporters to minor offices or would ensure they received lucrative public contracts. In the period before World War II machines were important providers of welfare and jobs to immigrant communities and were an integral part of the legitimate municipal or state political parties. Famous American bosses included William Tweed (*see* Tweed Ring) of Tammany Hall (q.v.), Richard Daley, Mayor of Chicago, and Governor Huey Long of Louisiana.

Boston Tea Party   Incident in December 1773 when colonial patriots, disguised as Native Americans, boarded British merchant ships in Boston Harbor and tipped into the sea their cargoes of tea in protest at the duties laid by the British government upon its import. The duty on tea was the only one remaining after the repeal of the more comprehensive Townshend Duties of 1767, but the Americans radicals were opposed to Parliament's right to levy *any* duty on the colonists without their consent. Furthermore, the direct importation of tea by the British East India Company, as permitted under the Tea Act of 1773, would have harmed the colonial merchants.

Brady Plan   Proposal made in 1989 by US Treasury Secretary Brady for co-ordinated action by the G7 group of leading capitalist economies to reduce or forgive the sovereign debt of developing countries.

Brains Trust   Originally the name of a private group of academic and business advisers assembled by President Franklin Roosevelt during the New Deal (q.v.); it included Professor Frankfurter of Harvard (later a Supreme Court Justice) and Rex Tugwell, Raymond Moley and Adolf Berle of Columbia University. The term is now generally applied to any such advisory group.

Bretton Woods (Conference)   Town in New Hampshire where representatives of 28 nations attended a conference called by President Franklin Roosevelt in July 1944 to organize a system of monetary co-operation in order to prevent financial crises such as that which had triggered the Great Depression (q.v.). The final agreement was largely based on the American plans and proposed convertibility of currencies and fixed exchange rates to encourage trade. The conference also led to the establishment of the International Bank for Reconstruction and Development (the World Bank) and the International Monetary Fund.

Brinkmanship   Term describing the policy of forcing a rival power to reach an accommodation by deliberately creating a severe risk of nuclear war. It was coined by US Secretary of State John Foster Dulles who, in January 1956, told *Life* magazine that to attain diplomatic goals statesmen needed 'the ability to get to the brink of war without getting into war'.

Brokered convention   A convention (q.v.) at which the decisions are made by the leaders of the party rather than by the delegates, often because of a deadlock in the voting.

Bull Moosers   *See* Progressive Party, p. 350 *and* Progressive Era.

Bullet vote   A ballot in which American electors confine their interest to a single issue or candidate.

Bunker Hill   First major battle of the American War of Independence (q.v.) in June 1775, in which the British troops under General William Howe, who were beseiged in Boston, managed to drive the colonial forces from the heights above the city but only at great cost to themselves.

Busing   Practice adopted in the 1970s of moving children from certain neighbourhoods to schools in different areas, in order to prevent educational facilities becoming entirely black or white as a result of the movement of a large proportion of the white population to the suburbs. The intention was to encourage racial harmony, but many white parents complained that the practice infringed their right to choose where their children were educated.

Cabinet   The group of the President's principal advisers. Its membership is determined according to the President's discretion, but it does include the heads of the principal departments of state who are appointed to such offices by him.

Camp David   Presidential retreat in Maryland and site in September 1978 of a conference arranged by the US President Jimmy Carter between Israeli Prime Minister Menachem Begin and Egyptian President Anwar Sadat. Their agreement at Camp David established the basis for the subsequent Egyptian–Israeli peace treaty.

Canal Zone   Area incorporating the 40-mile long Panama Canal in Central America and granted to the US in 1903. The Zone is under the control of the US Army, but by a treaty of September 1977 between the Panamanian leader General Torrijos and President Carter it was agreed that the Zone would be returned to the Republic of Panama by 2000.

Cannonism   Period of rule of the Republican Speaker of the House of Representatives Joseph Cannon, who exploited his power of appointment to the Rules Committee to decide the legislative agenda. In 1910 progressive Republicans formed an alliance with the Democrats to deprive the Speaker of this power.

Capitol The name given to the building in Washington, DC which houses the House of Representatives and the Senate of the United States; and to the counterparts in the capitals of each of the 50 states of the Union.

Carpetbagger Term of abuse applied during the era of Reconstruction (q.v.) to those Northern politicians and businessmen who migrated to the American South, many with the hope of being elected to Congress by the votes of the newly enfranchised black Americans. The term implied they had no interest in the South beyond their personal hand-baggage.

Casablanca Conference Meeting in 1943 between President Franklin Roosevelt and British Prime Minister Winston Churchill at Casablanca in Morocco. The conference was used to plan the military strategy for the Allied liberation of Europe. It has become notorious for the decision taken there to require the unconditional surrender of the Axis which, it is argued, unnecessarily prolonged World War II.

Caucus A meeting of party members in one of the houses of a legislative body for the purposes of making decisions on the selection of party leaders and on legislative business; or a meeting of party leaders in any state to choose electoral candidates. Republicans in Congress prefer to call their party meetings a 'conference'. The term 'to caucus' is also commonly used to describe any informal meeting of legislators seeking to reach agreement on a common course of action. The 'majority caucus' in each house makes important decisions regarding the organization of committees in Congress, the appointment of chairmen, and so forth, all of which are officially and formally endorsed when the full house meets in regular session.

CBO The Congressional Budget Office, an agency of Congress established in 1974 to make recommendations upon the federal budget and to advise Congress on fiscal policy generally and the consequences of any expenditure authorized by legislative measures.

CDF The Conservative Democratic Forum, a grouping in Congress of Southern Democrats.

CEA Council of Economic Advisers, a board of academic economists established in 1946 within the President's Executive Office, which advises the Administration on economic policy.

Chappaquiddick Affair   Scandal involving Senator Edward Kennedy of Massachusetts. In July 1969 Kennedy delayed reporting to the police an automobile accident which resulted in the drowning of his assistant Mary Jo Kopechne after he had driven off a bridge on Chappaquiddick Island, Massachusetts. This and subsequent allegations about Kennedy's personal judgement weighed heavily against him during the contest for the Democratic presidential nomination of 1980.

Chicago Martyrs   Eight anarchists arrested after the Haymarket Affair (q.v.). Found guilty on circumstantial evidence, four were hanged in November 1887, one committed suicide and three were imprisoned. The eight, who were pardoned on grounds of a miscarriage of justice in 1893, were the earliest martyrs of the American Left.

Chicago Seven   Leaders of disturbances at the 1968 Democratic National Convention held in Chicago. The convention was the scene of street protests against the Vietnam War (q.v.) which were violently suppressed by the police. The leaders were tried for incitement to riot in September 1969 and five were jailed; they were originally eight in number but Bobby Seale, chairman of the Black Panther Party (q.v.), was tried separately.

Chief of Staff   The head of the White House Office, who co-ordinates the activities of the Cabinet and frequently controls officials' access to the President. Historically individual Chiefs of Staff, such as Bob Haldeman under President Nixon, have been very powerful.

CIA   *See* p. 255.

Civil Rights Commission   A bipartisan federal commission established by the Civil Rights Act of 1957 whose function is to investigate the upholding of civil rights under law.

Civil Rights Movement   *See* p. 142.

Closed Primary   *See* Primary.

Cloture   The procedure employed to terminate a debate in Congress and bring the particular matter to a vote.

Coat tails   The term for the fact that in an election the leading candidate on a ballot may attract votes for other candidates of the same party affiliation running for lesser offices. For example, the presence of a presidential candidate may induce voters to vote for congressional candidates on the same ticket.

Collective security Term widely used in international diplomacy and first coined at the Geneva Conference of 1924 to denote a policy whereby the security of individual countries was guaranteed jointly by others. Under the Charter of the United Nations (q.v.) power to meet threats to peace is invested the Security Council, whose permanent members are the United States, Russia, the United Kingdom, France and China. However, as the Council cannot act if a member dissents, the principle of collective security is not fully established.

Color bar Separation of persons according to race, usually a reference to the legal prohibition in the Southern states up to the 1960s which forbade non-whites to frequent public areas and facilities reserved for whites. *See* Segregation.

Commander-in-Chief Article II, Section 2 of the US Constitution stipulates that the President shall be Commander-in-Chief of all the military forces of the United States, and of the state national guard units when called into federal service. In this position the President has at his disposal a vast array of 'war powers' which enables him to deploy American forces anywhere in the world. On many occasions Presidents have actually ordered troops into combat without securing a declaration of war by Congress. In reaction to this enormous power, Congress in 1969 passed the 'national commitments' resolution which required the President to have its approval to use United States' forces abroad; and in 1973 the War Powers Act (which President Nixon vetoed) which required him to do so only in a military emergency or after a declaration of war had been passed by Congress.

Commerce power The legal authority given to Congress by the US Constitution to regulate external and internal trade (i.e., between the several states). It has been used as the basis for federal regulation of and intervention in most economic activities.

Common Cause A pressure group founded in 1970 which campaigns for various causes it identifies as being in the public interest, for example the reform of the laws on electoral campaign finance.

Common Sense Political pamphlet written by Thomas Paine in 1776 which argued that the cause of the American colonists required not redress by the British Parliament or Crown but complete independence from Great Britain. Violently republican in tone, the pamphlet encouraged American political sentiment towards the Declaration of Independence (q.v.).

Compromise of 1877 In the presidential election of 1876 neither the Democratic candidate, Samuel Tilden of New York, nor the Republican

Rutherford Hayes of Ohio won a majority of votes in the electoral college and the result was disputed until a congressional electoral commission awarded the election to Hayes. The Democrats threatened to obstruct the business of Congress but then agreed to Hayes's election in return for the withdrawal of the federal troops from the Southern states and the effective termination of Reconstruction (q.v.).

Concurrent powers Those constitutional powers which may be possessed simultaneously by both the federal and local governments, for example, the power to levy taxes.

Confederate States of America Independent republic of the eleven Southern states which seceded from the United States in 1860 after the election of the first Republican President Abraham Lincoln. The South feared that the federal government, under a Northern political party antithetical to slavery, would seek its abolition and would restrict states' rights. In December 1860 South Carolina legally dissolved the Union between itself and the other states and was quickly followed by the rest of the Lower South; in February 1861 delegates from the secessionist states met in Montgomery, Alabama and drew up the constitution of a new union, the Confederate States of America. Jefferson Davis of Mississippi was elected President. The constitution of the new republic was actually closely modelled upon that of the USA. The Confederacy's attack upon the United States led to the American Civil War (q.v.); following its military defeat the individual states were readmitted to the Union during the era known as Reconstruction (q.v.).

Conference Committee A joint committee of members of both houses of Congress appointed by the Speaker of the House and the President of the Senate to reconcile the different versions of any legislative bill passed by each chamber. The compromise, known as a 'conference report', forms the bill which, if passed by both chambers, is sent to the President for signing into law.

Confirmation The power of a legislative body to approve nominations made to fill executive and judicial positions. Nominations for such offices made by the President must be confirmed by the Senate with a majority of votes cast. In addition, the Twenty-Fifth Amendment to the Constitution gives the President the power to fill a vacancy in the office of the Vice-President with the approval of both houses of Congress. Many of the appointments made by the Governors of the various states must also be approved by the upper houses of the state legislatures.

Congress *See* p. 76.

Constitutional convention A body called by Congress upon the application of the legislatures of two-thirds of the states which shall propose amendments to the US Constitution (as an alternative to Congress itself proposing them); or that body within each state which may subsequently ratify those amendments as an alternative to ratification by the legislature, as Congress shall choose. Only the Twenty-First Amendment of 1933 repealing prohibition has been ratified by conventions.

Containment Policy adopted by the USA in 1947 in response to Soviet expansionism after World War II, with the aim of containing communism within its existing territorial limits. Its clearest exposition was given by George Kennan of the State Department. Writing in the journal *Foreign Affairs* under the pseudonym 'X' in June 1947, Kennan argued that the USSR was more likely than Hitler had been to be deterred from expansion by a resolute stance. This policy was pursued by economic assistance to Europe under the Marshall Plan (q.v.) and by military intervention in Korea and Vietnam. *See* Truman Doctrine.

Continental Congress *See* p. 54.

Contract with America The right-wing Republican agenda which produced victory in the mid-term elections of 1994. The agenda is most closely associated with Newt Gingrich.

Contras Supporters of the right-wing Nicaraguan dictator Anastasio Somoza Debayle who was overthrown by the Sandinista revolutionaries in 1979. After Somoza's death in 1980, with American support, they mounted armed attacks in north-west Nicaragua from neighbouring Honduras but their position was weakened after 1984 when the US Congress refused to vote aid. However, the electoral defeat of the Sandinistas in 1990 led to negotiations with the new Nicaraguan government and the cessation of military activities by the contras.

Convention Both major parties hold a national convention every four years in order to nominate their respective presidential candidates and to adopt a 'platform'. In most states, both parties hold county and state conventions annually. In the national convention, delegates, who cast votes to select the party's candidate, are apportioned on the basis of state representation with bonuses for states showing voting majorities for the party in the preceding election. They are selected by party conventions or committees in approximately half of the states and by primaries in the other half. Both parties also accredit delegates from the District of Columbia, Puerto Rico and the Virgin Islands.

COPE   The Committee on Political Education, an agency of the AFL–CIO and the first political action committee established in the 1940s. *See* PAC.

Copperheads   Name given to those Democrats in the Northern states who sympathized with the Confederacy and opposed military action against the South during the American Civil War (q.v.). It derives from the venomous copperhead snake which does not produce a warning rattle before striking.

CORE   The Congress of Racial Equality was founded in 1942 and advocated non-violent civil disobedience in order to obtain civil rights for black Americans. *See also* p. 142.

County   With the exception of a small number of minor states, the county is the major unit of local government in the United States. They number over 3,000 in total. The powers and functions of the county vary widely depending upon the state, but typically they are responsible for law enforcement and the maintenance of courts, roads, schools and the local welfare agencies. Each county is governed by a county board which in most states is composed of a number of elected officials.

Coxeyites   The unemployed army led by 'General' Jacob Coxey who marched on Washington in April 1894 as the depression of 1893 was felt. The protest soon lost its impetus when Coxey was arrested.

Crittenden Compromise   Proposals made in 1861 by Senator John Crittenden of Kentucky to bring back into the United States those states which had seceded, by guaranteeing through a series of constitutional amendments their right to maintain slavery. The proposals were rejected by the Republican President-elect Abraham Lincoln. *See* Confederate States of America.

Cross of Gold Speech   Speech made by William Jennings Bryan at the Democratic National Convention in 1896 in support of the free silver platform. Opposing the gold standard with the celebrated remark 'You shall not crucify mankind upon a cross of gold', Bryan won the Democratic nomination but subsequently lost the presidential election to the Republican McKinley. *See* Bimetallism.

Cuban Missile Crisis   Period of extreme tension in the Cold War from 22 to 28 October 1962. Intelligence agencies in Washington, aware of increased Soviet interest in Cuban affairs, discovered on 16 October from aerial reconnaissance photographic evidence that Soviet ballistic missiles capable of delivering nuclear warheads on US cities were being installed in Cuba. During the previous month the Soviet government had admitted supplying arms to Cuba but denied that they were offensive in nature. On 22 October President Kennedy declared that the US Navy would blockade Cuba and requested the USSR to remove its missiles. The Soviet reply on 26 October was that they would be removed if NATO missiles were removed from Turkey. Kennedy found this offer unacceptable and the world faced a real threat of imminent nuclear war. Khrushchev, the Soviet leader, realizing perhaps that the USSR had 'overplayed its hand', agreed on 28 October to remove the missiles. Castro, the Cuban leader, would not allow UN observers into Cuba to check that they had been dismantled, but the US Defense Department accepted by the first week in November that they had been. The blockade was ended on 20 November following Soviet promises to remove bombers and missile technicians by the end of the month. Kennedy's resoluteness and calm during this period of great tension marked him as a leading statesman on the world stage.

Cumberland Road   The 'National Road' which ran westward from Cumberland, Maryland to link the Potomac and Ohio rivers. Its construction, which was voted by Congress in 1817, was one of the most significant examples of the policy known as the American System (q.v.).

Dark horse   A candidate for political office who makes an unexpected appearance (e.g., at a party convention) or rapidly achieves unforeseen prominence.

Dawes Plan   Plan presented by the American banker Charles Dawes to the Allied Reparations Committee in April 1924 for settlement of German war reparations by an annual payment of 2,000 million marks, thus allowing Germany to meet the harsh financial terms imposed upon her by the Allies at the Paris Peace Conference of 1919–20. *See* Young Plan.

Declaration of Independence   *See* p. 55.

Delegated powers   The powers which the US Constitution grants to the federal government, as stipulated in the first three Articles covering the legislative, executive and judicial branches.

Demilitarized zone   Any area which by agreement between two or more states may not be fortified nor contain any military forces. The term usually refers to the area (approximately following the 38th parallel) dividing North and South Korea which was demilitarized following the 1950–53 Korean War; and to the area along the 17th parallel between North and South Vietnam from 1954 to 1975.

Departments   The major administrative offices responsible for the conduct of government. In the federal government the departments are headed by officers who comprise the President's Cabinet. They include the Departments of the Treasury, State, Defense, Justice, Commerce, Labor, Agriculture, Interior, Health and Human Services, Education, Welfare, Housing and Urban Development, and Transportation. States and local governments also arrange their major administrative activities on departmental lines.

Dewline   Acronym for the Distant Early Warning Viewing Line, a comprehensive radar system established in 1957 by the North American Air Defense Command (NORAD) across the northern reaches of the hemisphere to detect the approach of Soviet nuclear missiles or aircraft. By the 1970s it had been rendered obsolete by the use of satellites in space to detect military movements.

DFL   Democratic-Farmer Labor Party, the branch of the Democratic Party in Minnesota. The upper states of the Mid-West have an abiding tradition of populist politics based upon the rural parties of the late nineteenth century.

Dies Committee   Alternative name for the House Un-American Activities Committee (q.v.) after its first chairman, Martin Dies of Texas.

Direct Primary   *See* Primary.

District Attorney   The public prosecutor acting on behalf of the state authority in each county of the United States (federal prosecutions are carried out by the US Attorneys). He or she is usually an elected official.

District of Columbia   The national capital district of the United States, home to the US Congress and other offices of the government, including the Executive Mansion (White House) and the Supreme Court. It was created in 1790 by the cessation of lands around the Potomac river which belonged to Virginia and Maryland. The intention was to create a permanent home for the national government which would be geographically midway between the Northern and Southern states and which would not be part of the territory of any of the states. Prior to that the US government had been itinerant. The official government of the District itself remains Congress.

Dixie   The Southern states of the USA. The name is derived from the Mason–Dixon line, the boundary between Pennsylvania and Maryland surveyed by Charles Mason and Jeremiah Dixon between 1763 and 1767.

Latterly the line marked the boundary between the Southern states which practised slavery and the Northern states which did not.

Dixiecrats Name given to those Democrats who insisted on the maintenance of racial segregation and white domination in the Southern states. During the 1950s they were important in delaying the Democratic Party's acceptance of civil rights for black Americans. The term is most probably derived from the name Dixie (q.v.).

DNC The Democratic National Committee. *See* National Committee.

Dollar diplomacy Term originally applied to the policy of President Taft (1909–13) in China, although Taft's policy had been foreshadowed by that of President Roosevelt (1905–09) towards the Caribbean. Taft stated in December 1912 that he intended 'substituting dollars for bullets' in the conduct of foreign policy, mainly by the selective encouragement of trade or the granting of aid. The term is now most commonly used to describe US policy with respect to Latin America, but may refer to any aspect of the conduct of American foreign policy primarily by monetary or economic means. *See* Alliance for Progress.

Domino Theory Theory referring to the existence of relations of political dependence between several states, specifically that should one of them fall under communist control its neighbours would be likely also to succumb, like a row of dominos falling. The first explicit formulation of this policy appeared in 1954 in support of arguments for American military assistance to non-communist regimes in Indo-China and ultimately American intervention in the Vietnam War (q.v.) after 1965. The credibility of the theory was undermined by the fact that following the reunification of Vietnam the whole of South-East Asia has not fallen to communism.

Dow Jones Index of prices of the 30 largest industrial stocks listed on the New York Stock Exchange (*see* Wall Street). It has been compiled by the Dow Jones Company since 1897.

Draft The popular term for Selective Service, the conscription system by which all US citizen males, upon attaining their majority, are required to register for military service; women are not subject to it. The draft was employed during World Wars I and II and again during the Vietnam War when it was highly unpopular and often avoided. Registration for Selective Service was restored in 1980 but those registered are not actually required to serve in the armed forces.

Dred Scott   Celebrated judgement of the US Supreme Court delivered in 1857 in the case of *Dred Scott v. Sandford*. Dred Scott was originally a slave from Missouri who, on being taken by his master to the Minnesota Territory where slavery was forbidden by the Missouri Compromise (q.v.), claimed that his residence there had automatically made him a free man. Chief Justice Taney ruled, however, that because Scott had not been a citizen of Missouri he could not sue in a federal court, and maintained moreover that slaves were property whose inviolability had been guaranteed by the Fifth Amendment to the Constitution. Congress therefore could not deprive a person (i.e., Scott's master) of his property 'without due process of law' and so could not legislate against slavery in the territories. By this decision the Court ruled the Missouri Compromise unconstitutional and greatly increased the political tension between North and South.

DSG   The Democratic Study Group, a group of liberal Democratic members of Congress established in 1959 to counteract the influence of the then dominant conservative bloc in both parties.

Dustbowl   Semi-arid area of high plains in south-central USA, which encompasses parts of the states of Texas, Oklahoma, Colorado and Kansas. It is periodically subjected to severe wind erosion during eras of drought, which badly affects agriculture in that area. *See* Okies.

Eisenhower Doctrine   In March 1957, following the collapse of Anglo-French power in the Middle East in the Suez Crisis, President Eisenhower feared that the Soviet Union would have an opportunity to increase its influence in the region. He therefore obtained the approval of Congress to extend US military or economic aid to any state threatened with aggression by 'any nation controlled by international communism'. This policy became known as the Eisenhower Doctrine.

Electoral College   The presidential electors from each state who meet to determine the election of the President in their respective state capitals following their popular election, and cast ballots for the offices of President and Vice-President. The electors never meet as a national group. They are chosen by the nomination of partisan groups of potential electors by party conventions or committees, or by primary election. The number of electors in each state is equal to its number of representatives in both houses of Congress, which, when added to the three allowed to the District of Columbia, represents a total vote in the electoral college of 538. In the presidential election, the whole group of electors receiving a plurality of votes in each state is elected. Presidential candidates receiving a majority of the electoral votes are declared the winners. If no one receives an actual majority, the election of the President is decided by the House of Representatives from among the three highest candidates. Because of the 'winner take all' system in each state, it is conceivable that a presidential candidate who receives less popular votes than a rival may nevertheless win more electoral votes and therefore the election. The possibility of this anomaly has given rise to proposals for the reform or even the complete abolition of the college.

Ellis Island   Island in Upper New York bay which from 1892 was the site of the city's immigration inspection depot. During the first half of the twentieth century millions of immigrants from Europe were landed there and examined for contagious diseases etc. before admittance to the United States.

Emancipation Proclamation   Declaration made in two parts by President Lincoln during the American Civil War (q.v.). The First Proclamation made on 22 September 1862 declared that, unless the Confederacy surrendered in the meantime, on 1 January of the following year all slaves held in those areas *still in rebellion* would be declared to be free persons. This edict was carried into effect by the Second Proclamation, of 1 January 1863. The legal authority of the President to abolish slavery was still in dispute (constitutionally it was not effected until the Thirteenth Amendment of 1865), so the Emancipation Proclamation was based upon Lincoln's powers as Commander-in-Chief of the US armed forces and was justified solely as a measure of military emergency. For this reason it 'freed' only those slaves still in the hands of the Confederate states and *not* those in areas already conquered by the US Army.

EPA   The Environmental Protection Agency, an independent agency which oversees federal programmes intended to control pollution and environmental integrity. It was established as an executive agency in 1970; in 1991 legislation was proposed to raise it to a Department of Cabinet rank.

EPIC   Acronym for End Poverty in California. The EPIC plan to alleviate the widespread suffering in the 1930s was the policy of former socialist author Upton Sinclair (1878–1968). Despite a bitter campaign against him, he sought and won the Democratic nomination for Governor in 1934.

Equal time   A legally enforceable right of political candidates to claim equal time on radio or television to answer opposing statements made in the course of a campaign.

ERA   The Equal Rights Amendment, a proposed amendment to the US Constitution which was passed by Congress in 1972 to provide that 'equality of rights under law shall not be denied or abridged by the United States or any state on account of sex'. It failed to receive the ratification of three-quarters of the states within the statutorily defined period.

Era of good feeling   The decade after 1815 (i.e., the end of the War of 1812 (q.v.)) which was marked by strong nationalism in the US and a collapse of the two-party system. The Federalists (q.v.) disappeared and the first Republican Party (*see* Democratic Party) under President Monroe enjoyed political dominance, although by 1820 regional divisions were again significant.

Executive agreement   An agreement between the President of the United States and the representative of a foreign power which does not require the approval of the US Senate. Such agreements usually cover non-controversial questions affecting, for example, trade and cultural exchanges. The Case Amendment of 1972 requires the President to inform Congress of every foreign commitment which he makes and may be explained as an attempt to prevent the extension of this presidential power which has no specific sanction in the Constitution.

Executive Office   The Executive Office was established by President Franklin Roosevelt under the Reorganization Act of 1939 to act as the principal staff for the President in the execution of his constitutional duties. Its main elements include the Office of Management and Budget, the White House Office, the National Security Council, the Council of Economic Advisers, the Office of Emergency Preparedness and the Domestic Council.

Executive order   A rule or regulation, issued by the President or some other administrative authority, which has the force of law. These rules are used to implement provisions of the Constitution, treaties or statutes and are published in the *Federal Register*. The use of the executive order has greatly increased in recent years as a result of the growing tendency of legislative bodies to leave the details of bills to the interpretation of the executive branch.

Executive privilege   The right of executive officials to refuse to appear before or otherwise withhold information from a legislative committee or court. Executive privilege is held to be enjoyed by those officials accorded the right by the President. Until 1974 there existed no legal restraints upon the exercise of the privilege, but a decision by the Supreme Court ordering President Nixon to release tape recordings connected with the

Watergate scandal established that the privilege could not be invoked if it was likely to impede the investigation or prosecution of a criminal offence.

External territories Territories are those areas which belong to the United States but which are not part of any individual state. The US Constitution specifies that Congress shall make rules regarding their government, and they are administered by the US Department of the Interior. A number are located overseas (hence 'external') and include Guam, Samoa, the US Virgin Islands and the Territory of the Pacific Islands. Puerto Rico is a commonwealth of the United States and the Panama Canal Zone is at present supervised by a bilateral commission.

Fair Deal Political programme advocated by President Truman, when running for his second term in 1948. A conscious continuation of the New Deal (q.v.) and designed to contain more collectivist and isolationist rivals, it was a progressive set of policies which proposed comprehensive education, housing and health programmes (e.g., national health insurance) as a means of extending social justice at home, and military and economic aid to ensure security abroad.

Fanny Mae The popular name for the Federal National Mortgage Association, a government corporation which finances mortgages.

Farm Belt Term for the Mid-West farming states dependent on agriculture and often a source of support for populist politicians.

Farmers' Alliances National and regional farmers' organizations which continued the agricultural protest movement of the Grangers (q.v.). The most important were the Southern Alliance in the cotton states and the Northwestern Farmers' Alliance in the 'wheat-belt'. They were significant in the 1880s but during the following decade they were incorporated into the People's Party (*see* p. 110).

Favorite son A state political leader, often the state Governor, whose name is placed in nomination for the presidency at a national party convention by members of his state's delegation. The nomination of a favorite son (who is not generally a serious candidate) is used either to honour the nominee or to delay the commitment of the delegation's vote to another candidate and so augment its bargaining power.

FBI The Federal Bureau of Investigation, an agency of the US Department of Justice founded in 1908. The FBI investigates alleged violations of federal law and as such it is responsible for dealing not only with inter-state crimes but also with acts of espionage and sabotage, and general internal state security. Its headquarters are in Washington, DC. It was known as the Bureau of Investigation until July 1935 and its longest-serving director was J. Edgar Hoover who held the post from 1924 until his death in 1972.

FDIC The Federal Deposit Insurance Corporation, the government body which insures personal deposits in clearing banks up to the sum of $100,000 for each account. It was established in 1933 as part of the emergency legislation of the New Deal (q.v.) to restore confidence in the banking system.

Federal Convention Great convention of states' delegates held at Philadelphia from 25 May to 17 September 1787 which, although charged only with the revision of the Articles of Confederation (q.v.), in fact drew up an entirely new constitution for the United States. *See* Founding Fathers, New Jersey Plan *and* Virginia Plan.

Federal Reserve System (Fed) The American equivalent of the Bank of England. The Federal Reserve System establishes banking policies and influences the amount of credit available and the amount of currency in circulation. It was created by Congress in 1913 and consists of twelve federal reserve banks, each located in one of the twelve federal reserve districts into which the United States is divided, and a central Board of Governors of seven members appointed by the President and confirmed by the Senate.

Federalism The political theory and system of government upon which the United States is based, by which authority is divided between a national government and a number of local governments according to the provisions of a constitution. The authority of each is therefore derived not from the other but from the constitution; therefore in the United States the federal government does not have the right to abolish, alter or abrogate the powers and privileges of the states.

Federalist Papers Collection of 85 political commentaries originally written for the New York press by Andrew Hamilton, John Jay and James Madison, which urged the adoption of the US Constitution during the national debate on its ratification by the states.

Federalists *See* Federalist Party p. 106.

Filibuster A method used in the Senate by which a minority of Senators seek to frustrate the will of the majority, by talking inconclusively until the time available for a bill's passage into law has expired. Senate Rule 22 allows unlimited debate on a motion before it can be brought to a vote. In 1975, a change in procedure occurred which made it easier to invoke closure of debate under Rule 22. *See* Cloture.

Fire Eaters Name applied by their opponents to extremist supporters of slavery and states rights in the Southern states during the decade prior to the American Civil War (q.v.).

Fireside chats Various radio addresses to the American people by President Franklin Roosevelt, in which he sought to explain his New Deal (q.v.) and restore political and commercial confidence. The first was on 12 March 1933 when Roosevelt described his Emergency Banking Relief Act and assured listeners that the banking system was once again solvent.

Food for Peace US foreign aid programme. The Congress established Food for Peace in 1954 to reduce domestic farm surpluses, establish foreign markets for American agricultural products, and increase the United States' influence with developing nations. Farm products are sold abroad for local currency, which is usually returned to the purchaser nation to ensure monetary stability.

Forty-Niners Prospectors of the Californian Gold Rush which followed the discovery of gold in the Sacramento Valley in January 1848. The influx of Forty-Niners raised the territory's population sufficiently for it to be admitted to the Union as a state in 1850.

Founding Fathers Delegates to the Federal Convention (q.v.) of 1787 who drew up the US Constitution. They included significant political theorists such as James Madison and Alexander Hamilton, but not the author of the Declaration of Independence (q.v.) Thomas Jefferson, who at the time was serving as the American minister to France.

Four Freedoms Principles enunciated as basic human rights by President Franklin Roosevelt in his State of the Union address to Congress in January 1941. They are the freedoms (1) of speech and expression; (2) of religion; (3) from want; and (4) from fear.

Fourteen Points Peace programme outlined to Congress by President Wilson on 8 January 1918 and accepted as the basis for an armistice with Germany and Austria-Hungary. The original Points were: renunciation of secret diplomacy; freedom of the seas; removal of economic barriers between states; general reduction of armaments; impartial settlement of colonial claims; evacuation of Russia by the Central Powers; restoration of Belgium; German withdrawal from France and the restoration of Alsace-Lorraine; readjustment of the Italian frontiers; self-determination for the nationalities of Austria-Hungary; evacuation of occupying forces from Romania, Serbia and Montenegro; free navigation of the Dardanelles and self-determination for the peoples of the Ottoman Empire; creation of an independent Poland; and establishment of a general association of states, the League of Nations.

Freedmen's Bureau   Federal agency established by Congress in March 1865 to provide humanitarian assistance to former slaves after the American Civil War (q.v.); and latterly to educate them and settle them on confiscated lands. The Congress allowed it to lapse in 1872 as Radical Republicanism declined. *See* Reconstruction.

Freedom Riders   Members of the Congress of Racial Equality (*see* CORE) who in May 1961 sought to test the effectiveness of a recent Supreme Court decision that restaurants in bus stations could not discriminate against interstate travellers on the basis of race. Attacks upon them by racist mobs as they travelled by bus to Birmingham, Alabama forced the US Justice Department to attempt to enforce desegregation at the appropriate facilities. *See* Segregation.

Freeze   A peace movement in the USA campaigning for a 'freeze' on the expenditure on and development of nuclear weapons (but accepting the maintenance of the number and current technology of such weapons), in order to limit the arms race.

French and Indian War   American term for the Seven Years' War (1756–63), which on the North American continent saw fighting between the French and British colonists and their native American allies. It led to the British conquest of Canada in 1760.

Frost Belt   Those northerly states of the USA which are subject to severe winters. *See* Sun Belt.

Fundamental Orders of Connecticut   First written constitution among the English colonists in North America, drawn up in 1639 among settlements in Connecticut.

Gadsden Purchase   Border territory bought from Mexico in 1853, a further addition to the continental territory of the United States. The purchase for $10 million was concluded by the US minister James Gadsden and the Mexican President Santa Anna to fix the border of the two states between El Paso in Texas and the Pacific Ocean, which had not been definitely settled after the Mexican–American War (q.v.).

Gag Rule   Rule of Congressional business adopted in 1836 at the instigation of Southern Congressmen that all petitions to Congress concerning slavery should be received but automatically tabled without debate.

GAO   The General Accounting Office, the independent government agency established in 1921 which monitors the operations of the federal administration and, as directed by Congress, audits its expenditures.

Gerrymandering   The practice of manipulating the boundaries of electoral divisions in such a way as to give an unfair advantage to one political party. It is named after its first noted proponent Elbridge Gerry, Governor of Massachusetts, who in 1812 created a district shaped like a salamander. Because it is the responsibility of each state legislature to decide the boundaries of both congressional and state districts, they are particularly suspect to gerrymandering by the majority party.

GI   Popular term for US soldiers from World War II onwards, derived from the stamp 'Government Issue' on their equipment.

Gilded Age   Title of minor novel of 1873 by Mark Twain which has come to be applied to the 1870s and 1880s. The last three decades of the nineteenth century witnessed the flowering of the Industrial Revolution in America, which brought with it both tremendous economic expansion and extensive political corruption. Various primary industrial sectors came to be dominated by large vertically integrated corporations under centralized control, which were known as 'trusts'; Carnegie in steel, Rockefeller in oil and Morgan in finance became household words and by 1895 the United States had emerged as the largest economy in the world. National politics was dominated by industrial interests; the Republican Party in particular pursued a high-tariff policy designed to help domestic producers against European competitors. Corruption was rife and certain captains of industry – most notoriously the railway operators Jay Gould and 'Commodore' Cornelius Vanderbilt – were dubbed 'robber barons' for their sharp business and political practices. The novelist Mark Twain named the era 'The Gilded Age' for its wealth and immorality.

The effective reintegration of the South into the national political system at the end of Reconstruction (q.v.) in 1877 had returned the Democratic Party to competitive two-party politics; and not until 1896 was any President to be elected with a majority of the popular vote. The Republicans drew their support largely from Protestant Americans of Northern European stock, the Democrats from Southerners and the new immigrants from Europe who were pouring into America's rapidly expanding industrial cities. Questions of civil service and currency reform and the tariff dominated the national agenda in the 1880s – especially in the contests between the Democratic President Grover Cleveland and his Republican successor Benjamin Harrison – but the parties were primarily divided from one another on ethnic, religious and cultural lines.

By the 1890s economic discontent among those who suffered relative losses during the process of industrialization – particularly farmers in the Mid-West and the South – led to broad-based movements for social and political reform. Agricultural communities were affected by over-production and a long-term decline in commodity prices, and farmers' organizations such as the Grange and, later, the Farmers' Alliance (q.v.) fought for industrial regulation (especially of railway freight charges) and currency reform to alleviate their indebtedness. In 1892 a new political party, the People's Party (q.v.), was formed to unite the farmers with the urban industrial working class – the first attempt in the United States to create a genuine labour party. The Populists (*see* p. 110) stood for industrial and workplace regulation, political reform and inflation of the currency through the free coinage of silver. The adoption of the silver policy by the Democrats at the presidential election of 1896 forced the Populists to support their charismatic candidate William Jennings Bryan; but Bryan's defeat at the hands of the Republican William McKinley broke Populism and established a Republican hegemony which lasted a generation.

Goldbugs   Name applied in the nineteenth and twentieth centuries to supporters of the gold standard. *See* Bimetallism.

Good Neighbor Policy   Foreign policy stance adopted by President Franklin Roosevelt (1931–45) involving a cautious move away from iso-lationism on the part of the United States and the promotion of better diplomatic relations, especially with South America.

Governor   The chief executive officer of a state. In all 50 states the Governor is popularly elected and serves for four years in some and two years in others. Approximately half the states limit the Governor to one or two terms in office. The Governor's powers include those of appoint-ment, preparation and execution of the budget, issuing of executive orders and general state law enforcement. As regards legislation, every state but North Carolina permits its Governor to exercise a veto.

Gramm–Rudman–Hollings   The popular title of the Balanced Budget and Emergency Deficit Control Act of 1985 (which required the pro-gressive elimination of deficits in the annual budget of the federal gov-ernment). The name is derived from those of its sponsors, Senators

Phil Gramm of Texas, Warren Rudman of New Hampshire and Ernest Hollings of South Carolina.

Grand Jury   A panel of citizens called (as for jury service) to hear evidence presented by the prosecuting attorney of any jurisdictional authority and to decide whether it warrants further proceedings against the accused. It still exists in a number of the American states.

Grand Old Party   Colloquial term for the Republican Party, usually abbreviated to GOP (*see* p. 92).

Grandfather Clause   Taken to mean any law intended to restrict the suffrage to adult males whose grandfathers or fathers had been entitled to vote before the era of Reconstruction (q.v.) and so to exclude black Americans. First adopted in Louisiana in 1898, the Grandfather Clause was technically a measure to re-enfranchise poor whites who were incidentally excluded by poll tax requirements or literacy tests aimed at blacks.

Grangers   Members of the National Grange of the Patrons of Husbandry, the first nation-wide farmers' body in the United States. Founded in 1867, it developed rapidly during the agricultural depression of the early 1870s and attempted to restore farmers' fortunes by promoting marketing co-operatives and even supporting political candidates sympathetic to the Grange's opposition to railroad monopolies. In 1873 and 1874 Grangers controlled the legislatures of eleven Mid-West states, but the organization's political influence declined in the 1880s with the return of prosperity.

Grant-in-aid   Grants made by Congress to state and local governments for the execution of certain statutorily defined functions (e.g., road maintenance). The recipient is required to match the grant with its own funds.

Great Awakening   Evangelical, Protestant religious reform movement which began in the Mid-Atlantic colonies in the 1720s and continued for some 20 years. It was marked by an emotional emphasis on the need for personal salvation and by criticism of the established churches. A Second Great Awakening occurred in the frontier region and New England in the period 1800–30 and led to the establishment of the Mormon church in 1830.

Great Compromise   Agreement reached at the Federal Convention (q.v.) in 1787 to settle representation in the new US Congress by compromising between the New Jersey and Virginia Plans (q.v.).

Great Depression   The severe economic recession which began after the Wall Street Crash (q.v.) of the New York Stock Exchange in 1929 and continued until the economy was revived by the demands of World War II. At its depth the Depression resulted in a fall of one-half in industrial production in 1932 and unemployment of 25% the following year. The policies of the New Deal (q.v.) ameliorated the social consequences of the Depression but did not succeed in fully restoring the economy.

Great Migration   Term used to denote both the English Puritan settlement of the American colonies from the 1620s to 1640s and the migration to the Mississippi Valley after the War of 1812.

Great Society   Expression first used in May 1964 by President Lyndon Johnson (1963–69) to describe the liberal society which he hoped would result from his Administration's progressive civil rights and welfare legislation. *See* War on Poverty.

Greenback   Slang expression for the US dollar note, derived from its colour. Greenbacks were first issued by the US Treasury in 1862 to assist the financing of the Union war-effort during the American Civil War.

Green Mountain Boys   Organized band of settlers from Vermont, formed in 1773 to resist encroachment by New Yorkers who claimed Vermont as part of their state territory under a charter of Charles II of England.

Gulf of Tonkin Resolution   Congressional resolution passed on 7 August 1964 which authorized President Lyndon Johnson to take 'all necessary measures' to ensure the security of US armed forces and to defeat aggression in South-East Asia. It arose from an attack by North Vietnamese torpedo boats upon US naval vessels and, although technically not a declaration of war, it was interpreted by Johnson as offering a legal basis for his commitment of US troops to Vietnam.

Gypsy Moths   Colloquial term for those liberal Republicans from Northern states who occasionally vote with the Democrats in Congress. They were especially prominent in the early 1980s in opposing certain pieces of Reaganite legislation.

Half-Breeds   Nickname given in 1881 by their opponents the Stalwarts (q.v.) to those Liberal Republicans who supported President Garfield in his campaign for civil service reform.

Hartford Convention   A meeting at Hartford, Connecticut in 1814 of delegates of those New England states which for economic reasons were opposed to war with Great Britain. They met to consider constitutional amendments to protect their commerical interests, but their political position was undermined by the coming of peace. *See* War of 1812, p. 240.

Havana Conference   Pan-American conference of 1940 at which the delegates agreed to the US policy of not recognizing the transfer of any territory in the western hemisphere from one non-American state to another. The intention was to prevent the Axis powers obtaining any colonies in the western hemisphere.

Hawks   Name given to those who wished to continue or escalate the US participation in the Vietnam War (1965–73), believing this to be the quickest and most effective way of ending it. The term became current in 1964 and is thought to have originated in the State Department.

Haymarket Affair   Anarchist outrage perpetrated on 4 May 1886 when a policeman was killed by a bomb during an attempt to disperse a mass meeting of anarchists and trades unionists in Haymarket Square in Chicago. *See* Chicago Martyrs.

HEW   The US Department of Health, Education and Welfare established by President Eisenhower in 1953. In 1979 it was divided into the Departments of Education and of Health and Human Services. HHS (including the Social Security Administration) has the largest budget of any governmental agency in the world, in excess of $400 billion or greater than the gross domestic product of many countries.

Hispanics   Americans of Spanish or Latin American descent. It is probable that by 2000 they will be the largest ethnic group in California.

Hollywood Ten   Group of movie writers and directors who refused to answer questions put to them by the House Un-American Activities Committee (q.v.) in October 1947. They were subsequently convicted of contempt of Congress and were fined or jailed.

Hooverville   Name for any of the shanty towns established by homeless unemployed during the Great Depression (q.v.). The term is an ironic reference to President Herbert Hoover, under whose Republican administration of 1929–33 the Depression began.

Hot Line   A direct telecommunications link between the White House and the Kremlin, which was set up by a memorandum of understanding signed by the United States and the Soviet Union in Geneva on 20 June 1963. The need for such a direct channel of communication for negotiations in time of crisis was demonstrated by the Cuban Missile Crisis of October 1962.

House of Representatives   *See* p. 76.

House Un-American Activities Committee   Committee of the House of Representatives, established in 1938 to investigate alleged Nazi spy rings in the United States. However it was HUAC's post-war hearings into communist activities in the United States during the Cold War (q.v.) which were especially notorious, being marked by the violent bullying of witnesses and the persecution of alleged Soviet sympathizers. In 1948 one of its members, Congressman Richard Nixon of California, exposed the former State Department official, Alger Hiss, as a Soviet spy. The climate of hysteria fed by HUAC's activities led to severe legal restrictions on left-wing political activities and civil liberties. *See* McCarthyism.

HUD   The US Department of Housing and Urban Development, created in 1965 to administer federal housing assistance programmes.

Hundred Days   Popular description for the first one hundred days of President Franklin Roosevelt's first Administration, beginning in March 1933, during which he launched his New Deal (q.v.) and Congress passed fifteen major bills.

Hunkers   *See* Old Hunkers.

Impeachment   A formal accusation made by the lower house of a legislative body that commits an accused public official for trial in the upper house. Impeachment is the first of a two-stage process, analogous in legal terms to indictment before trial. In the federal system, power of impeachment lies with the House of Representatives and the power to try impeachable offences lies with the Senate. All civil officers of the US government except members of Congress are liable to impeachment. The process begins with the formal presentation of charges by a member of the House, which will then be referred to the judiciary committee or a specially constituted investigating committee for detailed consideration. A simple majority of the House is required for impeachment and, if secured, 'Articles of Impeachment' are drawn up which represent the case for removal from office. The House will appoint managers who will try the case before the Senate and if the President is on trial the Chief Justice of the United States presides. A two-thirds majority in the Senate is necessary for conviction, but the only punishments open to the Senate are removal from office and disqualification from holding any public office in the future. In 1974 the then President, Richard

Nixon, resigned in the face of House preparations to begin impeachment proceedings.

Implied powers   Article I, Section 8 of the US Constitution grants to Congress the authority to make laws which are 'necessary and proper' in order to put into effect the powers granted to it or to other branches of the federal government by the other clauses of the Constitution. Therefore the government possesses powers which are implied by this clause as well as those explicitly granted it.

Impoundment   The action of a President in refusing to expend monies appropriated for certain uses by Congress. It has been adopted as a means of controlling the budget according to the priorities of the executive branch rather than those of Congress, but the Budget and Impoundment Control Act of 1974 severely restricted the circumstances in which the President might impound funds.

Independent Regulatory Commissions   Those agencies of the federal government which are not part of one of the major departments of state and which are responsible for regulating certain areas of activity under law. Examples include the Interstate Commerce Commission, the Federal Communications Commission and the Securities and Exchange Commission.

Indirect Primary   *See* Primary.

Inherent powers   That authority which the federal government possesses because the Untied States is a sovereign country, as opposed to those which are explicitly granted to it by the US Constitution.

Initiative   A procedure in a minority of states whereby the electors may (upon the petition of a statutorily defined number of qualified voters) present legislative proposals or constitutional amendments. These are placed upon the ballot at a general election and must be approved by whatever majority of voters is established by law. For example, in 1978 the voters of California enacted Proposition 13 which has restricted increases in local property taxes.

Interstate Compact   An agreement between any two of the states, which by the Constitution must be ratified by Congress, although many of a minor nature are not.

Intolerable Acts   Series of Acts passed by Parliament in 1774 in an attempt to re-establish the control of the British government over the colonies following the Boston Tea Party (q.v.). Specifically, the measures were the closure of the port of Boston, the revision of the charter of the colony of Massachusetts, the transfer of certain murder trials to English courts and a new act applying to all the colonies regarding the quartering of British troops. They were known as the Coercive Acts in Great Britain.

Iran–Contra affair   Political scandal of the second Reagan Administration (1985–89), in which it was alleged that the US government, in contravention of the law and its own stated policy, supplied arms to the government of Iran (then involved in a war with Iraq) and used the profits of these sales to fund the operations of the Contras (q.v.) in Nicaragua. The charges, which first arose in the press in November 1986, were investigated and largely substantiated by the Tower Commission (q.v.) in 1987 and subsequently by congressional committees. They resulted in criminal charges being laid against certain government officials, including the National Security Adviser Vice-Admiral John Poindexter and National Security Council staff member Colonel Oliver North. However it was not established that President Reagan had himself either sanctioned or known about the illegal activities.

Iran hostage crisis   Political crisis arising from the seizure by revolutionary students of 53 staff members at the US Embassy in Tehran in November 1979. The Americans were held hostage for 444 days in an attempt to force the US government to return the deposed Shah to Iran. The episode caused immense damage to the reputation of the then President Jimmy Carter and significantly weakened his re-electability in the 1980 presidential campaign. The hostages were only released in January 1981 at the moment that President Reagan was being sworn into office. A decade later it was being alleged that the Reagan election campaign had secretly conspired with the Iranian government (in an episode known as the 'October Surprise') to manipulate the issue to the Republicans' advantage.

Iron Curtain   Phrase first used in February 1945 by the Nazi Minister of Propaganda Joseph Goebbels, but brought into general use by its repetition in a speech by Winston Churchill at Fulton, Missouri on 5 March 1946 (in which he stated that 'From Stettin in the Baltic to Trieste in the Adriatic an iron curtain has descended across the continent'). It denoted the border which existed between Soviet-dominated Eastern Europe and the capitalist West from the end of World War II until 1990, and, more specifically, to the restraints placed upon the movement of persons and political activity by the communist regimes.

Irreconcilables Republican members of the US Senate who opposed the Treaty of Versailles when it was submitted for ratification in 1919, largely on the grounds that the United States' membership of the League of Nations would have been unconstitutional. The treaty was never in fact ratified and the United States therefore did not become a member of the League, despite the idea of it having been one of President Wilson's Fourteen Points (q.v.).

IRS The Internal Revenue Service, the division of the Department of the Treasury which is responsible for collecting federal taxes.

Isolationism Policy of avoiding alliances and having only a minimal involvement in international affairs. The United States remained largely an isolationist power outside of the western hemisphere until the early twentieth century (George Washington had advised the infant republic in his Farewell Address in 1796 to avoid foreign alliances). America returned to that policy in the 1920s following her involvement in World War I and refusal to join the League of Nations. However, the United States' position as the most economically and militarily powerful democracy forced an abandonment of isolationism after 1945 (*see* Cold War); but a return to the policy has been a recurring demand of many conservative Republicans, first in the early 1960s and again after the 1965–73 Vietnam War.

IWW The Industrial Workers of the World, an American labour movement formed in Chicago in 1905 and dedicated to the overthrow of capitalism. Its members were nicknamed 'Wobblies'. It was active in mainstream politics (its Detroit Conference of 1909 agreed to support the presidential campaign of the Socialist Eugene Debs), but other sections of the movement indulged in sabotage and sought to foment strikes. Such actions resulted in prosecutions and alienation of many potential supporters, allowing the government to label the IWW as 'red fanatics'. Between 1912 and 1915, when its influence was strongest, the IWW had 100,000 members but it declined rapidly after the Red Scare (q.v.).

Jacksonians Supporters of the Democrat President Andrew Jackson (1829–37). The Jacksonians represented a continuation of Jeffersonian (q.v.) republicanism in terms of policy, but were politically more populist and egalitarian. Jackson himself initially favoured limited government, but during his own terms of office he substantially increased the political power of the Presidency within the federal system – conceiving of it as the truest representative of the popular will – and his actions during the Nullification Crisis (q.v.) reveal the activist nationalism which underlay Jacksonian democracy.

Jeffersonians   Followers of Thomas Jefferson, US President (1801–09) and leader of the first Democratic Party (q.v.). Jefferson preferred a federal government of limited powers which would not extend upon the constitutional rights of the individual states and which would reduce government expenditure. In contrast to the Federalists (q.v.), who favoured a powerful central executive able to develop American industry and commerce, the Jeffersonians represented largely agrarian interests which Jefferson himself always identified as the cornerstone of political democracy.

Jim Crow   Colloquial term describing the laws which formerly provided for racial segregation in the United States. The first was passed in Florida in 1887, requiring separate accommodation in trains, and the Supreme Court upheld their legality in 1896, providing that the separate facilities were 'equal'. Such laws were finally swept away during the Civil Rights Movement (q.v.) of the 1950s and 1960s. *See* Segregation.

Judicial review   The power of the courts to declare acts of the legislative and executive branches of the government unconstitutional. No provision for this procedure exists within the US Constitution, but the Supreme Court established the precedent for it in the case of *Marbury v. Madison* in 1803. Judicial review places the Supreme Court in particular in a sensitive and powerful political position, but it also enshrines the principle that the Constitution is the supreme law of the United States and cannot be contravened by any authority.

Judiciary   One of the three branches of the US government, i.e., the courts and judges of the United States. Because of the federal system of government the judiciary collectively may be divided into national and state branches, each of which is independent of the other with the exception that the US Supreme Court may (in certain circumstances involving federal questions) review a state court decision.

Kent State   On 4 May 1970 four students were shot dead by National Guardsmen on the campus of Kent State University near Cleveland, Ohio during a violent demonstration by students against the recent movement of US troops into Cambodia (*see* Vietnam War). It was the most notorious and bloody episode in the widespread unrest over the war which affected American universities at that period.

Kentucky and Virginia Resolutions   First formal declaration of the right of the states to judge whether Acts of Congress did or did not infringe the US Constitution (*see* Nullification Crisis). In 1798 the legislatures of Kentucky and Virginia resolved that the Aliens and Sedition Acts (passed during an undeclared war with France) were unconstitutional, although neither state actually attempted to prevent their application.

Keynote speech   The major speech at a party convention setting out the programme by which the party or candidate will campaign, allocating priority to certain parts of it, and introducing or celebrating the candidate. It is usually given by a senior party figure.

King Cotton diplomacy   During the American Civil War the Confederate States (q.v.) deliberately restricted the export of their staple crop of cotton in order to depress the European textile industry (which relied upon American cotton) and so force the European powers to intervene and stop the war. The economic importance of the staple to the South earned it the name of 'King Cotton'.

Kitchen Cabinet   The term denoting the President's unofficial group of advisers, as opposed to the formal office-holding Cabinet. It was first used of the friends of President Andrew Jackson who between 1829 and 1831 were regarded as being more influential than the official body.

Knights of the Golden Circle   A society founded in the Southern states in 1859 to press for the annexation of Mexico, which was regarded as a suitable means of increasing the size of the slave-owning territories and thus countering the political influence of the industrial Northern states. It attracted many Copperheads (q.v.) and in 1863 it merged with the Order of American Knights, so becoming more opposed to the American Civil War (q.v.). In the following year it changed its name to the Sons of Liberty and a number of its members were tried for treason in Indianapolis, Indiana.

Knights of Labor   Early American trades union founded in Philadelphia in 1869. The Knights aimed to unite both skilled and unskilled workers into one centrally organized trades union rather than organized on the basis of individuals crafts; they sought progressive labour conditions but rejected socialist politics and made limited use of the strike weapon. However the Knights' power was damaged by the failure of a strike against the Gould railway syndicate in 1886 and by the Haymarket Affair (*see* Chicago Martyrs), and in the 1890s the organization was superseded by the American Federation of Labor, a loose federation of national craft unions founded in 1881 (*see* AFL–CIO).

Knights of the White Camelia   A Southern anti-Negro organization, similar to the Ku Klux Klan (q.v.) but less flamboyant, which was founded at Franklin, Louisiana in 1867. It established national headquarters in

New Orleans but was suppressed in the 1870s. In 1935 George E. Deatherage revived the organization in West Virginia; the main tenet of the new Knights was anti-Semitism.

Koreagate   Scandal exposed in 1977 when several US Congressmen were shown to have accepted bribes from South Korean agents in return for supporting continued economic and military aid to the repressive South Korean regime of President Park.

Ku Klux Klan (KKK)   Secret society formed in the Southern states shortly after the end of the American Civil War (q.v.) as a means by which whites could maintain political control over the black American population during the era of Reconstruction (q.v.). The Klan was founded as a social club in Pulaski, Tennessee in 1866 but reorganized on political lines in Nashville in 1867. A hierarchical system was devised to rule over the 'Invisible Empire of the South' (the Klan's leader was thus the Imperial Wizard) and white hoods were worn to hide the identity of members involved in violence against blacks which included whippings, shootings and hangings. The escalation of violence and the attack on federal authority led to the Force Act and 'Ku Klux Klan' Act of 1870 which allowed the President to use military force against the Klan and impose heavy penalties on members. It was thus effectively suppressed by 1880 but was revived in Atlanta, Georgia in 1915 during the wave of nativist hysteria occasioned by World War I. It remains a racist, anti-Semitic, anti-Catholic and anti-communist organization, but since the Civil Rights Movement (q.v.) of the 1950s and 1960s its political power has been significantly marginalized.

Labor Unions   The American equivalent of British trades unions. About 70% of those organized into labor unions are associated with the American Federation of Labor–Congress of Industrial Organizations (*see* AFL–CIO). The remainder of organized labour is organized in independent unions such as the Teamsters, Mine Workers, Longshoremen and Railroad Brotherhoods. The political alignment of the labor unions is traditionally with the Democratic Party, but at present less than 30% of the total workforce is unionized.

Lecompton Constitution   State constitution drawn up in 1857 by a convention of settlers in Kansas Territory meeting in Lecompton which allowed slavery within the new state. The anti-slavery settlers refused to participate in the referendum on the new constitution and it was theoretically ratified; but Congress refused to admit Kansas as a new state and the constitution was rejected the following year in a further referendum. *See* Bleeding Kansas.

Legislative veto A provision in certain Acts of Congress to give Congress the authority to overrule an action of the executive branch or any of its agencies. The legislative veto is mostly employed to review the activities of those regulatory commissions or other bodies which make federal regulations. In 1983 the Supreme Court ruled that the veto was unconstitutional because it violated the principle of the separation of powers.

Lend-Lease Act passed by Congress on 11 March 1941, authorizing President Franklin Roosevelt to lend or lease arms and military equipment to those countries 'whose defence the President deems vital to the United States'. This allowed Roosevelt to give military support to Great Britain, China and the USSR despite US neutrality.

Liberal Republicans *See* Liberal Republican Party, p. 107.

Lieutenant Governor The elected official who, in most states, succeeds to the governorship when that office is vacant between statutory terms of office. Usually the Lieutenant Governor presides over the senate of the state and casts the deciding vote in the event of a tie. He or she is elected at the same time and for the same term as the Governor.

Lima Declaration Declaration of the Pan-American Conference of 1938, meeting in the Peruvian capital Lima, that any threat to the peace or security of any American republic would be a matter of concern to all. By this Declaration, President Franklin Roosevelt succeeded in denying the Axis powers of Europe any support or colonial presence in the western hemisphere.

Little Big Horn Site in Montana where, on 25 June 1876, a scouting party of US cavalry under General George Custer was annihilated by the Sioux led by Chief Sitting Bull.

Little Boy Nickname of the first atomic bomb dropped on the Japanese city of Hiroshima by the USAF aircraft *Enola Gay* on 6 August 1945.

Little Rock City in Arkansas where in 1957 President Eisenhower mobilized federal troops to prevent mob violence and escort black children to school against the opposition of Governor Orval Faubus, who sought to prevent the desegregation of the public schools. *See* Civil Rights Movement.

Lobbyist A person who acts on behalf of an interest or pressure group and seeks to bring influence to bear on the passage of legislation.

The federal government requires the registration of lobbyists and the full disclosure of information regarding their employers, salaries and expenses.

Locofocos   Faction within the Democratic Party (q.v.), which arose in the 1830s in opposition to paper currency and the practice of depositing government funds in state banks. The name derived from a brand of match, used for light at one of their meetings after opponents had turned off the gas lamps.

Log rolling   The process by which legislators bargain for each other's support for measures in Congress.

Los Alamos   Site of US government nuclear research laboratories in New Mexico. It was a base for the Manhattan Project (q.v.) and the development of the hydrogen bomb.

Louisiana Purchase   Territory secretly bought by President Jefferson from France in 1803 for $15 million. The area concerned – most of which Spain had ceded to France in 1800 – stretched from Canada to the Gulf of Mexico and from the Mississippi River to the Rocky Mountains. Its purchase more than doubled the size of the USA and gave her control of New Orleans and the Mississippi River, which was vital to her commercial development and the settlement of the Western Territories.

Loyalists   American colonists – known to their opponents as Tories – who remained loyal to the British Crown during the American War of Independence (q.v.). Many fought for the British and as many as 100,000 emigrated to Canada, the Caribbean and England after the United States achieved her independence.

Machine politics   The organization of party politics by a well-organized group of party members under the direction of (frequently unelected) leaders. *See* Boss.

Majority Leader   The leader of the largest party in both the Senate or the House. He or she is elected by fellow party members in each chamber and is highly influential in organizing the legislative agenda and establishing the party's political priorities. The head of the smaller party is termed the Minority Leader.

Manhattan Project   Codename for the Allied project which developed the atomic bomb during World War II. It was based at laboratories in Oak Ridge, Tennessee and at Los Alamos (q.v.) in New Mexico, where the first experimental explosion – codenamed Trinity – was conducted on 16 July 1945. *See* Little Boy.

Manifest destiny   Phrase first used in 1845 by a New York newspaper editor to denote the popular belief that the United States had been divinely granted the right to control the entire North American continent. The doctrine was used to justify the acquisition of territories from other states and the destruction of Native American cultures and peoples.

Marshall Plan   US plan for the economic reconstruction of Europe after World War II, named after Secretary of State General George C. Marshall who announced the policy in a speech at Harvard on 5 June 1947. The Organization for European Economic Co-operation was established in April 1948 to administer American financial aid and encourage economic expansion, but the Soviet rejection of the Plan meant most of the money went to western Europe alone. Some $17,000 million was provided in all, mostly between 1948 and 1952.

Mason–Dixon Line   *See* Dixie.

Massive retaliation   Name given to defence doctrine announced by Secretary of State John Foster Dulles in January 1954 which stipulated that the appropriate way for the United States to respond to communist threats was 'vigorously at places and with means of our own choosing'. This implied that the United States might use her strategic nuclear forces directly against the USSR in retaliation for communist aggression anywhere in the world.

McCarthyism   Anti-communist hysteria which swept the United States during the 1940s and 1950s when the Cold War (q.v.) was at its height. The name is derived from Senator Joseph McCarthy of Wisconsin (1909–57) who rose to prominence by making unfounded accusations about the integrity of government employees. Following the earlier revelations before the House Un-American Activities Committee (q.v.), McCarthy's accusations were widely accepted and in February 1950 he claimed to know of 205 communists in the US State Department. Hundreds were imprisoned during four years of investigations but in 1954 the Senate censured McCarthy for bringing it into disrepute when he attempted to extend his criticisms to the US Army.

Military industrial complex   Phrase used by President Eisenhower in his retirement address in 1961, in which he warned of the excessive influence over economic and foreign policy which might accrue to the armed forces and defence manufacturers as a result of the United States' involvement in the Cold War (q.v.).

Minutemen   American colonial militiamen, founded in Boston in 1774 and active against the British during the American War of Independence (q.v.), particularly in Massachusetts. The name derives from the claim that they could turn out for military service at a minute's notice.

Miranda   In the case of *Miranda v. Arizona* of 1966 the Supreme Court ruled that, in order to perform a legal arrest, law enforcement authorities were obliged to make any person aware of his or her constitutional rights, particularly the right to remain silent without incrimination. To 'miranda' an arrested person is therefore to read him or her these rights.

Missile gap   Popular political term of the 1960s to refer to the United States' supposed deficiency in strategic nuclear weapons compared with the USSR.

Missouri Compromise   Congressional resolution of 1820 devised by Henry Clay by which the territory of Missouri was to be admitted to the Union as a slave state and Maine, formerly part of Massachusetts, was to be admitted as a 'free' state. Slavery was also forbidden within the Louisiana Purchase north of Missouri itself. The intention was to preserve the balance between the Northern and Southern states within the Senate and so reduce sectional conflict over the extension of slavery into the Western Territories. The Compromise was declared unconstitutional by the Supreme Court in the *Dred Scott* decision (q.v.) in 1857.

Molly Maguires   Secret Irish labour organization operating in the mining districts of Pennsylvania in the 1870s, which used violence during strikes and against political opponents. It was eventually suppressed when it was infiltrated by the Pinkerton detective agents.

Monroe Doctrine   Doctrine proclaimed to Congress in 1823 by President Monroe, who declared that 'The American continents, by the free and independent conditions which they have assumed and maintained, are henceforth not to be considered as subjects for future colonization by any European powers.' The statement was prompted by fears of renewed Spanish and French attempts on Latin America, but subsequently it has been used to justify US imperialism in the western hemisphere.

Moral Majority   Right-wing political pressure group influential in American politics in the 1980s which takes an often fundamentalist Christian position on social issues.

Morgenthau Plan   Proposal made by Secretary of the Treasury Henry Morgenthau at the Quebec Conference of September 1944. President

Franklin Roosevelt and British Prime Minister Winston Churchill accepted his idea that Germany should be 'pastoralized' – i.e., be deprived of its industrial capacity after the war – but both the US State Department and British Foreign Office rejected it as impractical.

Mormons   American religious sect, properly known as the Church of Jesus Christ of the Latter-Day Saints and founded in New York by Joseph Smith in 1830. Smith claimed he had been divinely directed to uncover a series of buried texts, later published as the *Book of Mormon*, which identified the Native Americans as the lost tribes of Israel and alleged Christ had appeared in America after his resurrection. Persecution and the murder of Smith in 1844 persuaded the Mormons under their new leader Brigham Young to embark upon a great migration to Salt Lake, Utah which was reached in 1847. They had hoped to establish there their own state of Deseret but the United States took control of the area as the Utah Territory in 1850. By the following year 50,000 Mormons had arrived and Salt Lake City was built as their headquarters. In 1896 when the Mormon Church consented to abandon polygamy, Utah was admitted to the Union as a state. It remains predominantly Mormon.

Muckrakers   Term, initially of rebuke, applied by President Theodore Roosevelt in 1906 to those journalists who uncovered illegal and exploitative activities in big business. The revelations helped engender public support for the reform legislation of the Progressive Era (q.v.).

Mugwumps   Term derived from the Native American word *mugguomp* or great chief and coined by New York journalist Charles Anderson Dana to describe members of the Republican Party (q.v.) who deserted James Blaine and chose to support the Democrat Cleveland in the presidential election of 1884, attracted by his advocacy of civil service reform. It is now used to denote independent members of any political party or those who temporarily change allegiance during an electoral campaign.

My Lai   Vietnamese village where US troops massacred the inhabitants on 16 March 1968 during operations against the Viet Cong (q.v.). The incident became public knowledge the following year and further undermined support for American participation in the Vietnam War (q.v.). In 1971 Lieutenant Calley was sentenced to life imprisonment for his part in the crime.

NAACP   National Association for the Advancement of Colored People, founded in 1909 to campaign for civil rights for black Americans. It specifically sought redress by legal and constitutional means and consequently during the 1960s was partly eclipsed by the more radical Black

Power (q.v.) movement, but remains the principal advocate for racial equality. *See* Civil Rights Movement.

NAFTA   The North American Free Trade Area, established by executive agreement between the United States and Canada in 1987 and subsequently ratified by the legislatures of those two states. Mexico subsequently became a member. It took effect on 1 Jan. 1994. The agreement provides for the abolition of all tariffs between them by 1999. Under NAFTA the US, Canada and Mexico become a single integrated market of nearly 400 million people.

Nat Turner Rebellion   Slave insurrection of 1831 in Virginia, which was led by the radical Negro preacher Nat Turner. Fifty-seven whites were killed before it was suppressed and it led to stricter 'slave codes' regulating the treatment and rights of slaves and, indeed, of free blacks.

National Committee   A standing committee of one of the two national political parties which co-ordinates the activities of the different state parties and is responsible for the organization of the nominating convention and presidential campaign. Its chairman is nominated by the President (or by the party's presidential nominee when 'in opposition'), and is regarded as the national spokesman of the party.

National Convention   *See* Convention.

National Guard   The militia of each of the states, composed of part-time volunteers. It is under the command of the state Governor unless called into federal service and in peacetime is frequently used for police purposes or to assist the authorities during emergencies or natural disasters.

National Security Council   A staff agency of the Executive Office of the President, established by the National Security Act of 1947, which advises the President on domestic and foreign matters involving national security. The statutory members of the Council are the President, the Vice-President, the Secretaries of State and of Defense, and the Director of the Office of Emergency Preparedness. It can issue directives to the CIA but its main role is to assess the objectives of US security policy with the aim of formulating specific and departmentally agreed proposals for action by the President.

NCPAC   The National Conservative Political Action Committee, the leading right-wing PAC (q.v.).

New Deal   Term describing the policies of the first and second Administrations of President Franklin Roosevelt (1933–41), which were aimed at alleviating the Great Depression (q.v.) and extending social and economic justice. The First New Deal (1933–35) was essentially an emergency stabilization programme which involved the devaluation of the dollar, the expansion of business credit through an Economy Act, the stabilization of the market for farm products by the Agricultural Adjustment Act, an Emergency Banking Relief Act to ensure the liquidity of banks and a Federal Emergency Relief Administration to provide welfare. Various public works projects were initiated to create employment, including the Civilian Construction Corps which provided two million jobs in reclamation work; the Civil Works Administration which provided four million on other public works; and the Tennessee Valley Authority or TVA which provided hydro-electric power to depressed areas of seven states. The Executive branch of government was given the authority to regulate industrial competition by the National Industrial Recovery Act, although this was later abandoned as impractical. The Second New Deal (1935–46) was designed to increase the social security of the industrial population and small farmers; for example, the National Labor Relations Act of 1935 strengthened the power of workers to form trades unions and the Social Security Act introduced a scheme of social insurance. The New Deal clearly failed to end the Depression (economy recovery was finally brought about only by the vast rearmament for World War II), but it did establish a 'safety net' for ordinary Americans. At the time it was condemned as 'socialist' (and measures such as the National Industrial Recovery Act were indeed declared unconstitutional by the Supreme Court), but in fact the New Deal represented a form of state capitalism based on economic regulation and counter-cyclical government spending. The period was also instrumental in forging a new electoral coalition which ensured the primacy of the Democratic Party (q.v.) for 30 years. *See* Alphabet agencies, Hundred Days, Fair Deal *and* Fireside chats.

New England Confederation   The Confederation of the United Colonies of New England was formed in 1643 among Massachusetts, Connecticut, Plymouth and New Haven to provide for their defence while England was preoccupied with her own civil war. It was the first federation in American history and was successfully maintained until 1684.

New Federalism   Policy elaborated by successive American presidents in the post-war era to devolve more responsibility for certain developments and social policies to the states and so reduce federal expenditure. President Nixon (1969–74) initiated a system of 'revenue sharing' by which certain tax revenues were to be granted to state and local governments to enable them directly to support health, education and welfare programmes. Under the more conservative President Reagan (1981–89) the federal government significantly reduced direct financial aid to the states.

New Freedom   Reform policy elaborated by Woodrow Wilson when Democratic presidential candidate in the election of 1912. Wilson criticized his opponent Roosevelt's New Nationalism (q.v.) as being too statist and advocated instead a legal prohibition on business monopolies.

New Frontier   Phrase of John F. Kennedy in his acceptance speech as presidential candidate to the Democratic Party Convention in 1960 in which he proclaimed a need for national service on the part of all Americans; and subsequently used to describe the policies of his Administration, which ostensibly sought social justice at home and resistance to oppression and international communism abroad.

New Jersey Plan   One of the two plans for the national legislature submitted to the Federal Convention (q.v.) of 1787. William Paterson of New Jersey proposed that the US Congress be a single legislature in which each state would have only one vote, thus restricting the influence of the more populous states and largely protecting state sovereignty as it existed under the Articles of Confederation (q.v.). *See* Virginia Plan.

New Nationalism   Policy first advocated by the former Republican President Theodore Roosevelt in 1910 in favour of the state provision of welfare and extensive federal regulation of business 'trusts'. It won him the support of the Progressives (q.v.) in the election of 1912.

New Right   Term embracing the conservative, Christian-based politics, an increasingly important section of the right, in the late 1970s. Later based around the Moral Majority (q.v.) organization founded by the Reverend Jerry Falwell in 1979. Often fundamentalist and evangelical, it bitterly opposed such things as abortion, pornography, gay rights, etc., and supported school prayers, anti-communism, etc.

Nixon Doctrine   Policy of distributing the burden of collective defence more equally between the United States and her allies. It was first enunciated by President Nixon in 1969 when, speaking of American intervention in South-East Asia, he expressed US willingness to give military supplies and economic assistance to friendly nations but not necessarily to commit troops to their defence.

Noraid   Acronym for the Northern Aid Committee which channels funds from sympathizers in the United States to Republican organizations in Northern Ireland. It is said by its critics that these include terrorist groups.

Normalcy Term first used by Republican presidential candidate Warren Harding before his election in 1920, expressing America's desire for a return to 'normal' conditions after World War I. This included in particular a policy of isolationism (q.v.) in foreign affairs.

NOW The National Organization for Women, established in July 1966 to campaign for equal rights for women.

Nullification Crisis Constitutional crisis provoked in 1832 when the state of South Carolina claimed the right to decide which Acts of Congress did or did not apply within that state. South Carolina, whose economic interests favoured free trade, asserted that the Tariff Acts of 1828 and 1832 were unconstitutional and would not be enforced within the state. Although President Jackson was a supporter of states' rights (q.v.) he threatened military action should South Carolina fail to collect the tariffs or secede from the Union; finally in 1833 South Carolina, mollified by new and lower tariffs, withdrew her 'nullification' of the Acts. The great principles underlying the crisis – whether or not Congress had power to make laws for all the United States and whether the union of the states was indissoluble – were to be at issue again during the American Civil War (q.v.).

OAS The Organization of American States, an international body made up of the United States and 34 other countries in the western hemisphere to encourage co-operation between members and provide a forum for the resolution of mutual problems. It was established at the Bogota Conference of 1948 and its secretariat, the Pan-American Union, is based in Washington DC.

Ohio Gang Those members of the Administration of President Harding (1921–23) who were his personal political supporters from his home state of Ohio. Some were subsequently found to be guilty of fraud and corruption. *See* Teapot Dome Scandal.

Okies Migrants to California between 1933 and 1935 from Oklahoma, Kansas, Colorado and Texas, whose agricultural livelihoods had been devastated by the Dust Bowl (q.v.).

Old Glory Popular term for the flag of the United States (*see* Stars and Stripes).

Old Hunkers Section of the New York Democrats between 1844 and 1848 which was extremely conservative and pro-slavery. After 1848 they were known as 'Hardshell Democrats'.

OMB   The Office of Management and Budget, the division of the Executive Office of the President established in 1970 to prepare the federal budget and supervise its execution and to advise upon the management of the various agencies of the Administration.

Open contest   Any election for public office in which the incumbent is not standing for re-election.

Open Door Policy   Policy proposed by Secretary of State John Hay in September 1899 for the economic development of China, which would preserve its independence and political unity. It was defined in the 1900 Anglo-German agreement as involving free access for all nations to the Chinese ports, in contrast to the practice of claiming exclusive spheres of interest by individual powers.

Open Primary   *See* Primary.

Oregon Country   Territory of North America which encompassed most of present-day British Columbia and the Pacific North West states of the USA. By agreement with Great Britain in 1818 it had been opened to settlers of both countries. During the late 1830s a substantial number of Americans began to migrate westward along the 2,000-mile Oregon Trail and in 1846 the Oregon Country was formally divided by treaty between the two countries along the 49th parallel.

Ostend Manifesto   Confidential report to the State Department from the American Ministers to Great Britain, France and Spain who had met as instructed at Ostend in Belgium in 1854 to discuss the means by which Spain might be induced to sell Cuba to the United States or otherwise cede it. The Manifesto was leaked to the American press, causing a storm of protest from abolitionists (q.v.) and Northern politicians who feared Cuba might be annexed as another slave territory.

Oval Office   The personal office of the President within the White House. It is located in the West Wing.

PAC   Political Action Committee, the term for any interest group which is active in raising funds for electoral candidates and financially supporting certain political causes. The first PAC was the liberal Committee on Political Education (*see* COPE) and many today are committees formed by corporations or labor unions rather than independent groups. Given the frequency of elections in the United States, PACs are extremely influential and there have been successive attempts to regulate their operations, particularly the 1971 Federal Election Campaign Act.

Palmer Raids   The 1920 raids by federal agents on communist head-quarters (so-called because they were authorized by Attorney General Palmer). More than one-third of the 6,000 arrested were later released because of lack of evidence, but more than 500 aliens were eventually deported.

Pardon   The President exercises complete pardoning power for federal offences except in impeachment cases. One of the most controversial presidential pardons was that granted by President Ford (1974–77) to his predecessor Richard Nixon for any crimes Nixon might have committed during his term of office.

Peace Corps   US agency which administers the foreign aid programme adopted in 1961 by which American volunteers are sent to developing countries to teach skills and generally to assist in raising living standards.

Pearl Harbor   US naval base in Hawaii which was attacked by Japanese aircraft on 7 December 1941 in an attempt to destroy the US Pacific Fleet. The United States lost 2,000 men, five battleships and 120 aircraft and declared war on Japan the following day.

Peculiar Institution   A term by which slavery was often known.

Pentagon   The headquarters of the US Department of Defense, located in northern Virginia on the outskirts of Washington DC. It is so-called because of the pentagonal shape of the building.

Pentagon Papers   Documents originating in the US Department of Defense (whose headquarters is the Pentagon building outside of Washington DC) which were leaked to the *New York Times* in 1971 by former Pentagon analyst Daniel Ellsberg. They appeared to reveal a government policy of deliberate misinformation about the Vietnam War (q.v.). The leak led President Nixon to go on to form the Plumbers (q.v.).

Philadelphia Charter   Declaration issued in Philadelphia, Pennsylvania in May 1944 by the International Labour Organization (now an agency of the United Nations) expressing the right of all people to freedom, dignity, economic security, material well-being, spiritual development and equal opportunity.

The Plumbers   Nickname for a secret unit created at the behest of President Nixon to carry out acts of espionage and prevent leaks of government information to the press. On 17 June 1972 five of its operatives were arrested by the police when they broke into the headquarters of the Democratic National Committee in Washington DC (*see* Watergate). The Plumbers were exposed to the public when all five were found to be members of CREEP, the Campaign to Re-Elect the President.

Plurality   That proportion or number by which the vote for the candidate with the largest number of votes in any electoral contest is greater than that of the candidate with the second largest number. In British usage this is frequently and incorrectly described as a candidate's 'majority' although in any contest in which there are more than two candidates it is often unlikely that the winner will in fact have received a majority (i.e., over half) of the votes cast.

Pocket Veto   *See* Veto.

Point Four   President Truman's programme of economic aid to underdeveloped countries begun in 1950.

Police powers   Within the US federal system, those powers by which the states have the authority to regulate the safety and welfare of the people. These include the power to regulate the local economy or protect public health.

Popular Sovereignty   Doctrine first expounded in 1847 by Lewis Cass of Michigan and taken up by Stephen Douglas, Democratic Senator for Illinois. It held that the question of whether to extend slavery into any of the Western Territories should be decided not by Congress (which was bitterly divided on the issue), but by the settlers in each area which sought to become a state. *See* Wilmot Proviso.

Populists   Name given to members of the People's Party (*see* p. 110).

Pork Barrel   Appropriations passed by Congress or state legislatures which are not required by the public interest but are carried out to generate political support for individual members (e.g., the building of public works to support employment in the member's congressional district).

Potsdam Conference   Last Allied conference of World War II, held at Potsdam outside Berlin from 11 July to 2 August 1945 between British Prime Minister Churchill (replaced by Attlee during the course of the conference), Marshal Stalin of the USSR and President Truman. The

Allies agreed at the conference to the partitioning of Germany between themselves into zones of military occupation.

Precinct   The basic unit in the United States in both the electoral process and for party organization. Cities and counties are divided into precinct polling districts, each containing from 200 to 1,000 voters and one polling station. The precinct also serves for the election or appointment of delegates to city or county party conventions.

Pressure group   An organized group in which members share a common interest and which seeks to influence government officials and policies in accordance. In 1946 Congress sought to limit their activity through the federal Regulation of Lobbying Act, which required registration of groups which sought to lobby officials. Thus many professional societies, racial and religious groupings, and veterans' organizations act as pressure groups as well as those representing business and labour interests, and different social and political activists. *See* PAC.

Primary   The primary election, an institution of US politics designed to safeguard against corruption. To prevent bosses or those with vested interests from securing the nomination of a particular candidate, in the early twentieth century reformers favoured the practice of holding a preliminary ballot at which qualified electors might choose a candidate to stand in the election (i.e., the election of party candidates by party members). Depending upon the laws of the state in which they are held, primaries may be 'closed', with only members of a particular party being allowed to vote for candidates, or 'open', in which the right to vote is not restricted to those who are registered as voters of the respective party. A *direct primary* is one in which candidates are chosen for the actual election itself. An *indirect primary* elects delegates on a candidate's behalf to a party's nominating convention, which then makes the choice; this is the method used in selecting the presidential nominee. Most of the states and the District of Columbia hold some form of presidential primary in the months preceding the conventions. Delegates are selected in the other states by political party conventions or committees. Delegates selected in the primaries may or may not be pledged to vote for a particular presidential aspirant. In some states delegates are selected by the party organization but are bound to support the candidate designated by the voters on a 'popularity' vote.

Proclamation Line   Boundary established along the line of the Allegheny mountains by a Proclamation of the British Crown in 1763. The American colonists were not permitted to settle west of the line, in order to protect the Native Americans and reduce the degree of conflict between them. It was soon violated by the colonists.

Progressive Era Era in American politics from the later 1890s until World War I, which was marked by a major movement for state intervention in social policy and the regulation of economic life. The election of 1896 established a Republican hegemony in the United States that lasted with one interruption until 1932. The politics of the era was dominated by the interests of industrial capitalism, but political society, and latterly the government itself, was energized by a reform movement that was known as 'Progressivism'. No single class or political group comprised the Progressives, but in large part they were urban middle-class activists who sought to address the social and economic dislocations caused by industrialization – such as immigration, the development of slums and the corruption of municipal government – and who desired a more efficient and democratic government. In matters of education, public health and safety, industrial working conditions (especially child labour), social order and policing, reformers were active at the municipal and state levels in the 1890s and 1900s. Some were guided by the religious creed of the 'Social Gospel'; popular support for reform was encouraged by investigative journalists, known as 'muckrackers' (q.v.), who exposed abuses, particularly in industry. In politics, reformers pressed for measures to strengthen the electoral control of government, such as the direct election of US Senators, the introduction of primary (q.v.) elections to select candidates and the use of referendums to allow the voters to make laws directly.

Progressivism in certain aspects was nonetheless a profoundly conservative, even anti-modern, movement. The majority of its supporters were middle-class professionals who, until the rise of industrial capitalism, had been the natural political and social leaders of their communities and who now sought a return to the supposedly morally superior values of Jeffersonian agrarianism and Jacksonian democracy. To achieve this they supported the abandonment of *laissez-faire* economics and the regulation of big business by the state and federal governments. In politics, moreover, their ideas for increasing electoral control of government were intended to benefit largely the middle classes, because these had the effect of concentrating power in the hands of those with the money and organization to participate in elections. The anti-working-class bias of the movement went further: reformers identified the city as the principal focus of political corruption and saw the new immigrants of the 1880s and 1890s as controlled by local 'bosses' (q.v.) of the existing political parties. The only adequate solution was both to restrict future immigration and to prevent existing citizens of non-American origin from being able to vote; thus the Progressives actively supported literacy tests to keep out voters who could not read English. In the South they supported the Democratic Party's attempts to remove the franchise from (uneducated) blacks.

Despite its humanitarianism, the Progressive movement wished not to change the existing social and political order but to preserve it from Populist or even independent socialist challenges. At the federal level it flowered during the second Administration of the energetic Republican Theodore Roosevelt (1905–09), when the first major federal laws affecting public and industrial health and conservation were enacted. Roosevelt voluntarily retired in 1908 but was disappointed in the conservatism of his Republican successor, William Howard Taft, and sought the Republican nomination for the 1912 election. When it was refused, Roosevelt created his own Progressive Party (or 'Bull Moose' party, after his nickname) to fight the election; however, he succeeded only in splitting the Republican vote and throwing the White House to the Democratic contender, Woodrow Wilson.

Wilson continued the reform movement, especially in the fields of industrial regulation, tariff and banking reform, labour legislation and support for agriculture. His political reputation, however, depended heavily on his claim to have kept the United States out of World War I. It carried Wilson to a second term in 1916 but when the US entered the war the following year Progressivism seemed compromised, even in victory. The American people did not share Wilson's liberal internationalism and the election of 1920 inaugurated a new era of conservative Republicanism.

Prohibition   The period between January 1920 and December 1933 when the manufacture, sale and distribution of liquor in the United States was outlawed. *See* pp. 160–1.

Proposition   An alternative name for the term Initiative (q.v.).

Proposition 209   Controversial law passed in California in November 1996 which would end racial quotas and hence reverse the so-called 'affirmative action' programme. The proposition bans preferences based on race or sex in public education, employment and contracting. The proposition was blocked by a US federal judge in December 1996.

Pujo Committee   Committee of the House of Representatives created in 1912 to investigate monopoly conditions in the banking system. Its report was influential in the establishment of the Federal Reserve Bank.

Pullman strike   Major railway strike in 1894, which began initially as an action against the Pullman Palace Car Company of Chicago. It was broken when President Cleveland sent in federal troops.

PUSH   People United to Serve Humanity, an organization founded by the Reverend Jesse Jackson to work for the economic development of black communities and as a political base for electoral campaigns.

Quebec Conference   Wartime meeting of August 1943 between President Franklin Roosevelt and British Prime Minister Winston Churchill in the Canadian city of Quebec, at which the Americans successfully insisted that the Allied invasion of western Europe, agreed upon for the late spring of 1944, should come in northern France rather than from the Mediterranean.

Reaganomics   Term describing the economic policies of the Republican Administrations of President Reagan (1981–89). The Reagan era was marked by an enormous increase in the federal debt (due to tax cuts simultaneous with an increase in defence spending), but the clearest theoretical feature of Reaganomics was its belief in micro-economic reform to improve the 'supply side' of the economy.

Recall Election   Procedure whereby a state will, upon the petition of a statutorily defined number of registered voters, conduct an election to determine whether an elected public (but not federal) official shall remain in office. If a majority of voters favours the official's 'recall', a successor shall be chosen by the same ballot or at a subsequent election.

Reconstruction   The era from 1865 to 1877 was dominated by the attempt of the federal government to reconstruct the constitutional order of the Union and re-integrate the defeated South into the American nation. This massive task was made all the more difficult by a combination of Southern recalcitrance and political resistance; divisions within the ruling Republican Party over how to treat the defeated Democrats; and the tremendous economic and social dislocations caused by the abolition of slavery and the collapse of the 'plantocracy' in the South. The assassination of President Lincoln at the very end of the Civil War removed perhaps the one politician who would have been able to reconcile the nation; his successor, Vice-President Andrew Johnson, was a Southern Democrat who rapidly fell out with the Radical Republicans then controlling Congress. Johnson's attempts to frustrate the Radicals' policies led to the imposition of military rule in the South in 1867 and the attempted impeachment of the President himself in 1868.

The Republicans successfully elected Union war hero Ulysses S. Grant in 1868, but he proved a weak President and his Administration became a by-word for corruption. The South at this time was ruled by state governments elected by universal male suffrage for the first time; and the Fourteenth and Fifteenth Amendments of 1868 and 1870 secured blacks' civil rights in law. Eventually, most Republicans tired of the massive Southern resistance (as shown by the notorious Ku Klux Klan) and the US Army was progressively withdrawn from the region. The outcome of the presidential election of 1876 was disputed, but the Democrats the following year agreed to a Republican President if the federal government withdrew its troops and allowed the re-establishment of Democratic state governments.

Red Scare   Period of popular fear of a communist or socialist uprising in the United States in 1919. Following the Bolshevik Revolution in Russia and World War I, there was a fierce swing in public opinion against foreigners, trades unionists and the political parties of the left. Industrial strikes were violently suppressed and Congress and state legislatures passed laws banning many socialist and syndicalist organizations.

Redistricting   The procedure of redrawing the boundaries of electoral districts to maintain proportionality between them (*see* Apportionment). In each state it is carried out by, or under the direction of, the legislature.

Regulators   Members of associations formed in eighteenth-century North Carolina to regulate such affairs as law enforcement and civil disputes, most of whom were settlers of the western boundary of the colony who had difficulty attending the courts in Charleston. After conflicts with the authorities in 1770–71 they migrated westwards to colonize Tennessee.

Representative   Members of the lower House of Congress or any of the state legislatures. The term of a Representative is two years; whenever there is a vacancy a special election is held.

Reserved powers   In the US federal system, the powers of the individual states according to the Tenth Amendment to the US Constitution, whereby the powers not delegated to the federal government are reserved to the states or to the people.

Resolution   An enactment of either or both Houses of Congress to express the collective will of that body. A *simple resolution* is passed by one chamber only and does not require the consent of the other or of the President; its use is restricted to changing procedural rules. A *joint resolution* is passed by both Houses and when signed by the President becomes law; it is used to approve or authorize executive actions, usually in the sphere of foreign policy (e.g., the Gulf of Tonkin Resolution (q.v.) of 1964). A *concurrent resolution* is passed by one House with the concurrence of the other and is used to express the will of Congress on certain issues.

Revolutionary War   *See* War of Independence, p. 239.

RNC   The Republican National Committee. *See* National Committee, p. 342.

Roaring Twenties   Popular phrase describing the period of economic and social vitality in the United States before the Wall Street Crash of 1929 (q.v.) and the Great Depression (q.v.), *see* Gilded age.

Robber Barons   Term of abuse applied in the latter part of the nineteenth century to industrialists (particularly railway owners) on account of their predatory commercial practices.

Roll call vote   A vote in any legislature in which it is recorded how each member has voted. It is the method required in any vote to override a presidential veto.

Roosevelt Corollary   Interpretation of the Monroe Doctrine (q.v.) proclaimed by President Theodore Roosevelt in 1904, by which he asserted that instability among other countries in the western hemisphere gave the United States an international 'police power' to intervene in their internal affairs. The following year it was used to justify forcing the Dominican Republic to pay its debts to US creditors.

Rugged Individualism   Policy of the Republican Party (q.v.) in the 1920s, stressing that competition among the strong would produce a socially optimum outcome and that government intervention in the economy and in society (e.g., through regulation) should be kept to a minimum.

Rust Belt   Those US states which were formerly heavily industrialized (i.e., those of the Mid-West) and which, particularly during the early 1980s, experienced precipitous economic decline.

SALT   Strategic Arms Limitations Talks between the United States and the Soviet Union which began in November 1969 and ended in May 1972 with a treaty restricting anti-ballistic missile systems. A second round opened in November 1974 and produced a treaty in June 1979 but this was not ratified by the US Senate because of the Soviet invasion of Afghanistan. *See* START *and* Cold War.

Scalawags   Term of abuse for those white Southerners who supported the Radical Republican governments or held political office during the era of Reconstruction (q.v.). Many of them, however, were not simple opportunists but rather were poor whites who had always opposed slavery and secession.

SDI Strategic Defense Initiative, announced by President Reagan in March 1983 when he revealed that research was being undertaken into the feasibility of protecting the United States from ICBM (intercontinental ballistic missile) attack by developing a chain of satellites in space able to destroy ground-launched missiles, and by other measures.

SEC The Securities and Exchange Commission, the regulatory commission of the financial industry established by the Securities Exchange Act of 1934.

Second Front Following the German attack upon the Soviet Union in June 1941, Stalin asked Britain to open a 'Second Front' by an invasion of western Europe in order to relieve the pressure on Russia. This Britain could not do without American support. The Second Front, agreed at the Quebec Conference of August 1943, was finally opened by the Allied landings in Normandy on 6 June 1944.

Secret Service The law enforcement section of the Treasury Department, which is responsible for the protection of the lives of the President and other officers of state and for the security of others designated by the President, such as visiting foreign dignitaries and foreign embassies in Washington DC.

Segregation Separation of white and black races in public and private facilities. Laws regarding segregation have at various times been on the statute books of several US states, not solely those in the South. In 1896 the Supreme Court ruled in *Plessy v. Ferguson* that such laws were constitutional if the separate facilities provided for each race were nonetheless equal. This produced a plethora of statutes preventing blacks enjoying schools, hospitals, public transport and forms of recreation reserved for whites. However, in 1954 the Court reversed the formula of *Plessy* by holding that segregation based on race was, in fact, incompatible with equality; and subsequent Court orders and legislation on civil rights in 1957, 1960, 1964, 1965 and 1968 have removed the edifice of legally sanctioned segregation. *See* Civil Rights Movement.

Select Committee Any committee of either chamber of Congress (or jointly of both) created for a special purpose and for a set period, as opposed to the standing committees.

Seniority Rule The custom almost always adhered to in both Houses of Congress of awarding the chairmanship of a committee to the member of the majority party with the greatest number of years of continuous service on the committee. Each party lists the ranking of its members of each committee strictly according to this principle of seniority. In 1973 Congress adopted a method of electing committee chairmen by caucuses of the respective parties, but seniority is still generally observed.

Separation of Powers   A fundamental principle of the government of the United States whereby power is divided between the three branches, namely the legislature, the executive and the judiciary. The officials of each branch are selected by different procedures, have different terms of office and are functionally independent of one another. Nevertheless the separation is not complete in that each branch participates in the functions of the others through a system of 'checks and balances' (e.g., the President nominates the members of the Supreme Court, which has the authority to rule upon the constitutionality of laws passed by Congress). The separation ensures different persons discharge the tasks of making the law, applying it and interpreting it.

Sharecroppers   System of cultivating land whereby tenants farm the landlord's property in exchange for a house, the necessary tools etc., and a share of the crop. Owing to a lack of credit which would have permitted a rental system based on money, it was a predominant feature of agriculture among both poor black and white tenants in the Southern states for 50 years after the American Civil War (q.v.).

Shays' Rebellion   Uprising of 1786–87 led among the heavily endebted farmers of western Massachusetts by Daniel Shay. The farmers wanted a paper currency to alleviate the contemporary deflation and an end to the attempt to pay off the state debt by taxation. It was one of several conflicts pitting rural classes against creditors in the aftermath of the War of Independence (q.v.) and lent further weight to the need to revise the Articles of Confederation (q.v.).

Slush fund   Money obtained from undeclared sources used by a US Congressman to maintain his office and for other administrative expenses.

Snow Belt   An alternative name for the Frost Belt (q.v.).

Soft-shell Democrats   Section of the Democratic Party (q.v.) in New York between 1848 and 1854 which opposed slavery. *See* Old Hunkers.

Solid South   Term referring to the fact that the Southern states of the USA had often tended to elect candidates of the Democratic Party (q.v.). In the post-war era this solidity has been undermined, first by the tendency of the more liberal Northern Democrats in the New Deal (q.v.) coalition to support civil rights for black Americans, and secondly by the ability in the 1980s of Republican candidates – initially at the presidential level – to appeal successfully to the more conservative social values of the Southern electorate.

Speaker   The leader of the House of Representatives or of the lower chamber of a state legislature who presides over its business. As presiding officer he interprets its rules and decides questions of order and has considerable influence in arranging the business of the chamber. The Speaker of the House is elected by the caucus of the majority party and, according to the Presidential Succession Act of 1947, succeeds to that office after the Vice-President.

Special Relationship   Chiefly a term of British usage to refer to the relationship between Great Britain and the United States, which is said to be especially deep on account of historical and sentimental links of culture and kinship.

Split ticket   The practice whereby electors vote for candidates of different parties for different offices, i.e., they do not vote the party line or 'straight ticket'.

Stalking horse   A candidate fielded in an election to draw votes from a rival in order to enable a preferred third candidate to win, or to cover the appearance of a more significant candidate.

Stalwarts   Section of the Republican Party (q.v.) led by Senator Conkling of New York which opposed President Garfield on the issue of civil service reform in 1881. Garfield was assassinated by the Stalwart Guiteau, who claimed he had acted to reunite the Republican Party which he believed the President had split.

'Star Wars'   Popular term for the Strategic Defense Initiative. *See* SDI.

Stars and Stripes   The title of the US National Anthem, taken from the colloquial name for the flag of the United States. The flag consists of 13 stripes signifying the original 13 states of the Union and 50 stars representing the present states. It has been the practice to add a star to the flag when a new state accedes to the Union. The most recent were added following the accession of Alaska and Hawaii in 1959.

START   Strategic Arms Reduction Talks, conducted intermittently between the United States and the Soviet Union during the 1980s. The

Soviets withdrew in December 1983 in protest at the American installation of middle-range nuclear missiles in Europe, but a treaty on intermediate range nuclear forces (INF) was concluded in 1987. *See* SALT *and* Cold War.

State of the Union Address   The President's annual message to Congress in which he proposes the programme of legislation which he would like to see enacted. It is customarily delivered in person at the beginning of the legislative session in January.

States' Rights   *See* State's Rights Democratic Party, p. 115.

Sun Belt   Those states in the South which have a Mediterranean or sub-tropical climate and which in the 1980s experienced substantial economic and population growth.

Sunset Laws   Those statutes which expire at the end of a specified period, unless renewed by the legislature.

Super Tuesday   A collection of presidential primary elections held simultaneously (on a Tuesday) by a number of states, the majority of which are in the South. Each state may determine when either of the political parties holds a primary election in that state and beginning in March 1988, a number of Southern states agreed to schedule their primaries simultaneously with the object of trying to increase the influence of the region upon the final choice of presidential candidate.

Supremacy Clause   Article VI of the US Constitution which asserts that the Constitution itself, any federal laws passed in accordance with the powers constitutionally delegated to the federal government, and all treaties are to be the supreme law of the land, above state law.

Tammany Hall   Headquarters of the Democratic Party in New York county and a byword for 'machine' control of the political process and the corruption that goes with it (*see* Boss). The Society of St Tammany was founded as a club in 1789, but by the early 1800s it had already become a political organization and under William Tweed it was the dominant influence in New York City in the 1860s. Its control extended beyond the city to embrace the state government of New York and until President Roosevelt specifically allied himself with the Republican Party in New York during the New Deal (q.v.), it exerted a sometimes decisive influence on national Democratic politics.

Teapot Dome Scandal   Political scandal during the Administration of President Harding (1921–23), which marked the nadir of the Ohio Gang (q.v.). Harding transferred control of naval oil reserves held at Teapot Dome, Wyoming from the Navy to his friend Albert Fall, Secretary of the Interior, who subsequently leased them to oil companies in return for a bribe. Fall was eventually imprisoned in 1929, following a Senate investigation, the first Cabinet minster to be criminally convicted.

Tehran Conference   Wartime meeting in Tehran, Persia from 28 November to 1 December 1943 between British Prime Minister Churchill, Marshal Stalin of the USSR and President Franklin Roosevelt, at which the Allied military strategy for the conduct of World War II in Europe and the Far East was agreed.

Tennis Cabinet   Popular term, at the time, for the unofficial advisers to Theodore Roosevelt.

Tet Offensive   Attack by the Viet Cong (q.v.) and North Vietnamese forces on Saigon and other South Vietnamese towns during the Tet lunar new year festival. It ran from 20 January to 25 February 1968 and although it was a military defeat for the communists it nonetheless significantly weakened the United States' commitment to the Vietnam War (q.v.).

Thirteen Colonies   The English colonies situated on the eastern seaboard of the North American continent which declared their independence from the British Crown in 1776 during the War of Independence (q.v.) and became the original United States of America. They were (in the order in which they ratified the subsequent US Constitution) Delaware, Pennsylvania, New Jersey, Georgia, Connecticut, Massachusetts, Maryland, South Carolina, New Hampshire, Virginia, New York, North Carolina and Rhode Island. Quebec, which had been captured from France by the British in 1760, remained loyal to the Crown and became the first colony of Canada.

Thousand Days   The period in office of President John F. Kennedy from his inauguration in January 1961 to his assassination in November 1963. Kennedy was the youngest ever elected President and his Administration seemed to mark a new period of activist, liberal government after the conservatism of the Republican Eisenhower era. Kennedy initiated social and civil rights legislation, proposed talks on a nuclear test ban, and resisted communist aggression in the Cuban Missile Crisis (q.v.). However, as President he also authorized the Bay of Pigs (q.v.) operation and increased US involvement in the Vietnam War (q.v.).

Three Mile Island   Site in Harrisburg, Pennsylvania where there was a serious leakage of radiation from a nuclear power station in March 1979.

Top Eleven   Leaders of the Communist Party of the United States who in October 1949 were convicted of conspiracy to overthrow the US government and sentenced to prison. Their convictions were upheld by the Supreme Court in 1951. However, in 1957 the Court applied a new standard of evidence to cases brought under the Smith Act (which had outlawed anti-government conspiracies) and the Justice Department dropped all further prosecutions. *See* House Un-American Activities Committee *and* McCarthyism.

Tory   *See* Loyalists.

Tower Commission   Commission of investigation appointed by President Reagan in November 1986 to investigate the role of the National Security Council during the Iran–Contra Affair (q.v.). It consisted of Lieutenant General Brent Scowcroft (National Security Adviser to President Ford), Edmund Muskie (Secretary of State to President Carter) and John Tower, a former Republican Senator of Texas who had chaired the Senate Armed Services Committee.

Trail of Tears   The great trek made by the several thousand Cherokee people in 1838 from their homeland in the East to territory in the West of the United States. By the terms of the 1830 Indian Removal Act, all tribes east of the Mississippi were obliged to cede their lands in exchange for areas in the West. Four thousand of the 13,000 Cherokee died of the great hardships suffered *en route*.

***Trent* Affair**   Diplomatic incident between Great Britain and the United States during the American Civil War (q.v.). In November 1861 the US Navy stopped the British ship *Trent* on the high seas and arrested its passengers Mason and Slidell, commissioners of the Confederate States (q.v.) *en route* to Europe. The British government protested against this breach of neutrality and for a while it seemed possible that Great Britain might enter the Civil War on the side of the Confederacy, but President Lincoln was eager to avoid hostilities and subsequently released the Confederate officers.

Truman Doctrine   Policy of the US government announced by President Truman in March 1947 that the United States would not attack the Soviet Union but would rather seek to contain communism within its present limits and actively prevent its extension into new countries. The policy was occasioned by Great Britain informing the United States that for economic reasons she could no longer support the anti-communist forces in the Greek Civil War, thus requiring Truman to offer American aid to Greece instead. The Doctrine was, however, soon shown to be inadequate by the failure of the Americans to prevent the fall of China to the communists in October 1949. *See* Cold War.

Trusts Business combines which prevailed in the late nineteenth century whereby shareholders in different companies delegated control of their shares to groups of trustees who might thereby control several firms. In 1891 the Sherman Anti-Trust Act was passed to control such potential oligopolistic behaviour, although it was also applied against trades unions.

TVA Tennessee Valley Authority, a controversial federal agency established in May 1933 as part of the New Deal (q.v.). It developed hydroelectric power in the Tennessee Valley, providing cheap electricity for rural industrialization and allowing land reclamation and the improvement of agriculture across seven states.

Tweed Ring Political machine of William Tweed, notorious boss (q.v.) of Tammany Hall (q.v.), who embezzled New York City of a million dollars a year in the later 1860s. Tweed was eventually exposed in 1871 and subsequently jailed.

U–2 Incident On 1 May 1960 an American Lockheed U–2 reconnaissance aircraft was shot down near Sverdlovsk in the Soviet Union while on a photographic mission. As a result, the Soviets cancelled a summit meeting with President Eisenhower planned for May 1960 in West Berlin and the Americans ceased U–2 flights over the USSR. The pilot, Gary Powers, was sentenced to ten years' imprisonment but exchanged for a Soviet spy in 1962.

Underground railroad In the era before the American Civil War (q.v.) Southern slave-owners alleged that Northern abolitionists (q.v.) were systematically helping the escape of fugitive slaves to the North. The organization supposedly responsible for this was dubbed the 'underground railroad', but it was largely fictitious; certain abolitionist clergymen were active in helping slaves escape, but most of the assistance was in fact provided by the ex-slaves themselves on a personal basis.

United Nations Term first used by the Allied powers of themselves in a joint pledge of 1 January 1942 that none of their number would make a separate peace with the Axis. A conference between China, Great Britain, the USSR and the USA in October 1943 recognized the need for an international organization, based on the principle of the sovereign equality of all peace-loving states, for the maintenance of international peace and security. After various further wartime discussions, the

United Nations Charter, the basis of the United Nations Organization, was drawn up by the 50 states at war with Germany in conference in San Francisco between 15 April and 26 June 1945. The participation of the United States and Russia has been instrumental in the success of the UN compared with the pre-war League of Nations. *See* Fourteen Points.

USIA The United States Information Agency, an independent executive agency established in 1953 to administer the overseas information and cultural programmes of the US government. Its critics often see it purely as a propaganda organization.

Valley Forge Site in eastern Pennsylvania near Philadelphia where the army of the Continental Congress (q.v.) wintered during 1777–78. General George Washington, despite the enormous privations endured by the colonial troops, with the assistance of European advisers, succeeded in re-organizing and re-equipping his men into an effective military force.

Veto The power vested in the President (and in the states in the Governor) to return a bill unsigned to the legislative body with reasons for his objections. The US Constitution provides that every bill which passes the House and Senate must carry the signature of the President before it becomes law. When the President receives a bill he has four courses of action open to him: he may sign the bill, in which case it becomes law; he may not sign it, in which case it becomes law after ten congressional working days; he may write 'veto' (i.e., I forbid, in Latin) across the bill and send it back to Congress, in which case it comes under reconsideration; or he may not sign it whereupon if Congress adjourns within ten days the bill falls (the so-called 'pocket veto'). Congress can override a presidential veto by repassing the legislation with a majority of no less than two-thirds of the votes cast in each chamber, or it may amend the sections of which the President disapproves to make it acceptable to him.

Viet Cong Name meaning 'Vietnamese Communists' given by the South Vietnamese government to the supporters of the Front for the Liberation of South Vietnam (founded 1960). The government was anxious to distinguish between the Communists and the Viet Minh, the nationalist independence league which had fought against the French colonial regime and had included non-communists. The Viet Cong took an active part in the Vietnam War (q.v.) against the forces of the South Vietnamese government and the Americans. They were responsible for attacks on US bases at Pleiku and Qui Nhon in February 1965 which escalated American involvement in the war and they participated in the Tet Offensive (q.v.).

Vietnamization   Policy of President Nixon, pursued from 1968–69 onwards, of reducing the involvement of American ground troops in the Vietnam War (q.v.) and transferring most of the responsibility for the defence of South Vietnam to the army of that republic.

Virginia Plan   One of the two plans for the national legislature submitted to the Federal Convention (q.v.) in 1787. James Madison and Edmund Randolph, both delegates from Virginia, proposed that the US Congress should consist of two houses in which representation was to be in accordance with population, thus giving more influence to the more populous states (such as Virginia). The Plan also envisaged a more centralized government than that which existed under the Articles of Confederation (q.v.). *See* New Jersey Plan.

Wall Street   Site of the New York Stock Exchange in New York City and a synonym for US finance and banking generally.

Wall Street Crash   Collapse of the New York Stock Exchange, beginning on 24 October 1929 (Black Thursday) when a two-year speculative boom finally faltered and 132 million shares were sold in panic trading. The Federal Reserve Bank failed to expand the money supply sufficiently quickly and by Tuesday 29 October shares had become valueless. The Wall Street Crash – sometimes known as the Great Crash – led directly to the Great Depression (q.v.) of the 1930s.

War on Poverty   Collective term for the series of social programmes enacted by the Johnson Administration (1963–69) as part of the Great Society (q.v.). These included the provision of health care for elderly and poor Americans, the expansion of job training for the disadvantaged, increased federal assistance to the states for education, and grants to cities for the development of urban areas. However, the fiscal strain caused by US involvement in the Vietnam War (q.v.) brought the War on Poverty to an untimely end.

War powers   Those powers granted explicitly in the United States Constitution concerned with protecting the nation from its enemies. War powers include those granted to Congress to tax and spend for the common defence, to declare war and to make rules concerning captures, to raise and support armies and provide a navy, to enact military law and to oversee the state militias. The President of the United States as Commander-in-Chief has the 'inherent power' to do whatever is necessary to protect the nation subject to judicial scrutiny. In times of crisis Congress can and has delegated certain of its powers to the President as 'emergency powers'.

WASP (White Anglo-Saxon Protestant) An acronym first brought into wide use by E. Digby Baitzell in *The Protestant Establishment* (1964). Traditionally, WASPS have been seen to dominate Wall Street (q.v.), major corporations and the Ivy League universities.

Watergate The most serious political scandal in American history, which followed the arrest in June 1972 of five White House operatives while burgling the headquarters of the Democratic National Committee in Washington DC (*see* The Plumbers). President Nixon's staff managed to keep the affair largely secret until November 1972 when the *Washington Post* uncovered their links with the Campaign to Re-Elect the President (CREEP). The Senate established a select committee to investigate the affair in February 1973, but as late as April Nixon was still meeting with his advisers to discuss further ways of preventing public disclosure. The President claimed that 'executive privilege' protected White House officials from having to testify to congressional committees, but on 30 April certain of them, including Chief of Staff Haldeman and Attorney General Kleindienst, were forced to resign. In July 1973 it was revealed to the Senate committee that Nixon had secretly recorded conversations in his office. The President delayed the surrender of these tapes (even dismissing Archibald Cox, the Attorney General's special prosecutor in the case) and only released them in their entirety on 24 July 1974 under threat of impeachment and on the direct order of the Supreme Court. On 27 July the House Judiciary Committee passed the first article of impeachment, charging Nixon with the obstruction of justice and on 29 and 30 July the second and final articles were passed. Nixon resigned the Presidency (the only man to have done so) on 9 August 1974 to forestall further proceedings. He was subsequently pardoned by his successor President Ford, an action which severely damaged Ford's reputation.

Watts Area of South Central Los Angeles, which was the scene in August 1965 of the most severe urban rioting in the United States since the Civil War, and the centre of even more widespread disturbances in April 1992 in which 58 people died. Racism and the lack of economic opportunities for the disadvantaged population were the essential causes of the rioting.

Weathermen Group on the extreme left of American politics which arose in the late 1960s and whose aim was the total overthrow of the US political system. It committed carefully planned acts of terrorism, including bombings and the murder of policemen. Members were generally drawn from the intelligentsia but little is known of the movement's origins. It appeared to have ceased activities in the early 1970s although bomb outrages were committed in its name in 1975.

West Point   Fortress on the Hudson River in New York state and site of the US Military Academy, founded in 1802.

Wetbacks   Illegal immigrants to the USA from Mexico, so-called because for many years they were forced to swim the Rio Grande River. They form a cheap source of labour, especially for agricultural producers in California.

Whigs   *See* Whig Party, p. 115.

Whiskey Rebellion   Insurrection in western Pennsylvania in 1794 against the heavy duty imposed upon distilled liquor. This measure had been introduced to finance Secretary of the Treasury Alexander Hamilton's plans to pay off debts incurred by the states and the Continental Congress (q.v.) during the War of Independence (q.v.).

White House   The name of the Executive Mansion in Washington DC, the official residence of the President of the United States, so called because it was whitewashed to disguise the damage caused when the British burnt the city in 1814. The White House Office contains the President's most immediate advisers and is directed by the Chief of Staff.

Whitecaps   Secret organization formed in Indiana in the late nineteenth century, whose original purpose was to serve as a vigilante society but which later committed many outrages.

Wilmot Proviso   Amendment to the appropriations bill introduced into Congress in 1846 to provide monies for the purchase of additional territory from Mexico during peace negotiations following the Mexican–American War (*see* p. 240). Proposed by David Wilmot of Pennsylvania, it prohibited slavery in any land to be acquired from Mexico. The amendment was defeated in the Senate but subsequently endorsed by many Northern states which opposed the expansion of slavery.

Wounded Knee   Scene of the massacre of at least 200 Hunkpapa Sioux, mostly women and children, by the US Seventh Cavalry shortly after Christmas 1890. The events at Wounded Knee Creek, South Dakota, now symbolize the end of the Plains Indians' resistance to American expansion.

Yalta Conference   Conference of the Big Three (q.v.) held at Yalta in the Crimea, 4–11 February 1945. Agreements were reached concerning the post-war world order: France was to be an equal partner in the Allied Control Commission for Germany; the Soviet Union was to be granted Russia's old rights in China (in order to ensure her entry into the war against Japan); and a United Nations (q.v.) Organization was to be established.

Yankee   Nickname first given to American colonists in New England, the derivation of which is obscure. In the USA it is used specifically with reference to persons from the Northern states; in other countries it is used more generally to mean an American.

Yippies   Close contemporaries of the 'hippy' but more actively involved in political action, particularly in protests against American action in the Vietnam War (q.v.) and the methods of American police forces. The term was coined by one of the movement's leaders, Jerry Rubin, and is derived from the initials of the Youth International Party and hippy. The movement's influence faded in the 1970s with US withdrawal from Vietnam.

Young Plan   Proposal made in June 1929 by US businessman Owen Young for settlement of German war reparations. Payments were to be reduced by 75% and made annually until 1988. Germany accepted the plan but Hitler refused to make any further payments after 1933. *See* Dawes Plan.

Zimmermann Telegram   Coded message of 19 January 1917 from German foreign minister Arthur Zimmermann to the German minister in Mexico urging the conclusion of a German–Mexican alliance in the event of a declaration of war on Germany by the United States following Germany's intended resumption of unrestricted submarine warfare on 1 February. Mexico would be offered the recapture of her territories lost in the Mexican–American War (q.v.). Intercepted by British Naval Intelligence, the telegram was released to the American press on 1 March, greatly inflaming feeling against Germany and helping to precipitate the US declaration of war against Germany on 6 April 1917.

Zoning   The division of a city or other unit of government into districts and the regulation by law of land use. Zoning concerns the nature of the actual buildings and the purposes for which they are erected. The instrument of zoning, enacted under the police power of communities, has political importance in that well-to-do suburban areas can, and have, excluded the possibility of the settlement of poorer minorities by imposing land-use requirements for further construction which only the wealthy can afford.

SECTION SEVEN

Topic bibliography[1]

[1] Compiled by Peter Thompson and David Waller.

Topics

Introductory note

Although the history of the independent United States is relatively short, its historical literature is particularly large. Any bibliography of this nature can only be introductory and selective. A policy has been followed of attempting to include the fundamental texts for any particular subject (which might be called classics) in addition to a representative selection of more recent works, on the grounds that these will be ones which can be most readily obtained. Likewise the bibliographies are restricted to works published originally in English, by for the most part American and British authors.

The following bibliographies are organized by chronologically successive episodes of political history, if only because the history of the United States is still predominantly written and taught in this manner. Thus the reader will not find separate thematic bibliographies, for example of the history of women in the United States or of ethnic minorities. Nevertheless an attempt has been made to include a representative selection of material on matters of social, racial and cultural history within each chronological section.

General texts

The history of the area of North America now known as the United States has been variously treated; it has been written in terms of European imperial history, colonial American history, the history of the indigenous cultures of the whole American continent, and of the independent federal republic of the United States. No single work has treated all aspects equally or in an integral manner. However a number of well-established histories of America may be recommended, such as *The Penguin History of the United States of America* (1986) by Hugh Brogan or *The Limits of Liberty: American History 1607–1980* (2nd edn, 1995) by Maldwyn A. Jones. Historical geography is served by Eric Homberger, *The Penguin Historical Atlas of North America* (1996). More detailed treatment can be found in a multi-volume series such as the *Oxford History of the United States*, the most recent of which (Vol. X) is James Patterson's *Grand Expectations: The United States, 1945–1974* (1996).

Shorter studies of more recent American history are numerous; particularly useful is William H. Chafe, *The Unfinished Journey: America since World War II* (3rd edn, 1995), a work of great sensitivity and learning. An excellent reference source for the immediately preceding period is Patrick Renshaw, *The Longman Companion to America in the Era of the Two World Wars, 1910–1945* (1996). The political history of the last quarter-century, marked as it is by common perceptions of the 'failure' of American liberalism, has been excellently described in Iwan Morgan, *Beyond the*

Liberal Consensus: A Political History of the United States since 1965 (1994). Works which treat two topics of particular importance to the 'shape' of America in the second half of the twentieth century – namely the changing nature of the American South and the fate of African-Americans – are Bruce Shulman, *From Cotton Belt to Sun Belt: Federal Policy, Economic Development, and the Transformation of the South, 1938–1980* (1995) and Nicholas Lemann, *The Promised Land: The Great Black Migration and How It Changed America* (1991).

America's place in the wider world should be studied in the four volumes of *The Cambridge History of American Foreign Relations* published in 1993: namely, *Volume I: The Creation of a Republican Empire, 1776–1865* by Bradford Perkins; *Volume II: The American Search for Opportunity, 1865–1913* by Walter LaFeber; *Volume III: The Globalizing of America, 1913–1945* by Akira Iriye; and *Volume IV: America in the Age of Soviet Power, 1945–1991* by Warren I. Cohen. Supplementary interpretative essays are available in Gordon Martel (ed.), *American Foreign Relations Reconsidered, 1890–1993* (1994).

American cultural history, in its broadest sense, has benefited from much recent scholarly activity. Two works indispensible to an understanding of the evolution of political culture since 1800 are Robert H. Wiebe, *Self-Rule: A Cultural History of American Democracy* (1995) and Michael Kazin, *The Populist Persuasion: An American History* (1995). Their own bibliographies are invaluable guides for any student of American political history since the Revolution. For the intellectual history of the country there is no better commentator than the late Christopher Lasch; in *The True and Only Heaven* (1991) he argues that American reform movements have historically been 'captured' by the middle classes, who have imposed their own ideals upon the forces of social change. The more recent history of American society is recorded by Michael Klein (ed.), *An American Half Century: Postwar Culture and Politics in the USA* (1994) and by Warren Susman, *Culture as History: The Transformation of American Society in the Twentieth Century* (1984).

Students of American history should also be students of American politics. Recommended introductory texts are Alan Grant, *The American Political Process* (5th edn, 1994), Tim Hames and Nicol Rae, *Governing America* (1996) and David McKay, *American Politics and Society* (3rd edn, 1993). A radical interpretation of the American political system is provided by Michael Parenti, *Democracy for the Few* (6th edn, 1995); see also Mike Davis, *Prisoners of the American Dream: Politics and Economy in the History of the US Working Class* (1986). For the history of electoral politics see Martin Shefter, *Political Parties and the State: The American Historical Experience* (1994) and Wilson Carey McWilliams, *The Politics of Disappointment: American Elections, 1976–94* (1995). Frances Fox Piven and Richard Cloward, *Why Americans Don't Vote* (1988) presents a radical analysis of the limits of American electoral democracy. Paul F. Boller, Jr, *Presidential Campaigns* (rev. edn, 1996) is a convenient single-volume account of all presidential elections up to 1992. John White, *Black Leadership in America: From Booker T. Washington to Jesse Jackson* (2nd edn, 1990) is a standard text on black political participation. In addition to these recent studies, American political science has produced several classic works of historical interpretation, notably Louis Hartz, *The Liberal Tradition in America* (1955), E.E. Schattschneider, *The Semisovereign People* (1960) and Theodore Lowi, *The End of American Liberalism* (1969). The individual author whose work has been most influential in understanding the contours of American politics in this century is Walter Dean Burnham; see *Critical Elections and the Mainsprings of American Politics* (1970) and *The Current Crisis in American Politics* (1982). Reference sources for the study of American government include William A. Degregorio, *The Complete Book of U.S. Presidents: From George Washington to Bill Clinton* (1994), Donald C. Bacon, Roger H. Davidson and Morton Keller, *The Encyclopaedia of the United States Congress* (4 vols, 1995) and Kermit L. Hall (ed.), *The Oxford Companion to the Supreme Court of the United States* (1993). A further source of much value for both history and politics is Jack C. Plano and Milton Greenberg, *The American Political Dictionary* (9th edn, 1992).

No reading of the history of the United States can be considered complete without some understanding of the development of adjacent regions and countries. The study of Canadian history can be begun with the two volumes of Alvin Finkel, Margaret Conrad, Cornelius Jaenen and Veronica Strong-Boag, *History of the Canadian Peoples* (1993). A recent comprehensive history of Mexico is Jaime Suchlicki, *Mexico: From Montezuma to NAFTA, Chiapas, and Beyond* (1996).

Finally, for students wishing to undertake independent research in American history the single most useful guide to available resources is Francis Paul Prucha, *Handbook for Research in American History: A Guide to Bibliographies and Other Reference Works* (2nd edn, 1994).

1. Colonial America

The standard introductory text for the history of the British colonies prior to independence is now Richard Middleton, *Colonial America: A History, 1607–1760* (2nd edn, 1996). This may be supplemented with Jack P. Greene and J.R. Pole (eds), *Colonial British America* (1984). Studies of the changing nature of American society through the colonial period are James Henretta and Gregory Nobles, *Evolution and Revolution of American Society, 1600–1820* (1987), and Gary B. Nash, *Red, White and Black: The Peoples of Early America* (1993) which considers the interaction of different racial traditions (albeit not on the basis of equality) in the construction of the new society.

The recent quincentenary of the Columbian discovery has produced much new writing on the European encounter with North America. Hans Konig, *Columbus, His Enterprise: Exploding The Myth* (1991) and David Standdard, *American Holocaust: Columbus and the Conquest of the New World* (1992) offer particularly critical accounts. See also James Axtell, *Beyond 1492: Encounters in Colonial North America* (1992), which is the author's third collection of essays. Anthony McFarlane, *The British in the Americas, 1480–1815* (1994), considers Britain's impact from the Caribbean to Canada, and Ian Steele, *Warpaths: Invasions of North America* (1996) uses ethnohistory and sociology to produce new perspectives on the military history of the continent.

The study of the effect of European migration upon the native peoples should be commenced with Frederick E. Hoxie (ed.), *Indians in American History: An Introduction* (1991) and James Axtell, *The Invasion Within: The Conquest of Cultures in Colonial North America* (1985). Leonard Dinnerstein, Roger L. Nichols and David M. Reimers, *Natives and Strangers: A Multicultural History of Americans* (3rd edn, 1996) is a study of the entire history of immigration up to the present day, but discusses Native Americans in its earlier parts. Richard Slotkin's classic *Regeneration Through Violence: The Mythology of the American Frontier, 1600–1860* (1973) reflects upon the importance of this contact within the development of American culture. Studies of English migration to the colonies are numerous. David B. Quinn, *Raleigh and the British Empire* (1947, repr. 1973) remains useful, as does Ralph Davis, *The Rise of the Atlantic Economies* (1973) which explains the economic forces within English and European societies that drove colonization. More recent is John J. McCusker and Russell R. Menard, *The Economy of British North America, 1607–1789* (1985). For the migrants themselves, see Bernard Bailyn's two volumes, *The Peopling of British North America: An Introduction* (1986) and *Voyagers to the West: Immigration to America on the Eve of the Revolution* (1986). The impact of the migration of non-Anglo populations is discussed in Ida Altman and James Horn (eds), *'To Make America': European Emigration in the Early Modern Period* (1991) and Bernard Bailyn and Philip D. Morgan (eds), *Strangers Within the Realm: Cultural Margins of the First British Empire* (1991). Darien J. Davis (ed.), *Slavery and Beyond: The African Impact on Latin America and the Caribbean* (1994) studies the effect upon the Americas of the (largely involuntary) African diaspora.

The nature of the multicultural society which resulted from these migrations is surveyed by Jack P. Greene, *Pursuits of Happiness: The Social Development of the Early Modern British Colonies and the Formation of American Culture* (1988). David H. Fischer, *Albion's Seed: Four British Folkways in America* (1989) considers the transmission and survival of British cultural forms, including aspects of physical culture such as building styles. For the social history of New England and its dominant Puritan tradition, useful introductions are Francis J. Bremer, *The Puritan Experiment: New England Society from Bradford to Edwards* (1976) and Sacvan Bercovitch (ed.), *The American Puritan Imagination: Essays in Revaluation* [sic] (1974). The 'failure' of that society as reflected in such infamous episodes as the Salem witch trials of 1692 is studied in John Demos, *Entertaining Satan: Witchcraft and the Culture of Early New England* (1982) and Carol F. Karlsen, *The Devil in the Shape of a Woman: Witchcraft in Colonial New England* (1987). For the important religious history of colonial America, particularly the revival of the early eighteenth century known as 'The Great Awakening', see Patricia Bonomi, *Under the Cope of Heaven: Religion, Society and Politics in Colonial America* (1986). Forrest Wood, *The Arrogance of Faith: Christianity and Race in America from the Colonial Era to the Twentieth Century* (1992) studies its interaction with racial questions.

The socio-economic history of British North America is indelibly bound up with the evolution of a variety of systems of unfree labour. David W. Galenson, *White Servitude in Colonial America: An Economic Analysis* (1981) examines the system initially employed in the colonies – indentured servitude. An incisive study of the entire history of American slavery is provided by Peter Kolchin, *American Slavery: 1619–1877* (1995). See also Lawrence Goodheart, Richard D. Brown and Stephen G. Rabe (eds), *Slavery in American Society* (1993). The work of Winthrop Jordan has been important in explaining the racial aspects of the adoption of the slave system; see his *White Over Black: American Attitudes Towards the Negro, 1550–1812* (1968, repr. 1977) and *The White Man's Burden: Historical Origins of Racism in the United States* (1974). Edmund Morgan, *American Slavery, American Freedom: The Ordeal of Colonial Virginia* (1975) explores the social structure of one colony and reveals how concepts of race were fundamental to its construction.

2. The Revolution, 1760–81

The massive history of the American Revolution has long been fertile territory for historians of competing historiographical and political traditions, from the Marxist to the neo-conservative. Any proper study of its origins in Anglo-American political culture must still begin with the pathbreaking work of Bernard Bailyn; see his *The Ideological Origins of the American Revolution* (1967) and *The Origins of American Politics* (1968). Jonathan Clark, *The Language of Liberty, 1660–1832* (1994) considers similar questions in a longer perspective. See also Edmund S. Morgan, *Inventing the People: The Rise of Popular Sovereignty in England and America* (1988). Gary B. Nash, *The Urban Crucible: Social Change, Political Consciousness and the Origins of the American Revolution* (1979) studies how socio-economic change in three American cities – New York, Boston and Philadelphia – produced the climate for revolution.

Excellent single volume studies of the Revolution itself are Colin Bonwick, *The American Revolution* (1991) and Edward Countryman, *The American Revolution* (1985). Gordon S. Wood's *The Creation of the American Republic, 1776–1787* (1969) carries its history through to the establishment of the Constitution, with an emphasis upon changes in political theory. The effect of war upon the American people is revealed in William Cumming and Hugh Rankin (eds), *The Fate of a Nation: The American Revolution Through Contemporary Eyes* (1975) and John Dann (ed.), *The Revolution Remembered: Eyewitness Accounts of the War for Independence* (1980). Peter D.G. Thomas has produced studies of the Revolution's impact upon the colonial power itself, with *British Politics and the Stamp Act Crisis: The First Phase of the American Revolution, 1763–1767* (1975) and *The Townshend Duties Crisis: The Second Phase of the American Revolution, 1767–1773* (1987). Ian Christie's *Crisis of Empire: Great Britain and the American Colonies, 1754–1783* (1966) remains a standard introduction to this subject. Jonathan R. Dull, *A Diplomatic History of the American Revolution* (1985) and Ronald Hoffman and Peter Albert (eds), *Diplomacy and Revolution: The Franco–American Alliance of 1778* (1981) should be consulted for the place of the War of Independence in an international context. Robert Middlekauf's *The Glorious Cause: The American Revolution, 1763–1789* (1982) provides a good account of the military history of the conflict. See also John Shy, *A People Numerous and Armed: Reflections on the Military Struggle for American Independence* (1976).

The vexed question of the 'character' of the Revolution can be studied in George Billias (ed.), *The American Revolution: How Revolutionary Was It?* (3rd edn, 1980) and Jack P. Greene (ed.), *The American Revolution: Its Character and Limits* (1987). Marc Egnal, *A Mighty Empire: The Origins of the American Revolution* (1988) claims that the Revolution was led by upper-class colonial expansionists who wanted a rapid development of the New World, something which would be best served by independence. Alternatively, Gordon S. Wood in *The Radicalism of the American Revolution* (1992) argues that the Revolution decisively overthrew the old order in America. The contribution of particular individuals to the revolutionary debate may be studied in Eric Foner, *Tom Paine and Revolutionary America* (1976) and Merril D. Paterson, *Adams and Jefferson: A Revolutionary Dialogue* (1976). Gary Wills, *Inventing America: Jefferson's Declaration of Independence* (1978) considers the 'rhetorical construction' of the new nation through a study of its most famous document.

The effect of war and revolution upon various 'minority' groups in society has received increased attention from scholars in recent years. Linda Kerber, *Women of the Republic: Intellect and Ideology in Revolutionary America* (1980) and Mary Beth Norton, *Liberty's Daughters: The Revolutionary Experience of American Women, 1750–1800* (1980) examine the changing position of women. Norton has also written on the experience of those who manifestly 'lost' the war in *The British-Americans: The Loyalist Exiles in England, 1774–1789* (1974). Paul Finkelman considers the great American dilemma in *Slavery and the Founders: Race and Liberty in the Age of Jefferson* (1996), which clearly indicates the very real limits to contemporary concepts of liberty. For the Revolution's impact upon native peoples, see Colin G. Calloway, *The American Revolution in Indian Country: Crisis and Diversity in Native American Communities* (1995). The broader social history of the age is treated in Stephanie G. Wolf, *As Various As Their Land: Everyday Life in Eighteenth Century America* (1993) and Kenneth Silverman, *A Cultural History of the American Revolution: Painting, Music and Literature* (1976).

3. The birth of the Republic

The intellectual climate in which America established self-government is detailed in Gordon S. Wood's classic *The Creation of the American Republic, 1776–1787* (1969). Developments at state level are surveyed in Willi Paul Adams, *The First American Constitutions* (1980) and J.R. Pole, *Political Representation in England and the Origins of the American Republic* (1966). National government under the Articles of Confederation is treated in Merrill Jensen, *The Articles of Confederation* (1940) and Richard B. Morris, *The Forging of the Union, 1781–1789* (1987).

The Convention which drafted the United States Constitution had no popular mandate and Antifederalists soon emerged to oppose its adoption. A selection of Antifederalist arguments can be found in Cecelia Kenyon, *The Antifederalists* (1985) and J.R. Pole, *The American Revolution: For and Against* (1987). Jackson Turner Main, *The Antifederalists* (1961) and Herbert J. Storing, *What the Antifederalists Were For* (1981) explore opposition to the Constitution. The classic statement of support for the Constitution can be found in [Publius] *The Federalist Papers* (1788). The ratification struggle is detailed in Robert Rutland, *The Ordeal of the Constitution* (1966). The origins of the Constitution continue to divide historians. Clinton Rossiter, *1787: The Grand Convention* (1973) paints a portrait of wise statecraft. Charles Beard's *An Economic Interpretation of the Constitution of the United States* (1913) details the framers' economic interests. Joyce Appleby, *Capitalism and a New Social Order* (1984) situates the Constitution within economic ideology while challenging accepted views of the Federalists. The Constitution's acceptance of slavery is investigated in Duncan Macleod's *Slavery, Race, and the American Revolution* (1974). The social and political concerns of urban workers are treated in Alfred F. Young, *The Democratic-Republicans of New York* (1967). In *Women of the Republic* (1980) Linda Kerber treats the issue of women's involvement in the revolutionary settlement. In *The Radicalism of the American Revolution* (1992) Gordon Wood challenges recent emphasis on the limitations of the revolutionary achievement by arguing for its transforming power.

Stanley Elkins and Eric McKitrick's *The Age of Federalism, The Early American Republic, 1788–1800* (1993) is an exhaustive treatment of government and society under Washington and Adams. Drew McCoy's *The Elusive Republic: Political Economy in Jeffersonian America* (1980) suggests that Jefferson and his supporters shared a cast of mind fundamentally different from that of their Federalist opponents. Richard K. Matthews, *The Radical Politics of Thomas Jefferson: A Revisionist View* (1984) offers different treatment. Forrest McDonald, *The Presidency of Thomas Jefferson* (1976) surveys Jefferson's period in office. Richard Ellis, *The Jeffersonian Crisis: Courts and Politics in the Young Republic* (1971) offers a valuable account of crucial Supreme Court decisions. Leonard Levy, *Jefferson and Civil Liberties: The Darker Side* (1963) surveys Jefferson's treatment of the Constitution.

Reginald Horsman, *The Causes of the War of 1812* (1962) and Roger Brown, *The Republic in Peril* (1964) treat the War of 1812. Steven Watts, *The Republic Reborn: War and the Making of Liberal America, 1790–1820* (1987) places the war within a larger cultural context.

4. Jacksonian America

John Mayfield, *The New Nation: 1800–1845* (1982), John R. Howe, *From the Revolution through the Age of Jackson* (1973) and Harry L. Watson, *Liberty and Power: The Politics of Jacksonian America* (1990) provide surveys of a period which witnessed the emergence of a two-party system and the rapid development of an expansive and industrializing commercial economy. A very well received recent study of the era is Daniel Feller, *The Jacksonian Promise: America, 1815–1840* (1995), which argues that Americans universally agreed their nation had a 'Manifest Destiny' but disagreed fundamentally over how to achieve it. Charles Sellers, in *The Market Revolution* (1991), examines changes in economic assumptions and behaviour in this period. Anthony Wallace, *Rockdale: The Growth of an American Village in the Industrial Revolution* (1978) considers the social impact of industrialization. Richard McCormick weaves together political and economic developments in *The Second American Party System: Party Formation in the Jacksonian Era* (1966).

The figure of Andrew Jackson dominates historical writing on this period. Was Jackson an astute populist who merely articulated the prejudices of his supporters, or was he the head of a coalition of interests which sought principled democratic reform? Edward Pessen, *Jacksonian America: Society, Personality, and Politics* (1969) questions whether Jacksonians sought, let alone achieved, reform. Douglas T. Miller, *Jacksonian Aristocracy* (1967) points to the emergence of a new capitalist elite in this period. Sean Wilentz, *Chants Democratic: New York City and the Rise of the American Working Class* (1984) details the emergence of an urban working class whose history and concerns distinguished them from Jackson's agrarian supporters. Ronald N. Satz, *American Indian Policy in the Jacksonian Era* (1975) details the injustices of American policy towards the Indians during this period. Richard E. Ellis, *The Union at Risk: Jacksonian Democracy, States' Rights, and the Nullification Crisis* (1987), Donald E. Fehrenbacher, *The South and Three Sectional Crises* (1980), and Glover Moore, *The Missouri Controversy, 1819–1821* (1953) describe the persistent influence of sectional considerations on national government policy.

Arthur M. Schlesinger, *The Age of Jackson* (1946), paints a favourable portrait of the period, claiming that it saw the interests of the common man advanced. Robert Remini, *Andrew Jackson* (1966) is an admiring biography. Remini's *The Revolutionary Age of Andrew Jackson* (1976) suggests that Jackson's supporters were, within the limits of their age, committed to democratic reform.

A number of studies illuminate the period without reference to Jackson or the Democratic Party. Daniel Walker Howe, *The Political Culture of the American Whigs* (1979), Paul Johnson, *A Shopkeeper's Millenium: Society and Revivals in Rochester, New York, 1815–1837* (1978) and Mary Ryan, *Cradle of the Middle Class* (1981) explore the pervasive influence of Protestant theology on politics and social reform.

5. The Peculiar Institution: American slavery, 1800–60

Recent comprehensive overviews of the question of 'The Peculiar Institution' have been provided by Robert W. Fogel, *Without Consent or Contract* (1988) and Peter Kolchin, *American Slavery: 1619–1877* (1995). William L. Van Deburg, *Slavery and Race in American Popular Culture* (1984) is a study of how black Americans have been depicted by others throughout American history, whereas Peter J. Parish, *Slavery* (1989) provides the best guide to historians' debates about American slavery. John Ashworth's *Slavery, Capitalism and Politics in the Antebellum Republic. Volume 1: Commerce and Compromise, 1820–1850* (1995) is the first in a projected two-volume interpretation which employs a neo-Marxist analysis to describe the contest between North and South as a struggle between two different class systems.

Slavery as a mature institution has been analysed in Kenneth M. Stampp's classic study, *The Peculiar Institution: Slavery in the Antebellum South* (1956), which did much to lay bare the conflictual relationship between masters and slaves. Stanley Elkins's controversial *Slavery: A Problem in American Institutional and Intellectual Life* (1959) led to a fundamental reassessment; he argued that slaves were so traumatized by the system that they were reduced to the childlike 'Sambo' of popular mythology, without culture or community. Elkins's work has subsequently been severely criticized, most importantly by John W. Blassingame, *The Slave Community: Plantation Life in the Antebellum South* (rev. edn, 1979), Herbert Gutman, *The Black Family in Slavery and Freedom, 1750–1925* (1976) and Lawrence W. Levine, *Black Culture and Black Consciousness: Afro-American Folk Thought from Slavery to Freedom* (1977). The work of Eugene D. Genovese is fundamental to the study of the subject; his *The Political Economy of Slavery: Studies in the Economy and Society of the Slave South* (1965) and particularly *Roll, Jordan, Roll: The World the Slaves Made* (1974) have famously analysed the slaves' own contribution to the construction of their social environment. Genovese's work has itself been attacked by James Oakes, *The Ruling Race: A History of American Slaveholders* (1982) and by Michael Tadman, *Speculators and Slaves: Masters, Traders, and Slaves in the Old South* (1989).

More recent studies include Larry E. Hudson, Jr, *Working Toward Freedom: Slave Society and Domestic Economy in the American South* (1995) and Brenda Stevenson, *Life in Black and White: Family and Community in the Slave South* (1996). On women and slavery, see Elizabeth Fox-Genovese, *Within the Plantation Household: Black and White Women of the Old South* (1988) and Patricia Morton (ed.), *Discovering the Women in Slavery: Emancipating Perspectives on the American Past* (1996). Ira Berlin, *Slaves without Masters* (1974) is the classic study of free blacks.

The economics of the institution are considered in a comparative study by Peter Kolchin, *Unfree Labor: American Slavery and Russian Serfdom* (1987); and, at a more advanced level, in the pathbreaking and controversial study by Robert W. Fogel and Stanley L. Engerman, *Time on the Cross: The Economics of Negro Slavery* (2 vols, 1974), which argued that both masters and slaves saw their relationship as more akin to that of factory-owner and worker. Gavin Wright, *The Political Economy of the Cotton South: Households, Markets and Wealth in the Nineteenth Century* (1978) and Fred Bateman and Thomas Weiss, *A Deplorable Scarcity: The Failure of Industrialization in the Slave Economy* (1981) situate slavery within the overall development of the Southern economy. Robert S. Starobin, *Industrial Slavery in the Old South* (1970) is the major work on its subject.

Recent writing on the abolitionist movement has stressed the role played by both black Americans and Northern women; see Benjamin Quarles, *Black Abolitionists* (1968), R.J.M. Blackett, *Building an Antislavery Wall: Black Americans in the Atlantic Abolitionist Movement* (1983), Blanche Hersh, *The Slavery of Sex: Feminist Abolitionists in Nineteenth Century America* (1978) and Aileen Kraditor, *Means and Ends in American Abolitionism* (1969). The *Narrative of the Life of Frederick Douglass* (1845) is a fascinating account of abolitionist activities and assumptions in New England, while Stanley Harrold, *The Abolitionists and the South, 1831–1861* (1995) considers their influence in the region of the country most hostile to the cause. The limits of the abolitionist understanding of the black condition, and the strength of opposition to abolitionism within Northern societies, emerge in Leonard D. Richards, *'Gentlemen of Property and Standing': Anti-Abolitionist Mobs in Jacksonian America* (1970) and George Fredrickson, *The Black Image in the White Mind* (1971). The politics of anti-slavery activism cannot be understood without Eric Foner's *Free Soil, Free Labor, Free Men: The Ideology of the Republican Party Before the Civil War* (1970), which considers the ways mainstream opinion in Northern states came to judge the continued existence of slavery as a threat to the values of a white agrarian republic. By way of contrast, Drew Faust treats Southern defences of slavery in *The Ideology of Slavery* (1981). Bruce Collins, *White Society in the Antebellum South* (1985) is an excellent synopsis of the society and culture which the Peculiar Institution helped to shape.

6. The Civil War, 1861–65

The great conflict which divided the American Union in the middle of the nineteenth century is probably the single most popular episode in its history and its literature is particularly large. Kenneth M. Stampp, *The Imperiled Union* (1980) and James McPherson, *Ordeal by Fire* (1982) offer distinguished surveys of the crises of the 1850s. Barbara Fields, *Slavery and Freedom on the Middle Ground* (1985) argues that the crisis was caused as much by the moral implications of the continued existence or expansion of slavery as by the political problems it posed. Donald Fehrenbacher, *The Dred Scott Case: Its Significance in American Law and Politics* (1978) investigates every aspect of the Supreme Court ruling which destroyed the Second Party System. Gabor S. Boritt (ed.), *Why the Civil War Came* (1996) is a recent collection of essays on the roots of the War – political, institutional, and cultural – and questions whether it could have been avoided; and Brian Holden Reid, *The Origins of the American Civil War* (1996) studies its politico-military background in detail. William J. Cooper, *Liberty and Slavery: Southern Politics to 1860* (1983) is a very useful synopsis of recent studies of the role of the South within national politics, while Wilbur J. Cash's classic interpretative essay, *The Mind of the South* (1941), remains as yet unsurpassed in its explanation of the Southern psyche. William W. Freehling, *The Road to Disunion: Secessionists at Bay, 1776–1854* (1990) traces the long history of the politics of disunion, while William E. Gienapp, *The Origins of the Republican Party, 1852–1856* (1987) studies a critical period in the anti-slavery politics of the North.

James McPherson, *Battle Cry of Freedom: The Civil War Era* (1988) provides an outstanding survey of the United States from the mid-1840s until the end of the War and is probably the best single introduction for the general reader. Historians have advanced a number of explanations for the outcome of the conflict, for example David Donald, *Why the North Won the Civil War* (1960) and Richard Beringer *et al.*, *Why the South Lost The Civil War* (1986). Grady McWhiney and Perry Jamieson link military and cultural history in *Attack and Die: Civil War Military Tactics and the Southern Heritage* (1982), as does Michael Adams in *Our Masters the Rebels* (1978), an explanation of why Union armies almost lost the War. Stephen Crane's short novel *The Red Badge of Courage* (1895) and the motion picture *Glory* (TriStar, dir. Edward Zwick, 1989) offer accurate and moving portrayals of the effects of military service.

Eric Foner, *Politics and Ideology in the Age of the Civil War* (1980) offers a comprehensive political history. During the War the Republican Party hardened its opposition to slavery, a process detailed in Hans L. Trefousse, *The Radical Republicans: Lincoln's Vanguard for Racial Justice* (1969). Opposition to the War is analysed in Joel Silbey, *A Respectable Minority: The Democratic Party in the Civil War Era* (1977). Howard Jones, *Union in Peril: The Crisis over British Intervention in the Civil War* (1992) is a recent study of Anglo-American relations which places events in their international context. The most recent single-volume biography of President Lincoln is David H. Donald's well-received *Lincoln* (1995); the standard study of his opponent is William Davis, *Jefferson Davis: The Man and the Hour* (1990). Gary Willis, *Lincoln at Gettysburg: The Words that Remade America* (1992) is a provocative work which explores Lincoln's own understanding of the meaning of the War.

There are numerous local studies of the War's impact upon particular regions and states; excellent recent examples include Stephen V. Ash, *When the Yankees Came: Conflict and Chaos in the Occupied South, 1861–1865* (1995) and William Gillette, *Jersey Blue: Civil War Politics in New Jersey, 1854–1865* (1995). Emory M. Thomas, *The Confederate Nation, 1861–1865* (1979) narrates the history of the whole South, underlining the ultimate failure of Southern nationalism.

The social and cultural effects of the Civil War, which were considerable, have a wide literature. See Maris A. Vinovskis, *Toward a Social History of the American Civil War: Exploratory Essays* (1990). Margaret Ripley Wolfe, *Daughters of Canaan: A Saga of Southern Women* (1995) begins before the Civil War and continues into the twentieth century, while Catherine Clinton and Nina Silber (eds), *Divided Houses: Gender and the Civil War* (1992) is a collection of essays examining changing roles for women during the War itself. The momentous experiences of black Americans during this period are studied in Leon Litwack, *Been in the Storm So Long: The Aftermath of Slavery* (1979). The history of the War in the longer perspective is considered in Jim Cullen, *The Civil War in Popular Culture: A Reusable Past* (1995); Edmund Wilson's *Patriotic Gore* (1961) is the classic study of its impact upon American literature.

7. Reconstruction, 1865–77

The political history of the era is described in John Hope Franklin, *Reconstruction After the Civil War* (2nd rev. edn, 1995). Kenneth M. Stampp's *The Era of Reconstruction, 1865–1877* (1965) remains a standard text. A more recent interpretation is given by Eric Foner, *Reconstruction: America's Unfinished Revolution* (1988), which emphasizes slavery as a cause of the War. James M. McPherson's *Abraham Lincoln and the Second American Revolution* (1991) argues that the War fundamentally changed the nature of the Republic. The career of President Johnson is covered by Hans L. Trefousse, *Andrew Johnson: A Biography* (1989); his impeachment by Michael Les Benedict, *The Impeachment and Trial of Andrew Johnson* (1973).

The Republican Party's view of the South is considered in Richard H. Abbott, *The Republican Party and the South, 1855–1877: The First Southern Strategy* (1986); for the North as a whole, see Nina Silber, *The Romance of Reunion: Northerners and the South, 1865–1900* (1993). Michael Les Benedict, *A Compromise of Principle: Congressional Republicans and Reconstruction* (1974) is a study of the Radicals in Congress; see also James C. Mohr, *Radical Republicans in the North: State Politics During Reconstruction* (1976). Daniel E. Sutherland, *The Confederate Carpetbaggers* (1988) and Richard N. Current, *Those Terrible Carpetbaggers* (1988) examine Republican Party supporters in the South. The experience of the South in this period can be studied in Michael Perman, *The Road to Redemption: Southern Politics, 1869–1879* (1984), Dan T. Carter, *When the War Was Over* (1985), and George C. Rable's *But There Was No Peace: The Role of Violence in the Politics of Reconstruction* (1984). Jonathan M. Bryant, *How Curious A Land: Conflict and Change in Greene County, Georgia, 1850–1885* (1996), through its detailed study of one particular area, shows how the Old South became the New and how this affected its people, both white and black.

The effect of Reconstruction on black Americans is given a succinct treatment in Michael Perman, *Emancipation and Reconstruction, 1862–1879* (1987); a more detailed study is Leon Litwack, *Been in the Storm So Long: The Aftermath of Slavery* (1979). Howard N. Rabinowitz's *Race Relations in the Urban South, 1865–1890* (1978) considers the developing metropolitan areas. W.E.B. Du Bois's *Black Reconstruction in America, 1860–1880* (1935) remains a classic. See also Eric Foner's *Nothing but Freedom: Emancipation and Its Legacies* (1983) and *Politics and Ideology in the Age of the Civil War* (1980). Joel Williamson's *The Crucible of Race: Black–White Relations in the American South since Emancipation* (1984) examines the longer perspective.

The Compromise of 1877, which ended Reconstruction, received a classic treatment in C. Van Woodward's *Reunion and Reaction* (1951), which can be read with William Gillette, *Retreat from Reconstruction, 1869–1879* (1979). The career of the 'compromise president' himself can be studied in Ari Hoogenboom, *Rutherford B. Hayes: Warrior and President* (1995). The consequences of Reconstruction are examined in J. Morgan Kousser, *The Shaping of Southern Politics: Suffrage Restriction and the Establishment of the One-Party South, 1880–1910* (1974). Relevant discussions can also be found in Alexander Saxton, *The Rise and Fall of the White Republic: Class Politics and Mass Culture in Nineteenth Century America* (1990), and Joel H. Silbey, *The American Political Nation, 1838–1893* (1991).

Richard Bensel's *Yankee Leviathan: The Origins of Central State Authority in America, 1859–1877* (1991) examines the effect of the War and Reconstruction on the growth of the federal government. The history of the Ku Klux Klan is considered in Wyn Craig Wade, *The Fiery Cross: The Ku Klux Klan in America* (1986); and the federal government's response by Everette Swinney, *Suppressing the Ku Klux Klan: The Enforcement of the Reconstruction Amendments, 1870–1877* (1987). Allen W. Trelease, *White Terror: The Ku Klux Klan Conspiracy and Southern Reconstruction* (1971) looks at other organizations as well as at the Klan itself.

8. The new American nation: American society and culture, 1865–1900

There is an extensive literature on the South in this era. The starting points remain W.J. Cash, *The Mind of the South* (1941) and C. Vann Woodward, *Origins of the New South, 1877–1913* (1951), which may be supplemented with Edward L. Ayers, *The Promise of the New South: Life After Reconstruction* (1992) and Gaines M. Foster, *Ghosts of the Confederacy: Defeat, the Lost Cause, and the Emergence of the New South, 1865–1913* (1987). An abridged version of Ayers's text has been published for students as *Southern Crossing: A History of the American South, 1877–1906* (1996). The political history of the era should be followed in Dewey W. Grantham, *The Life and Death of the Solid South: A Political History* (1988). The political origins and consequences of racial exclusion are analysed in J. Morgan Kousser, *The Shaping of Southern Politics: Suffrage Restriction and the Establishment of the One-Party South, 1880–1910* (1974). The history of segregation is treated in C. Vann Woodward, *The Strange Career of Jim Crow* (3rd edn, 1974); Vann Woodward's thesis has since been modified by Howard N. Rabinowitz's *Race Relations in the Urban South, 1865–1890* (1978) and Joel Williamson's *The Crucible of Race: Black–White Relations in the American South since Emancipation* (1984). The leading black political figures of the period are treated in Louis R. Harlan, *Booker T. Washington: The Making of a Black Leader, 1865–1901* (2 vols, 1983) and Elliott M. Rudwick, *W.E.B. Du Bois* (2nd edn, 1969). On the economy, see James C. Cobb, *Industrialization and Southern Society, 1877–1984* (1984), Gavin Wright, *Old South, New South: Revolutions in the Southern Economy since the Civil War* (1986) and Douglas Flamming, *Creating the Modern South: Millhands and Managers in*

Dalton, Georgia, 1884–1984 (1992). Roger L. Ransom and Richard Sutch, *One Kind of Freedom: The Economic Consequences of Emancipation* (1977) considers Southern agriculture.

For the West, the standard source is now Clyde A. Milner II, Carol A. O'Connor and Martha A. Sandweiss (eds), *The Oxford History of the American West* (1994), which should serve as a guide for further study and reading. Milner is also the editor of a collection of historiographical essays, *A New Significance: Re-Envisioning the History of the American West* (1996). William Cronon, George Miles and Jay Gitlin (eds), *Under the Open Sky: Rethinking America's Western Past* (1992) and Patricia Nelson Limerick, *The Legacy of Conquest: The Unbroken Past of the American West* (1987) also consider the 'new history' of the region, emphasizing its cultural dimensions. For the impact of the West on the nation as a whole, see Anne F. Hyde, *The American Vision: Far Western Landscape and National Culture, 1820–1920* (1990) and William H. Truettner (ed.), *The West as America: Reinterpreting Images of the Frontier, 1820–1920* (1991). For the history of the Native Americans, Robert H. Berkhofer, Jr's, *The White Man's Indian: Images of the American Indian from Columbus to the Present* (1978) remains relevant to this period, as does Francis Paul Prucha, *The Great Father: The United States Government and the Indians* (1984). The best single-volume history of the Plains Indian culture is Wilcomb E. Washburn, *The Indian in America* (1975); Janet A. McDonnell, *The Dispossession of the American Indian, 1887–1934* (1991) studies the deleterious effects of the Dawes Act which sought to 'Americanize' natives. For various aspects of white settlement and exploitation of the West, see Susan Armitage and Elizabeth Jameson (eds), *The Woman's West* (1987), William R. Savage (ed.), *Cowboy Life: Reconstructing an American Myth* (1980), David Dary, *Cowboy Culture* (1989) and Duane A. Smith, *Mining America: The Industry and the Environment* (1987). A study of a later period of colonization which introduces a cross-national perspective is John W. Bennett and Seena B. Kohl, *Settling the Canadian–American West, 1890–1915: Pioneer Adaptation and Community Building* (1995).

The history of urban America in this period must begin with the contemporary account of the social reformer Jane Addams, *Twenty Years at Hull House* (1910). Eric H. Monkkonen, *America Becomes Urban: The Development of U.S. Cities and Towns, 1780–1980* (1988) provides an overview. For the politics see John M. Allswang, *Bosses, Machines, and Urban Voters* (rev. edn, 1986) and Paul Boyer, *Urban Masses and Moral Order in America, 1820–1920* (1978). The emerging culture of the city is analysed in David Ward, *Poverty, Ethnicity, and the American City, 1840–1925* (1989), Stanley K. Schultz, *Constructing Urban Culture: American Cities and City Planning, 1800–1920* (1989) and Alexander von Hoffman, *Local Attachments: The Making of an American Urban Neighbourhood, 1850 to 1920* (1994). William Cronon's *Nature's Metropolis: Chicago and the Great West* (1991) and Philip Ethington's *The Public City: The Political Construction of Urban Life in San Francisco, 1850–1900* (1994) examine distinctive examples of the period.

The great immigration of the last quarter of the century has its standard histories in Maldwyn A. Jones, *American Immigration* (2nd edn, 1992), Leonard Dinnerstein and David M. Reimers, *Ethnic Americans: A History of Immigration and Assimilation* (2nd edn, 1982), Thomas J. Archdeacon, *Becoming American: An Ethnic History* (1983), Roger Daniels, *Coming To America: A History of Immigration and Ethnicity in American Life* (1990) and Leonard Dinnerstein, Roger L. Nichols and David M. Reimers, *Natives and Strangers: Blacks, Indians and Immigrants in America* (2nd edn, 1990). Walter Nugent's *Crossings: The Great Transatlantic Migrations, 1870–1914* (1992) discusses this period in particular. For an example of how immigrants affected the urban America they encountered, see Frederick Binder and David M. Reimers, *All The Nations Under Heaven: An Ethnic and Racial History of New York City* (1995). Judy Yung, *Unbound Feet: A Social History of Chinese Women in San Francisco* (1995), which covers the first half of the twentieth century, is a major study of a much neglected aspect of the important Asian immigration.

The origins of the new mass culture of the age are discussed in Alan Trachtenberg, *The Incorporation of America: Culture and Society in the Gilded Age* (1982), Daniel E. Sutherland, *The Expansion of Everyday Life, 1860–1876* (1989) and Maury Klein, *The Flowering of Third America: The Making of an Organizational Society, 1850–1920* (1993). The impact of industrial capitalism and its technology on the domestic scene is studied in Jessica Foy and Thomas J. Schlereth (eds), *American Home Life, 1880–1930* (1992) and Olivier Zunz, *Making America Corporate, 1879–1920* (1990). Finally, John E. Finding, *Chicago's Great World's Fairs* (1994) and Robert Muccigrosso, *Celebrating the New World: Chicago's Columbian Exposition of 1893* (1993) examine one of the most important cultural events of the age, the World's Fair of 1893.

9. The Gilded Age: industrialization and politics, 1877–96

Two classic accounts of the stresses and strains which the Industrial Revolution imposed upon America's social and political fabric are Samuel P. Hays's *The Response to Industrialism, 1885–1914* (1957) and Robert H. Wiebe's *The Search for Order, 1877–1920* (1967). More recent introductions to the period are Sean Dennis Cashman, *America in the Gilded Age: From the Death of Lincoln to the Rise of Theodore Roosevelt* (1988), Neil Painter, *Standing at Armageddon* (1987) and Charles W. Calhoun, *The Gilded Age: Essays on the Origins of Modern America* (1995).

The politics of the era are placed in their wider context by Alexander Saxton, *The Rise and Fall of the White Republic: Class Politics and Mass Culture in Nineteenth Century America* (1990). Joel H. Silbey, *The American Political Nation, 1838–1893* (1991) and Richard L. McCormick, *The Party Period and Public Policy: American Politics from the Age of Jackson to the Progressive Era* (1989) consider the evolution of political parties in this period. Gerald W. McFarland, *Mugwumps, Morals, and Politics, 1884–1920* (1975) examines the importance of the question of political reform. The literature on the Populist movement is particularly extensive. Two classic texts are John D. Hicks, *The Populist Revolt: A History of the Farmers' Alliance and the People's Party* (1931) which characterizes the Populists as prototypes of twentieth-century liberalism, and Richard Hofstadter's *The Age of Reform: From Bryan to FDR* (1955), which by contrast emphasizes their anti-modernist tradition. Lawrence Goodwyn, *The Populist Movement: A Short History of Agrarian Revolt in America* (1978) and Steven Hahn, *The Roots of Southern Populism: Yeoman Farmers and the Transformation of the Georgia Upcountry, 1850–1890* (1983) discuss the agrarian origins of the movement. Jeffrey Ostler, *Prairie Populism: The Fate of Agrarian Radicalism in Kansas, Nebraska, and Iowa, 1880–1892* (1993) considers its mature phase. The racial dimension is considered in Gerald H. Gaither, *Blacks and the Populist Revolt* (1979). Useful summaries of recent research are William F. Holmes (ed.), *American Populism* (1994) and Robert C. McMath, *American Populism: A Social History, 1877–1898* (1993).

On the election of 1896 see Robert F. Durden, *The Climax of Populism: The Election of 1896* (1965) and Paul W. Glad, *McKinley, Bryan, and the People* (1964). For Bryan himself, see Louis W. Koenig, *Bryan: A Political Biography of William Jennings Bryan* (1971) and for his opponent, Lewis L. Gould, *The Presidency of William McKinley* (1980).

The impact of the Industrial Revolution is assessed by Walter Licht, *Industrializing America: The Nineteenth Century* (1995); and the response of government by Martin Sklar, *The Corporate Reconstruction of American Capitalism, 1890–1916: The Market, the Law, and Politics* (1988). For a study of the classic example of an industrial 'trust', see Maury Klein, *Unfinished Business: The Railroad in American Life* (1994). Trevor Lummis, *The Labour Aristocracy, 1851–1914* (1994) and Kim Voss, *The Making of American Exceptionalism: The Knights of Labor and Class Formation in the 19th Century* (1993) examine the important history of organized labour in this period. See also Leon Fink, *Workingmen's Democracy: The Knights of Labor and American Politics* (1983). Ardis Cameron's *Radicals of the Worst Sort: Laboring Women in Lawrence, Massachusetts, 1860–1912* (1994) considers the oft-neglected history of female workers and the important question of how class interacted with gender in determining their relationship with the world of work. The contentious relationship between labour and the judiciary in the late Gilded Age is studied by William G.

Ross, *A Muted Fury: Populists, Progressives, and Labor Unions Confront the Courts, 1890–1937* (1994).

Theda Skocpol, *Protecting Soldiers and Mothers: The Political Origins of Social Policy in the United States* (1992) studies the early development of the welfare state at the end of the nineteenth century. The work of David Montgomery is indispensible to an understanding of this period; see *The Fall of the House of Labor: The Workplace, the State, and American Labor Activism, 1865–1925* (1987) and *Citizen Worker: The Experience of Free Workers in the United States and the Free Market during the Nineteenth Century* (1995).

10. The Progressive Era: the age of reform, 1896–1920

Suitable introductory texts are Arthur S. Link and Richard L. McCormick, *Progressivism* (1983) and Lewis L. Gould, *Reform and Regulation: American Politics, 1900–1916* (2nd edn, 1986). Samuel P. Hays's *The Response to Industrialism, 1885–1914* (1957) and Robert H. Wiebe's *The Search for Order, 1877–1920* (1967) remain relevant for this period. Richard Hofstadter's classic *The Age of Reform: From Bryan to FDR* (1955) considers the origins of Progressivism to be a middle-class concern at the loss of political and social control; Gabriel Kolko, *The Triumph of Conservatism* (1963) argues that Progressivism primarily served business's interests.

For the politics of the age William E. Leuchtenburg's *The Perils of Prosperity 1914–1932* (1958) is still the best introduction. The history and development of parties can be found in Richard L. McCormick, *The Party Period and Public Policy: American Politics from the Age of Jackson to the Progressive Era* (1989) and Kenneth Allen, *Components of Electoral Evolution: Realignment in the United States, 1912–1940* (1988). Martin Sklar, *The United States as a Developing Country: Studies in U.S. History in the Progressive Era and the 1920s* (1992) is a collection of useful interpretative essays. James Weinstein, *The Decline of Socialism in America, 1912–1925* (1967) examines the often overlooked but very important history of left-wing politics in the United States in this era.

For specific presidents, see John Morton Blum, *The Progressive Presidents: Roosevelt, Wilson, Roosevelt, Johnson* (1980) and his *The Republican Roosevelt* (2nd edn, 1977); the latter can be supplemented by Lewis L. Gould, *The Presidency of Theodore Roosevelt* (1991). For Wilson, Kendrick A. Clements's *The Presidency of Woodrow Wilson* (1992) is a good introduction, but reference may still be made to the work of the official biographer Arthur S. Link, *Wilson* (1947–65). See also John Milton Cooper, Jr and Charles E. Neuneu (eds), *The Wilson Era: Essays in Honor of Arthur S. Link* (1991); Cooper's *The Warrior and the Priest* (1983) discusses the Republican and Democratic presidents together. Lawrence W. Levine, *Defender of the Faith: William Jennings Bryan, The Last Decade, 1915–1925*

(1987) examines the later career of the Populist leader. For the end of the Progressive era, see Wesley M. Bagby, *The Road to Normalcy: The Presidential Campaign and Election of 1920* (1968).

Varieties of Progressive reform in different regions of the United States may be studied in William A. Link, *The Paradox of Southern Progressivism, 1880–1930* (1992), which looks at the urban scene, Dewey Grantham, *Southern Progressivism: The Reconciliation of Progress and Tradition* (1983), Richard M. Abram, *Conservatism in a Progressive Era: Massachusetts Politics, 1900–1912* (1964) and Richard L. McCormick, *From Realignment to Reform: Political Change in New York State, 1893–1910* (1981).

On economic policy – which figured so highly in Progressive concerns – Edwin C. Rozwenc (ed.), *Roosevelt, Wilson and the Trusts* (1950) remains useful. For specifically trade union politics, see Irving Greenberg, *Theodore Roosevelt and Labor, 1900–1918* (1988). Martin Sklar, *The Corporate Reconstruction of American Capitalism, 1890–1916: The Market, the Law, and Politics* (1988) considers contemporary developments in their broader political context. See also Morton Keller, *Regulating A New Society: Public Policy and Social Change in America, 1900–1933* (1994). There are numerous studies of different aspects of social reform. Alan Dawley, *Struggle for Justice: Social Responsibility and the Liberal State* (1991) places the issue in its wider historical context. John D. Buenker, *Urban Liberalism and Progressive Reform* (1973) and Paul Boyer, *Urban Masses and Moral Order in America, 1820–1920* (1978) should be consulted for an introduction to urban Progressivism; and for the considerable contribution made by women Progressives to the reform movement, see Ellen Fitzpatrick, *Endless Crusade: Women Social Scientists and Progressive Reform* (1990). Samuel P. Hays, *Conservation and the Gospel of Efficiency: The Progressive Conservation Movement, 1890–1920* (1959) examines the rise of environmental issues.

The place of Progressivism in American cultural and intellectual history can be studied in Peter Conn, *Divided Mind: Ideology and Imagination in America, 1898–1917* (1989) and Roderick Nash, *The Nervous Generation: American Thought, 1917–1930* (1990). For discussion of certain reactionary elements in contemporary society, see Wyn Craig Wade, *The Fiery Cross: The Ku Klux Klan in America* (1986) and Michael Woodiwiss, *Crime, Crusades and Corruption: Prohibitions in the United States, 1900–1987* (1988).

11. America confronts the world, 1870–1920

The best single volume introductions to the topic for this period are now Walter LaFeber, *The Cambridge History of American Foreign Relations Volume II: The American Search for Opportunity, 1865–1913* (1993) and Akira Iriye, *The Cambridge History of American Foreign Relations, Volume III: The Globalizing of America, 1913–1945* (1993). These may be supplemented by William Appleman Williams, *The Tragedy of American Diplomacy* (2nd edn, 1972), a now classic text which stresses the economic determinants of foreign policy; and Robert L. Beisner, *From the Old Diplomacy to the New, 1865–1900* (2nd edn, 1986).

The fundamental causes of American expansion have attracted much research. Michael H. Hunt, *Ideology and U.S. Foreign Policy* (1987) examines the psychology of imperialism in its American variant. For studies of how expansion reflected and reinforced the political culture of the age, see Emily S. Rosenberg, *Spreading the American Dream: American Economic and Cultural Expansion, 1890–1945* (1982), Richard H. Collin, *Theodore Roosevelt, Culture, Diplomacy, and Expansion: A New View of American Imperialism* (1985) and Robert C. Hilderbrand, *Power and the People: Executive Management of Public Opinion in Foreign Affairs, 1897–1921* (1981).

For the Spanish–American War, see David F. Trask, *The War with Spain in 1898* (1981), John Offner, *An Unwanted War* (1992), and Joseph Smith, *The Spanish–American War: Conflict in the Caribbean and the Pacific, 1895–1902* (1994). H.W. Brands, *Bound to Empire: The United States and the Philippines* (1992) and Richard E. Welch, *Response to Imperialism: The United States and the Philippine–American War* (1979) examine its Pacific aspect. Relations between the United States and Central America in this period are examined in David McCullough, *The Path Between the Seas: The Creation of the Panama Canal, 1870–1914* (1977), Lester D. Langley, *The United States and the Caribbean, 1900–1970* (1980), Thomas Schoonover, *The United States in Central America, 1860–1911* (1991) and Lester D. Langley and Thomas Schoonover, *The Banana Men: American Mercenaries and Entrepreneurs in Central America, 1880–1930* (1995). America's 'Open Door' policy towards China should be studied in Michael H. Hunt, *The Making of a Special Relationship: The United States and China to 1914* (1983) and Warren I. Cohen, *America's Response to China* (2nd edn, 1980).

The literature on the United States' involvement in World War I is extensive. Reinhard R. Doerries, *Imperial Challenge: Ambassador Count Bernstorff and German–American Relations, 1908–17* (1989) considers the breakdown with Germany and Lloyd C. Gardner, *Safe for Democracy* (1984) treats the growing rapprochement with Great Britain. On Woodrow Wilson, a good summary may be found in Robert H. Ferrell, *Woodrow Wilson and World War I, 1917–1921* (1985). Arthur S. Link, *Woodrow Wilson: Revolution, War, and Peace* (1979) is sympathetic towards Wilson personally; Thomas J. Knock, *To End All Wars: Woodrow Wilson and the Quest for a New World Order* (1992) reflects upon the links between Wilson's internationalism and domestic Progressivism. On the experience of the war itself, see Edward M. Coffman, *The War to End All Wars: The American Military Experience in World War I* (1968), Ronald Schaffer, *America In The Great War: The Rise of the War Welfare State* (1991) and Ellis W. Hawley, *The Great War and the Search for a Modern Order: A History of the American People and Their Institutions, 1917–1933* (2nd edn, 1992). David Kennedy,

Over Here: The First World War and American Society (1982) considers the repercussions on the American people themselves.

The failure of the Versailles Treaty is considered by Arthur J. Walworth, *Wilson and his Peacemakers* (1986) and Lloyd E. Ambrosius, *Woodrow Wilson and the American Diplomatic Tradition: The Treaty Fight in Perspective* (1987). Robert David Johnson, *The Peace Progressives and American Foreign Relations* (1995) is an important study of an attempt to construct an 'anti-imperialist' doctrine of foreign policy in the interwar years. Discussions of the United States' contemporary relations with two of the major alien powers are Klaus Schwabe, *Woodrow Wilson, Revolutionary Germany, and Peacemaking, 1918–1919* (1985) and John L. Gaddis, *Russia, the Soviet Union, and the United States* (1978).

12. The age of normalcy, 1921–33

The end of the Great War saw a reaction in America against internationalism and the rise of both cultural and political isolationism in the face of revolution in Europe. The resulting retreat from Progressivism and the desire for a return to normality produced a new conservative politics whose roots are examined in William E. Leuchtenburg's established text *The Perils of Prosperity, 1914–32* (1958). A recent introductory history to the whole inter-war period is provided by Michael E. Parrish, *Anxious Decades: America in Prosperity and Depression, 1920–1941* (1992), which also has a good bibliographical essay. For the development of party politics in this era, see John D. Hicks, *Republican Ascendancy, 1921–1933* (1960), David Burner, *The Politics of Provincialism: The Democratic Party in Transition* (1968) and Douglas R. Craig, *After Wilson: The Struggle for the Democratic Party, 1920–1934* (1992). On elections, see Wesley M. Bagby, *The Road to Normalcy: The Presidential Campaign and Election of 1920* (1968) and Allan J. Lichtman, *Prejudice and Old Politics: The Presidential Election of 1928* (1979) which emphasizes the importance of ethnic politics in this era. Martin Sklar's *The United States as a Developing Country: Studies in U.S. History in the Progressive Era and the 1920s* (1992) provides an advanced commentary upon relevant historiographical debates. Foreign affairs in this decade of isolationism are surveyed in Warren I. Cohen, *Empire Without Tears: America's Foreign Relations, 1921–1933* (1987).

Of the major political figures of the time Warren Harding, whose brief Presidency is often regarded as a failure, has not received recent attention; his best biography is still Francis Russell's *The Shadow of the Blooming Grove: Warren G. Harding in His Times* (1968). See also Eugene P. Trani and David L. Wilson, *The Presidency of Warren G. Harding* (1977). For his successor Coolidge, no study has yet displaced William Allen White's classic *A Puritan in Babylon: The Story of Calvin Coolidge* (1938), but for a more recent account of his Administration see Donald R.

McCoy, *Calvin Coolidge: The Quiet President* (1967). Herbert Hoover's early career has been covered by the two published volumes of George H. Nash's biography *The Life of Herbert Hoover: The Engineer, 1874–1914* (1983) and *The Humanitarian, 1914–1917* (1988). His Administration is examined by Martin L. Fausold, *The Presidency of Herbert C. Hoover* (1985).

The impact of the Bolshevik Revolution upon the mass politics of the Left in America has been recently illuminated in Harvey Klehr, John Earl Haynes and Fridrikh I. Firsov, *The Secret World of American Communism* (1995), which offers excellent documentary sources. The politics of the racist, culturally reactionary Right is explored in David Chalmers, *Hooded Americanism: The History of the Ku Klux Klan* (1987), Nancy MacLean, *Behind the Mask of Chivalry: The Making of the Second Ku Klux Klan* (1994) and Kathleen M. Blee, *Women and the Klan: Racism and Gender in the 1920s* (1991). For a revealing recent study of the revived Klan in the North of the United States, the region in which it was strongest in this era, see Shawn Lay, *Hooded Knights on the Niagara: The Ku Klux Klan in Buffalo, New York* (1995). The Klan was reinvigorated by contemporary concerns about immigration and the growth of alien communities in America; John Higham, *Strangers in the Land: Patterns of American Nativism, 1860–1925* (1955) remains a classic study and many of the sources described in the bibliography for 'The new American nation' are still relevant for this period.

The cultural history of the inter-war period was dominated by questions of social conformity, material development and racial tension. The literature relating to the prohibition of alcohol is particularly large. Jack S. Blocker, *Retreat from Reform: The Prohibition Movement in the United States, 1890–1913* (1976) surveys the period before the Eighteenth Amendment of 1919, and Michael Woodiwiss, *Crime, Crusades and Corruption: Prohibitions in the United States, 1900–1987* (1988) places the movement in its larger context. See also Norman H. Clark, *Deliver Us From Evil: An Interpretation of American Prohibition* (1976) and John J. Rumbarger, *Profits, Power, and Prohibition: Alcohol Reform and the Industrializing of America, 1800–1930* (1989). For the history of American labour the best source remains Irving Bernstein, *The Lean Years: A History of the American Worker, Volume I: 1920–1933* (1960), but see also Robert H. Zieger, *American Workers, American Unions, 1920–1985* (1986). George Marsden, *Fundamentalism and American Culture: The Shaping of Twentieth-Century Evangelism, 1870–1925* (1980) is a study of contemporary religious history.

On the experience of the 'Jazz Age', see Kathy H. Ogren, *The Jazz Revolution: Twenties America and the Meaning of Jazz* (1989). Nathan I. Huggins, *Harlem Renaissance* (1971) and Gilbert Osofsky, *Harlem: The Making of a Ghetto* (1971) remain important studies of the new black urban culture, while August Meier and Elliott Rudwick, *From Plantation to Ghetto* (1962) is vital for understanding the history of African-Americans in this transitional period. Judith Stein, *The World of Marcus Garvey: Race and Class in Modern Society* (1986) reflects upon the importance of the major black leader of the era. Daniel J. Boorstin, *The Americans: The Democratic Experience* (1973) and Roland Marchand, *Advertising the American Dream* (1985) are invaluable on the importance of the consumer in the development of capitalist culture, while Ronald Edsforth, *Class Conflict and Cultural Consensus* (1987) argues that consumerism dulled the militancy of the working class. On women's history, see Dorothy M. Brown, *Setting A Course: American Women in the 1920s* (1987) and Nancy F. Cott, *The Grounding of Modern Feminism* (1987). The intellectual history of the era is explored by Roderick Nash, *The Nervous Generation: American Thought, 1917–1930* (1990). Among numerous studies of the growth of mass culture, Sumiko Higash's *Cecil B. DeMille and American Culture: The Silent Era* (1994) is a recent examination of arguably the century's most important development in how Americans used their leisure time – the cinema.

13. The Great Depression and the New Deal, 1933–39

The cataclysm of the Great Depression which devastated the United States after the Wall Street Crash of 1929 and the federal government's response in Franklin Roosevelt's New Deal programme from 1933 onwards fundamentally changed the relationship of state and society. John Kenneth Galbraith's popular study *The Great Crash, 1929* (1961) remains a useful introduction. The economic history of the decade is summarized by Jim Potter, *The American Economy Between the World Wars* (rev. edn, 1985); John A. Garraty, *The Great Depression* (1987) is especially valuable for putting the American experience into its international context. More technical studies are available in Milton Friedman and Anna J. Schwartz, *Monetary History of the United States, 1867–1960* (1963) and Peter Temin, *Did Monetary Forces Cause the Great Depression?* (1976). The attempts of the Hoover Administration to address the crisis are sympathetically interpreted in Albert U. Romasco, *The Poverty of Abundance: Hoover, the Nation and the Depression* (1965), which also emphasizes the continuities with the later period.

An excellent introduction to every major aspect of the subsequent New Deal era – and a useful synopsis of the relevant literature and historiographical debates – is provided by Anthony J. Badger, *The New Deal: The Depression Years, 1933–1940* (1989). Older, equally valuable, studies include Arthur M. Schlesinger, Jr, *The Age of Roosevelt* (3 vols, 1957–61) and William E. Leuchtenburg, *Franklin D. Roosevelt and the New Deal* (1963). Most interpretations of the New Deal have been sympathetic, but Gary Dean Best's *Pride, Prejudice, and Politics: Roosevelt versus Recovery* (1991) argues that it contributed little to the eventual economic recovery. The Administration's often controversial relations with the judicial branch are explored in Richard M. Maidment, *The Judicial Response to the New Deal* (1991) and Peter H. Irons, *The New Deal Lawyers* (1982); William E. Leuchtenburg, *The Supreme Court Reborn: The Constitutional Revolution in the Age of Roosevelt* (1995) is the author's collected essays. Classic studies of FDR's own role include James MacGregor Burns, *Roosevelt: The Lion and the Fox* (1956) and various accounts by those who served in his Administration; especially valuable are Frances Perkins, *The Roosevelt I Knew* (1946) and Rex Tugwell, *FDR: Architect of an Era* (1967).

The importance of the political history of the New Deal era cannot be overstated; its role in fashioning a Democratic majority in the United States – and the waning of that majority – are examined in Steve Fraser and Gary Gerstle (eds), *The Rise and Fall of the New Deal Order, 1930–1980* (1989). Sean J. Savage, *Roosevelt: The Party Leader, 1932–1945* (1991) examines FDR's attempt to rebuild his own party as an explicitly liberal one. The career of one of the President's most influential advisers has been recently studied in Jeanne Nienaber Clarke, *Roosevelt's Warrior: Harold L. Ickes and the New Deal* (1996). Kenneth Finegold and Theda Skocpol, *State and Party in America's New Deal* (1995) examines the importance of political structures in implementing the Administration's policies for agriculture and industry. Other studies which consider the era's role in reshaping American politics are Stanley M. Milkis, *The President and the Parties: The Transformation of the American Party System since the New Deal* (1993) and David Plotke, *Building A Democratic Political Order: Reshaping American Liberalism in the 1930s and 1940s* (1996). The fate of the 'opposition party' in this decade can be studied in Clyde P. Weed, *The Nemesis of Reform: The Republican Party during the New Deal* (1994). The history of opposition to the New Deal from radical and populist sources is summarized in Alan Brinkley, *Voices of Protest: Huey Long, Father Coughlin, and the Great Depression* (1982). See also Harvey Klehr, *The Heyday of American Communism: The Depression Decade* (1984).

The important history of American labour in this decade is placed in its larger context by Robert H. Zieger, *American Workers, American Unions, 1920–1985* (1986), which supplements the standard history by Irving Bernstein, *The Turbulent Years: A History of the American Worker, 1933–1941* (1969); Zieger's *The C.I.O., 1935–1955* (1995) is a study of the growth of industrial unionism. Excellent accounts of labour's development in specific localities are to be found in David Wellman, *The Union Makes Us Strong: Radical Unionism on the San Francisco Waterfront* (1995) and Lizabeth Cohen, *Making A New Deal: Industrial Workers in Chicago, 1919–1939* (1990), which discusses the growth of a working-class consciousness. Stanley Vittoz, *New Deal Labor Policy and the American Industrial Economy* (1987) considers labour's role in transforming the political economy of the workplace; Patrick Renshaw, *American Labour and Consensus Capitalism, 1935–1990* (1991) extends the analysis into the post-war era.

The development of public welfare during the New Deal is explained in James T. Patterson, *America's Struggle Against Poverty, 1900–1980* (1981) which remains the best introduction to the political and historical debates on this subject. A comparative perspective is now available in Desmond S. King, *Actively Seeking Work? The Politics of Unemployment and Welfare Policy in the United States and Great Britain* (1995). Harvard Sitkoff, *A New Deal for Blacks: The Emergence of Civil Rights as a National Issue. Volume I: The Depression Decade* (1978) concludes that the New Deal had a positive legacy for African-Americans. Its effect upon other minorities is explored in Donald L. Parman, *Navajos and the New Deal* (1976), Graham D. Taylor, *The New Deal and American Indian Tribalism: The Administration of the Indian Reorganization Act, 1934–45* (1980), Cletus Daniel, *Bitter Harvest: A History of the California Farm Workers, 1870–1941* (1981) and George J. Sanchez, *Becoming Mexican American: Ethnicity, Culture, and Identity in Chicano Los Angeles: 1900–1945* (1993).

Analysis of the New Deal's impact at the regional level may be found in Jack T. Kirby, *Rural Worlds Lost: The American South, 1920–1960* (1987), Douglas L. Smith, *The New Deal in the Urban South* (1988) and Bruce J. Schulman, *From Cotton Belt to Sunbelt: Federal Policy, Economic Development, and the Transformation of the South, 1938–1980* (1991). Recent studies of the Depression in the West include Kevin Starr, *Endangered Dreams: The Great Depression in California* (1996) and Pamela Riney-Kehrberg, *Rooted in Dust: Surviving Drought and Depression in Southwestern Kansas* (1994).

The impact of the Great Depression upon American society and culture has a vast literature. Studs Terkel, *Hard Times* (1970) remains an unsurpassed oral history. Aspects of cultural history are explored in Richard H. Pell, *Radical Visions and American Dreams: Cultural and Social Thought in the Depression Years* (1973), which focuses upon intellectuals, and Heinz Ickstadt, *The Thirties: Politics and Culture in a Line of Broken Dreams* (1987). Still invaluable are the classic accounts of Frederick L. Allen, *Since Yesterday* (1940) and Robert S. and Helen M. Lynd, *Middletown in Transition: A Study in Cultural Conflicts* (1937). Susan Ware, *Holding Their Own: American Women in the 1930s* (1982) is the best introduction to the history of women in the Depression; it should be supplemented by Lois Scharf, *To Work and to Wed: Female Employment, Feminism, and the Great Depression* (1980), Winifred D. Wandersee, *Women's Work and Family Values, 1920–1940* (1981), and Laura Hapke, *Daughters of the Great Depression: Women, Work, and Fiction in the American 1930s* (1995). Studies of various forms of cultural expression in this era include Andre Bergman, *We're in the Money: Depression America and its Films* (1971), Matthew Baigell, *The American Scene: Painting in the 1930s* (1974), Malcolm Goldstein, *The Political State: American Drama and the Theatre of the Great Depression* (1974), and Martin Williams, *Jazz in Its Own Time* (1989).

14. America at war, 1935–53

America's long march from isolationism to superpower during the 1930s and 1940s has produced a wealth of scholarship on US diplomacy, war aims, mobilization for war and the troubled relations with her fellow victors. The impact of war upon the American state system and the militarization of American society are explored in Michael Sherry, *In the Shadow of War: The United States since the 1930s* (1995), which provides an excellent guide to the historical literature for the period. An important study of the fate of progressive ideals in government during the later 1930s and the subsequent decade is Alan Brinkley, *The End of Reform: New Deal Liberalism in Recession and War* (1995).

Standard histories of this era in relation to subsequent periods are Robert D. Schulzinger, *American Diplomacy in the Twentieth Century* (3rd edn, 1994) and Stephen E. Ambrose, *The Rise to Globalism: American Foreign Policy since 1938* (7th edn, 1993). Robert Dallek's well-established study, *Franklin Roosevelt and American Foreign Policy, 1932–1945* (1979), presents a sympathetic treatment of the President's policy. On FDR himself, see Warren F. Kimball, *The Juggler: Franklin Roosevelt as Wartime Statesman* (1991). The events which directly propelled America into World War II are examined in Akira Iriye, *The Origins of the Second World War in Asia and the Pacific* (1987); John Dower, *War Without Mercy: Race and Power in the Pacific War* (1986) is an excellent analysis of the racist views which the Americans and Japanese had of one another's cultures during the war years. Patrick Hearden, *Roosevelt Confronts Hitler: America's Entry into World War II* (1987) emphasizes the economic aspects of foreign policy in the 1930s.

The military history of the war may be followed in I.C.B. Dear and M.R.D. Foot (eds), *The Oxford Companion to the Second World War* (1995). On America's war in the Pacific see, in addition to Dower, Ronald H. Spector, *Eagle Against the Sun: The American War with Japan* (1987). Michael J. Hogan, *Hiroshima in History and Memory* (1996) is a recent study of the controversial decision to use the atomic weapon and should be used as a guide to the extensive literature and historical debate on this topic. On the USA's relationship with Great Britain, see David Reynolds, *The Creation of the Anglo–American Alliance, 1937–41* (1981), which emphasizes how co-operation arose from, but also reinforced, competition between the two powers. Recent studies of particular aspects of the wartime alliance are Helen Leigh-Phippard, *Congress and US Military Aid to Britain: Interdependence and Dependence, 1949–56* (1995) and Inderjeet Parmar, *Special Interests, the State and the Anglo–American Alliance 1939–1945* (1995). Randall Bennett Woods, *A Changing of the Guard: Anglo–American Relations, 1941–1946* (1990) focuses upon the economic aspects of the relationship. The impact of the war upon the US domestic economy as a whole is explained in Harold Vatter, *The U.S. Economy in World War II* (1985).

The breakdown of America's alliance with the Soviet Union and the growing confrontation between the superpowers has produced a rich historiography; John Young, *The Longman Companion to Cold War and Detente, 1941–91* (1993) is a useful guide to the debate. Traditional interpretations such as John Lewis Gaddis, *The United States and the Origins of the Cold War, 1941–1947* (1972) may be weighed against the revisionist studies of Walter LaFeber, *America, Russia and the Cold War* (rev. edn, 1993) and Gabriel Kolko, *The Limits of Power: The World and United States Foreign Policy, 1945–1954* (1972) which are more critical of American policy. Richard Crockatt, *The Fifty Years War: The United States and the Soviet Union in World Politics, 1941–1991* (1996) follows the history up to the demise of the Soviet Union. Thomas McCormick, *America's Half-Century: United States Foreign Policy in the Cold War* (1989) emphasizes America's economic interest in internationalism; and US post-war policy towards Europe is studied in Michael J. Hogan, *The Marshall Plan: America, Britain and the Reconstruction of Western Europe, 1947–1952* (1987). Specific military aspects of the Cold War are treated in Steven T. Ross, *American War Plans, 1945–1950* (1996) and Samuel R. Williamson, Jr and Steven L. Rearden, *The Origins of U.S. Nuclear Strategy, 1945–1953* (1993). Wilson D. Miscamble, *George F. Kennan and the Making of American Foreign Policy, 1947–1950* (1992) and Melvyn P. Leffler, *A Preponderance of Power: National Security, the Truman Administration, and the Cold War* (1992) both study the American policy-makers themselves in detail.

The USA's growing engagement in Asia and the resulting conflict should be followed in Michael Schaller, *The American Occupation of Japan: The Origins of the Cold War in Asia* (1985). Richard Whelan, *Drawing the Line: The Korean War, 1950–1953* (1990) provides an introduction for the general reader; Bruce Cumings, *The Origins of the Korean War* (2 vols, 1981, 1990) is the more comprehensive standard history. For the domestic history of the United States in this era, Robert Donovan's *Conflict and Crisis: The Presidency of Harry S. Truman, 1945–1948* (1976), is a standard account of Truman's first term. More recent studies are Alonzo L. Hamby, *Man of the People: A Life of Harry S. Truman* (1996), and William E. Pemberton, *Harry S. Truman: Fair Dealer and Cold Warrior* (1989) which is particularly critical of its subject. Michael Lacey (ed.), *The Truman Presidency* (1989) offers essays on individual aspects of the Administration. For aspects of the politics of the Left in this period, see Maurice Isserman, *Which Side Were You On? The American Communist Party during the Second World War* (1982) and Nelson Lichtenstein, *Labor's War at Home: The CIO in World War II* (1982).

The American home front was fundamentally transformed by the economic and demographic upheavals of the war years. Geoffrey Perrett,

Days of Sadness, Years of Triumph: The American People, 1939–1945 (1973) remains the best introduction. Richard Polenberg, *War and Society: The United States, 1941–1945* (1972) and his *One Nation Divisible: Class, Race, and Ethnicity in the United States since 1938* (1980) are standard histories of the war's impact upon society, the latter being particularly insightful. See also John Morton Blum, *V Was For Victory: Politics and American Culture during World War II* (1976). The fate of minorities in the United States is studied in Robert Hill, *Racon: Racial Conditions in the United States during World War II* (1995), Roger Daniels, *Concentration Camp USA: Japanese Americans during World War II* (1962) and Alison R. Bernstein, *American Indians and World War II: Toward a New Era in Indian Affairs* (1991). On the previously 'silent majority' who were now conscripted for the war effort, see Karen Anderson, *Wartime Women* (1994); other studies of American women for earlier periods remain relevant. Of numerous explorations of the impact of the Cold War upon American society, Stephen J. Whitfield, *The Culture of the Cold War* (2nd edn, 1996) is the most balanced. See also, Paul Boyer, *By the Bomb's Early Light: American Thought and Culture at the Dawn of the Atomic Age* (1985) and the relevant parts of Robert Wuthnow, *The Restructuring of American Religion: Society and Faith since World War II* (1988).

15. The Eisenhower years, 1953–61

Nineteen-fifties' America was, on the surface, a nation of cultural and political conformity, enjoying unparalleled prosperity. Yet beneath there was a tremendous social and racial ferment as the strains of the Cold War and rapid economic growth produced a new materialism which seemed to challenge deep-seated traditions. The best single-volume history of American society in the post-war era is William H. Chafe, *The Unfinished Journey: America since World War II* (3rd edn, 1995), an excellent synthesis of social and political history. The leadership of Dwight Eisenhower has in recent years received renewed attention as historians have come to judge the President more politically capable than did his contemporaries. A personal account is provided in the memoirs of his Chief of Staff, Sherman Adams, *First Hand Report: The Inside Story of the Eisenhower Administration* (1962). The second volume of Stephen Ambrose's biography, *Eisenhower: The President* (1984), is the best single study of the Administration. One of the leading revisionists, Fred I. Greenstein, argues in *The Hidden-Hand Presidency: Eisenhower as Leader* (1982) that Eisenhower was an activist President despite his public image as the reverse. Chester J. Pach and Elmo Richardson, *The Presidency of Dwight D. Eisenhower* (1991) studies various aspects of the Administration in more detail. John W. Sloan, *Eisenhower and the Management of Prosperity* (1991) and Iwan Morgan, *Eisenhower versus 'The Spenders': The*

Eisenhower Administration, the Democrats and the Budget, 1953–60 (1990) should be consulted on economic policy. See also Gary W. Reichard, *Politics as Usual: The Age of Truman and Eisenhower* (1988) for Eisenhower's relationship with the preceding Administration. On judicial politics see, among studies of the civil rights movement noted below, Bernard Schwartz, *Super Chief: Earl Warren and His Supreme Court* (1983).

The political history of the 1950s is synonymous with the name of Senator Joseph McCarthy. Richard M. Fried, *Nightmare in Red: The McCarthy Era in Perspective* (1990) is the best available synthesis of existing scholarship. Other excellent studies of particular aspects are Robert Griffith, *The Politics of Fear: Joseph R. McCarthy and the Senate* (1987) and Ellen Schrecker, *No Ivory Tower: McCarthyism and the Universities* (1986). Jeff Broadwater, *Eisenhower and the Anti-Communist Crusade* (1992) argues that Eisenhower was sympathetic to the prevalent politics of anti-communism and could have done more to dislodge McCarthy had he so desired. The wider history of conservatism in this decade is described by Nicol Rae, *The Decline and Fall of the Liberal Republicans* (1989), Patrick Allitt, *Catholic Intellectuals and Conservative Politics in America, 1950–1985* (1993) and M.J. Heale, *American Anticommunism: Combating the Enemy Within, 1830* [sic]*–1970* (1990).

For America's relations with the Soviet Union, the standard histories of the Cold War are still relevant; see also Saki Dockrill, *Eisenhower's New-Look National Security Policy, 1953–61* (1996) and Michael Beschloss, *Mayday: Eisenhower, Khrushchev, and the U-2 Affair* (1986). Rosemary Foot, *A Substitute for Victory: The Politics of Peacemaking at the Korean Armistice Talks* (1990) describes the circumstances of the end of one war, and Loren Baritz, *Backfire: A History of How American Culture Led Us into Vietnam and Made Us Fight the Way We Did* (1985) those of the beginning of another, the latter in a particularly critical fashion. Eisenhower's own responsibility for the subsequent tragedy is assessed by David Anderson, *Trapped By Success: The Eisenhower Administration and Vietnam* (1991). See Walter A. McDougall, *The Heavens and the Earth: A Political History of the Space Age* (1985) for an account of the United States' response to the Soviets' launch of Sputnik. Tom Wolfe, *The Right Stuff* (1975) is a popular account of the developing space race.

The flowering in the 1950s of the long struggle for civil rights for minorities, especially for African-Americans, is placed in its historical context in Robert Weisbrot, *Freedom Bound: A History of America's Civil Rights Movement* (1990). Aldon D. Morris, *The Origins of the Civil Rights Movement: Black Communities Organizing for Change* (1984) emphasizes the 'grass roots' nature of the movement, and Frederick Burk, *The Eisenhower Administration and Black Civil Rights* (1984) criticizes the Administration's slow response. See also Harvard Sitkoff, *The Struggle for Black Equality, 1954–1992* (1993). The experience of Native Americans is examined in Larry W. Burt, *Tribalism in Crisis: Federal Indian Policy, 1953–1961* (1982) and Donald Fixico, *Termination and Relocation: Federal Indian Policy, 1945–1970* (1986). The history of poverty in the United States in this period is best studied in Jacqueline Jones, *The Dispossessed: America's Underclass from the Civil War to the Present* (1992) and the state's response in James T. Patterson, *America's Struggle Against Poverty, 1900–1980* (1981). J. Wayne Flynt, *Dixie's Forgotten People: The South's Poor Whites* (1979) examines another, often ignored, 'minority'.

Studies of the culture of the Cold War continue to be relevant for this period. The way in which material abundance had changed American economic life was noted by contemporaries – John Kenneth Galbraith's *The Affluent Society* (1958) remains the starting point for any serious study. The changing demography of the country is examined by Landon Jones, *Great Expectations: America and the Baby Boom Generation* (1980) and its residential patterns in Kenneth Jackson's excellent *Crabgrass Frontier: The Suburbanization of the United States* (1985). Elaine Tyler May, *Homeward Bound: American Families in the Cold War Era* (1988) examines how the Cold War affected gender roles; William H. Chafe, *The American Woman: Her Changing Social, Economic, and Political Roles, 1920–1970* (rev. edn, 1988) focuses upon the persistence of discrimination. For the development of modern culture, see Larry May (ed.), *Recasting America: Culture and Politics in the Age of the Cold War* (1989), W.T. Lhamon, *Deliberate Speed: The Origins of a Cultural Style in the American 1950s* (1990) and Robert Wuthnow, *The Restructuring of American Religion: Society and Faith since World War II* (1988). On specific aspects of social behaviour and on the new technology of leisure, see Ella Taylor, *Prime-Time Families: Television Culture in Postwar America* (1989), James Baughman, *The Republic of Mass Culture: Journalism, Filmmaking, and Broadcasting since 1941* (1992), Cynthia G. Dettelbach, *In the Driver's Seat: The Automobile in American Literature and Popular Culture* (1976), Ray Pratt, *Rhythm and Resistance: The Political Uses of American Popular Music* (1994), Simon Reynolds and Joy Press, *The Sex Revolts: Gender, Rebellion and Rock 'n' Roll* (1995), Malcolm Bradbury, *The Modern American Novel* (1984), and for art, among other forms of cultural expression, Douglas Tallack, *Twentieth-Century America: The Intellectual and Cultural Context* (1991), which offers an excellent annotated bibliography.

16. America in the sixties: the New Frontier and the Great Society, 1961–69

John Morton Blum, *Years of Discord: American Politics and Society, 1961–1974* (1991) is a useful one-volume introduction to the decade which broke the mould of American politics and saw almost unprecedented social and cultural turmoil. William H. Chafe, *The Unfinished Journey:*

America since World War II (3rd edn, 1995) continues to be an excellent source for the interrelation of national and social history and is particularly reliable on the civil rights movement. Alan J. Matusow, *The Unraveling of America: A History of Liberalism in the 1960s* (1984) is a critical but comprehensive analysis of the failings of the dominant liberal tradition. For the political history of this and subsequent eras an incisive introduction is provided by Iwan Morgan, *Beyond the Liberal Consensus: A Political History of the United States since 1965* (1994).

The short Presidency of John F. Kennedy has attracted much academic and popular writing. An insider's account is given by Arthur M. Schlesinger Jr, *A Thousand Days: John F. Kennedy in the White House* (1965). The circumstances of Kennedy's election are described in Theodore H. White's *The Making of the President 1960* (1961), the first in a series of accounts of successive elections by one of America's leading journalists. Hugh Brogan, *Kennedy* (1996) considers JFK's as a 'Cold War presidency' and contrasts his foreign policy with his predecessor's. James J. Giglio, *The Presidency of John F. Kennedy* (1991) is an important study which judges Kennedy favourably while admitting his numerous personal faults. Irving Bernstein, *Promises Kept: John F. Kennedy's New Frontier* (1991) considers him to have been a successful President domestically, but should be compared with the more critical study by Thomas Reeves, *A Question of Character: A Life of John F. Kennedy* (1991). The established account of the President's assassination remains William Manchester, *The Death of the President* (1967). Paul R. Henggeler, *In His Steps: Lyndon Johnson and the Kennedy Mystique* (1991) studies JFK's relationship with his successor.

The early career of Lyndon Johnson is scathingly treated by Robert Caro, *The Years of Lyndon Johnson: Means of Ascent* (1990) and more objectively by Robert Dalleck, *Lone Star Rising: Lyndon Johnson and His Times, 1908–1960* (1991). The domestic history of the Johnson Presidency and the launching of the Great Society programme are discussed in Doris Kearns, *Lyndon Johnson and the American Dream* (1977), Robert A. Divine (ed.), *Exploring the Johnson Years: Foreign Policy, the Great Society, and the White House* (1981), D. Zarefsky, *President Johnson's War on Poverty: Rhetoric and History* (1986) and E. Berkowitz and Kim McQuaid, *Creating the Welfare State* (1992), to which must now be added Irving Bernstein, *Guns or Butter? The Presidency of Lyndon Johnson* (1996), a superlative narrative history of American politics from Kennedy's assassination to Nixon's election. Bernstein identifies Johnson's debt to Kennedy for his legislative agenda, but also argues that Johnson's prosecution of the Vietnam War meant abandoning the New Deal legacy that the President had so wished to preserve and extend. Bruce J. Schulman, *Lyndon B. Johnson and American Liberalism: A Brief Biography with Documents* (1995) is also a useful source. A full biography of Johnson's Republican opponent in 1964, *Barry Goldwater* (1995) by Robert Alan Goldberg, is now available; it provides a useful insight into the development of American conservatism and the rise of its libertarian wing.

The domestic politics of the United States in the 1960s were dominated by the question of race. In addition to the histories of the civil rights movement already noted for the 1950s, reference should be made to Hugh Davis Graham, *The Civil Rights Era: Origins and Development of National Policy, 1960–1972* (1990), which considers the state's response at the federal level, and to Mark Stern, *Calculating Visions: Kennedy, Johnson, and Civil Rights* (1992), which suggests that successive Presidents advanced reform with a keen eye on the potential electoral advantages. Richard H. King, *Civil Rights and the Idea of Freedom* (1992) discusses the broader political culture of the movement and William L. Van Deburg, *New Day In Babylon: The Black Power Movement and American Culture, 1965–1975* (1992) examines the origins of its more radical elements. The contributions of individual major participants are explored in Lea E. Williams, *Servants of the People: The 1960s Legacy of African-American Leadership* (1997), Stephen B. Oates, *Let the Trumpet Sound: The Life of Martin Luther King, Jr.* (1982), Adam Fairclough, *To Redeem the Soul of America: The Southern Christian Leadership Conference and Martin Luther King, Jr.* (1987) and Mark V. Tushnet, *Making Civil Rights Law: Thurgood Marshall and the Supreme Court, 1936–1961* (1996). The personal writings of major participants remain important sources: Alex Haley (ed.), *The Autobiography of Malcolm X* (1965), Eldridge Cleaver, *Soul on Ice* (1967) and Stokely Carmichael and Charles Hamilton, *Black Power: The Politics of Liberation in America* (1967). For an introduction to the history of the growing Hispanic communities and cultures, see Rodolfo F. Acuna, *Occupied America: A History of the Chicanos* (3rd edn, 1988), Mario T. Garcia, *Mexican–Americans: Leadership, Ideology and Identity, 1930–1960* (1989) and Juan Gomez-Quinones, *Chicano Politics: Reality and Promise, 1940–1990* (1990).

For the histories of the political and cultural protest movements which convulsed American society in this decade, see Terry H. Anderson, *The Movement and the Sixties: Protest in America from Greensboro to Wounded Knee* (1996). James J. Farrell, *The Spirit of the Sixties: Roots and Routes of Sixties Radicalism* (1997) is an exploration of radical political culture from the participants' perspective. Aspects of the New Left are considered in Wini Breines, *Community and Organization in the New Left: 1962–1968* (1982), James Miller, *'Democracy is in the Streets': From Port Huron to the Siege of Chicago* (1987) and Peter B. Levy, *The New Left and Labor in the 1960s* (1994). Stanley Aronowitz, *The Death and Rebirth of American Radicalism* (1996) considers the New Left's legacy and how it failed to meet the challenge of a revived conservatism. The writings of numerous of the participants themselves are instructive; an excellent personal memoir is

Todd Gitlin's *The Sixties: Years of Hope, Days of Rage* (1987). The politics of the women's movement are considered in Nancy Cott, *The Grounding of Modern Feminism* (1987) and Alice Echols, *Daring To Be Bad: Radical Feminism in America, 1967–1975* (1989), but the starting point for any investigation must remain contemporary texts such as Betty Friedan's *The Feminine Mystique* (1963) and Kate Millett's *Sexual Politics* (1971). See also Sara Evans, *Personal Politics: The Roots of Women's Liberation in the Civil Rights Movement and the New Left* (1980).

17. The world in crisis, 1961–69

The domestic upheavals of the 1960s were mirrored abroad by crises in the United States' relations with other countries, not least the nightmare of the war in Vietnam. The outlook and policies of successive Presidents are examined in two excellent collections, Thomas G. Paterson (ed.), *Kennedy's Quest For Victory: American Foreign Policy, 1961–1963* (1989) and Warren I. Cohen and Nancy B. Tucker (eds), *Lyndon Johnson Confronts the World: American Foreign Policy, 1963–1968* (1994); the latter finds that Johnson, whose principal goal was to preserve American 'credibility', was in fact more restrained than his predecessor had been. On the US relationship with the Soviet Union see Michael Beschloss, *The Crisis Years: Kennedy and Khrushchev, 1960–1963* (1991) which concludes that, despite the rhetoric of his own Inaugural Address, JFK was quite pragmatic when dealing with the United States' principal opponent.

America's troubled relationship with her immediate neighbours are surveyed in John D. Martz (ed.), *United States Policy in Latin America: A Quarter Century of Crisis and Challenge, 1961–1986* (1988). On policy towards Cuba, see Robert Smith Thompson, *The Missiles of October: The Declassified Story of John F. Kennedy and the Cuban Missile Crisis* (1992), Mark J. White, *The Cuban Missile Crisis* (1995) and Thomas G. Paterson, *Contesting Castro: The United States and the Triumph of the Cuban Revolution* (new edn, 1995). Sebastian Balfour, *Castro* (2nd edn, 1994) is now established as the standard introduction on the revolutionary leader himself. Abraham F. Lowenthal, *The Dominican Intervention* (2nd edn, 1995) is the best book on the 1965 episode now overshadowed by the Vietnam War.

The tragedy of Vietnam has produced an enormous literature reflecting the vigorous debate among politicians and participants, as well as historians. A recent contribution from one of the leading US policymakers is Robert S. McNamara's much-criticized but indispensible, *In Retrospect: The Tragedy and Lessons of Vietnam* (1995). Marilyn B. Young, *The Vietnam Wars, 1945–1990* (1991) is a recent comprehensive survey; older but still incisive in its judgements is George C. Herring, *America's Longest War: The United States and Vietnam, 1960–1975* (rev. edn, 1985). David W. Levy, *The Debate Over Vietnam* (1991) and David L. Di Leo,

George Ball, Vietnam, and the Rethinking of Containment (1991) study the policy-makers and their debates over intervention; Larry Cable, *Unholy Grail: The US and the Wars in Vietnam, 1965–8* (1991) criticizes the interventionists. For specific periods of US involvement, see David L. Anderson, *Trapped By Success: The Eisenhower Administration and Vietnam, 1953–1961* (1991) – which concludes that 'Ike' was responsible for judging Vietnam to be vital to America's security and for making the major commitment – and Larry Berman, *Planning A Tragedy: The Americanization of the War in Vietnam* (1982) and *Lyndon Johnson's War: The Road to Stalemate in Vietnam* (1989). Defences of American policy include Norman Podhoretz, *Why We Were in Vietnam* (1982) and Leslie H. Gelb and Richard K. Betts, *The Irony of Vietnam: The System Worked* (1979).

The impact of the war upon the Americans who fought it and those who protested against it at home is considered in Christian Appy, *Working-Class War: American Combat Soldiers and Vietnam* (1993), which makes extensive use of the testimony of veterans, and Adam Garfinkle, *Telltale Hearts: The Origins and Impact of the Vietnam Antiwar Movement* (1995). See also Kenneth J. Heineman, *Campus Wars: The Peace Movement at American State Universities in the Vietnam Era* (1993). Melvin Small, *Johnson, Nixon, and the Doves* (1988) is useful for the Presidents' reactions to the Anti-War Movement. Michael Charlton and Anthony Moncrieff, *Many Reasons Why: The American Involvement in Vietnam* (1978) is an excellent oral history. For the reaction of the media, see Daniel C. Hallin, *The 'Uncensored War': The Media and Vietnam* (1986), Michael Anderegg (ed.), *Inventing Vietnam: The War in Film and Television* (1991) and Clarence R. Wyatt, *Paper Soldiers: The American Press and the Vietnam War* (2nd edn, 1995). Michael D. Shafer (ed.), *The Legacy: The Vietnam War in the American Imagination* (1990) and Susan Jeffords, *The Remasculinization of America: Gender and the Vietnam War* (1989) consider aspects of the war's impact on popular culture. Bruce H. Franklin, *M.I.A. or Mythmaking in America* (rev. edn, 1993) examines the politically important issue of missing American servicemen, and Thomas A. Bass, *Vietnamerica: The War Comes Home* (1996) the fate of Vietnamese children born to American fathers.

18. From Nixon to Carter, 1969–81

For an introduction to the political history of the era, the previously cited texts John Morton Blum, *Years of Discord: American Politics and Society, 1961–1974* (1991) and Iwan Morgan, *Beyond the Liberal Consensus: A Political History of the United States since 1965* (1994) should be consulted. William Berman, *America's Right Turn: From Nixon to Bush* (1994) surveys the rise of the New Right. Peter Carroll, *It Seemed Like Nothing Happened: America in the 1970s* (1982) is a good study of the whole decade written close to the events it describes.

The momentous election of 1968, which marked the dissolution of the New Deal Democratic majority and inaugurated an era of conservatism at the presidential level, is analysed in Lewis L. Gould, *1968: The Election That Changed America* (1993). Excellent contemporary accounts of the campaign are Norman Mailer, *Miami and the Siege of Chicago* (1968) and Joe McGinniss, *The Selling of the President, 1968* (1969). Kevin Phillips, *The Emerging Republican Majority* (1969) is another contemporary text which argued that the socio-economic changes of the preceding decade had fundamentally altered America's political demography, to the advantage of the Grand Old Party. Dan T. Carter, *The Politics of Rage: George Wallace, the Origins of the New Conservatism, and the Transformation of American Politics* (1995) is an important study of the populist Governor of Alabama who split the Democratic Party in 1968.

For the career of the victor of '68 a good starting point is his own account, *RN: The Memoirs of Richard Nixon* (1978); it may be compared with another account – Henry A. Kissinger, *The White House Years* (1979). Of the recommended Nixon biographies, Stephen E. Ambrose's *Nixon: Ruin and Recovery, 1973–1990* (1991) is the final volume of a trilogy and is largely devoted to the Watergate crisis. Roger Morris, *Richard Milhous Nixon: The Rise of an American Politician* (1990) is the first volume of another trilogy; it covers Nixon's career up until 1952 and largely confirms accepted interpretations of him. A major revisionist study of the Nixon Presidency by Joan Hoff, *Nixon Reconsidered* (1994), argues that the Watergate scandal has obscured the successes of his domestic as well as foreign policies. Stanley I. Kutler, *The Wars of Watergate: The Last Crisis of Richard Nixon* (1990) is the best single account of this episode, interpreting it as representative of the President's whole career and not as an aberration. John Robert Greene, *The Limits of Power: The Nixon and Ford Administrations* (1992) is a good survey of the Republican governments; *The Presidency of Gerald R. Ford* (1995) is the same author's contribution to an established series of presidential histories.

The Carter Presidency has not yet been an area of much scholarship, one observer (Sherry, 1995) commenting that he 'seemed such an anomaly that historians have largely discarded him'. A good study is provided by Burton I. Kaufman, *The Presidency of James Earl Carter, Jr.* (1993). John Dumbrell's *The Carter Presidency: A Re-evaluation* (1993) is a sympathetic treatment which identifies Carter's support of human rights as central to his domestic as well as foreign policies. Leo P. Ribuffo, *Right, Center, Left: Essays in American History* (1992) has useful chapters; and the President's often difficult relationship with a Democratic Congress is explored in Charles O. Jones, *The Trusteeship Presidency: Jimmy Carter and the United States Congress* (1988). See also Erwin C. Hargrove, *Jimmy Carter as President: Leadership and the Politics of the Public Good* (1988) and, for the accounts of those who served in his Administration, Kenneth

W. Thompson (ed.), *The Carter Presidency: Fourteen Intimate Perspectives of Jimmy Carter* (1990).

The relative success of American foreign policy in the Nixon years is surveyed in Robert D. Schulzinger, *Henry Kissinger: Doctor of Diplomacy* (1989) and its greatest reversal in Arnold Isaacs, *Without Honor: Defeat in Vietnam and Cambodia* (1983). Arthur M. Schlesinger, Jr, *The Imperial Presidency* (1973) relates Nixon's downfall in Watergate to a presidential system which gave the incumbent enormous discretion in the conduct of foreign policy. For the momentous opening to the People's Republic of China in 1972, see Gordon H. Chang, *Friends and Enemies: The United States, China, and the Soviet Union, 1948–1972* (1990) which places these dramatic events in their historical context and concludes that Nixon's visit represented the logical outcome of a relatively pragmatic US policy. The subsequent history of the relationship is explored in Robert S. Ross, *Negotiating Cooperation: The United States and China, 1969–1989* (1995). A recent survey for the whole Carter period is John Dumbrell, *American Foreign Policy: Carter to Clinton* (1996). Gaddis Smith, *Morality, Reason, and Power: American Diplomacy in the Carter Years* (1986) is the best single-volume study of the policy of *détente* in this decade. Contemporary nuclear strategy and arms control policy is analysed in John Newhouse, *War and Peace in the Nuclear Age* (1989).

Students seeking information on post-1973 developments in the armed forces should consult Jerry K. Sweeney (ed.), *A Handbook of American Military History* (1996).

19. The Republican ascendancy, 1981–96

Garry Wills, *Reagan's America: Innocents at Home* (1987) is the best single-volume introduction to the history of the Reagan era. Of the numerous memoirs by members of the Administration, Peggy Noonan's *What I Saw at the Revolution: A Political Life in the Reagan Era* (1990) is an imaginative account by the President's speechwriter. An insight into the history of economic policy in the 1980s is provided by David A. Stockman, *The Triumph of Politics: How the Reagan Revolution Failed* (1986). David Mervin, *Ronald Reagan and the American Presidency* (1990) considers Reagan's role in reviving the authority of the Presidency and his relative success as a policy-maker; it should be compared with the highly critical account by Haynes Johnson, *Sleepwalking Through History: America in the Reagan Years* (1991) which argues that the Administration was quite undistinguished. See also Michael Schaller, *Reckoning with Reagan: America and its President in the 1980s* (1992). Paul Boyer (ed.), *Reagan as President: Contemporary Views of the Man, His Politics, and His Policies* (1990) and Joseph Hogan (ed.), *The Reagan Years: The Record in Presidential Leadership* (1990) are useful collections of essays, as is Michael P. Rogin, *'Ronald Reagan, The*

Movie' and Other Episodes in Political Demonology (1987) which suggests that Reagan's own view of the Presidency was moulded by roles that he had played during his Hollywood career. Daniel Wirls, *Buildup: The Politics of Defense in the Reagan Era* (1992) argues that the growth of defence spending was largely determined by political rather than military needs. Larry M. Schwab, *The Illusion of a Conservative Reagan Revolution* (1991) contends that, whatever the personal popularity of President Reagan, his conservative policies did not attract wide support in the 1980s. The landslide of Reagan's re-election is detailed in Jack W. Germond and Jules Witcover, *Wake Us When It's Over: Presidential Politics of 1984* (1985). Theodore Draper, *A Very Thin Line: The Iran–Contra Affair* (1991) is a substantial study of the major scandal of the era. Geoffrey Smith, *Reagan and Thatcher* (1990) examines the President's single most influential relationship with a foreign leader and emphasizes how Margaret Thatcher's international position depended upon her ally's support.

For Reagan's successors, David Mervin, *George Bush and the Guardianship Presidency* (1996) describes his former Vice-President as seeking to preserve the *status quo* against political and social challenges, but also as one who provided concrete leadership within his Administration in pursuit of his objectives. The circumstances of Bush's election are described by Jack W. Germond and Jules Witcover, *Whose Broad Stripes and Bright Stars? The Trivial Pursuit of the Presidency 1988* (1989). Colin Campbell and Bert A. Rockman (eds), *The Bush Presidency: First Appraisals* (1991) is a useful collection of essays, as is *The Clinton Presidency: First Appraisals* (1996) compiled by the same editors. Stanley A. Renshon, *The Clinton Presidency: Campaigning, Governing, and the Psychology of Leadership* (1995) identifies a particular style of government in the Clinton Presidency related to electoral politics. A life of the President is provided by David Maraniss, *First In His Class: A Biography of Bill Clinton* (1995). Peter B. Levy, *Encyclopedia of the Reagan–Bush Years* (1996) is a comprehensive reference source.

Wider socio-economic changes in the later 1970s and the 1980s are analysed critically in Kevin Phillips, *The Politics of Rich and Poor: Wealth and the American Electorate in the Reagan Aftermath* (1990) and Thomas Byrne Edsall and Mary D. Edsall, *Chain Reaction: The Impact of Race, Rights, and Taxes on American Politics* (1991). For the transformation of American conservatism in the preceeding 20 years, an introduction is provided by William Berman, *America's Right Turn: From Nixon to Bush* (1994). Mary C. Brennan, *Turning Right in the Sixties: The Conservative Capture of the GOP* (1995) describes how conservatism – previously the preserve of intellectuals – was built into a popular movement with its own grassroots organization within the Republican Party. See also Jerome L. Himmelstein, *To the Right: The Transformation of American Conservatism* (1990) and J. David Hoeveler, Jr, *Watch On the Right: Conservative Intellectuals in the Reagan Era* (1991).

For aspects of the history of 'oppositional politics' in this era, see Mike Davis and Michael Sprinker, *Reshaping the US Left: Popular Struggles in the 1980s* (1988), Allen D. Hertzke, *Echoes of Discontent: Jesse Jackson, Pat Robertson, and the Resurgence of Populism* (1993) and Richard M. Merelman, *Representing Black Culture: Racial Conflict and Cultural Politics in the United States* (1995). See also Dennis Heyck (ed.), *Barrios and Borderlands: Cultures of Latinos and Latinas in the United States* (1993) and Pyong Gap Min, *Asian Americans: Contemporary Trends and Issues* (1995). Important issues of contemporary social politics are described in Arlene S. Skolnick, *Embattled Paradise: The American Family in an Age of Uncertainty* (1991), Christopher Pierson, *Beyond the Welfare State? The New Political Economy of Welfare* (1991), Roger Rosenblatt, *Life Itself* (1992) on abortion, Philip Shabecoff, *A Fierce Green Fire: The American Environmental Movement* (1993), and Christopher Jencks, *The Homeless* (1994).

The transformation of American foreign policy with the end of the Cold War is surveyed in John Dumbrell, *American Foreign Policy: Carter to Clinton* (1996); the same author's *The Making of US Foreign Policy* (1990) usefully explains the political process. For the longer-term implications of the demise of the Soviet Union, see John Lewis Gaddis, *The United States and the End of the Cold War: Implications, Reconsiderations, Provocations* (1994) and Michael J. Hogan (ed.), *The End of the Cold War: Its Meanings and Implications* (1992) – two good studies on what is already an overwritten topic. Specific aspects of policy under Reagan are examined in Leslie Cockburn, *Out of Control: The Story of the Reagan Administration's Secret War in Nicaragua* (1987), John D. Martz (ed.), *United States Policy in Latin America: A Quarter Century of Crisis and Challenge, 1961–1986* (1988) and Thomas Carothers, *In The Name of Democracy: U.S. Policy Toward Latin America in the Reagan Years* (1991), which sees policy becoming more flexible and pragmatic. See also Kenneth Mokoena (ed.), *South Africa and the United States: The Declassified History* (1993). The future of foreign policy is suggested by Eric Nordlinger, *Isolationism Reconfigured: American Foreign Policy for a New Century* (1995); see also Joseph Nye, *Bound To Lead* (1990) and Henry Nau, *The Myth of America's Decline* (1990), two texts which have attracted public attention for challenging the thesis suggested by Paul Kennedy's *The Rise and Fall of the Great Powers* (1987) that American hegemony is temporary. Rhodri Jeffreys-Jones, *Changing Differences: Women and the Shaping of American Foreign Policy, 1917–1984* (1995) studies a little-examined aspect of policy-making.

The social history of the last 20 years and the increasing diversity of American society have provoked numerous studies of the changing climate of moral opinion and cultural identity, among which see particularly James Davison Hunter, *Culture Wars: The Struggle to Define America* (1991). The contemporary question of whether multi-culturalism is undermining the unity of the United States is addressed by journalist

Michael Lind in *The Next American Nation: The New Nationalism and the Fourth American Revolution* (1995). Robert Hughes, *Culture of Complaint: The Fraying of America* (1993) and Arthur M. Schlesinger, Jr, *The Disuniting of America: Reflections on a Multicultural Society* (1993) are two insightful polemics, the first a devastating critique of the intellectual foundations of 'political correctness'. The continuity of traditional morality is assessed in Robert Wuthnow, *The Restructuring of American Religion: Society and Faith since World War II* (1988), which is now the standard work on the subject, and by Paul Boyer, *When Time Shall Be No More: Prophecy Belief in Modern American Culture* (1992), an important study of apocalyptic thought. There is a large literature on religion (particularly Protestant Christianity) and politics; a useful introduction is provided by Steve Bruce, *The Rise and Fall of the Christian Right: Conservative Protestant Politics in America, 1978–1988* (1988). Susan Jeffords, *Hard Bodies: Hollywood Masculinity in the Reagan Era* (1994) is an important study of this aspect of popular culture. Randy Shilts, *And the Band Played On: Politics, People, and the AIDS Epidemic* (1987) is a journalistic account of the (culturally and politically) most important public health issue of the age.

Appendices

Appendix I: Constitution of the United States of America

PREAMBLE

WE THE PEOPLE of the United States, in order to form a more perfect Union, establish justice, insure domestic tranquility, provide for the common defense, promote the general welfare, and secure the blessings of liberty to ourselves and our posterity, do ordain and establish this Constitution for the United States of America.

ARTICLE I

SECTION 1. All legislative powers herein granted shall be vested in a Congress of the United States, which shall consist of a Senate and House of Representatives.

SECTION 2. The House of Representatives shall be composed of members chosen every second year by the people of the several States, and the electors in each State shall have the qualifications requisite for electors of the most numerous branch of the State Legislature.

No person shall be a representative who shall not have attained to the age of twenty-five years, and been seven years a citizen of the United States, and who shall not, when elected, be an inhabitant of that State in which he shall be chosen.

Representatives and direct taxes shall be apportioned among the several States which may be included within this Union, according to their respective numbers which shall be determined by adding to the whole number of free persons, including those bound to service for a term of years, and excluding Indians not taxed, three-fifths of all other persons. The actual enumeration shall be made within three years after the first meeting of the Congress of the United States, and within every subsequent term of ten years, in such manner as they shall by law direct. The number of representatives shall not exceed one for every thirty thousand, but each State shall have at least one representative; and until such enumeration shall be made, the State of New Hampshire shall be entitled to choose three, Massachusetts eight, Rhode Island and Providence Plantations one, Connecticut five, New York six, New Jersey four, Pennsylvania eight, Delaware one, Maryland six, Virginia ten, North Carolina five, South Carolina five, and Georgia three.

When vacancies happen in the representation from any State, the executive authority thereof shall issue writs of election to fill such vacancies.

The House of Representatives shall choose their Speaker and other officers; and shall have the sole power of impeachment.

SECTION 3. The Senate of the United States shall be composed of two senators from each State, chosen by the legislature thereof, for six years and each senator shall have one vote.

Immediately after they shall be assembled in consequence of the first election, they shall be divided as equally as may be into three classes. The seats of the senators of the first class shall be vacated at the expiration of the second year, of the second class at the expiration of the fourth year, and of the third class at the expiration of the sixth year, so that one-third may be chosen every second year; and if vacancies happen by resignation, or otherwise, during the recess of the legislature of any State, the executive thereof may make temporary appointments until the next meeting of the legislature, which shall then fill such vacancies.

No person shall be a senator who shall not have attained to the age of thirty-years, and been nine years a citizen of the United States, and who shall not, when elected, be an inhabitant of that State for which he shall be chosen.

The Vice President of the United States shall be President of the Senate, but shall have no vote, unless they be equally divided.

The Senate shall choose their other officers, and also a President pro tempore, in the absence of the Vice President, or when he shall exercise the office of President of the United States.

The Senate shall have the sole power to try all impeachments. When sitting for that purpose, they shall be on oath or affirmation. When the President of the United States is tried, the Chief Justice shall preside: And no person shall be convicted without the concurrence of two-thirds of the members present.

Judgment in cases of impeachment shall not extend further than to removal from office, and disqualification to hold and enjoy any office of honor, trust or profit under the United States; but the party convicted shall nevertheless be liable and subject to indictment, trial, judgment and punishment, according to law.

SECTION 4. The times, places and manner of holding elections for senators and representatives, shall be prescribed in each State by the legislature thereof; but the Congress may at any time by law make or alter such regulations, except as to the places of choosing senators.

The Congress shall assemble at least once in every year, and such meeting shall be on the first Monday in December, unless they shall by law appoint a different day.

SECTION 5. Each House shall be the judge of the elections, returns and qualifications of its own members, and a majority of each shall constitute a quorum to do business; but a smaller number may adjourn from day to day, and may be authorized to compel the attendance of absent members, in such manner, and under such penalties as each House may provide.

Each House may determine the rules of its proceedings, punish its members for disorderly behaviour, and, with the concurrence of two-thirds, expel a member.

Each House shall keep a journal of its proceedings, and from time to time publish the same, excepting such parts as may in their judgment require secrecy; and the yeas and nays of the members of either House on any question shall, at the desire of one-fifth of those present, be entered on the journal.

Neither House, during the session of Congress, shall, without the consent of the other, adjourn for more than three days, nor to any other place than that in which the two Houses shall be sitting.

SECTION 6. The senators and representatives shall receive a compensation for their services, to be ascertained by law, and paid out of the Treasury of the United States. They shall in all cases, except treason, felony and breach of the peace, be privileged from arrest during their attendance at the session of their respective Houses, and in going to and returning from the same; and for any speech or debate in either House, they shall not be questioned in any other place.

No senator or representative shall, during the time for which he was elected, be appointed to any civil office under the authority of the United States, which shall have been created, or the emoluments whereof shall have been increased during such time; and no person holding any office under the United States shall be a member of either House during his continuance in office.

SECTION 7. All bills for raising revenue shall originate in the House of Representatives; but the Senate may propose or concur with amendments as on other bills.

Every bill which shall have passed the House of Representatives and the Senate, shall, before it becomes a law, be presented to the President of the United States; if he approve he shall sign it; but if not he shall return it, with his objections to that House in which it shall have originated, who shall enter the objections at large on their journal, and proceed to reconsider it. If after such reconsideration two-thirds of that House shall agree to pass the bill, it shall be sent, together with the objections, to the other House, by which it shall likewise be reconsidered, and if approved by two-thirds of that House, it shall become a law. But in all such cases the votes of both Houses shall be determined by yeas and nays, and the names of the persons voting for and against the bill shall be entered on the journal of each House respectively. If any bill shall not be returned by the President within ten days (Sundays excepted) after it shall have been presented to him, the same shall be a law, in like manner as if he had signed it, unless the Congress by their adjournment prevent its return, in which case it shall not be a law.

Every order, resolution, or vote to which the concurrence of the Senate and House of Representatives may be necessary (except on a question of adjournment) shall be presented to the President of the United States; and before the same shall take effect, shall be approved by him, or being disapproved by him, shall be repassed by two-thirds of the Senate and House of Representatives, according to the rules and limitations prescribed in the case of a bill.

SECTION 8. The Congress shall have the power to lay and collect taxes, duties, imposts and excises, to pay the debts and provide for the common defense and general welfare of the United States; but all duties, imposts and excises shall be uniform throughout the United States;

To borrow money on the credit of the United States;

To regulate commerce with foreign nations, and among the several States, and with the Indian tribes;

To establish an uniform rule of naturalization, and uniform laws on the subject of bankruptcies throughout the United States;

To coin money, regulate the value thereof, and of foreign coin, and fix the standard of weights and measures;

To provide for the punishment of counterfeiting the securities and current coin of the United States;

To establish post offices and post roads;

To promote the progress of science and useful arts, by securing for limited times to authors and inventors the exclusive right to their respective writings and discoveries;

To constitute tribunals inferior to the Supreme Court;

To define and punish piracies and felonies committed on the high seas, and offenses against the law of nations;

To declare war, grant letters of marque and reprisal, and make rules concerning captures on land and water;

To raise and support armies, but no appropriation of money to that use shall be for a longer term than two years;

To provide and maintain a Navy;

To make rules for the government and regulation of the land and naval forces;

To provide for calling forth the militia to execute the laws of the Union, suppress insurrections and repel invasions;

To provide for organizing, arming, and disciplining, the militia, and for governing such part of them as may be employed in the service of the United States, reserving to the States respectively, the appointment of the officers, and the authority of training the militia according to the discipline prescribed by Congress;

To exercise exclusive legislation in all cases whatsoever, over such district (not exceeding ten miles square) as may, by cession of particular States, and the acceptance of Congress, become the seat of the Government of the United States, and to exercise like authority over all places purchased by the consent of the legislature of the State in which the same shall be, for the erection of forts, magazines, arsenals, dock-yards, and other needful buildings; – And

To make all laws which shall be necessary and proper for carrying into execution the foregoing powers, and all other powers vested by the Constitution in the Government of the United States, or in any department or officer thereof.

SECTION 9. The migration or importation of such persons as any of the States now existing shall think proper to admit, shall not be prohibited by the Congress prior to the year one thousand eight hundred and eight, but a tax or duty may be imposed on such importation, not exceeding ten dollars for each person.

The privilege of the writ of habeas corpus shall not be suspended, unless when in cases of rebellion or invasion the public safety may require it.

No bill of attainder or ex post facto law shall be passed.

No capitation, or other direct, tax shall be laid, unless in proportion to the census or enumeration herein before directed to be taken.

No tax or duty shall be laid on articles exported from any State.

No preference shall be given by any regulation of commerce or revenue to the ports of one State over those of another; nor shall vessels bound to, or from, one State, be obliged to enter, clear, or pay duties in another.

No money shall be drawn from the Treasury, but in consequence of appropriations made by law; and a regular statement and account of the receipts and expenditures of all public money shall be published from time to time.

No title of nobility shall be granted by the United States: And no person holding any office of profit or trust under them, shall, without the consent of the Congress, accept of any present, emolument, office, or title, of any kind whatever, from any King, Prince, or foreign State.

SECTION 10. No State shall enter into any treaty, alliance, or confederation; grant letters of marque and reprisal; coin money; emit bills of credit; make any thing but gold and silver coin a tender in payment of debts; pass any bill of attainder, ex post facto law, or law impairing the obligation of contracts, or grant any title of nobility.

No State shall, without the consent of the Congress, lay any imposts or duties on imports or exports, except what may be absolutely necessary for executing its inspection laws: and the net produce of all duties and imposts, laid by any State on imports or exports, shall be for the use of the Treasury of the United States; and all such laws shall be subject to the revision and control of the Congress.

No State shall, without the consent of Congress, lay any duty of tonnage, keep troops, or ships of war in time of peace, enter into any agreement or compact with another State, or with a foreign power, or engage in war, unless actually invaded or in such imminent danger as will not admit of delay.

ARTICLE II

SECTION 1. The executive power shall be vested in a President of the United States of America. He shall hold his office during the term of four years, and, together with the Vice President, chosen for the same term, be elected, as follows:

Each State shall appoint, in such manner as the legislature thereof may direct, a number of electors, equal to the whole number of senators and representatives to which the State may be entitled in the Congress; but no senator or representative, or person holding an office of trust or profit under the United States, shall be appointed an elector.

The electors shall meet in their respective States, and vote by ballot for two persons, of whom one at least shall not be an inhabitant of the same State with themselves. And they shall make a list of all the persons voted for, and of the number of votes for each; which list they shall sign and certify; and transmit sealed to the seat of the Government of the United States, directed to the President of the Senate. The President of the Senate shall, in the presence of the Senate and House of Representatives, open all the certificates, and the votes shall then be counted. The person having the greatest number of votes shall be the President, if such number be a majority of the whole number of electors appointed; and if there be more than one who have such majority, and have an equal number of votes, then the House of Representatives shall immediately choose by ballot one of them for President; and if no person have a majority, then from the five highest on the list the said House shall in like manner choose the President. But in choosing the President, the votes shall be taken by States, the representation from each State having one vote; a quorum for this purpose shall consist of a member or members from two-thirds of the States, and a majority of all the States shall be necessary to a choice. In every case, after the choice of the President, the person having the greatest number of votes of the electors shall be the Vice President. But if there should remain two or more who have equal votes, the Senate shall choose from them by ballot the Vice President.

The Congress may determine the time of choosing the electors, and the day on which they shall give their votes; which day shall be the same throughout the United States.

No person except a natural born citizen, or a citizen of the United States, at the time of the adoption of this Constitution, shall be eligible to the office of President; neither shall any person be eligible to that office who shall not have attained to the age of thirty-five years, and been fourteen years a resident within the United States.

In case of the removal of the President from office, or of his death, resignation, or inability to discharge the powers and duties of the said office, the same shall devolve on the Vice President, and the Congress may by law provide for the case of removal, death, resignation, or inability, both of the President and Vice President, declaring what officer shall then act as President, and such officer shall act accordingly, until the disability be removed, or a President shall be elected.

The President shall, at stated times, receive for his services, a compensation, which shall neither be increased nor diminished during the period for which he shall have been elected, and he shall not receive within that period any other emolument from the United States, or any of them.

Before he enter on the execution of his office, he shall take the following oath or affirmation: – 'I do solemnly swear (or affirm) that I will faithfully execute the office of President of the United States, and will to the best of my ability, preserve, protect and defend the Constitution of the United States.'

SECTION 2. The President shall be Commander in Chief of the Army and Navy of the United States, and of the militia of the several States, when called into the actual service of the United States; he may require the opinion, in writing of the principal officer in each of the Executive Departments, upon any subject relating to the duties of their respective offices, and he shall have power to grant reprieves and pardons for offenses against the United States, except in cases of impeachment.

He shall have power, by and with the advice and consent of the Senate, to make treaties, provided two-thirds of the Senators present concur; and he shall nominate, and by and with the advice and consent of the Senate, shall appoint ambassadors, other public ministers and consuls, judges of the Supreme Court, and all other officers of the United States, whose appointments are not herein otherwise provided for, and which shall be established by law: but the Congress may by law vest the appointment of such inferior officers, as they think proper, in the President alone, in the courts of law, or in the heads of departments.

The President shall have power to fill up all vacancies that may happen during the recess of the Senate, by granting commissions which shall expire at the end of their next session.

SECTION 3. He shall from time to time give to the Congress information of the state of the Union, and recommend to their consideration such measures as he shall judge necessary and expedient; he may, on extraordinary occasions, convene both Houses, or either of them, and in case of disagreement between them, with respect to the time of adjournment, he may adjourn them to such time as he shall think proper; he shall receive ambassadors and other public ministers; he shall take care that the laws be faithfully executed, and shall commission all the officers of the United States.

SECTION 4. The President, Vice President and all civil officers of the United States, shall be removed from office on impeachment for, and conviction of, treason, bribery, or other high crimes and misdemeanors.

ARTICLE III

SECTION 1. The judicial power of the United States shall be vested in one Supreme Court, and in such inferior courts as the Congress may from time to time ordain and establish. The judges, both of the supreme and inferior courts, shall hold their offices during good behaviour, and shall, at stated times, receive for their services, a compensation, which shall not be diminished during their continuance in office.

SECTION 2. The judicial power shall extend to all cases, in law and equity, arising under this Constitution, the laws of the United States, and treaties made, or which shall be made, under their authority; to all cases affecting ambassadors, other public ministers and consuls; to all cases of admiralty and maritime jurisdiction; to controversies to which the United States shall be a party; to controversies between two or more States; between a State and citizens of another State; between citizens of different States; between citizens of the same State claiming lands under grants of different States, and between a State, or the citizens thereof, and foreign States, citizens, or subjects.

In all cases affecting ambassadors, other public ministers and consuls, and those in which a State shall be party, the Supreme Court shall have original jurisdiction. In all the other cases before mentioned, the Supreme Court shall have appellate jurisdiction, both as to law and to fact, with such exceptions, and under such regulations as the Congress shall make.

The trial of all crimes, except in cases of impeachment, shall be by jury; and such trial shall be held in the State where the said crimes shall have been committed; but when not committed within any State, the trial shall be at such place or places as the Congress may by law have directed.

SECTION 3. Treason against the United States, shall consist only in levying war against them, or in adhering to their enemies, giving them aid and comfort. No person shall be convicted of treason unless on the testimony of two witnesses to the same overt act, or on confession in open court.

The Congress shall have power to declare the punishment of treason, but no attainder of treason shall work corruption of blood, or forfeiture except during the life of the person attainted.

ARTICLE IV

SECTION 1. Full faith and credit shall be given in each State to the public acts, records, and judicial proceedings of every other State. And the Congress may by general laws prescribe the manner in which such acts, records and proceedings shall be proved, and the effect thereof.

SECTION 2. The citizens of each State shall be entitled to all privileges and immunities of citizens in the several States.

A person charged in any State with treason, felony, or other crimes, who shall flee from justice, and be found in another State, shall on demand of the executive authority of the State from which he fled, be delivered up, to be removed to the State having jurisdiction of the crime.

No person held to service or labor in one State, under the laws thereof, escaping into another, shall, in consequence of any law or regulation therein, be discharged from such service or labor but shall be delivered up on claim of the party to whom such service or labor may be due.

SECTION 3. New States may be admitted by the Congress into this Union; but no new State shall be formed or erected within the jurisdiction of any other State; nor any State be formed by the junction of two or more States, or parts of States, without the consent of the legislature of the States concerned as well as of the Congress.

The Congress shall have the power to dispose of and make all needful rules and regulations respecting the Territory or other property belonging to the United States; and nothing in this Constitution shall be so construed as to prejudice any claims of the United States, or of any particular State.

SECTION 4. The United States shall guarantee to every State in this Union a republican form of Government, and shall protect each of them against invasion; and on application of the legislature, or of the executive (when the legislature cannot be convened) against domestic violence.

ARTICLE V

The Congress, whenever two-thirds of both Houses shall deem it necessary, shall propose amendments to this Constitution, or, on the application of the legislatures of two-thirds of the several States, shall call a convention for proposing amendments, which, in either case, shall be valid to all intents and purposes, as part of this Constitution, when ratified by the legislatures of three-fourths of the several States, or by conventions in three-fourths thereof, as the one or the other mode of ratification may be proposed by the Congress; provided that no amendment which may be made prior to the year one thousand eight hundred and eight shall in any manner affect the first and fourth clauses in the Ninth Section of the First Article; and that no State, without its consent, shall be deprived of its equal suffrage in the Senate.

ARTICLE VI

All debts contracted and engagements entered into, before the adoption of this Constitution, shall be as valid against the United States under this Constitution, as under the Confederation.

This Constitution, and the laws of the United States which shall be made in pursuance thereof; and all treaties made, or which shall be made, under the authority of the United States, shall be the supreme law of the land; and the judges in every State shall be bound thereby, anything in the Constitution or laws of any State to the contrary notwithstanding.

The senators and representatives before mentioned, and the members of the several State legislatures, and all executive and judicial officers, both of the United States and of the several States, shall be bound by oath or affirmation, to support this Constitution; but no religious test shall ever be required as a qualification to any office or public trust under the United States.

ARTICLE VII

The ratification of the conventions of nine States shall be sufficient for the establishment of this Constitution between the States so ratifying the same.

Done in convention by the unanimous consent of the States present the seventeenth day of September in the year of Our Lord one thousand seven hundred and eighty-seven and of the Independence of the United States of America the twelfth. In witness whereof we have hereunto subscribed our names.

Appendix II:
The Bill of Rights

Amendments to the Constitution

ARTICLE I

Congress shall make no law respecting an establishment of religion, or prohibiting the free exercise thereof; or abridging the freedom of speech, or of the press; or the right of the people peaceably to assemble, and to petition the Government for a redress of grievances.

ARTICLE II

A well regulated militia, being necessary to the security of a free State, the right of the people to keep and bear arms, shall not be infringed.

ARTICLE III

No soldier shall, in time of peace be quartered in any house, without the consent of the owner, nor in time of war, but in a manner to be prescribed by law.

ARTICLE IV

The right of the people to be secure in their persons, houses, papers, and effects, against unreasonable searches and seizures, shall not be violated, and no warrants shall issue, but upon probable cause, supported by oath or affirmation, and particularly describing the place to be searched, and the persons or things to be seized.

ARTICLE V

No person shall be held to answer for a capital, or otherwise infamous crime, unless on a presentment or indictment of a grand jury, except in cases arising in the land or naval forces, or in the militia, when in actual service in time of war or public danger; nor shall any person be subject for the same offense to be twice put in jeopardy of life or limb; nor shall be compelled in any criminal case to be a witness against himself, nor be deprived of life, liberty, or property, without due process of law; nor shall private property be taken for public use, without just compensation.

ARTICLE VI

In all criminal prosecutions, the accused shall enjoy the right to a speedy and public trial, by an impartial jury of the State and district wherein the crime shall have been committed, which district shall have been previously ascertained by law, and to be informed of the nature and cause of the accusation; to be confronted with the witnesses against him; to have compulsory process for obtaining witnesses in his favor, and to have the assistance of counsel for his defense.

ARTICLE VII

In suits at common law, where the value in controversy shall exceed twenty dollars, the right of trial by jury shall be preserved, and no fact tried by a jury, shall be otherwise re-examined in any court of the United States, than according to the rules of the common law.

ARTICLE VIII

Excessive bail shall not be required, nor excessive fines imposed, nor cruel and unusual punishments inflicted.

ARTICLE IX

The enumeration in the Constitution, of certain rights, shall not be construed to deny or disparage others retained by the people.

ARTICLE X
(Articles I to X were adopted in 1791)

The powers not delegated to the United States by the Constitution, nor prohibited by it to the States, are reserved to the States respectively, or to the people.

Maps

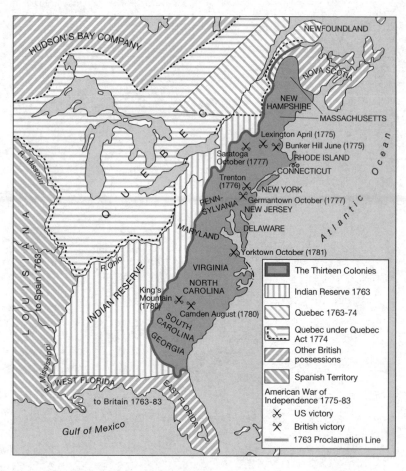

1 British North America, 1763–1783
From Geoffrey Barraclough (ed.), *The Times Atlas of World History*
(London, 1978). © Times Books. 1978. Reproduced with permission
of HarperCollins. MM–0797–06

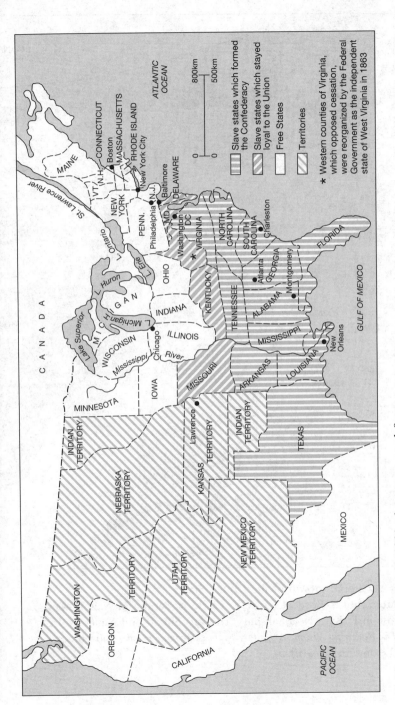

2 The United States in 1861: slave states and free states
After Brian Holden Reid, *The Origins of the American Civil War* (London, 1996)

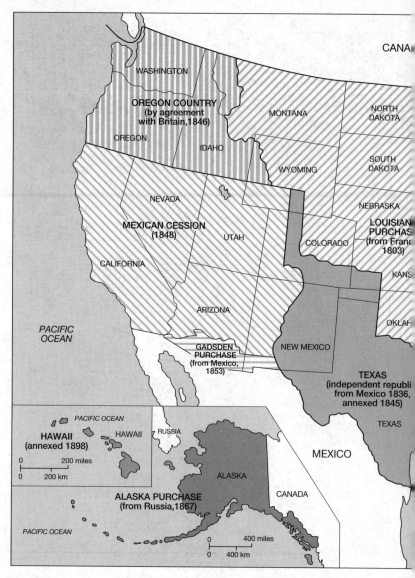

3 Territorial growth of the United States
After Paul S. Boyer, Clifford E. Clark, Jr, Sandra McNair Hawley,
Joseph F. Kett, Neal Salisbury, Harvard Sitkoff and Nancy Woloch,
The Enduring Vision: A History of the American People, 2nd edition
(Lexington, MA, 1995)

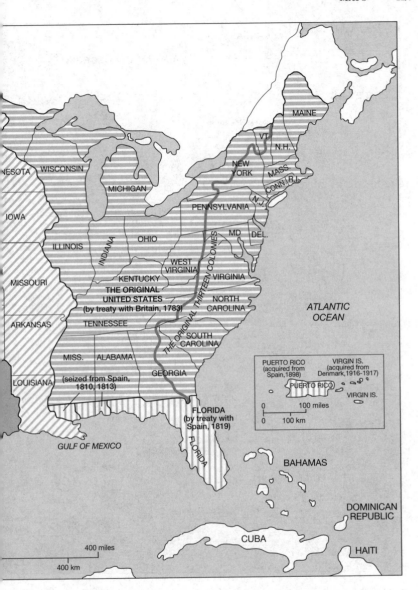

MAINE

VT

N.H.

NEW
YORK

MASS.

CONN. R.I.

MINNESOTA

WISCONSIN

MICHIGAN

PENNSYLVANIA

N.J.

IOWA

ILLINOIS

INDIANA

OHIO

MD.

DEL.

WEST
VIRGINIA

THE ORIGINAL THIRTEEN COLONIES

VIRGINIA

ATLANTIC
OCEAN

MISSOURI

KENTUCKY

THE ORIGINAL
UNITED STATES
(by treaty with Britain, 1783)

NORTH
CAROLINA

ARKANSAS

TENNESSEE

SOUTH
CAROLINA

MISS.

ALABAMA

GEORGIA

PUERTO RICO
(acquired from
Spain,1898)

VIRGIN IS.
(acquired from
Denmark,1916-1917)

PUERTO RICO

VIRGIN IS.

LOUISIANA

(seized from Spain,
1810, 1813)

0   100 miles

0   100 km

FLORIDA
(by treaty with
Spain, 1819)

GULF OF MEXICO

FLORIDA

BAHAMAS

DOMINICAN
REPUBLIC

400 miles

CUBA

400 km

HAITI

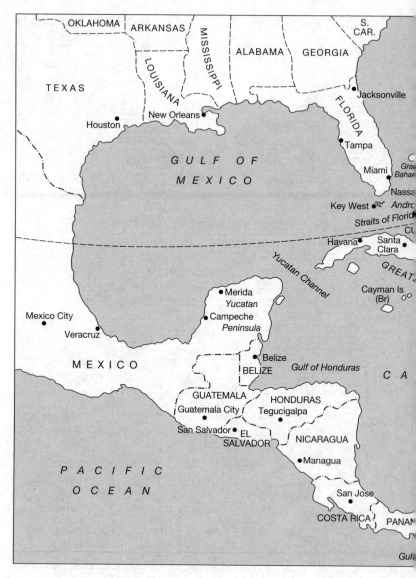

4 The Caribbean and Central America
After Chris Cook and John Stevenson, *The Longman Handbook of World History since 1914* (London, 1991)

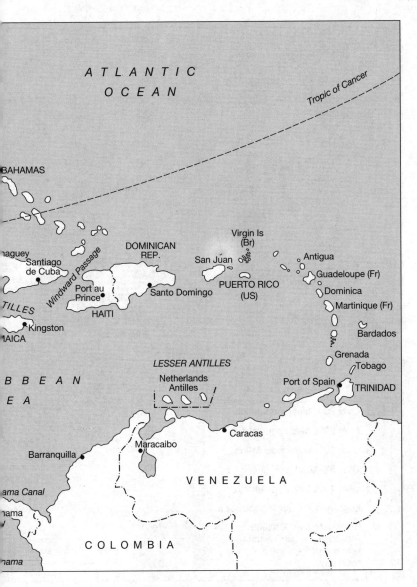

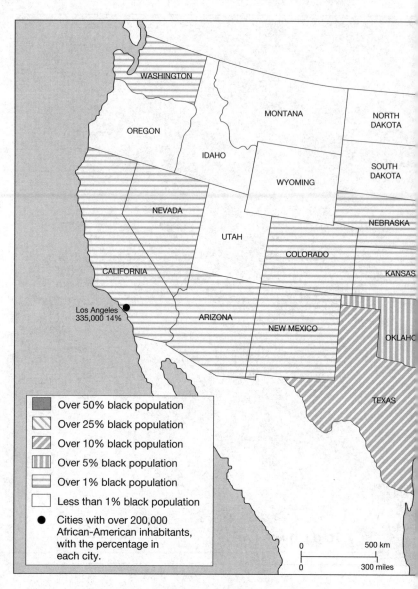

5 USA: African-American population, 1965
After Martin Gilbert, *American History Atlas* (London, 1968)

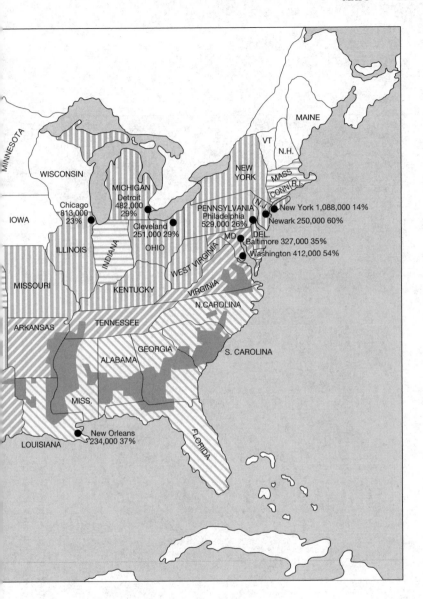

MAINE

VT

N.H.

MINNESOTA

WISCONSIN

MICHIGAN
Detroit
482,000
29%

NEW
YORK

MASS

CONN R.I.

N.J.

New York 1,088,000 14%

Chicago
813,000
23%

IOWA

Cleveland
251,000 29%

ILLINOIS

INDIANA

OHIO

PENNSYLVANIA
Philadelphia
529,000 26%

Newark 250,000 60%

MD

DEL.
Baltimore 327,000 35%
Washington 412,000 54%

MISSOURI

KENTUCKY

WEST VIRGINIA

VIRGINIA

N.CAROLINA

ARKANSAS

TENNESSEE

S. CAROLINA

ALABAMA

GEORGIA

MISS.

New Orleans
234,000 37%

FLORIDA

LOUISIANA

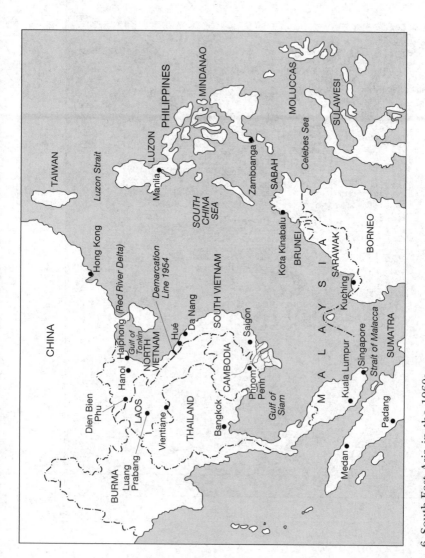

6 South-East Asia in the 1960s
After Chris Cook and John Stevenson, *The Longman Handbook of World History since 1914* (London, 1991)

Index

Notes: readers are referred to the list on pages 13–14 for abbreviations.
Bold type indicates main location, for ease of reference, where helpful